THE ARCHITECTURE OF DIPLOMACY

The
Architecture
of Diplomacy
Building America's Embassies

Jane C. Loeffler

AN ADST-DACOR DIPLOMATS AND DIPLOMACY BOOK

PRINCETON ARCHITECTURAL PRESS   NEW YORK

Published by
Princeton Architectural Press
37 East Seventh Street
New York, NY 10003
+1.212.995.9620

For a free catalog of books published by Princeton Architectural Press,
call toll free 1.800.722.6657 or visit www.papress.com

This book was supported in part by the Graham Foundation for Advanced Studies
in the Fine Arts and by the Nelson B Delavan Foundation

Editor: Mark Lamster
Jacket design: Sara E. Stemen
Book design: Sara E. Stemen & Mark Lamster
Index: Susan Fels
Special thanks to Jennifer Thompson, Deb Wood, Paul Wagner, John Myers,
Katharine Myers, Russell Fernandez, and Joe Weston of Princeton Architectural
Press—Kevin C. Lippert, publisher

Library of Congress Cataloging-in-Publication Data

Loeffler, Jane C. 1947–
      The architecture of diplomacy / Jane C. Loeffler. — 2nd ed.
          p.   cm.
      An ADST-DACOR Diplomats and Diplomacy Book
      Includes bibliographical references and index.
          ISBN 978-1-56898-984-6
      1. Embassy buildings—United States. 2. Diplomatic and consular
service, American—Buildings. 3. Architecture and state—United States.
4. Architecture, American. 5. Architecture, Modern—20th century.
6. United States. Dept. of State—History. 7. United States—Foreign relations.
I. Title
      NA 4441.L64 1998
      725'. 17—DC 21   97-45032
                                                          CIP

THE ADST-DACOR DIPLOMATS AND DIPLOMACY SERIES

FOR MORE THAN 230 years extraordinary men and women have represented the United States abroad under all kinds of circumstances. What they did and how and why they did it are not well known by their compatriots. In 1995 the Association for Diplomatic Studies and Training (ADST) and DACOR, an organization of foreign affairs professionals, created a book series to increase public knowledge and appreciation of the involvement of American diplomats in the events of world history. The series seeks to demystify diplomacy by telling the story of those who have conducted our foreign relations, as they saw and lived it. The present volume relates the saga of those who created diplomacy's physical settings.

Jane C. Loeffler, a scholar in architectural history and American civilization, has written an extensively researched study of the history and politics of the design and building of U.S. embassies, focusing on the years following World War II. These high-profile, often controversial structures—projections abroad of American art, culture, and political philosophy—have formed the settings for the conduct of U.S. diplomacy in the latter half of the twentieth century. In this widely praised account of the State Department and the Congress, of architects and changing times, Dr. Loeffler dissects the interplay of domestic politics, international affairs, and an array of functional and symbolic requirements. Her book adds greatly to our understanding of architecture and diplomacy. Since publication of the first edition in 1998, it has become recognized as the standard work on the subject.

Kenneth L. Brown, President, ADST
Edward M. Rowell, President, DACOR

PREFACE

A VISIT TO THE NEW Embassy of Finland in Washington, D.C., brings to mind the qualities that made the architecture of American embassies so noteworthy during the early postwar years. Located on Embassy Row across from the vice president's house and near several other sedate looking diplomatic buildings, the recently completed Finnish embassy is a real eye-catcher. A green-hued glass box trimmed in copper, bronze, and highly polished granite, it is framed by tall trees and is screened on its front by a metal trellis already partially covered with flowering vines. The highly-crafted building, designed by Finnish architects Mikko Heikkinen and Markku Komonen, has been compared to a "glittering jewel box," and when it opened in 1994 it was hailed as a local landmark. Since then, Washingtonians have vied for invitations to visit the unusual new building—to enjoy the view from its glass-walled interior, to walk down its sweeping central staircase, to sit under its whimsical canvas canopy, and to peek into its well-publicized sauna. Everyone agrees that the building represents a diplomatic "coup" for Finland. Anyone who tours the new Finnish building realizes instantly that Finland is a thoroughly modern place. Everything about the architecture of the new embassy is high-tech and calls attention to the quality of Finnish workmanship and the excellence of Finnish design—accomplishing at a glance what a multitude of pamphlets, books, films, travel posters, and formal exchange programs might only hope to do.

In much the same way as that new building serves as a showcase for the art and culture of Finland, American embassies serve as showcases for the art, culture, and political philosophy of the United States. Visiting the Finnish embassy today recalls what it must have been like to visit an American embassy in the 1950s, when openness was both a top design priority and a diplomatic objective. By the mid-1960s, priorities had shifted and the foreign building program felt the impact of a changing and more threatening world. The embassy in Dublin, completed in 1964, was the last of the American projects for which an architect was able to put design ahead of the many other factors that shape embassy architecture.

One of the biggest differences between American embassies and the embassies of most other nations has been an underlying assumption, articulated first in 1954, that American embassies should "fit in" and reflect their surroundings. While new diplomatic buildings in Washington made no particular effort to look "American," American architects tried hard to capture the "foreignness" of faraway places in their designs for U.S. embassies abroad. Some American officials may have felt the need to claim local authenticity out of a belief that such architecture would win approval from its hosts. They also wanted to avoid the accusation that foreign buildings were mere "exports." Another circumstance contributing to the professed interest in local architecture (the Taj Mahal, for example) was that architects, like all artists, are always on the lookout for ways to innovate, and the most daring build their careers on bold gestures. These and other factors combine to complicate the analysis of architectural meaning.

This book aims to provide a groundwork for future study of diplomatic architecture and its history. It provides evidence that will fuel many debates—including the already heated debate over cultural imperialism and whether or not the U.S. diplomatic building program represents a form of domination. Some will argue that the stated American policy of "fitting in" was an honest, if self-conscious, response by a nation that found itself uncomfortable with its status as a world power, while others are sure to suggest that the policy was nothing less than an expression of arrogance by a nation that trivializes the exotic and tends to view other cultures as if they were exhibits at a theme park. If architecture is indeed an assertion of power, then the building program represents a mode of conquest—but not necessarily a sinister one, nor one backed by a well-orchestrated plan. It is simplistic to presuppose such organized intent. As this book will show, numerous individuals both in and out of government separately contribute to what might be described as the planning process. Moreover, if exports (movies, fashion, foreign aid) are elements of cultural conquest, so too are imports (oil, cars, computers). Some are perceived to be essential to the national interest, some are not. There may be an irony in the effort to export democracy, but it is still worth exporting.

In searching for meaning in the appearance of U.S. embassies, I have tried to penetrate the surface to examine policies and programs that shape the architecture. The client is not one, but many, and meanings vary depending on which one speaks. Minoru Yamasaki's Eastern Airlines Terminal at Boston's Logan Airport, for example, bore a striking resemblance to a number of prominent U.S. embassy buildings when it was completed in 1969 (see fig. 54). When *Boston Globe* critic Robert Campbell described the landmark as "a pompous and silly building," an "arrogant" statement that conveyed a message of "narcissism" (13 August 1993), he was not suggesting that the entire city of Boston was either arrogant or narcissistic. It is similarly difficult to make inferences about the entire State Department, let alone the whole U.S. government or its people, from the interpretation of the architecture of one embassy or another. But there is much to learn from the overall history of the program.

Aside from adding to debate, it is my hope that this book will also stimulate further research. There is much territory left to explore. A historical assessment of Wayne Hays would be useful. Others who merit similar scrutiny include former members of Congress Frances Bolton, John Rooney, and Sol Bloom. Then there are the architects about whom we know next to nothing. The fact that so few architects' biographies exist is regrettable, as is the tendency of such books to focus on work to the exclusion of personality. Studies are already underway on the history of the Office of the Supervising Architect of the Treasury and the history of Harvard's Graduate School of Design, and both will be welcome.

Whether or not embassies should be protected under preservation statutes is another matter of interest. Because of the ever-shifting international situation, the legitimate need for security improvements that alter or affect architecture, the relatively small foreign affairs budget, and the concomitant need to sell existing real estate to finance new projects, it may make no sense to try to "preserve" such structures as historical artifacts. But they are historic American buildings, and they do need to be recognized as such. Before more of them are sold, lost, or abandoned, they should at least be documented so the State Department can hold onto its history and future historians can better interpret this dimension of diplomacy.

—Jane C. Loeffler, Washington, DC, May 1998

PREFACE TO THE REVISED SECOND EDITION

Soon after the first publication of this book, events occurred that caused us to rethink U.S. embassies. It was not the tragic events of 11 September, 2001, that fundamentally reshaped the State Department's embassy building program, as many suppose, but the suicide bombing attacks before that on August 7, 1998, at U.S. embassies in Nairobi, Kenya and Dar es Salaam, Tanzania. Those attacks, which killed 220, injured thousands, and destroyed prominent symbols of America's foreign presence, led the Department to revamp its capital construction agenda. With strong congressional support, the Department launched sweeping new plans to replace vulnerable and outdated facilities with up-to-date and secure infrastructure. In the relatively short interval since this book was first published in 1998 more than seventy new embassies have opened worldwide and some 20,000 people have been moved into safe, modern workplaces as part of a construction program that is scheduled to extend through 2018 and possibly beyond. This is already a staggering accomplishment by any measure. It is all the more impressive when examined against the program's earlier history that is chronicled here.

At the height of the Cold War, when buildings were bold, eye-catching, trendy, and sometimes egotistical statements, U.S. embassy architecture embraced modernism as a way of representing America's openness, its forward-looking outlook, and its commitment to individual talent and creativity. Security was a concern, but did not dictate design. Consciously planned as an alternative to traditional-looking Soviet buildings, America's embassies, like world's fair pavilions of that era, drew attention to themselves and their designers. In the aftermath of the bombings in East Africa and scores of similar, if less devastating, events, the same no longer holds true. Recent embassies still call attention to themselves, but largely because of their size, homogeneity, and imposing presence—not because of striking or individualistic designs. Security is now the rationale behind the entire building program. The Standard Embassy Design has sped production and rebranded America, giving it a recognizable new foreign presence. Examples of recent projects are included in this second edition. If there is talk about why these facilities resemble fortresses and how defensiveness can translate into fear, there is also recognition that secure workplaces are essential if U.S. diplomats are to continue their work under threatening circumstances. But given the isolation of so many new embassies and the formidable security that surrounds them, these are no longer welcoming places that encourage or even support interaction between local citizens and American diplomats. The tension between security and the work of diplomacy has never been more apparent.

It is hard to project optimism when foes are determined to attack our overseas outposts as a way of attacking American values and ultimately as a way of reaching us here at home. But the recently selected design for a new U.S. embassy in London is one positive statement. Maybe we are headed in a new direction? It is too soon to tell. What is positive about all of the new embassies, though, is that they represent continued engagement in the international arena despite growing risk. They are evidence of continued commitment to diplomatic discourse in a fractured world.

The study of architecture gives us a way of looking at history in tangible terms. Buildings are markers. They signify purpose and they symbolize presence. The enormous change in the embassy building program merits critical attention. Just as embassy architecture was impressive in the early postwar years, it is impressive today, albeit in a very different way. While it is early to be assessing events of the past decade as history, this revised edition of *The Architecture of Diplomacy* is intended as a first step in that direction.

—Jane C. Loeffler, Washington, DC, May 2010

ACKNOWLEDGMENTS

IF MY FATHER had not been a builder, I might not have developed a fascination with buildings, but watching the construction of his many projects in and around Boston, I acquired a lasting interest in architecture. This book is the outcome of that enthusiasm.

For consistently championing my cause, I owe sincere thanks to Richard W. Longstreth, George Washington University Professor of American Civilization. Of the many others who provided invaluable assistance, I am especially indebted to four: William Z. Slany, the State Department's Historian, who backed the project from its inception; Paul Claussen, Chief of the Special Projects Division, Office of the Historian, a true ally; Patrick W. Collins, Chief Architect in the Office of Foreign Buildings Operations (FBO), who made every effort to provide me with the data needed to insure that this history is accurate and complete; and Charles Rex Hellmann, the former Chief Architect, who introduced me to previously unexamined files and minutes.

For sharing their recollections, I am grateful to architects Robert E. Alexander, Lawrence Anderson, Edward Larrabee Barnes, Robert Beatty, Jean Paul Carlhian, Alan Jacobs, John M. Johansen, George E. Hartman, D. Rodman Henderer, Francis Lethbridge, Stuart L. Knoop, William Metcalf, Nobuaki Miyata, Tatsuya Okura, Joseph Passonneau, Ladislav Rado, Ralph Rapson, Chloethiel Woodard Smith, Hugh Stubbins, Alan Y. Taniguchi, John Carl Warnecke, Gerald A. Winkler, and others. For their assistance, I also thank Marjorie Belluschi, Dorothy Goodman, Don Homsey, Catherine Jacobs, Donna Rado, and Philip Will. Special thanks go to architects Rapson and Johansen for lending copies of original drawings and to Shepley Bulfinch Richardson and Abbott and the Shepley family for their generosity.

By good fortune, I spoke with seven former FBO directors: Leland King, James Johnstone, Ralph Scarritt, William Slayton, Richard Dertadian, Jerome Tolson, and Joseph Sikes. Current and former FBO staff members who helped me included James Capen, Sal DiGiacomo, William Gallagher, Jay Holleran, Anita Moeller Laird, Jennifer Loynd, William McCullough, Lore Mika, William Miner, Michael Minton, Robert Parke, Carl Petchik, Paul Serey, Kevin Spence, Joseph Toussaint, and Kevin Lee Sarring, who has added his artistry to the book's illustrations. I have also benefited from conversations with former Ambassador Nicolas M. Salgo, and with three Assistant Secretaries of State for Diplomatic Security, Sheldon Krys and his successors Anthony C. E. Quainton and Eric J. Boswell. For answering my unending questions with thoroughness and diplomatic good humor, I thank them all.

Of the many Foreign Service officers and others who assisted me on travels and fact-finding, I extend particular appreciation to Gloria Berbena and Martha Droge (Rome); Brian E. Carlson and Stephen L. Roberts (London); Victoria R. Cordova (Brussels); Jeri Guthrie-Corn (Paris); Kathryn Koob and Eugene A. Trahan Jr. (Munich); Jean Rylands (Dublin); William Breer, Robert A. MacCallum, Jonathan McHale, and Donna Wright (Tokyo); William V. Parker and John L. Whitney (New Delhi); and Arthur S. Berger and Ton Heijneman (The Hague). For advice on the relationship between the State Department and Congress, I am grateful to former Ambassador Ronald D. Palmer and to Thomas Stern, former Special Assistant to Deputy Under Secretary of State William J. Crockett.

Helpful colleagues, teachers, and friends included Laura Wood Roper, Sally Cutler, Peter P. Hill, Carol Krinsky, Richard Guy Wilson, and Bates Lowry, who first introduced me to this subject. My appreciation to Richard Arndt, Susanne K. Bennet, Simon Bourgin, Kristin Cogar, Lois Craig, Walter Creese, Gaston De Los Reyes, Norma Evenson, Peter Fergusson, Joshua Freed, Eliot Frost, Willy Hill, Charles Stuart Kennedy, Leonard and Betty King, Magali Kline, Monica Korab, J. L. Sibley Jennings, Judith Lanius, Lawrence K. Larkin, Camille Larson, Antoinette Lee, Michael Marcus, Sharon McCauley, James E. Miller, Jeffrey Miller, Henry Millon, Anne Nissen, Ruth Ross, Rob Rowe, Andrew L. Steigman, and Rhoda and Peter Trooboff; to librarians and archivists, including Mary F. Daniels at Harvard and Tony Wrenn at the AIA; and to Lawrence J. Vale, Elizabeth Grossman, Jeff Cody, and Ron Robin for pioneering efforts to understand America's public face abroad. Thanks, too, to my mother Blanche Canter for her guidance and to Susan Fels for her excellent index and editorial expertise.

A generous grant from the Graham Foundation for Advanced Studies in the Fine Arts provided me with funds used to assemble and reproduce the many fine illustrations in this volume. Two other awards provided financial and moral support for this project—the Harriet A. Shaw Graduate Fellowship from Wellesley College and the American Studies Alumni Award from George Washington University.

Giving credit where it is due, I thank Stephen Low, former President of the Association for Diplomatic Studies and Training, for commending the book. I am honored to be included in the ADST-DACOR publication series, and I thank ADST Publishing Coordinator Margery Boichel Thompson for so ably representing both book and author. No acknowledgments would be complete without thanks to Princeton Architectural Press and editor Mark Lamster. It has been a pleasure working with such imaginative and committed professionals.

SINCE ITS FIRST PUBLICATION this book has enjoyed enthusiastic support from reviewers and from many touched by the subject. For their continued assistance, I thank everyone at the State Department, including Jay Anania, Melanie Berkemeyer, Patrick Collins, Patrick Donovan, Christine Foushée, Christina Maier, William Miner, Adam Namm, Russ Norris, Kevin Lee Sarring, Richard Shinnick, Virginia Shore, Gregory Starr, and Joseph Toussaint—with special thanks to Jonathan Blyth. I also thank Mike Boyer of *Foreign Policy,* John Chapman, Jennifer Duncan, Susan Fels, Paul Foldi, Frances Halsband, Dan Hamilton, Ambassador William C. Harrop, Bob Ivy of *Architectural Record,* Suman Sorg, Ambassador Clyde D. Taylor, and Margery Thompson. I am grateful to Cathy Barks, William Dorland, Katherine Russell, Barbara Thorne, and other colleagues in the Honors College at the University of Maryland for providing me with such an excellent academic home. For sharing their complementary work, I thank Gabriella Paulix, Julia Klemeit, and Wijnand Galema. I am indebted to my editor/publisher Kevin Lippert for making a commitment to this book. Above all, I thank the Nelson B. Delavan Foundation, concerned about the quality of American diplomacy, for supporting this endeavor and making this second edition possible.

I dedicate the book to my husband Bob who has shared happily in this learning adventure and to my sons James and Charles who also saw the importance of the work and consistently encouraged me to pursue it.

THE ARCHITECTURE OF DIPLOMACY

INTRODUCTION

IN MARCH 1946, when Winston Churchill warned of an "Iron Curtain" being drawn across Europe, the Cold War was already taking shape in the minds of politicians and policy-makers. It was soon clear that Soviet moves would compel the United States to enter a conflict that lacked the boundaries of traditional battlefields. The Truman Doctrine, aimed at containing Soviet expansion in Europe, was one response. The creation of the United States Information Agency (USIA) was another. A much expanded embassy building program was yet another response to the challenges that faced the American nation at that time. This book traces the history of U.S. representation through its buildings, focusing on the building program that commenced in 1926. It examines America's first efforts to establish a foreign presence; the confident years following World War II, when the program reached its peak in terms of scope and popularity; the turmoil of the 1960s and 1970s, marked by political doubts and a rising concern for security; and recent developments including terrorist attacks and ever-changing commitments that shape the post–Cold War diplomatic landscape.

The embassy building program was, and remains, part of America's larger effort to define its world role. Like the Fulbright educational exchange program—designed to promote international understanding and widely praised as a goodwill gesture—new embassies have been hailed as evidence of American goodwill and commitment, and their modern architecture, introduced in the late 1940s, has come to symbolize the openness of public diplomacy.

Embassies are symbolically charged buildings uniquely defined by domestic politics, foreign affairs, and a complex set of representational requirements. As office buildings, they differ from ordinary projects not only in terms of their unusual programs and locations, but also in terms of their clients; they have not one, as is usual, but many. The State Department, the Foreign Service, congressional oversight committees, host governments, and individual ambassadors all consider the buildings to be their own, as do

American taxpayers. Foreign Service officers who actually work in the buildings often have the least input into the process through which new embassies are created. Not surprisingly, then, the history of the embassy building program is marked by competition and compromise.

Unlike authoritarian regimes and also unlike most other democratic nations, in which parliaments oversee diplomatic practice but exert little influence on it, the United States boasts diplomacy in which an elected congress plays a key role. The diplomatic decision of where to locate an embassy, what it should cost, and even what it should look like is the result of the push and pull between the executive departments and the Congress. It is impossible to examine the building program or its architecture without understanding the role played by elected officials and the way in which seemingly unrelated matters are joined politically.

The fact that Congress initially funded the postwar building program with nontax dollars, for example, is critically important to this study. Between 1946 and 1958, the State Department financed most of its overseas construction with postwar foreign credits generated by lend-lease settlements, sale of surplus property, war assets agreements, and Economic Cooperation Administration counterpart funds. This novel arrangement, first proposed by Frederick A. Larkin, chief of the department's Office of Foreign Buildings Operations (FBO), tapped into the reservoir of "frozen" funds, a reservoir of many hundreds of millions, to finance land acquisition and the construction abroad of American embassies, diplomatic and consular office buildings, and staff housing. Congressional oversight was minimal and the opportunity for architectural innovation was greatest while credits financed the building program. As Congress earmarked more and more of those funds for military use the supply dwindled, resulting in a curtailment of new construction and bitter, if sometimes useful, debate on matters of architectural style and taste.

The United States did not build more than a handful of its own embassies until late in the 1920s, when Congress first recognized the necessity to upgrade representation abroad. The need for foreign buildings existed prior to World War II, but not until after the war did the United States recognize its vastly increased global interests, and not until then did the funds exist to make a large-scale building program possible. FBO responded to the urgent postwar need for office space with an impressive array of modern office buildings, officially called chanceries, but popularly referred to as embassies.[*]

---

[*]Following popular custom, this book refers to embassy office buildings or chanceries as *embassies*. The term *embassy* can refer to a nation's overall representation, to its

Architectural modernism became linked with the idea of freedom after the war, and American architects emerged as leading proponents of the modern movement. In a radical departure from government practice at home, FBO began to showcase modern architecture in its first major postwar projects. As the most powerful nation in the world, the United States was proud of its accomplishment but also ambivalent about its widening world role and its growing power. Both a sense of pride and a sense of guilt were expressed in contemporary architecture, as in art. The desire to design high-profile buildings was coupled, for instance, with concern about negative impressions created by projects that were dramatic or ostentatious-looking. The desire to display and promote the freedom and ingenuity of American artists was coupled with doubts about the correctness of that art and what it represented.

Part of what makes the early postwar period so remarkable is the striking difference between its architectural history and its art history. In 1946, for example, in order to share the newest and most exciting works of American art with people around the world, the Office of International Information and Cultural Activities at the Department of State purchased a collection of paintings representing American artists. This was precisely when FBO was shifting course and inaugurating its new building program. With a budget of $49,000, State Department staff member Leroy Davidson selected the art, including works by Stuart Davis and Marsden Hartley. The works were first exhibited in October 1946 at New York's Metropolitan Museum of Art and widely praised in the art world. "The State Department was congratulated," wrote Aline Louchheim in the *New York Times*, "for deliberately eschewing the safe and tiresome cross-sectional view in favor of advanced painting."[1] Half of the collection then traveled to Paris, the other half to Havana, where, according to the *Times*, the paintings were enthusiastically received.

By the time the two exhibitions had reached Prague and Port-au-Prince a few months later, loud opposition from Congress rose to a crescendo, forcing the State Department to recall the paintings, cancel the show, fire the curator, and eventually sell the paintings at auction. As an attack on freedom of artistic expression, it was a devastating episode, the first of many. At issue was the style of painting, which was branded "distorted," "unintelligible," "unreal," and "ugly." Congressman Fred Busbey (R-Ill.) called it "weird," and even President Truman poked fun at it.[2] But the debate turned

---

ambassador's residence, to the ambassador's offices, and also to the ambassador. Here, it refers specifically to the office building, which may include consular as well as diplomatic offices. Here, too, the distinction between office and residential properties is noted and residences are identified as such.

vicious, and it was not long before critics linked avant-garde painting, and the artists themselves, to political subversion. The "formalist" works of Picasso, Matisse, Chagall, and other "cubists" were condemned as weapons of communist propaganda, and the artists, particularly those who were immigrants, were called communists. Secretary of State George C. Marshall declared in 1947 that the department would spend "no more taxpayers' money for modern art."[3] Accusations swirled around the exhibit of modern painting as Congressman George Dondero (R-Mich.), aided by the Hearst newspapers, an array of other leading publications, and vociferous groups of traditionalist artists, led a campaign against modern art in general and the State Department's cultural programs in particular. Dondero denounced modern art as a communist conspiracy to destroy traditional art and values, leveling special attacks at the Museum of Modern Art and Harvard's Fogg Art Museum. Interestingly enough, he did not attack the Fogg's neighbor, Harvard's Graduate School of Design, though the GSD was busy turning out the first generation of American modernist architects—a group that included John Carl Warnecke, Edward Larrabee Barnes, John Johansen, I. M. Pei, and Paul Rudolph. Those architects, as well as their famed teachers, Bauhaus masters Walter Gropius and Marcel Breuer, all went on to win major embassy commissions from the State Department.

While the State Department was building marble-clad towers and glass-walled boxes in Rio de Janeiro, Havana, and Antwerp, and about to begin similar projects in Madrid, Stockholm, and Copenhagen, Dondero did not turn his animus toward overseas architecture, nor did the others who so loudly faulted modern art as cultural degeneracy. The most obvious explanation for this is that the buildings were far away. Dondero, for instance, did voice objections to modern architecture on the Mall in Washington. Though congressional critics labeled some foreign buildings showy or frivolous, they never linked them to communism, never condemned the architects personally nor tried to connect them to any sort of subversive activity, and made no effort to trace the architecture to its socialist roots in Germany.

Architectural Forum provides one clue as to why critics did not reject modern overseas architecture along with the rest of modern art. In March 1953, in an article that clearly depicted export architecture as a diplomatic tool, the magazine's editors lavishly praised FBO's building program. The article, the first major feature on FBO architecture, was subtitled "Modern Design at Its Best Now Represents This Country in Foreign Lands." The point was underscored in the text:

No country can exercise political world leadership without exercising a degree of cultural leadership as well. Whether consciously or not, the US Government has now made US architecture a vehicle of our cultural leadership.[4]

Of all the architectural journals, *Architectural Forum* was the most likely to serve as a forum for Cold War rhetoric. A publication of Time, Inc., it was owned by Henry Luce, who openly used his better known magazines, *Time, Life,* and *Fortune,* to spread his anticommunist gospel. Luce's personal interest in architecture had prompted him to invest in architectural publishing, and he made no secret of his enthusiasm for modernism. More than an endorsement of political purpose, the *Forum* article was an endorsement of a design direction.

By the early 1950s, members of Congress who inspected new overseas projects came to differ strongly with Luce's assessment. Pressed by stinging congressional criticism, the State Department launched an effort to diminish the autonomy of FBO and directed the office to abandon its flirtation with modernism. Surprisingly, that is *not* what happened. Instead, the postwar design program maintained its course and even expanded its commitment to the new aesthetic.

No single factor is more important to an understanding of this turn of events than the extent to which architectural modernism became identified with democracy in the years following World War II. Modernism slowly acquired credibility in the United States through association with the leading architecture schools and through a series of well-publicized competitions and exhibitions. Still, there were only a handful of major modern buildings to be seen here in the late 1940s. While private corporations were willing to associate themselves with the new look, most American patrons, the U.S. government foremost among them, were still afraid to use modern architecture domestically.

When the State Department moved to its new headquarters in 1946, it moved into a large nondescript building with a stark four-story portico as its entrance and symmetrically arranged floors of offices on either side. The practical and traditionally-planned building was designed in 1941 to house the War Department, which had decided instead to build the Pentagon, an even less inviting and more massive installation across the Potomac. To the editors of the *Foreign Service Journal,* the State Department's move to Foggy Bottom marked a transition between "the leisurely days of Victorian gingerbread, swinging doors and isolationism to the faster pace of functional architecture, air-conditioning and leadership in foreign affairs."[5] In terms of design, the new building seemed cautious and conservative to architects at home, but the size of the building was an indication of an expanded mission and signaled a new era abroad. Due in large measure to the Cold War and ensuing competition between East and West, architecture became a part of the newness.

As Soviet architects renewed their commitment to the traditionalist forms of "Stalinist architecture" and glorified grandeur, high classical vocabulary, and lavish—if ponderous—architectural ornament, American architects were eager to move in the opposite direction. No longer interested in the association between democracy and ancient Greece or Rome, the Americans found it convenient as well as appropriate to equate democracy with newness, openness, abstraction, ambiguity, and technological innovation. Professional journals and magazines hailed their steps in this direction. In its 1953 coverage, for example, *Architectural Forum* underscored the East/West confrontation by contrasting a sketch of Eero Saarinen's proposed U.S. embassy in Helsinki with a photograph of the new Soviet embassy in the same city, and by pairing a photograph of the starkly modern American Consulate in Bremen, designed by Skidmore, Owings & Merrill, with the classically-detailed Soviet Monument in Berlin. With the illustrations, the magazine added text calling attention to how FBO displayed to the rest of the world "a colorful picture of a young, progressive and modern-minded America.... The lesson will not be lost," it observed, "upon those who may have received a different impression from Soviet propaganda."[6]

American embassies became symbols of the United States and its desire to be perceived as an energetic and future-oriented nation. Thus the buildings themselves served as cultural advertisements, propaganda perhaps, but nothing less than reflection of architectural theory married to political necessity. Not surprisingly, the symbols themselves were ambiguous—at once elegant and refined, decorative and flamboyant. Though often concealed behind wood, metal, or masonry screens, the buildings called attention to themselves with the openness of their glass walls, their overall accessibility, and their conspicuous newness.

While some diplomatic historians have examined cultural exchanges, concerts, broadcasts, language training, and other programs that took place in or around embassies, none has touched upon the diplomatic implications of the architecture itself. Critics in the 1960s described U.S. educational and cultural policy abroad as "the neglected aspect" of its foreign affairs, and the subject is overlooked still. According to William Z. Slany, historian of the Department of State, "the building program in the 1950s was the emblem of America's pretensions to superpower status. The results were social, cultural, financial, bureaucratic, and psychological.... The complex picture of the United States abroad," writes Slany, "has been little studied and is poorly understood."[7]

To date there has been no scholarly assessment of this chapter in diplomatic and architectural history—no investigation into the connection between domestic politics and foreign buildings, nor an appraisal of the history or significance of America's overseas landmarks. Even FBO has failed to maintain careful records of construction projects or other documents that might constitute an institutional history for itself. This book represents a step toward providing that history.

Chapter One: The Early Years relates how outcry from businessmen and others appalled at conditions at American posts abroad prompted Congress to pass legislation authorizing public funds for the purchase and construction of foreign buildings. Until then, American diplomats and consular officials paid for their own homes and offices abroad. The Porter Act created the Foreign Service Building Commission (FSBC) in 1926 and launched the foreign building program, headed after 1936 by Frederick A. Larkin.

Chapter Two: Postwar Expansion shows how the building program, financed with war debts, grew rapidly after World War II, how FBO purchased historic properties, how it bought land for upcoming projects, how it first built traditional-looking residences and traditional-looking chanceries, and how it then began to build modern office buildings.

Breaking with government building tradition, in 1948 Larkin's chief architect Leland W. King retained well-known modernists Wallace K. Harrison and Max Abramovitz to design embassies in Rio de Janeiro and Havana. Chapter Three: Modernism at the State Department explores those projects, and why so many in Congress objected to these buildings, which they often compared to the new United Nations tower in New York. This chapter also examines the work of two young American architects, Ralph Rapson and John van der Meulen, hired by King and sent to Europe to design half-a-dozen new embassy office buildings and staff apartment projects. Although these buildings won awards from design professionals, congressional critics quickly pointed out that they seemed to shun their surroundings, and they condemned them—along with the Rio and Madrid projects—for failing to properly represent the United States.

Facing the task of forging strong alliances and counterbalancing Soviet interests, the United States confronted the added challenge of aiding reconstruction and promoting democracy in the territories of its former foes, Germany and Japan. Chapter Four: America Exports Democracy focuses on that effort and the ways in which it affected the building program. It

examines how new staff housing in Tokyo by Raymond & Rado symbolically affirmed America's commitment to a modern Japan and how the architecture of the German program—projected to include forty buildings at
an estimated cost of $19 million—was similarly intended to demonstrate
commitment to Germany. A 1952 congressional investigation into the program was just the beginning of the troubles that ultimately toppled King and
threatened the entire building program. Chapter Five: Modern Architecture
Under Fire examines the events surrounding the Republican victory in
1952 and its impact on the foreign building program. Although King had
won a new $90 million authorization in 1952 before the election, after
it he lacked strong support on Capitol Hill, and newly appointed State
Department officials moved to tighten their control over FBO, an office
that had enjoyed unusual autonomy for years. In a witch-hunt atmosphere,
created in part by the McCarthy hearings, King was charged with mismanagement. Newly appointed State Department officials condemned the "so-
called International Style" and ordered him to return to designs modeled on
Renaissance palaces. As outside consultants came in to run FBO, ongoing
work was suspended.

Chapter Six: Power Shifts looks into why the building program
expanded as it did, why architects became its staunchest champions, and
why congressional critics were so worried about what they considered to
be ostentatious architecture. It also examines how changing foreign policy affected the building program, and sketches how political and aesthetic
power was distributed among the various institutions and individuals whose
decisions shaped public policy: congressmen, State Department administra-
tors, White House officials, Foreign Service officers, ambassadors, foreign
leaders, architects, local planning officials, and the general public, both in
America and abroad; all considered themselves to be the "clients" for these
design commissions.

As part of a political reorganization, the State Department established a
design review panel of prominent "experts" to buffer the building program
from congressional criticism. Chapter Seven: The Architectural Advisory
Committee introduces the first panelists and examines how they selected new
architects for the many projects on their agenda, how they evaluated designs,
and what the panel chairman contributed to the effort. It also looks at how
architects added yet another political dimension to the program, maintaining, as usual, that their efforts were "apolitical." Guided by the new panel,
FBO continued to build conspicuously modern buildings. The focus here
is on the significance of the newly drafted design policy and how it aimed
to further foreign policy objectives by creating "friendly" and "inviting"

American buildings that represented the United States and also reflected the "foreignness" of faraway places.

FBO's new design policy directed project architects to carefully consider climate, site, and local customs and history in preparing their schemes. Buildings were supposed to "fit in" and not stand out as alien intrusions. Chapter Eight: The Program at Its Peak provides an overview of the program during 1955, 1956, and 1957, and explains why, by the following year, the program had passed its prime. The chapter questions the extent to which architects really considered climate, and how they tried to adapt the modernist's glass box to the tropics. It also asks how they incorporated local customs into their work. Disdaining eclecticism in theory, modernists nonetheless borrowed readily from local traditions in efforts to reconcile the international style with regional differences. Did they create "authentic" regional architecture or were they merely playing loosely with exotic themes? Could international style architecture provide an appropriate expression of place?

Chapter Nine: Architects Assert Themselves examines case studies of projects by Edward Durell Stone, Eero Saarinen, and Marcel Breuer. In a design that became his trademark, Stone captured history and fantasy in a way that made the New Delhi embassy memorable as a symbol of the U.S. commitment to India in the 1950s. FBO hoped to duplicate New Delhi's "success" in London and held a juried design competition for the London chancery in which eight firms were invited to participate. Saarinen won first place with a scheme that was faulted by critics for being both too bold and not bold enough. Context was the key problem for Breuer in The Hague, where the new embassy faced a historic square.

Ohio Democrat Wayne Hays directed his wrath against John Johansen's Dublin design, and used that project to augment his own power over the State Department in general and the building program in particular. Chapter Ten: Deadlock Over Dublin, details how the building program became caught in a power struggle only marginally related to architecture, and how a fiscal crisis developed as the supply of credits dried up and FBO was forced to turn to Congress for new funds. It examines Johansen's Dublin design, Hays's objections to it, and how President Kennedy finally broke the deadlock. FBO's design policy was revised in 1961 in response to concern about security at posts abroad. This chapter looks at the new policy and its implications and also at ways in which domestic politics came to play an increased role in the building program.

Chapter Eleven: Targets for Terror traces the impact of security on embassy architecture and how new security standards began to turn embassies into the modern equivalent of frontier stockades. It examines new standards drawn up in the aftermath of the 1983 bombings in Beirut—the so-called "Inman standards"—how those standards reshaped embassy design and why they were never fully implemented. It also looks at the scandals involving U.S. properties in Cairo and Moscow that tarnished the image of FBO and cost it congressional support, and it assesses events surrounding the opening of an array of embassies in the newly independent states of the former Soviet Union. Security constraints and the scarcity of funds and sites significantly limited the Department's options at that time.

Chapter Twelve: Since 1998 explores the recent past and the dramatic changes that have occurred since terrorist bombs destroyed U.S. embassies in Nairobi and Dar es Salaam in 1998. As part of its response to the twin attacks, the State Department reorganized its building program creating a new Bureau of Overseas Buildings Operations (OBO) to replace the former FBO. OBO then drew up standard specifications aimed at speeding production, controlling costs, and increasing security at new embassies worldwide. The ramifications of the shift to a standard model merit serious scrutiny as they have taken the building program in a new and very different direction. The size and cost of new facilities, alone, sets them apart from anything that came before and represents a newly defined U.S. presence on the international landscape. This chapter outlines the scope of work and identifies recent projects from Berlin to Baghdad—already more than sixty new embassies built to protect U.S. personnel who work under menacing circumstances. It may be too soon to fully assess these developments, but it is not too soon to try to place them in an historical context.

To understand how architecture and diplomacy interact, and the meaning of the far-reaching changes that are now occurring, it is necessary to look back to the early years of this century when Congress was first persuaded to provide offices and residences for American diplomats abroad. The buildings that followed—whether exuberant or wary, open or impenetrable, beautiful or banal—are the subject of the following chapters. Their history adds to our understanding of the present as new constraints define diplomatic architecture, new nations rapidly emerge from older ones, and nationalism increasingly serves as a potent force in world affairs.

CHAPTER ONE

The Early Years

IN 1821 THE SULTAN OF MOROCCO gave the United States a building in Tangier as a gift. It became the American legation, and thereafter the oldest diplomatic property continuously owned by this country (fig. 1). But the Tangier legation was an exception.[1] Before 1821, and for a long while after, the United States owned no property abroad and provided no official residences for its foreign envoys, whose salaries and allowances were so small that men often refused to serve due to the financial burden involved. The history of the State Department's overseas building program dates from the creation of the Foreign Service Buildings Commission in 1926. While there were American foreign buildings before that date, they were few and far between.

President George Washington appointed American diplomats to France (1779), Spain (1779), Great Britain (1785), Portugal (1791), and the Netherlands (1792), but as Secretary of State Thomas Jefferson explained to the Senate, those diplomats carried the "lowest grades admissible" to keep costs to a minimum.[2] American envoys to Paris and London were called ministers, rather than ambassadors, because the young republic chose not to designate its representatives with aristocratic-sounding titles. U.S. missions were soon dispatched to Prussia (1797), Russia (1809), and Sweden (1814). Since embassies were official residences associated with ambassadors, and since no U.S. diplomats carried the rank of ambassador until late in the nineteenth century, there were no actual U.S. embassies until that time. Instead, the United States was among those nations represented abroad by diplomatic delegations led by lower ranking diplomats, generally ministers, who lived and worked in buildings known as legations.

Ever anxious to economize, Congress questioned the need for permanent diplomatic representation; still, the number of foreign missions grew slowly but steadily. Between 1823 and 1827, the United States sent representatives to Argentina, Brazil, Chile, Colombia, Denmark, Mexico, Peru, and the combined entity known as the Central American States. Prior to 1840, it had established diplomatic representation in the two Sicilies, Belgium,

Austria, Turkey, and in 1837 had even sent a *chargé d'affaires* to the independent nation of Texas.

A number of prominent public figures served abroad in the country's earliest years, including Benjamin Franklin, John Adams, John Quincy Adams, Thomas Jefferson, and John Jay. Literary figures included novelists Washington Irving and the poet Joel Barlow. Irving served as secretary to the American legation in London (1829–32), then as minister to Spain (1842–46). During his Spanish travels, he lived at least part of the time at the Alhambra, the famed Moorish castle in Granada. As a diplomat, however, he certainly did not live in a government-owned residence. Like the others, he rented space to suit his needs and his pocketbook. It was assumed that American diplomats had the independent means to pay for entertainment, travel, more than minimal rent, and other necessities of diplomatic life abroad. For example, Lucius Foote, designated as "envoy extraordinary and minister plenipotentiary," was the first Western diplomat to establish residence in Seoul when he arrived there in 1883 with his wife and a small staff. His annual salary was $5,000 and his allowance for rent, salaries for his secretary and translator, and other legation expenses consisted of $3,000. Given the absence of suitable facilities for foreigners, initially Foote may have lived in a guest house provided by the king. If he expected Congress to buy him a residence, he was disappointed; when Congress failed to appropriate the funds by 1884, Foote purchased a residence and a legation himself. The residence had a history dating back three hundred years and may have formerly housed royal concubines. In 1887, Congress passed a special appropriation for the acquisition of property in Seoul, and Foote deeded his purchases to the U.S. government in 1888.[3] American envoys with fewer personal resources were less fortunate.

Diplomatic and consular services existed apart until 1924. While diplomats concerned themselves with matters of representation, consuls handled passports, visas, and related business matters. Consular posts were established wherever Americans were involved in commerce or wherever commercial possibilities seemed ripe. By 1840 there were 145 consular posts, compared with twenty diplomatic posts. By 1860, the number of consular posts climbed to 279, with an increase to thirty-three diplomatic posts. Consuls, often businessmen promoting their own commercial interests, collected fees that they were permitted to keep in lieu of salary. Where fees were ample, men of limited means were able to live abroad in relative comfort. American author Nathaniel Hawthorne served as the American consul in Liverpool (1853–57) and managed to save enough money in little over four years to finance a two-year vacation in Italy.[4]

In 1893 Thomas F. Bayard became the first American to hold the rank of ambassador when the Senate confirmed President Grover Cleveland's appointment of Bayard as ambassador to Great Britain. Bayard was secretary of state in Cleveland's first administration, but Cleveland did not want to reappoint him to that position; as consolation, he offered him the first ambassadorial appointment. London thus was the site of the first American embassy, though the ambassador himself was still responsible for renting or buying his own home and office. Later that year the United States similarly established embassies in Paris, Berlin, and Rome.

Expanded trade and the need to protect American Christian missionaries prompted the United States government to begin to purchase and lease residences for its agents and ministers in the Far East. By 1895, the government had properties in Tokyo and Amoy (China), but neither was remotely adequate to its task. Two gifts followed in 1896: a property in Tahiti (a gift from the queen of the Society Islands) and a property in Bangkok (a gift from the king of Siam). That same year President Cleveland called for the purchase of official residences in major capitals, declaring:

> The usefulness of a nation's diplomatic representative undeniably depends much upon the appropriateness of his surroundings, and a country like ours, while avoiding unnecessary glitter and show, should be certain that it does not suffer in its relations with foreign nations through parsimony and shabbiness in its diplomatic outfit.[5]

Cleveland asked Congress to consider the provision of official residences in messages to Congress on 2 December 1895 and 7 December 1896. Despite the President's pleas, however, there was no sign of congressional willingness to accept his challenge.

Since nearly all American representatives were expected to buy or rent their own premises, foreign service was an option only for those with independent incomes. Thus, it was not a question of living amidst opulence; at many consular posts it was a question of not living in squalor. The system hardly favored ability and seemed singularly inappropriate to a democracy. Speaker of the House Nicholas Longworth condemned it in 1906 as "an aristocracy purely and solely of the dollar."[6] Longworth was in a position to do something about the problem: not only was he Speaker of the House, he was also the son-in-law of Theodore Roosevelt, who was then president.

Soon after 1900, as a trend toward professionalism spread through all sectors of American life, Secretary of State Elihu Root reorganized the diplomatic and consular services into a system that required entry exams and offered promotion based on merit for all but top positions. For the first time, the Department of State also established geographic divisions: Latin America, the Far East, the Near East, and Western Europe, reflecting the regions of greatest interest and concern. When Theodore Roosevelt was president, American businessmen drilled for oil in Venezuela, mined copper and silver in Mexico, and sought new markets in the Far East. Meanwhile, the government authorized construction of the Panama Canal to link the oceans, and President Roosevelt brought representatives of Russia and Japan together at Portsmouth, New Hampshire, to sign the treaty ending the Russo-Japanese War. The United States felt confident and expansive, a mood reflected in the classical grandeur of the World's Columbian Exposition, built on the banks of Lake Michigan in 1893. That vision of Beaux-Arts splendor, made out of white plaster, lingered in the minds of many. Translated into white marble, it established the classical vocabulary as the one best able to express the aspirations of American business and government in the years that followed.

Embarrassed and inconvenienced by the lack of support facilities abroad, American businessmen organized the American Embassy Association (AEA) in 1909 "to promote and encourage the acquisition by the United States of permanent homes for its Ambassadors in foreign capitals."[7] Arguing that it was undemocratic to require personal wealth as a prerequisite to foreign service, the association also made a strong case for the need to promote appropriately dignified embassy buildings. Rep. Frank O. Lowden (R-Ill.) voiced this concern to the Congress. He appealed to his fellow House members in 1910 to allow Americans serving abroad to do so on equal terms with emissaries of other nations and to do so on the basis of merit. "No position should be beyond the reach of the trained but poor man," he declared, echoing a theme associated with the progressive movement. "We have boasted through our history that this is a country of homes," Lowden declared. "Shall the nation alone be homeless?"[8]

In 1910, with its business interests worldwide, the United States still owned diplomatic properties in only four foreign capitals—Constantinople, Peking, Tokyo, and Bangkok—and in the International Zone of Tangier. Of those properties, only Constantinople (now Istanbul) and Peking (now Beijing) were considered "suitable" or even "adequate."[9] While there was no generally accepted prototype for embassy architecture, it was understood that a classical model was appropriate. The Peking legation was designed by a government architect who traveled there to supervise construction, and most of the materials were imported from the United States. It was described by Paul S. Reinsch, American minister to China, as "simple but handsome, in stately colonial Renaissance style, its interior admirably combining the spaciousness needed for official entertaining with the repose of a real home."

Reinsch was thankful for the comforts he enjoyed, noting that many an American diplomat has "no place to lay his head except in a hotel."[10]

Lowden's voice was heard in Congress, and on 11 February 1911 a bill was passed enabling the government to buy land and erect buildings abroad for the first time. Known as the Lowden Act, the bill authorized a maximum of $500,000 to be spent annually, and limited the amount that could be spent in any one place to $150,000. The first appropriations under the act were for the acquisition of sites in Mexico City and Tokyo in 1914.

The Mexico City project proceeded under the supervision of the Office of the Supervising Architect of the Treasury, which prepared working drawings and directed construction of a spacious villa designed by the American architect J. E. Campbell. The Tokyo project did not proceed, however, because the $100,000 appropriated for a new residence/office was considered inadequate, especially after existing buildings in Tokyo were destroyed in the earthquake of 1923. As part of its plan for the 1924 World's Fair, the United States built a spacious two-story building in Rio de Janeiro in 1923. Architect Frank L. Packard, of Columbus, Ohio, designed the structure so that it could eventually be used as an embassy office building.[11] But that project was an exception. Despite pressing needs elsewhere, by 1924 only six additional embassy and legation sites or buildings were acquired under the Lowden Act.

Property was purchased in Paris, Oslo, Havana, San José, San Salvador, and Santiago. Funds appropriated for these projects totaled approximately $1 million. Three additional properties, in Panama City, Paris, and London, were acquired at no cost: The War Department transferred a building in Panama City to the State Department in 1916 to be used as a legation; Ambassador Myron Herrick, formerly the head of U.S. Steel, lived in a spacious *hôtel* on the Avenue D'Iena facing the Trocadero in Paris, and donated the house to the U.S. government for use as an embassy residence in 1917 (formerly the home of the French president, it remained the American ambassador's residence until 1970, when it was sold for $2.5 million); and J. Pierpont Morgan donated his choice London home at 13/14 Prince's Gate to the government for use as a permanent residence in 1921.

The United States had a special regard for diplomatic and consular needs in the Far East, given its extensive and growing economic ties to that region and the constant cry of resident Americans for protection from the hostile Chinese, targets of zealous exploitation by foreigners. Though weakened by internal rebellion and external harassment, China was already regarded as a potentially valuable market. As early as 1916, consular officials were pleading with the State Department for better facilities. That year, in congressional hearings on the Diplomatic and Consular Appropriations bill, the port of Shanghai was described as the future "London of the Orient," and Congress was urged to approve the purchase of property there. After the House failed to include an appropriation for Shanghai, Rep. Whitmell Martin (Progressive-La.) received a plea from Secretary of State Robert Lansing urging suitable buildings for the consulate general, the consular court, and other government buildings in Shanghai, and stressing that the United States was the only great government with no permanent and suitable consular and court buildings in that city. Lansing indicated that the lease for the waterfront property then held by the United States and available for purchase was to expire in July 1916, and that the property was likely to fall into other hands, "in which case the Cons. [consulate] will have to be moved from the vicinity of the Consulates of other great nations and find a location outside the American concession and probably in an undesirable location. The result would be a loss of prestige not only for the Cons. and the Court, but, what is vastly more important, for the US in its commercial and political relations with China."[12] Soon after, Congress appropriated $355,000 for Shanghai, and funds for modest consular facilities in the southern Chinese port of Amoy, the Manchurian capital of Mukden, and the Japanese port city of Yokohama.

Appalling conditions generated demand for improved facilities in these cities. Americans were profoundly embarrassed by their diplomatic and consular properties compared to the installations of other nations, notably England, France, Japan, and Germany. In Mukden, for instance, where Japan boasted an "imposing" consulate and British personnel operated out of an "excellent" consulate general, the Americans, with inadequate allowances and no provision of funds for the purchase or leasing of decent facilities worked and lived in temporary quarters available to them through the "charity" of the local military warlord. The *China Weekly Review* cited the "disgrace" of the collapse of the American consular building in Antung, and criticized the State Department and Congress for their stubborn lack of interest.[13]

Although authorized to provide funds for better buildings, Congress was cautious. Every authorization bill that passed had annual spending limits that curtailed the State Department's ability to move quickly in response to Foreign Service needs or real estate opportunities, and moreover, even as Congress approved some spending requests, it flatly denied others. Despite efforts to improve facilities worldwide, the number of places where needs were never met far exceeded the number of places where the United States purchased or built new facilities. The total number of U.S. diplomatic and consular posts peaked at 413 in 1920 when there were forty-five diplomatic posts and 368 consular posts worldwide. In 1931, in the Far East alone, the State Department's list of posts still lacking minimally adequate office and residential quarters included: Canton, Changsha, Chefoo, Foochow, Hankow, Harbin, Nanking, Swatow, Tientsin, Tsinan, Tsingtao, and Yunnanfu (all in China); Dairien (Manchuria); Kobe and Nagoya (Japan); Taihoku (Formosa); and Hong Kong.[14] To some extent, the slow congressional response to State Department requests reflected America's growing isolationist sentiment.

BEFORE THE GOVERNMENT COULD BUILD ABROAD, it needed a mandate to do so. In 1911, Congress granted it that mandate, but no building program was formally established. A major reform bill, the Rogers Act, created the career Foreign Service in 1924. In passing the Rogers Act, Congress recognized that more and better facilities for work and residence were necessary if the Foreign Service was going to be able to fulfill its mission. Two years later, on 7 May 1926, the 69th Congress passed the Foreign Service Buildings Act. Despite the reputed isolationism of the 1920s, Congress recognized America's growing worldwide diplomatic role and the exigency of meeting the needs of the Foreign Service. Named the Porter Act, after its chief sponsor, Rep. Stephen G. Porter of Pittsburgh (R-Pa.), chairman of the House Committee on Foreign Affairs, the bill established for the first time a commission to oversee the purchase and construction of foreign buildings and a fund to finance such projects. It authorized the sizable sum of $10 million for the purchase, alteration, and initial repair of property and buildings for use as diplomatic and consular establishments. It also limited to $2 million the amount that could be appropriated in any one year. Members of the first commission included Secretary of State Frank Kellogg, Secretary of the Treasury Andrew Mellon, Secretary of Commerce Herbert Hoover, and ranking members of House Foreign Affairs and Senate Foreign Relations committees. Since the act provided no technical organization for design work, Secretary Mellon arranged for the Supervising Architect of the Treasury to prepare working drawings and specifications for projects submitted by the commission.[15]

Later the same month, on 25 May, Congress passed the Public Buildings Act, a massive authorization for the design and construction of government buildings. The Supervising Architect's office was similarly charged with implementation of this act, which included $50 million for construction of projects in Washington, D.C. Private, non-government architects did not want to see the Supervising Architect in control of all of this new design work. Fearing standardization and re-use of plans that would further diminish design opportunities, the American Institute of Architects (AIA) led the effort to maximize private input and harshly criticized the work of the Treasury Office as inferior. In response to aggressive lobbying, Congress amended the Public Buildings Act with the Keyes-Elliott bill of 1930, which increased Treasury's authority to contract with private architects.[16] The tug-of-war between the architectural profession and the Supervising Architect's office was not a reflection of stylistic differences as much as it was an economic battle and a struggle for professional autonomy. Eventually, private firms won most major commissions, highly prized for their visibility and symbolic importance.

The situation with foreign buildings differed little from that of the domestic buildings. Private architects sought the overseas commissions with the same vigor as those who pursued domestic jobs. The problems faced abroad, however, far exceeded those associated with domestic projects. The travel alone required coordination and planning. Disposition and ownership of overseas real estate raised issues that were more complex than usual and required special expertise.

In 1928, Representative Porter offered an amendment to the 1926 Act to permit the Foreign Service Buildings Commission (FSBC) to dispose of real estate and to hire staff for technical assistance. "Any commercial real estate office handling so many properties at such a distance would have power to buy, sell, or exchange properties as conditions change so as to protect their holdings," Porter argued in a report prepared by the Committee on Foreign Affairs.[17] On 29 May 1928, Congress passed Public Law 586, which enabled the State Department to dispose of properties by exchange.[18] Though real estate conditions varied widely and values fluctuated as politics and economics changed, the legislation did not enable the department to sell undesired properties and use the proceeds to purchase other properties or to finance other needed projects. Congress chose not to recognize the Foreign Service Buildings Office as a true real estate operation.

Defending the request for $5,000 a year for technical assistance, Porter's report observed:

> The work in the foreign buildings office is almost wholly without precedent. It is true we own some Government buildings. These, however, were acquired piecemeal and not as part of a broad, general policy to provide the Government with Government-owned buildings wherever our officials abroad are located.[19]

To support the commission, the Secretary of State set up a real estate office in the Department of State. Its fledgling staff consisted of one Foreign Service officer, Keith Merrill, on loan from consular work, and three clerks, on loan from the department. The staff, not the commission itself, was charged with the task of gathering data and preparing budgets and plans, but commission members—mainly the congressmen taking advantage of summer recesses—embarked on wide-ranging international inspection trips, often accompanied by Merrill.

Merrill was brought up in the real estate business. A graduate of Harvard Law School, he served as vice-consul in London and consul in Madrid, and then joined the State Department to work on preparations for hearings on the Foreign Service Buildings Act in 1926. Once the commission was established, Porter appointed Merrill as its executive secretary. Under questioning by Rep. Sol Bloom (D-N.Y.) of the Foreign Affairs Committee, Merrill explained that the Treasury Department was responsible for contracts and audits regarding foreign buildings. Outside architects, he said, were selected from across the country and retained to make preliminary studies for 3 percent of cost or less. He explained:

> Those studies, if approved by the Foreign Service Buildings Commission, are sent to the Supervising Architect's Office, where the final work is done on the drawings and the specifications. They then go out for bids, the contract is let, and the work is completed. The maximum allowed under the original buildings act for that architectural and technical services is 5 per cent. When that work is done completely by outside architects, the preliminary studies and final drawings are subject to review by the Supervising Architect.[20]

Merrill emphasized the role of the Supervising Architect, although his comments suggest that the FSBC retained outside architects on a regular basis, as the record shows.

Saying that he did not want the new fund to pay for his travel until he knew more about the work and its problems, in the summer of 1927 Porter traveled at his own expense to inspect sites in Guatemala City, Tegucigalpa, Corinto, Panama, Bluefields, Santiago de Cuba, Havana, Matanzas, Nuevitas, and Cienfuegos. Later that summer, he traveled to Paris to select a site for the new U.S. embassy office building there, and entered into negotiations for a site on the Place de la Concorde. That acquisition led to one of the first large-scale construction projects funded under the new act. Porter and Merrill returned to Paris in 1928 and then went on to Berlin, where they arranged to purchase the Bluecher Palace and its grounds, a property earlier selected by Porter and Rep. J. Charles Linthicum (D-Md.). Aside from these few transactions in Europe, the commission focused its attention on the first priority of providing facilities at "unhealthful" posts and posts in South America and the Far East. Linthicum, also a member of the House Foreign Affairs Committee, visited Rio de Janeiro, Buenos Aires, Santiago, Lima, Panama, and Montevideo in 1928. Robert J. Phillips, who had come over to the Foreign Service Buildings Office on loan from the Commerce Department, inspected property in Rio de Janeiro, Buenos Aires, Valparaiso, Santiago, La Paz, Panama, Lima, and Montevideo in the same year. The following year Merrill visited Belize, Managua, Panama, Guayaquil, Lima, La Paz, Buenos Aires, Montevideo, Rio de Janeiro, and Trinidad.

By 1931, Secretary of State Henry Stimson pointed to an impressive list of accomplishments abroad, including: acquisition of the site for an office building in Paris, site acquisition and approval of plans for an office building in Buenos Aires, acquisition of the Bluecher Palace for use as an embassy in Berlin, approval of previously drawn plans for a consulate at Amoy, approval of plans for an office building in Rio de Janeiro, acquisition of a site for an ambassador's residence in Lima, the beginning of construction of a consular building at Yokohama, and approval of plans for an embassy compound in Tokyo (construction was 70 percent complete in 1931). In addition, the FSBC had authorized purchase of a site for an office building in Ottawa, purchase of sites for consulates in Aden and Corinto, construction of consulates in Panama and Mukden, purchase of a site for a legation in Monrovia, purchase of sites for offices and residences in Managua and Calcutta, purchase of land and buildings in Tehran, Matanzas, and Santiago, furnishing of a government-owned ambassador's residence in Seville, and rehabilitation of the legation in Tangier (acquired by gift). Projects already completed by 1931 included purchase, repair, and furnishing of an ambassador's residence in Buenos Aires, furnishing of the ambassador's residence in London (acquired by gift), remodeling of the ambassador's residence in Paris (likewise, acquired by gift), and acquisition, remodeling, and repair of consulates at Penang and Nagasaki.

When asked about architect selection, Merrill said that the FSBC tried to pick architects from all across the country.[21] Since many projects never reached completion or lacked clear attribution, it is hard to know the extent to which geography really was a consideration. The commission also tried to hire American architects with work experience in other countries. For example, Secretary of State Frank B. Kellogg requested that Porter approve the appointment of Cass Gilbert to design the embassy in Ottawa, citing Gilbert's "great experience in construction work in Canada."[22] Though Gilbert's prior experience was never identified and may never have occurred, he did get the job and presented sketches to the commission on 22 June 1928. The embassy was built in the early 1930s, and took its cue from the classical model much favored in Washington. Supervising Architect of the Treasury Louis Simon prepared the working drawings for the building, which was prominently sited directly across from the Canadian Houses of Parliament (fig. 2).

Architect Robert Trimble, who had traveled and worked in the Far East, was selected to inspect overseas properties for the FSBC. On one trip in 1929, Trimble visited Shanghai, Calcutta, Rangoon, Bombay, and Aden. Elliott Hazzard, like Trimble, was an American architect experienced in the Far East. Hazzard went to China after World War I and set up practice in Shanghai. He designed the Amoy consulate and also served as the contractor for the project, completed in 1929. Later, the consul general at Shanghai asked Hazzard about revising the Amoy plans for use at Mukden. The plans were sent to the Office of the Supervising Architect for modifications to the façade and layout, but on 9 November 1928, instead of changes, the commission requested a new scheme for a consular building "in the manner of Westover mansion," an elegantly proportioned Virginia plantation house of red brick. If one is able to read anything into the decision not to reuse the Amoy plans it would be the desire to have an equally impressive but better proportioned and more dignified scheme. Trimble also designed the consulate general in Shanghai between 1928 and 1931, despite protest from his professional foe Hazzard, who wanted the commission himself.

The State Department was still trying to win approval to complete the project at Shanghai in 1935, arguing that it was urgent to proceed. Over $723,000 remained in its authorization, but those funds needed to be *appropriated* before they could be spent. Assistant Secretary of State Wilbur J. Carr claimed that "Our failure to construct a suitable building in the great city of Shanghai is regarded there not as a simple reluctance to expend money, but as a lack of permanent interest, and gives rise to speculation as to how long and to what extent the United States will continue to manifest any interest at all in that part of the world." In defense of the project, Carr also maintained that construction of an "imposing building upon our very prominent site" would also "serve as an exhibit of American construction, manufacture and equipment." He mentioned, for instance, that all of the mechanical equipment, heating, plumbing, wiring, and conduits, as well as electrical apparatus would be manufactured in the United States for use in China, and continued:

> The practical value of this kind of exhibit…is illustrated by the fact that after the installation in the American Embassy at Buenos Aires of a complete electrical kitchen with electric ice-boxes, stoves, et cetera, all large apartment houses subsequently designed or constructed in that city have included these American electrical inventions.[24]

No doubt primitive conditions and the widespread lack of electricity would have limited the usefulness of ice-boxes in China. Prestige compelled the urgency of this project, as did the hope of bettering the already strong trading position of the United States there. In the 1920s, before the crash that rocked the worldwide economy and put a check on overseas expansion, America's business interests were largely synonymous with its diplomatic interests. Four thousand Americans lived in the treaty port of Shanghai in 1935, and most were businessmen prospering or attempting to prosper from advantageous trade agreements. But the Americans could do little to influence the worsening internal situation in China, with or without a prestigious building in Shanghai. In 1936 work on the Shanghai project was permanently suspended. Its funds were reallocated to the embassy residence at Rio, and to projects in Panama, Lima, and Havana.[25]

BEFORE THE UNITED STATES BEGAN TO BUILD EMBASSIES, when the State Department could only purchase buildings to serve as residences and offices, generally the only sort of buildings available were large, even palatial, houses. The department purchased a handsome villa in Oslo in 1924, for example (fig. 3). Built in 1911 by former Norwegian Consul General Hans Olsen and his wife Mina Nobel Olsen (niece of Alfred Nobel), the villa was designed by Norway's most noted national romantic architect, Henrik Bull. The department also purchased the seventeenth-century Schoenborn Palace in Prague in 1925 for use as an embassy chancery. Many new embassies, including those received as gifts, were predictably grand. When the government began to design and build its own embassies, architects looked to these properties as models. Palatial homes were also the buildings popularly associated with diplomatic discourse. The signing of the Treaty of Versailles in the Hall of Mirrors in 1918 is one well-known diplomatic event associated with a royal residence.

When the department began to build its own embassies, its architects turned to well-known and widely admired American houses as models. In addition to Westover, those that were particularly influential were Carter's Grove (James City County, Va.), Monticello (Charlottesville, Va.), Homewood (Baltimore, Md.), and the White House, already an American architectural icon. Members of the FSBC greatly admired the American colonial tradition. Representative Porter also offered the suggestion that all foreign buildings be white, in keeping with landmark buildings in Washington. The *Pittsburgh Press* interpreted Porter's remark as a call for replicas of the White House. At least one building designed and built by the United States government was such a replica, the consulate in Yokohama, built in the early 1930s. The FSBC selected architect Frederick Brooke to design a consulate in Bluefields

(Nicaragua) to resemble Carroll House (Homewood), and Harrie T. Lindeberg patterned the embassy in Helsinki (1936) after Westover (fig. 4). The Baghdad legation was also modeled after the White House, but it was not a U.S.-built building. Rather, it was designed and built in 1938 by an Iraqi businessman who leased it to the State Department. William C. Bullitt, the first U.S. ambassador to the Soviet Union, proposed a replica of Jefferson's Monticello for a site on the Lenin Hills promised to him by Stalin in 1934, but Stalin never provided the site and Bullitt's plans were never realized.[26]

When the embassy was divorced from its residential purpose, however, houses no longer offered necessarily useful prototypes. Architects faced the problem of creating a new building type—of designing structures planned around an array of functions, some private and some public, some ceremonial and some routine and ordinary. For the new Paris embassy, for example, architects were asked to incorporate public-oriented spaces, such as consular offices, and ceremonial spaces, including an elaborate entrance vestibule, a grand staircase, and ornate reception rooms. While the ambassador's office and other prominent spaces were paneled in French oak and furnished with marble mantels and impressive crystal chandeliers, other parts of the building were "treated in the manner of an ordinary American office building with movable wood and glass partitions."[27] It was not a typical office building, by any definition. New structures, such as the Paris project, also had to incorporate the latest technology and innovative systems for heating, lighting, ventilation, and sanitation.

For the first major embassy construction projects in Tokyo and Paris, architects were guided by Beaux-Arts principles that emphasized clarity of plan, unity of parts, and appropriateness of expression. For Paris, Delano & Aldrich designed a Renaissance palazzo adapted as a modern office building. For Tokyo, Raymond & Magonigle also drew upon historical precedent, but their project included a chancery, staff apartments, as well as a separate ambassador's residence, all related by design. The two projects were very different, but their plans shared organizing principles, and to differing degrees, their designs were both classically-inspired.

Prior to passage of the Porter Bill, under a special appropriation in 1925, Congress authorized funds for diplomatic and consular buildings in Tokyo. Strictly speaking, the start of the Tokyo project preceded the creation of the FSBC, but after the new program was established, the Tokyo project ranked with Paris as one of the commission's earliest and most notable accomplishments. Architects for the project were H. Van Buren Magonigle, a New Yorker with impressive credentials, and Antonin Raymond, who had worked in Magonigle's office in 1916 and had since moved to Japan and established a thriving practice there. Magonigle was highly regarded by his traditionalist peers as a forward-looking architect. Contemporaries described him as a courteous and cultured gentleman. Together, Magonigle and Raymond formed an odd but outstanding pair.[28]

Much younger than Magonigle, Raymond was a Czech émigré later described as impetuous, emotional, and self-involved. But he was a clever designer with a special understanding of structure and a real appreciation for the possibilities of modernism. A native of Bohemia, Raymond studied at the Prague Polytechnic and made his way to New York in 1910 to work in the office of Cass Gilbert on the Woolworth Building. By 1914 he was working for Frank Lloyd Wright, whose designs he had known and admired as a student. After service in the United States Army during the war, Raymond reunited with Wright and moved to Tokyo to assist him on the Imperial Hotel. Once there, he stayed and established his own practice. He heard about the embassy commission from a friend posted there and was determined to participate in it. The embassy site, purchased in 1925, was directly across from his own house, on a hill with a commanding view of the landscape and the Japanese Parliament Building across the valley.[29] Magonigle traveled to Tokyo from New York in 1926 to inspect the site. He prepared the designs, while Raymond was responsible for site planning and eventually all of the construction supervision. In his autobiography, Raymond notes that he was forced "to change the structural design completely in order to comply with earthquake conditions." With his prior experience there, he was in a far better position than his partner to understand the requirements of the local building code and the seismic situation (figs. 5–6).

The Tokyo project consisted of a three-story chancery flanked by two similarly styled apartment buildings facing a courtyard. The apartments were for senior officers. Further up the steep hill was an L-shaped ambassador's residence opening onto gardens, planned with American principles using Japanese materials, according to Raymond (figs. 7–8). "The Embassy buildings are not modern in their design," he wrote, "but neither do they reflect any period."[30] Actually, the design fused Beaux-Arts planning, modern structure, and traditional ornament drawn from Japanese precedent. The architects used white stucco over reinforced concrete for all the walls, which were topped by highly ornamented decorative bands of precast stucco. The bands, alternating solids and voids, are reminiscent of Wright's ornamental work. Small mosaic tiles frame the windows with bands of color, graded from light blue below the bottom sills to dark blue at the top. Even a minor entrance to the ambassador's residence has splendid bronze doors surrounded by a frame of small mosaic tiles. The project is also significant for its elaborate fence of cast and wrought iron and its lead roofs bordered by friezes of black-glazed terra cotta. At completion in 1931, the Great Seal of the United

States, lavishly reproduced in bronze, was installed above the entrance in a setting of black and white tiles and purple marble.

Despite the elegant and elaborate details, Ambassador W. Cameron Forbes, the first to occupy the residence, faulted it for its shortage of bedrooms and baths, and complained that electric light fixtures had not arrived and carpentry work was still unfinished. Improbable though it sounds, the polo-playing Brahmin from Boston also called the architect, Raymond, to bemoan the fact that "he could not bring his horse into the living room to show his guests, as he was accustomed to do in his establishment in the United States."[31] No architect could have anticipated such needs.

Aside from Tokyo, the FSBC's most significant project was the design and construction of the U.S. Embassy in Paris. According to Merrill, when the FSBC was established its four biggest projects of immediate importance were Paris, Berlin, Rome, and Buenos Aires.[32] Of the four, Paris was the first to proceed, and from the outset, it was recognized as a project of the highest diplomatic value. The building site, selected personally by Representative Porter and purchased for the sum of $200,000, was the prized location on the northwest corner of the Place de la Concorde.

After Porter, who pushed the first major foreign building legislation through Congress in 1926 and promoted the program until his death in 1930, Rep. Sol Bloom was probably the most influential member of the House Foreign Affairs Committee until Wayne Hays (D-Ohio) joined its membership in 1955. Bloom was once a young impresario who brought exotic dancers to the 1893 World's Columbian Exposition in Chicago and premiered the famous "Hootchy Kootchy," a dance that captivated popular audiences. He was born in 1870 in Pekin, Illinois, the son of Jewish immigrants from Poland. A bookkeeper by the age of thirteen, he was a talented performer and entrepreneur, who wrote and produced plays and owned his own theater by the time he was nineteen. After the Exposition, he built businesses in sheet music and copyrights, promoted boxing matches, and amassed a fortune. When he moved to New York in 1910, he was already a wealthy man. He retired in 1920, at the age of fifty, and thereafter devoted himself to public service, winning his first Congressional election in 1923 with the support of Tammany Hall. He became an eccentric and industrious congressman recognized as a spokesman for the entertainment industry and as a strong New Deal advocate, and he was a key member of the Foreign Affairs Committee, serving as its chairman from 1939 until 1947, and again in 1949. He was also an *ex officio* member of the FSBC. All State Department authorizations had to win backing from the Foreign Affairs Committee, so Bloom's interest was essential.

As early as 1931, when the Foreign Affairs Committee held hearings on a proposed increase in the authorization for foreign buildings, Bloom's questions and comments show him to be a man who had a serious concern about foreign affairs, and a sincere interest in foreign buildings. If anything, his desire to review the minute details of certain projects irked his colleagues, who were satisfied with general facts and vague assurances.

Plans for the proposed Paris office building particularly concerned Bloom, and he closely questioned Merrill on the subject. Bloom wanted to know why Merrill did not buy the adjacent property when it was certain to be necessary someday to the United States. Merrill replied that his funds were limited, and he maintained that the purchased site was already ample in size. Bloom pressed him on the design restrictions imposed on the site by French law and on the preordained limits to expansion. Rep. Morton D. Hull (R-Ill.) interrupted and accused Bloom of wasting the committee's time. Bloom persisted. He wanted a clear understanding of how much space the building required and what functions it had to include, and he insisted that Merrill spell out the building's numerous functional needs, which included space for the consulate general, a commercial attaché, a military attaché, and a naval attaché; U.S. Customs and public health offices; the Advisory Commission on Aeronautics; the Battle Monuments Commission; offices related to reparations, rents, requisitions, and claims; diplomatic reception rooms; offices for the ambassador and his staff; and space for the building manager. The building would also contain a large library, dining rooms, kitchens, extensive storage space for archives, and underground parking for fifty cars. It was by far the most elaborate program that the FSBC had yet reviewed.

When another congressman tried to stop discussion of the Paris project, Bloom became furious. For him, it was imperative that the FSBC recognize the real problems of building in a historic zone, and he wanted the record to show the facts. "It does not make any difference to me," he said, "but these gentlemen are showing the plans here and naturally it is to be expected that the committee criticize the plans and ask questions. If you do not want to see them, it does not make any difference to me." Rep. Cyrenus Cole (R-Iowa) then asked Merrill if he would be able to add to the top of the completed building if more space was necessary, and Merrill replied that it could be done using a step back. Bloom was skeptical. He knew Merrill was wrong, and offered the following unusual observation:

> I was originally going to buy this property for myself, and I know the restrictions. You can not get more space than you have if you want to go up two extra stories. The authorities there will not allow you to do it. They are very particular about that property, and if you were permitted to do it and

should do it, the French people would feel very, very much dissatisfied. That is a fact because that particular corner, the French people are very, very careful about having its uniformity maintained around there.[33]

Although plans for the new building were already approved by Paris officials, Bloom urged Merrill to recognize the seriousness of the design controls at the Place de la Concorde and the need for future expansion. The 1931 discussion shifted to other matters when Representative Linthicum declared, "I think there will be abundant space for all time there," and Bloom's words were forgotten.

The New York firm of Delano & Aldrich designed the Paris Embassy in 1929, construction began in 1931, and it was completed by 1932. Merrill claimed that the Delano & Aldrich firm was selected because of its plans for the Japanese Embassy in Washington, and also because of its admirable plan for the proposed Post Office Department building in Washington's Federal Triangle. William Adams Delano, a graduate of the École des Beaux-Arts, had spent many years in France. Victor Laloux, Delano's former teacher, served as consulting architect to the project (figs. 9–10).

As Bloom noted, strict Parisian design controls accompanied the site and guided the choices available to the architects. Jacques-Ange Gabriel had designed buildings at two corners of the Place de la Concorde between 1753 and 1755—the Hôtel Saint-Florentin, once Talleyrand's residence at one end of the rue de Rivoli, and the other flanking the rue Royale. A Parisian law of 1757 required all future buildings surrounding the Place de la Concorde to conform to Gabriel's established design plan.[34] Taking their cue from Gabriel's original scheme, Delano & Aldrich created a classically detailed Beaux-Arts building guarded by monumental American eagles that flanked the entrance to a fenced forecourt. The building consisted of five stories above grade, and two stories below.

Built of steel and concrete, the embassy featured a doughnut plan and a central courtyard covered with glass over the first floor. On the ground floor, which housed consular offices, the courtyard was used as general office space for dealing with American citizens with consular business. Above, it served as a light well to the offices arranged on its periphery. Plans of the scheme show how tightly organized the design was. The ground floor consulate was open to the public. Two lesser entrances at this level also led directly from the street to offices devoted to immigration and consular invoices. The mezzanine contained offices for bookkeepers, stenographers, file clerks, and others whose duties were both consular and diplomatic. The second floor housed a Treasury Department office and the extensive offices then needed by the commercial attaché. The third floor housed the chancery, or the diplomatic offices, accessible via the central staircase and also via elevator. With the highest ceiling height and tallest windows, this floor contained the ambassador's private office, located on the southwest corner of the building and shown on the plan as "*Chambre de Reception Privée*," and the main reception room, shown on the plan as "*Ambassadeur*." (The original plan was amended, and the spaces were reversed after the building was finished.) The top floor contained offices of the various military attachés and others, including the Graves Registration Commission and Battle Monuments Commission.

The State Department selected an American contractor to build the Paris embassy, but all of the plans were converted to metric units and translated into French to facilitate the work of French subcontractors. The materials were both American and French in origin. The elevators, much of the mechanical equipment, tiles, and most of the flooring came from the United States. Floors in key rooms were created from beams removed from the Louvre during recent renovation. All of the limestone and marble was French. Contemporary accounts praised the United States for utilizing French materials and for allowing French workmen to complete much of the work. The whole was solid, simple, and symmetrical, an instant image of permanence and importance hailed by French and American critics as an asset to Paris and widely praised for its dignified and appropriate presentation.[35]

History proved Linthicum to be wrong—and Bloom correct. In less than fifteen years, the United States needed to expand its space in Paris. When American officials failed to heed Bloom's prescient warning about French sensibilities and the importance of maintaining design unity, they did so at great cost. The French reacted in horror at the later American intention to demolish a prominent French landmark nearby and replace it with a modern office building. In 1931, however, the FSBC and the Foreign Affairs Committee were not thinking about long-range plans or about modern-looking buildings. Their members shared two goals: to provide for immediate office and residential needs, particularly in places considered to be unhealthful, and to produce American buildings that would compare favorably with those of other great powers. They took a short-term view of each project and had no real way of anticipating future needs. They wanted to accomplish these goals while spending as little as possible. With admiration, and also envy in his voice, Chairman Henry W. Temple (R-Pa.) described Great Britain's new embassy in Washington as "the finest, and possibly the most expensive embassy or legation building to be found anywhere."[36] Temple and his colleagues made it clear in their remarks that they recognized the embassy on Massachusetts Avenue, designed by Edwin Lutyens in the traditional manner of a great country house, as the ultimate expression of what an embassy should be (fig. 11).

Bloom's advice stands out because of its prescience and because of his realistic assessment of how little the State Department could expect to accomplish without large-scale spending. In 1931, he urged the committee to consider the notion of buying property as available and holding it for future use. He also argued the benefits of owning diplomatic and consular properties—as opposed to leasing them—and he pointed out the advantages of combining diplomatic and consular offices at one site. Such an arrangement, he maintained, was more efficient and less costly. All of these ideas were recognized as important by the late 1930s and became policy thereafter when Bloom became chairman of the Foreign Affairs Committee in 1939.

SOON AFTER THE Office of the Supervising Architect moved from the Bureau of Construction at the Treasury Department into the Public Buildings Branch of the Procurement Division at Treasury, Frederick A. Larkin joined the staff of the newly created Public Buildings office as an inspection engineer. Larkin, known as "Fritz," was the man who masterminded the vast expansion of the foreign building program, and his arrival in 1935 signaled the beginning of a new phase in the program's history.

In 1935, Congress approved two modest authorization bills providing the building program with a total of $1,625,000 for a period of seven years.[37] Merrill resigned his position in 1936, and Larkin was appointed Chief of the Foreign Service Buildings Office, still an adjunct to the FSBC. Two years later, in 1938, Congress approved another, somewhat larger authorization of $5 million with a spending limit of $1 million per year. By the late 1930s, as a result of structural and personnel changes, the FSBC assumed a role that was largely advisory, and its administrative staff, headed by Larkin, took over direction of the building program. Thus Larkin had ample funds to work with as he began the task of turning the tiny office into a major real estate operation.

Larkin's strength grew rapidly. He had studied some architecture and engineering and had an interest in architecture, but his talents lay elsewhere, and most of his professional experience came from his years in the construction business supervising projects at home and abroad. Any explanation of his later success has to take into account the force of his personality and the power he derived from forging close ties to key Democratic congressmen. His overall influence came from his staunch congressional support and not from his position or rank at the Department of State, or as a result of any broad-based directive from Secretary of State James F. Byrnes or any other appointed public official. Two key congressional committees had and still have oversight over the budget of the Department of State: the House Committee on Foreign Affairs (now the House Committee on International Relations), which authorizes funds, and the House Appropriations Committee, which follows with actual appropriations each fiscal year. Both committees have subcommittees that review proposed legislation and budget requests. Larkin's two strongest allies in Congress were Democrats Sol Bloom, chairman of the House Foreign Affairs Committee, and John J. Rooney (D-N.Y.), chairman of the Subcommittee on the State and Justice Departments, the Judiciary and Related Federal Agencies of the House Appropriations Committee. Both men, especially Rooney, also happened to be his frequent traveling companions. Rooney chaired the Appropriations subcommittee from 1943 to 1953 and from 1955 to 1975, giving him control of the State Department's purse strings for thirty years. His disdain for what he considered to be waste was well-known, but his closeness to Larkin meant a virtual guaranty of support for foreign buildings until Larkin's retirement in 1952. At taxpayer expense, Rooney and his wife toured constantly with the energetic Larkin, accompanying him on trips to inspect, evaluate, and buy diplomatic properties and sites for future use—and on trips that may have had less specific purposes as well.

From the earliest years of U.S. diplomatic representation, Americans showed a suspicion of "unnecessary" comforts and expenditures for alleged frills. For example, the Tokyo embassy, recognized as the finest American building compound abroad and admired for its beauty as well as its practicality, was severely criticized in Washington. Its spacious rooms, elegant gardens, and fine ornamental motifs gave cost-conscious congressmen a target for ridicule. The display of architectural opulence, appreciated by the personnel at the post and highly regarded in the host country, was censured in Congress and described as "Hoover's Folly."[38]

The problems that Larkin faced in the 1930s largely involved improving upon designs to make them better fitted to their foreign sites and lowering the architectural profile so that the buildings were less likely to prompt criticism at home. He argued, for example, that the site purchased by the State Department in 1930 for an office building in Buenos Aires was too expensive, and he pointed out that a new subway line already ran beneath part of the property. He urged the selection of a "more modest" property in that city.[39] He also suggested that plans for the Monrovia legation made construction there too expensive. Scrutiny of the sorts of projects that were revised or reevaluated at that time reveals that Larkin made a conspicuous move away from schemes that might have appeared overly ostentatious or grand. He had a clear mandate to build practical rather than elaborate foreign buildings. Other projects moved ahead during the decade of the 1930s, and all were conspicuously traditional and straightforward. Wyeth & Sullivan designed the U.S. legation in Tirana, Albania, for example, as an unadorned two-story house with two small one-story wings bordering an open court (fig. 12).

When the FSBC met at the home of Assistant Secretary of State George S. Messersmith on 21 February 1938 the agenda labeled plans for the new legation in Montevideo "unnecessarily elaborate and expensive," although the Baltimore firm of Perring & White had submitted plans that had been approved in 1932.[40] Once bids came in, however, and it became apparent that available funds would not cover the cost of the building as designed, Larkin asked permission to turn the project over to Treasury architects. When the FSBC approved drawings for the legation in Managua in 1937, the commission stipulated that the same drawings were to be used for legations at Ciudad Trujillo and Port-au-Prince, but conditions at those posts had since proven to be radically different from those at Managua. Larkin described the Managua scheme as too elaborate and asked the commission to authorize new designs for Ciudad Trujillo and Port-au-Prince. He suggested the need for "simpler and more practical structures entailing less expense for maintenance and repair, though at the same time providing the proper degree of architectural merit and imposing appearance." At the same meeting, he requested approval of a plan to exchange the U.S.-owned site in the worst section of Managua for another healthier site, permission to re-allocate funds from Shanghai to build a new embassy residence in Rio de Janeiro (to replace a deteriorating and architecturally undistinguished building) and an embassy in Lima (on an already owned site). Other funds from Shanghai would finance the purchase of sites and construction of office buildings at Panama City and Havana, the purchase of a site for a legation residence at Panama City, and a site for an embassy residence at Havana. In response to conditions at the posts and priorities set by State Department area offices, the commission also considered funding construction of a legation at Vienna and purchase of leased property as a consulate in Mexico City.

When the House Committee on Foreign Affairs held hearings on the FSBC's $5 million authorization request on 22 March 1938, both the committee and witnesses for the State Department made it clear that they wanted to see diplomatic and consular offices combined where possible for the sake of efficiency and economy. The aim was to have the fewest number of separate properties to staff and maintain.[41]

Questioned by Bloom, Messersmith agreed that office space was poor and residential conditions were unacceptable at Athens, Bangkok, Bogotá, Calcutta, Havana, Lima, Mukden, Panama City, Rome, Santiago (Cuba), and Tehran. Bloom urged the State Department to invest in small jobs, many in South America, where needs were urgent, not just the major projects such as Paris. He was also highly critical of the situation in which American ministers found themselves unable to afford the cost of living at various posts. In Calcutta, where nearly all other consular staffs moved to the mountains for the summer months, the Americans were stranded in the heat. In an exchange with Rep. George Dondero, Messersmith explained that Americans had inadequate rental allowances to ease the financial burden of finding acceptable housing in Calcutta, let alone to accompany the rest of the government and its foreign representatives in their seasonal migration. He told the committee that the situation was the same in Belgrade, where the whole Yugoslavian government moved for the summer, similarly leaving the Americans behind. Congressmen who had visited foreign cities agreed that American diplomats were among the lowest paid in the world and thus unable to secure decent rental accommodations. The low pay further justified the need for the building program which aimed to provide a badly needed ambassador's residence at Lima, and combined office buildings and residences in cities including Ankara, Athens, Bangkok, Buenos Aires, Calcutta, Havana, Mukden, Panama City, and Tehran.[42]

For Berlin, the FSBC was prepared to spend $1 million, an amount equal to its entire annual appropriation. The U.S. government had purchased the Bluecher Palace property there in 1931. According to FSBC records, it was "probably the finest site in the city of Berlin," at the center of the city, adjoining the Brandenburg Gate.[43] (It is the site on which the United States opened its new embassy in 2008.) For hearings before the Foreign Affairs Committee, the State Department outlined its plan to erect a new office building on the part of the property facing the Pariser Platz, and also a new residence on the section that fronted upon the avenue then called Hermann Goering Strasse. The department also planned to renovate existing buildings for staff housing or demolish and replace them. "As you know," Messersmith told Bloom, "the German government has fantastic plans for changing Berlin, especially the center of the city."[44] Although Hitler wanted to buy the U.S.-owned property, Messersmith said, it was too valuable to sell. Rep. Samuel D. McReynolds (D-Tenn.), the committee chairman, said that he had asked the ambassador to try to arrange an exchange with the Nazi government. German plans prompted other moves, too, and Messersmith told the committee that several governments were eyeing a site across from the American property. "I am telling you," he said, "right next to the French Embassy is the house of one of the most distinguished Jewish personages which several governments are contemplating for Embassy purposes." No one in the hearings asked or seemed to want to know what had happened to the owners of that house. Soon thereafter, the French embassy was vacant, too, and questions concerning the value of the Bluecher property were no longer relevant. Hitler invaded Poland on 1 September 1939, and military issues quickly replaced diplomatic ones.

Two months earlier, in a move unrelated to the worsening situation in Europe, President Roosevelt had introduced a government reorganization plan that transferred the FSBC and its functions to the State Department.[45] The FSBC, once empowered to choose sites, select architects, and approve plans, lost its independent status and became an advisory body to the secretary of state and the small Foreign Service Buildings Office, headed by Larkin. The reorganization plan was the first in a series of steps that strengthened Larkin's position considerably, but there was little he could do as war brought a virtual halt to construction in many parts of the world.

IF LARKIN PROVIDED the real estate expertise for the postwar building program, Leland W. King Jr., provided its design direction. King, Larkin's assistant, was a young Arizona architect who also arrived at the Treasury Department in 1935 after completing the design of the Wyatt Clinic, a small, private medical facility in Tucson. Featured in the June 1935 issue of *Architectural Forum*, the clinic was the first building in the region to use steel-clad insulation over a welded light-weight steel frame. Its entire skeleton—window frames, door frames, and roof deck—was prefabricated. On the south, east, and west, its windows were made of a new type of plate glass capable of absorbing the sun's heat, probably the first use of this new product in the United States. According to the *Forum* account, the building's commercial value was enhanced by its clean, functional lines and use of up-to-date technology. In every way, it was recognized as a "modern" building.[46]

King moved to Washington to join the Supervising Architect's staff, which was best known for its designs for U.S. post offices, strongly traditional in character. In August 1937, he moved over to Larkin's staff as a field construction supervisor and set off on his first foreign assignment to Turkey. Between 1937 and 1940, he inspected diplomatic buildings in Europe, the Middle East, and Latin America. The Supervising Architect of the Treasury had been responsible for nearly all embassy designs until 1941. Even on projects for which architects in private practice were retained, approval by Treasury architects had been necessary, and that office almost always prepared the working drawings and specifications. But when King returned to Washington in 1941, he took over supervision of design work and assumed the position of chief architect for foreign buildings.[47] By the mid-1940s, Larkin's unit was known as the Office of Foreign Buildings Operations (FBO), and he and King and a staff of six were working out of the former State, War, and Navy Building adjacent to the White House.

King himself designed few buildings, but he was responsible for the proposed U.S. pavilion for the Exhibition International d'Haiti, a project that again demonstrated his interest in modernism. Few of his colleagues shared that interest. Like the Treasury architects, King's chief designer Paul Franz Jaquet was a committed traditionalist. As the building program shifted its focus to the American Republics, Jaquet designed a number of embassy residences, including one in Havana in 1939. King and Jaquet collaborated on an embassy residence in Asunción and another in Lima (fig. 13), described by King as "Spanish Baroque." Other projects from that era included residences in Montevideo, Managua, Port-au-Prince, Ciudad Trujillo, and Panama City.

While war raged in Europe and the Far East, the State Department shelved plans for embassies and consulates in Berlin, Athens, Ankara, Rome, Tehran, Bangkok, Calcutta, Mukden, and Shanghai.[48] Though still in its formative years, the foreign building program had already established its scope and begun to prove its usefulness. It was certain to expand as American interests and responsibilities grew. After the war, King was poised to explore the possibilities of modern architecture as the department moved to meet the demand for facilities worldwide.

CHAPTER TWO

Postwar Expansion

"THROWN INTO A position of leadership in the world." So Rep. Frances Bolton (R-Ohio) described the way the United States found itself just after World War II.[1] As a member of the House Foreign Affairs Committee, Bolton was keenly aware of postwar shifts in the geopolitical landscape when she made her comments in 1952. Responding to the requisites of that position—the need to strengthen itself and its allies, rebuild its former foes, and prevent the growth of Soviet hegemony—the United States vastly increased its overseas real estate holdings by purchasing sites and building offices and residences for diplomatic personnel and the growing number of representatives of the many other government agencies and departments being sent abroad.

The period between 1946 and 1954 was a time of transition for the foreign building program. The market was glutted with property at good prices, purchase funds were readily available, and FBO was able to acquire sites in the expectation of future use. FBO grew from one tiny Washington office to a worldwide operation with regional offices in Paris, The Hague, London, Bonn, Tokyo, and Rio de Janeiro, and additional field supervisors in Eastern Europe, North Africa, and the Middle East. And though the first postwar projects were designed in-house by cautious and tradition-minded architects, more and more jobs were awarded to private firms whose work was recognized as being both architecturally distinguished and boldly modern. There is no way to explain the celebrated program of the 1950s without reference to the events that took place during these years as the nation began to meet its new commitments.

When President Truman called for the containment of Soviet expansion in 1947, it was clear that the United States would be committing extensive economic and military resources to halt Soviet moves and the spread of international communism. The United States launched a massive effort to build democracy in Germany, Austria, Italy, and Japan and to turn its former foes into solid and productive allies as the Soviet Union used its military might to seal off Eastern Europe. The United States also had to wrestle with its own perceived need to maintain and expand free market economies and the concomitant need to increase pro-American sentiment and build worldwide support for the democratic model. Military and diplomatic objectives included postwar plans for an array of military bases, strategic defense pacts, economic aid, and information dissemination. Each of these had direct or indirect impact on the foreign building program, which became part of the larger effort by the United States to strengthen its postwar position and the position of its allies.

In the first years of the postwar building program, when Soviet containment was at the top of the foreign policy agenda, the State Department moved ahead with major projects in Germany, Greece, Turkey, Iran, India, and Pakistan. These nations, which bordered the Soviet Union and its satellites, were seen as prime targets for Communist infiltration. The Truman Doctrine, with its call to "support free peoples who are resisting attempted subjugation by armed minorities or by outside pressures," was the Truman administration's first step toward systematizing its opposition to what it perceived to be Soviet efforts to destabilize the West. It was coupled with a request for $400 million in military aid to Greece and Turkey. Not surprisingly, early postwar plans also called for new embassies in Athens and Ankara. And India, whose position of neutrality especially angered American officials, was the site of the first major embassy project approved during the Eisenhower years. When so much effort was going into telling America's story abroad, Prime Minister Jawaharlal Nehru's subsequent praise for the chancery in New Delhi and Indian public enthusiasm for its architecture represented a lasting diplomatic coup for the United States.

Even before the war ended, American military strategists recognized the need for U.S. control of both the Atlantic and Pacific oceans, and they called for the construction of an array of overseas airbases. Pentagon plans contained recommendations for the construction of military bases at sites that included American Samoa, Bora Bora, the Azores, Trinidad, Iceland, the Canary Islands, the Galapagos Islands, the Hawaiian Islands, Cape Verde, Dakar (French West Africa), and Monrovia (Liberia), as well as Edmonton and Fairbanks.[2] The base construction plan was never fully implemented, but its existence answers certain puzzling questions concerning the choice of some embassy and consulate locations procured after the war. The plan may help to explain, for example, why the State Department moved quickly to build a consulate general office building at Port of Spain on the sparsely populated Caribbean island of Trinidad, and why it decided at the same time to build a major embassy in the remote city of Reykjavik. Though the Reykjavik project was never completed, when it was commissioned soon after the war ended it ranked in importance with similar projects in Brussels,

Madrid, and Rio de Janeiro. The base plan may also help to explain why, out of all the cities in Africa, the Department selected Dakar and Monrovia as its first priority embassy sites. FBO never directly received any such plan, nor did military matters figure directly in FBO decisions, but those decisions were based upon requests from the various posts and also on recommendations from the State Department's area offices, where national security would have played a key role in the determination of priorities.

In his analysis of the origins of the Cold War, diplomatic historian Melvyn Leffler not only details the base system plan, but points out a less known but equally significant American strategic initiative designed to add to military capability. That initiative involved a plan to secure air transit and landing rights for American aircraft at key cities along a route that ran from Casablanca through Algiers and Tripoli to Cairo, east to Dhahran, on to Karachi, across India to New Delhi and Calcutta, then southeast to Rangoon, and across Southeast Asia to Bangkok, Saigon, and ending in Manila. All of the cities were considered strategically important to the United States. Although, coincidence may have played a role, the plan to secure transit and landing rights appears to have had an impact on the FBO building program. Leland King has stated that FBO was not influenced by military considerations after the war, but he does not deny that such considerations may have motivated decisions made at a higher level within the department. In fact, subsequent State Department plans included proposed projects, new embassies, or supplemental facilities at all of the twelve cities on that route. During the 1950s, FBO completed projects in Dhahran, Karachi, New Delhi, Calcutta, Bangkok, and Manila and suspended or delayed other projects scheduled for Algiers, Bangkok, and Saigon. Strategic interest in oil was responsible for the much of the interest in Saudi Arabia, and similar concern prompted plans for a large new embassy in Iran.

Soon after the proclamation of the Truman Doctrine, Secretary Marshall unveiled the administration's plan for broader economic aid to Western Europe. In approving the so-called Marshall Plan of 1948, Congress subsequently voted $17 billion over four years to stimulate European recovery and thereby counteract what Churchill called "a breeding ground of pestilence and hate." Prompted in part by events such as the Berlin Blockade (1948–49), the United States resolved to build consulates, information centers, and housing across Germany. The North Atlantic Treaty Organization (NATO) established a sizable permanent U.S. military presence in Europe in 1949 and generated a further need for support facilities for the thousands of American servicemen and their families stationed at European bases. These commitments drew the United States into the struggle that came to be called the Cold War. The Alger Hiss trial and the

House Un-American Activities Committee's pursuit of alleged communists in the State Department brought that battle to the home front.

The proliferation of new nations following the end of World War II provided another reason for the expansion of FBO operations. Right after the war it was essential for the United States to assert its presence in Europe. Soon after, though, with the rapid decolonization precipitated by the war, there was an urgent need for an increased American presence in South Asia, the Far East, and Africa. While the United States already had ministerial representation in some of these places, the anticipation of independence prompted plans for new consular office buildings in cities such as Leopoldville (Belgian Congo), Lagos (Nigeria), and Dakar as early as 1954. Two years later, FBO began planning for a new embassy in the Gold Coast, which in 1957 changed its name to Ghana after becoming the first of the European colonies in Africa to gain independence. Between 1948 and 1964, forty-seven new nations joined the world community.[3] In 1960, newly independent African nations included Gabon, Ivory Coast, Upper Volta, Somalia, Niger, Cameroon, and Togo. That year, also, the Belgian Congo became the independent nation of Zaire, French West Africa became Senegal, and Lagos became the capital of the newly independent Nigeria.

As the former colonies proclaimed their independence, even where there was scant evidence of national cohesion and the location of the capital city was less than certain, the United States faced pressure from its foreign hosts to upgrade its representation to the highest level. Regardless of size, each new nation expected appropriate U.S. diplomatic and consular representation in its capital city, and sometimes also consular representation in other cities. In terms of personnel, this meant an exchange of ambassadors, not simply of consuls or ministers; and in terms of buildings, it meant that existing facilities were upgraded to embassies, and wholly new facilities were planned to meet needs generated by the vastly expanded foreign aid program. The U.S. consulate general in Leopoldville, designed in 1954 and built in 1957, was upgraded to become an embassy when Leopoldville (renamed Kinshasa) became the capital of independent Zaire in 1960.

In the context of the Cold War, new embassy construction was seen by the State Department as part of the effort to counterbalance Soviet influence in the Third World. Some officials, such as Representative Hays, saw the threat of Soviet subversion as the sole factor driving the American commitment of aid to Africa. The Russians, he said, were welcome to try to build solid alliances with shaky new regimes, but the Americans were "idiots" for thinking that the United States could or would be able to do so. Hays opposed spending in places that appeared to be "unstable."[4] Because FBO was short of funds by the time that the need for new facilities in Africa peaked in the late 1950s and early 1960s, and because the issue of allocating funds for new African capitals became caught up in a larger power struggle between Congress and the State Department, some new capitals had to settle for less than others.

As THE STAFF at American embassies grew, facilities were expanded to meet the growing need for office space. Truman's "Point Four" program, for example, brought an influx of economic and agricultural advisors to India as part of one of the earliest postwar foreign aid plans designed to provide economic assistance to economically impoverished countries. The advisors added significantly to the size of the staff at the New Delhi embassy, a small rented facility for which the lease was soon expiring. The situation called for immediate construction of a new U.S. government-owned building.

In addition to its other expanded commitments, the State Department also had obligations to its own personnel, who often operated out of facilities that were pitifully inadequate. Complaints from Foreign Service officers and staff at posts abroad naturally influenced the location of new facilities, though probably to a lesser extent than the Foreign Service might have wished. Many existing facilities were old, dilapidated, or otherwise inappropriate. As a top priority, the State Department targeted its hardship posts, typically the most inaccessible with the worst climates and the fewest amenities, such as air-conditioning. In addition, congressmen returned from official and unofficial overseas travel with complaints about American buildings and became advocates for improvements at posts they had visited. In 1954, for example, Rep. Prince H. Preston Jr. (D-Ga.), returned from an investigative tour and decried the "substandard" condition of the existing U.S. embassy in Karachi, a rundown office located a flight of stairs above a garage and an automobile shop. He called for immediate action to replace it with a new building on a site already purchased for that purpose.[5] When his committee finally appropriated the relatively modest sum of $3 million for capital projects in fiscal 1955, nearly half of that amount went toward the construction of an impressive new chancery in Karachi.

The early postwar years saw a shift away from leased quarters on scattered sites toward consolidated U.S. government-owned quarters, and a shift from an emphasis on ambassadorial residences to office buildings. The new office buildings were designed to provide security against theft and fire, but terrorist attacks and suicide bombings were unknown at the time and therefore not taken into consideration. According to former U.S. Ambassador David D. Newsom, night watchmen at the embassy in Karachi routinely slept through the night, awaking themselves occasionally "to rise up or cough at intervals so possible intruders knew of their presence." In

1948 they went so far as to hire a band of musicians for entertainment and to keep themselves awake.[6] Violent incidents directed at U.S. embassies or staged in front of them were viewed as anomalies. When a mob attacked the U.S. Information Office in Baghdad to protest a treaty between the United Kingdom and Iraq in 1952, the incident was dismissed by State Department officials as an aberration.

In addition to the traditional State Department offices that handled diplomatic and consular services, new embassy offices had to accommodate representatives from many government agencies—a list headed by the Department of Defense and others from Commerce, Agriculture, and Justice (including the Federal Bureau of Investigation); the Public Health Service; the Veterans' Administration; and various commissions related to science, economic development, reparations, and war memorials. The presence of so many agencies meant that embassies often functioned like mini-U.S. governments, outposts of Washington with their own miniature Pentagons. As at home, the various agencies competed for prime office space and battled over parking.

The presence of Central Intelligence Agency agents was an additional factor that swelled many embassy staffs at the time. Counterintelligence agents had operated out of some U.S. embassies during World War II, but the need for information and access did not end with the war, and the CIA was created in 1947 to coordinate overseas intelligence operations. Diplomats may not have wanted to play a role in covert activities, but with John Foster Dulles heading the State Department and his brother Allen Dulles leading the CIA, the opportunity for cooperation between the two was maximized. In the early 1950s, the CIA was responsible for two coups, ousting leftist leaders in Iran (1953) and Guatemala (1954). In his biography of the Dulles brothers, Leonard Mosley notes: "Never before or since has the CIA had more support from the State Department, or, because Secretary Dulles was so powerful, more freedom to infiltrate U.S. embassies, consulates, and the U.S. Information Agency (USIA) offices in foreign countries." Mosley goes on to cite the illuminating fact that by 1954, there were four hundred CIA agents operating out of the U.S. embassy in London alone, and out of that number, thirty-eight "had diplomatic passports and positions in the embassy hierarchy."[7]

The increased use of sophisticated communications equipment also led to larger embassies with more complicated plans. To protect sensitive political activities and the new communications equipment used to gather, store, and transmit sensitive data, new embassies also needed secure areas. Such areas had to be specially designed with regard to soundproofing, climate control, and access. Strategic fortification was not yet considered necessary.

Even then, though, to accommodate new equipment and related activities, embassies had to balance an increasing need for privacy and physical security with the need for public access to consular and information services. Some embassies even became command centers for on-going military operations, such as the U.S. intervention in Lebanon in 1958, when Lebanese president Camille Chamoun called upon President Eisenhower to save his toppling regime and Eisenhower sent in the Marines.

The United States Information Agency was another presence that swelled embassy staff and size. Staffers, researchers, writers, teachers, librarians, and others were sent to counter the communist challenge through the dissemination of information about the United States, its democratic values, history, culture, and arts. This sort of diplomacy has been labeled "public diplomacy" to distinguish it from more traditional diplomatic practice.

Unlike traditional diplomacy, which consisted of polite discourse (sometimes confidential) among small numbers of well-mannered diplomats, public diplomacy involved large numbers of people and was directed sometimes at elites within a nation, and sometimes at mass audiences in one nation or many. The Fulbright Act of 1946, utilizing foreign credits to finance travel and study by foreign and American students, researchers, and teachers, was among the first of the U.S. exchange programs. In the United States Information and Educational Exchange Act of 1948, Congress gave the State Department a mandate to "promote the better understanding of the United States among the peoples of the world and to strengthen cooperative international relations."[8] This legislation, the Smith-Mundt Act, created the USIA and its overseas arm, the United States Information Service (USIS). Located at first within the State Department, the USIA was directed to tell the American story abroad through articles, films, and radio broadcasts. In 1953 it became a separate agency that took over administration of most information-related programs, including radio broadcasts by the Voice of America, libraries (such as the American library, which had served as a vital source of public information in wartime London), and the many outreach activities associated with the America House program in Germany. Commenting on the circumstances that led to the creation of USIA, Newsom writes that traditional diplomacy seemed inadequate after the war in light of the communications revolution and the increasingly important role of public opinion *vis à vis* national policy. "Embassies were seen as restricted to government contacts," he says, "and as distant from 'the people.' "[9] It was up to USIS personnel to reach out and touch the people in faraway places and introduce them to the United States, its government, and its culture.

USIS functions were incorporated into most new embassies, so in addition to expanded offices, the new buildings contained libraries, exhibition space, auditoriums equipped for audio-visual presentations, and reception spaces to which foreign guests, such as writers, journalists, musicians, and artists, were invited to meet and mingle with Americans as part of the new U.S. agenda to cultivate friends and promote democracy.

IN EARLY 1950 President Truman gave the green light to the U.S. hydrogen bomb project, and ordered a new assessment of U.S. foreign policy and military preparedness. Paul H. Nitze, director of the Policy Planning Staff at the State Department, drafted that report for Truman. Known as *NSC-68,* the report called for increased military spending and policies aimed at building the strength of the free world in order to "frustrate the Kremlin design of a world dominated by its will."[10] Four months later, on 25 June 1950, North Korean Communist forces armed with Soviet-made weapons invaded South Korea. Just five years after its World War II victory, when the world looked to Americans as saviors and protectors of the peace, the United States was drawn into a new and costly war.

Following World War II, the national mood was high and self-confident. But as the United States expanded its foreign commitments, Americans began to reassess their postwar role. Within the short interval between the end of the war and the beginning of the Eisenhower years in 1953, the mood shifted dramatically as a sense of self-doubt began to replace postwar elation and self-confidence. The emergence of the Soviet Union and "Red" China as demon-foes, the proliferation of nuclear capability, new global alliances, a costly no-win war in Korea, and the four-year scourge of Senator Joseph McCarthy—all combined to test American strength and resolve abroad and to weaken the sense of internal security at home. The resultant self-consciousness, though not so pronounced as the shame and doubt that accompanied the war in Vietnam, had its origins in the early 1950s when Americans, who had since 1945 felt secure as the world's foremost superpower, began to sense the onus of that burden.

The public euphoria that followed V-E Day did not accompany the end of hostilities in Korea. Nor did hostilities really cease with the signing of the armistice on 26 June 1953 at Panmunjon. American leaders, and the public as well, knew that the truce in Korea was an uneasy one. And that knowledge contributed to the sense of insecurity that emerged in public debate and private doubts about America's mission and the future of democracy. The war led Americans to wonder about American prominence and the extent to which they wanted to be or could afford to be identified with omnipotent power—especially when such power was available to their leaders but went unused in the Korean conflict. Calling upon nations to liberate themselves from communism was one thing, but offering anything more than encouragement was quite another.

By the early 1950s critics in Congress had become wary of foreign buildings that appeared to be conspicuous, assertive, or bold. At a time when they were beginning to question the limits of power, there was an interest in buildings that downplayed connotations of American strength and might—but still called attention to themselves as outposts of America.

WITH AN EYE for a bargain, FBO director Fritz Larkin moved quickly to buy overseas properties, both developed and undeveloped, after the war. He purchased building sites in Accra, Ankara, Le Havre, Marseille, and Tehran, leased sites in Jiddah and Dhahran, and bought a villa in Nice, a palace in Prague (the former Petschek Palace), and a manor house in Dublin. Though some of the older buildings were in disrepair, Larkin chose them because they were prominently located, spacious, available, and relatively cheap.

Just months after he secured his funding package in 1946, Larkin purchased prime property adjacent to the U.S. embassy in Paris at 4 Avenue Gabriel (formerly the Arts Club), an undeveloped site on the bank of the Tigris River near the royal palace in Baghdad for an embassy office/residence compound, and an office building in Tokyo. He also arranged for the purchase of two historic properties in Rome—the Villa Taverna for use as a residence and the Palazzo Margherita for use as a chancery (fig. 14). Under the newly enacted legislation, he completed the Rome transaction using Italian lire credited against an assortment of surplus American Army property, including vehicles. Though in disrepair, the palazzo was a prime acquisition. Built on land once owned by Julius Caesar and later the site of splendid Roman gardens, the palazzo was designed by the architect Gaetano Koch and built in 1885 for Prince Boncompagni-Ludovisi, who also built the two adjoining villas (earlier acquired for consular offices and today housing the U.S. consulate and USIS offices). Home to Margherita, queen of Italy, from 1900 to 1926, the palazzo was used as a Fascist headquarters building before it was acquired by the United States government. It was so sorely neglected when purchased that no one suspected the richness of its art collection, which includes Giambologna's *Venus* (1583), now standing in the main entrance foyer. Furthermore, no one expected to find a frescoed Roman cryptoportico (currently under restoration) deep underground, beneath the embassy's parking garage and motor pool.[11] Where history is such a visible part of the landscape and so highly valued, the American diplomatic presence has been much enhanced by association with this carefully restored Roman landmark.

Larkin approved the purchase of a beautiful and strategically located property, formerly an Italian estate, for use as a consulate and consular residence in Asmara (Ethiopia). In Brussels, he acquired a handsome house for use as the American ambassador's residence, paying approximately $182,000 in April 1947 for the historic property designed by Barnabe Guymard in 1781. He also purchased property behind the house as a site for an office building. For these purchases he used Belgian francs credited against surplus American military property in Belgium. The house was renovated in 1950 while construction of the new embassy proceeded on the adjacent parcel. In Paris, Larkin purchased the former Hôtel Pontalba at 41 rue du Faubourg Saint-Honoré in 1948 for use as an embassy residence and a property known as L'Hôtel Talleyrand at 2 rue St. Florentine in 1950 for use as an office annex. The Talleyrand property was designed by Jean François Chalgrin and Jacques-Ange Gabriel in 1767. (After renovations by Washington architect Hugh Newell Jacobsen in 1984, it became the U.S. consulate.)

Larkin's style, brutal at times, generally brought him what he wanted. Like the proverbial Yankee peddler, he traveled about making deals. A small man who sported a black fedora, he lived out of a suitcase as he moved from capital to capital and post to post, staying long enough to examine property and participate in often delicate negotiations, then moving on—frequently leaving bewildered ambassadors and Foreign Service officers in his wake. He reputedly had a prodigious memory for facts, and was known also for his dry humor. Foes and admirers referred to him with either affection or awe as a "little czar" or a "dictator." Chiefs of mission were particularly aware of how tightly he held the FBO purse strings. Helsinki, for example, was at one time the target of Russian air attacks. The American Legation made an urgent appeal to FBO for a bomb shelter. Even after inspecting the post, Larkin was unmoved, but when four Russian bombs fell near him and blew him down a flight of stairs at the legation, he changed his mind. According to one version of the story, Larkin picked himself up, telephoned the minister, and barked: "You can consider your damn bomb shelter already half built."[12]

Diplomats and State Department officials marveled at Larkin's ability to make binding financial decisions on his own, wherever he was, in whatever corner of the world. James Johnstone, former FBO director, recalls that Larkin "carried his budget in his hat."[13] He was used to operating with minimal interference from State Department superiors. After all, he had his own close working relationship with the key congressmen who authorized and appropriated funds for his budget. His decisions on behalf of FBO determined which ambassadors received new and refurbished homes, which posts added new office buildings, which gained staff housing, and also which were to receive everything from beds to dinnerware.

With such largesse under his control, Larkin was also able to cultivate allies throughout the diplomatic corps. As would be expected, he had close friends and bitter foes. He pointed out in an internal State Department report that "for more than 15 years after the initiation of the foreign buildings program, the officer responsible for its operation reported directly to the Assistant Secretary of State in charge of Administration and, in a number of matters, dealt directly with the Secretary and the Under Secretary."[14] He liked that arrangement and saw no reason why intermediaries should oversee his day-to-day operations.

Firmly allied with Congressmen Sol Bloom and John Rooney, Larkin was in a position to balk at subordination to the Office of Foreign Service. An internal report of 1947 observes: "Mr. Larkin and Mr. King attend only infrequently the weekly staff meetings held by the Office Director and it is apparent that they are irritated by the so-called 'red tape' of administrative procedures with which they are required to comply as part of the OFS structure." Both men argued that the technical nature of their work necessitated administrative independence, and they tended to ignore bureaucratic procedures that hindered the efficiency of their program.

In the twenty years since Congress passed the first authorization for the construction of foreign buildings in 1926, there had been a relatively small rise in the number of embassy office buildings owned by the United States: from six to only thirty-one, while the total number of residential units rose from thirty to eighty-three. In the five-year period between 1946 and 1951, however, with Larkin at the helm, the overall total quickly climbed to 604, including 114 government-owned office buildings; fifty-five embassy and legation residences; and 435 residential properties, with 375 individual apartment units providing housing for 837 Foreign Service officers and employees and attachés of other federal agencies accredited to foreign governments through the embassies. In that same period, FBO grew from a staff of six to a staff of twenty, four of whom were architects.

By 1949 FBO had operations in sixty-eight countries and 240 cities, and was transacting business in approximately sixty different currencies worldwide. Between 1947 and 1949 alone, FBO property acquisitions totaled 386 individual buildings and forty-six unimproved lots, bringing the total value of purchased property to approximately $70 million. By 1952, there were 737 government-owned buildings, ninety-two additional sites purchased for construction, and thirty-six buildings actually under construction.[15] Between 1926 and early 1952, investment in overseas construction and property acquisition totaled nearly $130 million, but most of that amount, at least $111.5 million was spent between 1946 and 1952, and most was in foreign credits, not dollars.

The State Department never could have expanded its postwar building program as it did, nor could it have moved daringly in the direction of newness, had it not been for one crucial event—the 1946 congressional authorization to use foreign credits for the acquisition of foreign buildings. That year Congress authorized $125 million for foreign buildings—$15 million in dollars to be spent over twelve years and $110 million in credits to be spent over five years. Not only did those funds finance Larkin's travels and his array of acquisitions and construction projects, but they insulated FBO from the usual budget review process, allowing it to function free from extensive bureaucratic supervision. Two additional events that also paved the way for the postwar mission to build were the structural reorganization at the State Department that created FBO in 1944, and the passage of legislation that increased FBO's authority in 1945.

Even before the end of World War II, the State Department announced a reorganization.[16] The plan marginalized the Foreign Service Buildings Commission, which no longer functioned as an independent body, and created the office known thereafter as the Office of Foreign Buildings Operations.[17] Larkin was to continue to serve as executive secretary of the FSBC in its advisory capacity, but the commissioners no longer reviewed his decisions, recommended priorities, or approved the selection of architects.

In 1945, legislation further strengthened the new office and provided Larkin the flexibility he needed to run a large-scale real estate operation. It gave the secretary of state authorization to sell buildings and grounds purchased as diplomatic and consular establishments; and more significantly, it permitted FBO to apply the proceeds of such sales to the acquisition, construction, and furnishing of other government-owned properties. Until that time, Larkin had been able to exchange properties or sell them with proceeds going to the Treasury, but he had no way to sell them and recoup the proceeds to benefit his own program. As the scale of U.S. operations grew after the war, and as it became increasingly necessary to centralize overseas programs and personnel in combined office buildings, the ability to dispose of obsolete, deteriorated, or otherwise undesirable properties became ever more important.

In the early 1950s members of Congress argued forcefully that the government should not be in the business of real estate speculation and urged FBO to sell off all properties for which there was no immediate use. Such views were astoundingly short-sighted. In fact, a key reason why American embassies were well located was because Larkin had moved so quickly after the war to acquire valuable properties at bargain prices—using credits. Had he not, the United States would not today own the former Palazzo Margherita in Rome and other similarly prized properties viewed today as diplomatic assets. Moreover, if Congress had been less short-sighted and had approved initial State Department requests, it would have been far easier and less costly to add office space in Paris and it would have made it possible to prevent an office tower from being located adjacent to embassy offices in Mexico City.

The extraordinary aspect of the 1946 authorization was that $110 million of the total amount was to come from foreign credits owed to the United States Treasury as a result of the lend-lease settlements, various counterpart funds, and the disposal of surplus war property, including in one instance a shipload of post exchange (PX) beer. According to the *Foreign Service Journal*, the beer was traded for a house for a deputy chief of mission in a Pacific port city after American troops departed, leaving the beer behind.[18] It was Larkin's clever idea to utilize these funds, and together he and King had little trouble convincing key congressmen of the wisdom of recouping assets that would be otherwise lost to American taxpayers.

On behalf of FBO, King argued the case for the use of so-called "blocked" or "frozen" funds in testimony before the Senate Foreign Relations Committee on 19 June 1946.[19] Foreign nations owed hundreds of millions of dollars to the United States Treasury as a result of war debts. But as King pointed out, those sums were unlikely ever to be recaptured. By arranging to pay for goods and services in foreign currencies, or credits, he said, FBO could buy and build abroad with minimal use of dollars. In other words, a foreign country that owed the U.S. government for wartime loans allowed the U.S. Treasury to exchange its much devalued foreign currency for equipment, materials, and labor purchased within that country. In this way, FBO later acquired teak from Burma and marble from Greece and Italy; foreign currency was also used to pay architectural fees to foreign architects and to American architects working abroad.

It would be fair to say that congressional interest in the bill (H. R. 6627) was less an endorsement of the foreign buildings program itself than it was approval of a means of recouping American assets. As Sen. Claude Pepper (D-Fla.) remarked in response to King's testimony, "I think this would be a very salutary use that we could make of our surplus property so that we will have something permanent to show for it."[20] The bill authorizing expenditure of $110 million in credits and $15 million in dollars easily passed both houses of the 79th Congress. Between 1926 and July 1946, Congress had authorized expenditures totaling $16,625,000. The new spending figure was seven and a half times greater than that amount, and represented a tremendous victory for Larkin, who was assisted by his ally Sol Bloom, who had played a key role in originally granting funds for lend-lease and was among President Roosevelt's closest congressional advisers during the war years.

Credits were available for immediate use in Australia, Austria, Canada, France, Greece, Hungary, India, Iran, Norway, Poland, Italy, Turkey, and the United Kingdom and its colonies. Agreements were pending for the use of funds tied up in Belgium, Czechoslovakia, China, Denmark, Egypt, the Netherlands, and the USSR. Some of the early projects financed with credits included embassies in Bangkok, Ankara, Stockholm, and Copenhagen; an embassy/residence in Madrid; an embassy and prefabricated housing in Tehran, consulates in Antwerp, Curaçao, and Le Havre; apartments in Bombay, Tokyo, and Paris; prefabricated housing in Lahore; site acquisition in Lagos; and construction of an embassy and sea-wall reinforcement in Manila. Other projects that proceeded without foreign credit financing included the purchase of property in Lima, construction of an embassy in Managua, and the renovation of a residence in Dublin. In 1949, using credits, Larkin purchased property for future use in Dakar, Algiers, Hanoi, Saigon, and The Hague.

Larkin's transactions in Saudi Arabia illustrate how he operated, what sorts of problems FBO faced, and why these transactions were at times extremely difficult. Saudi Arabia had only one paved road in 1947, for example, when Larkin initiated plans to lease two sites for American diplomatic buildings in that desert nation. The road led from Jiddah to Mecca, the pilgrimage route, and it was because of the heavy traffic of pilgrims that the United States and other nations located consular offices in Jiddah. The other consular site was at Dhahran, near the principal Saudi oil drilling region, the base of the Anglo-American Oil Company, and adjacent to a newly established American military airbase. Foreign governments could not own land in Saudi Arabia. According to former ambassador Parker Hart, Larkin had already negotiated with the Saudi Minister of Finance an agreement granting the U.S. government tax-free use of two sites for a period of twenty-five years.[21] After that time, the United States agreed to pay rental fees for the use of the land.

Ambassador Hart was a junior Foreign Service officer with the American legation in Jiddah when Larkin contacted him in 1947 to identify two sites and negotiate the long-term rental fees with the Saudi finance minister and, if needed, with King Abd al-Aziz (also known as "Ibn Saud") himself. Hart was told to accept a figure of three percent of the cost of construction and nothing higher. Larkin was distressed that the Saudis were talking about a ten percent fee and the American ambassador had already derailed negotiations by suggesting publicly that a five percent figure would be acceptable.

In this, as in other instances, Larkin bypassed the ambassador in order to strike a better deal. With permission from the State Department, Hart crossed the Saudi peninsula—in a trip that took a week—and set up a meeting with the king. When Hart arrived in Dhahran, the king sent a C-47, loaned from the U.S. Army Air Corps, to fly him to Hofuf, the administrative capital of the eastern region where the king was taking sulphur baths. Hart met the king at his retreat and eventually received approval of the 3 percent fee. A year later, Larkin joined Hart in Saudi Arabia, and they worked out the details of site selection.

For Jiddah, Larkin and Hart selected a site northwest of the old city, far into what was little more than desert wilderness at that time. In Dhahran, they selected a seemingly remote site 300 feet above sea-level on a rock formation 6 miles inland from the Persian Gulf. Although the site was far from any developed area, it was a prime location and Larkin saw that like the Jiddah site, it would be part of the city one day. According to Hart, once Larkin made up his mind, he was unstoppable. A top oil executive in Dhahran disputed Larkin's choice. "Fritz Larkin gave him hell," Hart recalls. "It was a total personality clash." The oil company official gave in, Hart says, when he saw that it was useless to argue with Larkin. Not only did Larkin end up with the preferred site, but he also made sure that the site consisted of four to five times the needed space so there would be some to give up or exchange as needed.

By any standards, building conditions were primitive in Saudi Arabia. To begin with, there was no wood in the country, forcing wooden poles to be imported from India or Africa to reinforce local buildings, nearly all of which were made of fossilized coral that lay beneath the desert sand. Vernacular buildings of coral and mud, known as *chundles*, had little or no reinforcement at all and tended to lean one way or the other. FBO began site preparation in Dhahran in 1949. The proximity of oil company facilities made it easier to work there than in Jiddah. Hart pointed out that the discovery of limestone outcroppings further aided the Dhahran project, although FBO had to import masons from Syria to quarry and cut the stone.

The Dhahran compound included a consulate general, a consul general's residence, a vice consul's residence, staff apartments, a utility compound with a warehouse, a generator house, servants' quarters, a water tower, and other necessary structures—eighteen buildings in all. The Jiddah compound consisted of nineteen buildings, including an office building, counselor's residence, ambassador's residence, prefabricated staff houses, refrigerated storage, and laundry facilities. In Jiddah, all of the buildings were simple, one-story structures made of concrete blocks fabricated on the site. The Dhahran buildings were equally unremarkable in terms of design, but in terms of construction they were unusual. As Leland King later noted, "These construction projects imposed every known problem of design, assembly of materials, labor, and supervision of construction."[22] Congressional investigators later forced King to defend the higher than normal costs and the use of war surplus credits in Saudi Arabia (a country that receives dollars for its oil).

After his sojourn in Saudi Arabia, Larkin flew via military aircraft to Iran to arrange for a site for a new embassy. Invited to travel with him, Hart had another glimpse of Larkin in action. Problems in Tehran included negotiations over water rights and the use of *qanats*, ancient underground water tunnels lying beneath the sand and rock of the compound site. While Hart himself got along well with Larkin, he was sympathetic to those who found him difficult and arbitrary in his decisions. "Fritz took an instant like or dislike to people," Hart recalled. "He had very strong preferences." Others were less charitable in their assessment of Larkin and FBO. Many Foreign Service officers hated FBO, Hart says bluntly, because they felt it was not responsive to the practical needs of living abroad.[23]

AFTER THE WAR, when Embassy officials realized that existing facilities would never suffice in Paris, officials began the task of adding to U.S. holdings there. In 1948, Larkin had arranged for the United States to purchase the residence owned by the Rothschild family that was formerly known as the Hôtel Pontalba (figs. 15–6). This purchase illustrates some of the hazards that faced FBO when it dealt with historic properties—hazards related both to finance and the fluctuating value of the dollar, and those related to architectural authenticity and cultural possessiveness. Furthermore, it demonstrates the difficulty of defending a purchase based on its projected use, as opposed to its immediate use, and the difficulty of defending long-term objectives and investments to short-sighted superiors whose frame of reference was usually one term in Congress or the length of one presidential administration.

The Paris property was originally designed in 1842 by Ludovico Visconti, the architect who designed Napoleon's tomb and the newer wings of the Louvre; it was rebuilt and enlarged by Felix Langlais in the 1870s for Baron Edmond de Rothschild, its new owner. The valuable site consisted of 2.5 acres in the middle of Paris adjoining the British embassy, near to the Elysée Palace, and also convenient to the American embassy. Visconti's portals and gatehouse remained intact in 1948, but the house was in sad repair: the Germans had seized it in 1941, forcing its Jewish owners to flee. The house was then at least partially stripped by the Germans, who had used it as a club for the Luftwaffe. After the war, the Allies rented it from the Rothschild family, using it first as a British Royal Air Force Club and then as U.S. government office space.[24]

Alan B. Jacobs, a young colonel in the U.S. Army Engineers, joined FBO in 1947 as head of the Paris regional office. Jacobs had served on General Eisenhower's staff and was a special assistant to the American ambassador in Paris when he joined FBO. He was also an architect who had been involved in building bases in the Near East and Ethiopia during the war. And he was someone who could "settle the feathers" raised by Larkin's frequent foreign travels. Jacobs visited the Rothschild property in 1948 after being contacted about a possible sale. He realized that it was a prize and reported to Larkin, who advised him to buy it at once. Jacobs negotiated a deal to purchase the property as it stood. When he found added bronze handrails, wrought iron trim, and hand-carved wood paneling missing, Jacobs immediately contacted Larkin in Washington and asked him whether or not to proceed. "Buy it," Larkin told him. "It's a good investment."[25]

The night before the deal was to be signed, a Treasury attaché at the embassy told Jacobs that the French government was about to devalue the franc. According to Jacobs, the deal almost fell through in the morning because of the devaluation (fortunately for the Americans, the purchase contract was in French and Belgian francs, not in U.S. dollars), but FBO managed to close the deal paying an amount equivalent to $2,111,783 for the property. Even if the newly replaced paneling was made of plaster, the house and its grounds represented a splendid asset, and Larkin knew that he had found a bargain. (Much of the original grillwork, including the main staircase balustrade, was later found and reinstalled.) He expected no second-guessing from Congress, especially because the entire sum came out of foreign currency credits rather than appropriated tax dollars.

But by 1952 congressional critics were objecting to the Rothschild purchase. On the House floor, Rep. John Phillips (R-Calif.) declared his belief that the ambassador did not want the property, and did not want to live in it. "The Rothschild house," he said, "was too big and expensive for the French to maintain, so they sold it to us."[26] As much as anything, such bickering reflected partisan, election-year efforts to discredit Secretary of State Dean Acheson, the State Department, and the Foreign Service. But the objections did not stop after the election. They continued for years, as various members of Congress found the "mansion" a convenient target of ridicule. John Rooney was one who advised FBO to sell the property in 1957 after condemning it as an extravagance.[27]

For nearly two decades, the United States Information Service used the former Hôtel Pontalba as its Paris headquarters. During that time, FBO tried to upgrade its facilities and proposed a number of plans for using it as part of an overall expansion of the Paris post. As early as 1952, FBO considered demolishing the building and replacing it with a modern office building designed to accommodate all of the U.S. office needs on a single site. At that time, FBO had little interest in historic preservation and seemed unfazed by Parisian design controls that protected local buildings and spaces, and equally indifferent to public attachment to local landmarks. At least some of the Americans must have known that the French were not about to permit large-scale destruction of the historic urban fabric of the area, but as late as 1960, when Henry Shepley prepared a report on the property for FBO, plans still called for construction of a large new building on the site. Oddly enough, Wayne Hays, a vociferous FBO critic, was one of the first to call for rehabilitation of the former Rothschild house, which he claimed needed only an interior fix-up and new floors. When FBO proposed a scheme to demolish all but the "Napoleonic façade," Hays declared that he would never allow FBO "to put up a monstrosity" on the erstwhile Rothschild property, which he described as "the most valuable site in Paris."[28] Hays's idea of a monstrosity was Eero Saarinen's recently completed U.S. chancery in London, so his interest in rehabilitation represented less support for historic preservation than opposition to modern architecture. It also represented his opposition to FBO director William Hughes. Possibly, Hays's own dream of one day living in the house as the U.S. ambassador figured in his thinking, too.

In 1964, FBO hired Pietro Belluschi to reexamine the building and consider ways to rehabilitate it rather than replace it. But by then it had already swallowed up an $875,000 appropriation that paid only for a new roof and cleaning and repair of the exterior stonework. Congressional critics refused additional funds for interior renovations. Finally, between 1966 and 1972, the house was carefully restored and outfitted with fine furnishings. Largely through the efforts of private American contributors, it was transformed into a prestigious residence for the American ambassador, who now uses it for conferences, press briefings, receptions, luncheons, dinners, and garden parties, including an annual Fourth of July reception for two thousand people. It is also equipped to handle programs of art and music, including presentations by visiting American artists and orchestras, and designed to accommodate visiting government officials and dignitaries as overnight guests. As Larkin imagined in 1948, it is now regarded as an invaluable asset to the United States and its representation in Paris.

LELAND KING WAS a tall and distinguished looking man, who set high standards and expected much from those with whom he worked. Born in 1907 in Michigan, he studied architecture at the Georgia School of Technology and the Armour Institute of Technology, and apprenticed in the architectural office of his grandfather Ernest W. Arnold in Battle Creek, Michigan. Though his training did not include juries critiqued by teachers like Gropius or Breuer, he was nonetheless interested in contemporary architectural thought and through his government career came to know, respect, and enjoy the friendship of many prominent architects.

Given the fact that the new embassies were far away, given Larkin's virtual immunity to congressional oversight, and given King's own penchant for modern design, architectural change became a possibility—even if Larkin did not share King's enthusiasm for modernism. The earliest diplomatic buildings were residences, so architects modeled many of the prewar projects after large houses; but the postwar need for large, multipurpose office buildings made the residential prototype obsolete. The exigencies of the Cold War, coupled with the need for a new type of diplomatic building that could accommodate a growing overseas program, soon made change inevitable.

As assistant director and supervising architect of FBO, King was in a position to shape the office's design policy, and that is precisely what he did. He moved cautiously at first. The first postwar projects were traditional in appearance, though they differed markedly from one another. They included office buildings in Canberra, Tehran, and Brussels, designed by FBO staff architects, and two others in Naples and Ankara designed by outside architects. His staff in Washington and in the several FBO regional offices provided design supervision. At the time, FBO maintained such offices in Paris, The Hague, London, Vienna, Frankfurt, Hong Kong, Tokyo, and Rio de Janeiro. Central America was handled from Washington, and a roving regional director handled projects in the Near East and Africa.

Paul Franz Jaquet, head of King's small in-house design staff, was responsible for the chancery in Canberra (1946), a red brick building of two stories topped with two large chimneys and a steeply pitched roof punctuated by deep dormer windows (fig. 17). It fit well with its neighbor, the embassy residence, which Jaquet had designed earlier (in 1941) as a Tidewater mansion, complete with columned portico. Most striking about the Canberra chancery is that it was a designated office building designed to resemble a house. King admired Jaquet's design, and felt that its "colonial" connotation and domestic association were particularly "appropriate." But in comments published in 1955 in *Architectural Record*, MIT Dean John Ely Burchard condemned the design and disdained the notion that there is such a thing as universally appropriate architecture. The Canberra terrain, he said, had nothing in common with the James River landscape of Virginia, and it made no sense to build a Williamsburg colonial there. "It was a disastrous decision by our country to build such a building," he declared, and he added the curious comment, "It is equally disastrous that many Australians like it."[29] Like other architectural critics, he argued for a careful consideration of purpose, place, materials, and time, a critique equally applicable to colonial reproductions as to subsequent examples of the international style. Architect Milton Grigg added two annexes to the Canberra group in 1957, maintaining the "Williamsburg tradition." The only later FBO project designed in the Georgian manner was a Warsaw residence designed by FBO staff architect Sal DiGiacomo in 1967.

With the Canberra project under way, King commissioned two other major embassy office buildings, one in Tehran and the other in Ankara. The Tehran project was designed by FBO architect Ides Van der Gracht in 1948 (fig. 18). It was a long, low, two-story brick structure, the standard sort of institutional building seen in American cities in the 1930s or 1940s. In fact, it so resembled a typical American public high school of that vintage that it was dubbed "Henderson High" after Loy Henderson, who arrived as ambassador to Iran in 1951, just after construction was completed. The lack of building supplies and the absence of workmen skilled in Western construction techniques forced FBO to import prefabricated housing units for Tehran and contributed to the choice of embassy design. Critics included King, who thought the embassy looked old-fashioned and lacked the dignity associated with the diplomatic mission.

Eggers & Higgins, successors to the practice of John Russell Pope, designed the embassy in Ankara (1948–53), a study in Beaux-Arts monumentality (fig. 19). Not surprisingly, it resembled some buildings in Washington, notably the Folger Shakespeare Library by Paul Cret and Alexander Trowbridge (1932). Neither like a house nor a school, this was the first of the projects to express importance and public purpose in a small office building. King attributes the Naples consulate (1947–53) to George Howe, former Supervising Architect of the Treasury, though the building hardly resembles Howe's work from this period. The unusual feature of the Naples project was that it combined office and residential functions, resulting in a five-story office block topped with a residential penthouse. This arrangement posed logistical problems due to the need to restrict public access to various parts of the building. When it was later proposed as a solution for a consulate in Palermo, it was rejected as an unworkable plan. Italian architect Mario di Renzi did the working drawings for Naples. To make maximum use of foreign credits, FBO often tried to retain foreign architects as consultants who could be paid in foreign currency. A number of postwar projects involved such foreign architects, sometimes working alone, sometimes in conjunction with Americans.

Paris regional director Alan Jacobs supervised the renovation of the recently purchased eighteenth-century mansion as a residence in Brussels, as well as the design and construction of a new embassy office building on the adjacent lot. The seven-story office block was connected to the residence by a ground-floor corridor. In comparison to the elegant and ornate residence, the office building was spare and efficient in appearance. Though hardly prominent in the cityscape today, the Brussels office building was a major American landmark in Europe when it was built in 1950.

The two Brussels projects would have caused no stir if not for the furnishings Jacobs selected for the embassy office building. He admired Hans Knoll and was interested in the growing furniture business he had launched in 1946. Backed by King, Jacobs selected Knoll furniture, manufactured abroad and purchased under credit agreements. According to congressional reports, the first ambassador to use the embassy objected strenuously to the fashionable but starkly modern furniture, which he disliked for its appearance and also for what he claimed was flimsy construction.[30] Brussels was not the only post to use Knoll furnishings. The chancery in Havana (1950–52) was furnished from top to bottom with Knoll pieces that were soon after ridiculed in Congress.

King directed more work to architects in private practice in the belief, he said, that this course was the most economical and that these men could provide the best design solutions. As he did so, he began to look for architects whose celebrity could generate positive publicity and augment the impact of the building program. By the time that King took the bold step of offering embassy commissions to well-known modernists, FBO was fully stocked with a supply of overseas real estate, a network of regional offices, and most important of all, plenty of money to pay design fees and construction costs. Between 1948 and 1952, King established the reputation of his program as a showcase for modernism.

In 1948, King retained Washington architect Charles Goodman to design an embassy in Reykjavik. The project in Iceland, King says, was probably "the first truly modern building" that he tried out on the department and it drew no comment or opposition. However, as the result of what he described as a bidding collusion scheme in which contractors attempted to boost the cost of the project, FBO refused to proceed with any of them and it was never built.[31] Goodman designed the embassy as a five-story tower perpendicular to a lower wing. The top floor of the tower was a glazed penthouse (intended as a residence) recessed slightly at one end and topped with a roof that was nothing more than a thin plane of concrete. Unlike those that preceded it, the building was asymmetrical. Aside from a single, large sculpture, its only ornament was the a rail enclosing the rooftop terrace. Although unbuilt, the Goodman project links the more traditional embassy office buildings that came before and the more expansively contemporary ones that followed.

Circumventing his own staff, whom he disdained as "entrenched civil

servants," King hired architects Ralph Rapson and John van der Meulen
for a number of projects that were supervised by FBO regional offices in
Europe. During the several years that they worked under contract to FBO,
the two Americans operated with considerable independence and made
important design decisions on their own. FBO's regional offices also established their own priorities and operated with an autonomy unusual for
a government program. Between 1949 and 1953, the number of projects
assigned to private architects grew from five to twenty-one, and with the
completion of working drawings for seventeen additional projects, the total
reached thirty-eight.[32] Through these designs modern architecture became
symbolically associated with the postwar effort to find new and better ways
to represent American interests abroad.

   If State Department superiors objected to nontraditional architecture,
they did not interfere with King during the years when Larkin was still
in charge of FBO. Though members of King's own staff did question his
increased use of private architects, there were no serious objections raised
by anyone from outside the department until well after March 1952, when
King assumed the duties of FBO chief upon Larkin's retirement.[33] Even
after Eisenhower's November 1952 election and the predictable government shake-up that ensued, King felt that he had "*carte blanche*" at FBO.
He selected architects as he pleased, and offered those architects generous
budgets and the opportunity to design important public buildings with an
unusual degree of spontaneity and freedom.

   King retained the New York firm of Harrison & Abramovitz to design
major embassy office buildings in Rio de Janeiro (1948) and Havana
(1950) just after the firm completed supervision of the design of the widely
publicized United Nations headquarters in New York; and he approved the
choice of Gordon Bunshaft of Skidmore, Owings & Merrill for an array
of new American projects in Germany (1952) while Bunshaft was still
basking in the acclaim surrounding his design of the New York corporate
headquarters of Lever Brothers. Additionally, he entered into negotiations
with Edward Durell Stone for the design of the embassy compound in New
Delhi. Though the architectural innovation associated with New Delhi was
later attributed to King's successors, Stone's final contract was prepared
while King still headed FBO in 1953 and awaited only the completion of
site acquisition.[34] Most important of all to FBO, after Larkin's retirement
and just before Eisenhower's election, King won congressional approval
for an authorization of $90 million—all in credits—a sum that sustained
the building program for nearly a decade.

FIG. 1 (TOP LEFT): Former U.S. Legation, Tangier, Morocco (acquired 1821). Currently the American Legation Museum.

FIG. 2 (TOP RIGHT): Former U.S. Embassy, Ottawa, Canada. Cass Gilbert (1928–32).

FIG. 3 (ABOVE): U.S. Ambassador's Residence, Oslo, Norway (acquired 1924). Henrik Bull (1909–11). Formerly owned by Hans Olsen.

FIG. 4 (LEFT): U.S. Embassy, Helsinki, Finland. Harrie T. Lindeberg in association with the Supervising Architect of the Treasury (1936–38). Modeled after Westover.

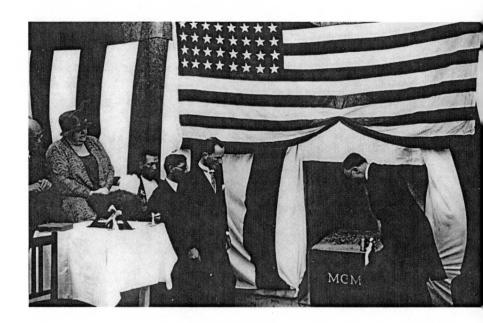

FIG. 5 (TOP): Former U.S. Embassy, Tokyo, Japan. Cornerstone laying ceremony with Ambassador William Castle, Mrs. Castle, architect Antonin Raymond, and Captain G. D. Stamp of the U.S. Army Corps of Engineers officiating (26 May 1930). Stamp supervised contruction of the new buildings. Others attending the ceremony included Prince Tokugawa, president of the America-Japan Society, and Baron Shidehara, Japanese foreign minister.

FIG. 6 (BOTTOM): Former U.S. Embassy, Tokyo, Japan. Raymond & Magonigle (1926–31). Demolished and replaced by new chancery building designed by Cesar Pelli with Gruen Associates in 1971. Ambassador's residence on hill in upper left.

FIGS. 7 & 8: U.S. Ambassador's Residence, embassy compound, Tokyo, Japan. Raymond
& Magonigle (1926–31). (TOP) Reception room where General Douglas MacArthur
received Emperor Hirohito in their historic encounter of 1945. (BOTTOM) Garden
entrance. Americans were interned at the residence throughout World War II.

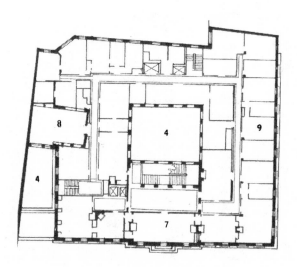

FIG. 9: U.S. Embassy, Paris, France. Delano & Aldrich (1929–32). (ABOVE) Ground floor. (BELOW) First floor. Plans after drawings in *Architecture* (1934).

1. ENTRANCE
2. RECEPTION
3. CONSUL GENERAL
4. COURT
5. PASSPORTS
6. VISAS
7. MAIN RECEPTION
   ROOM
8. LIBRARY
9. ADMINISTRATIVE
   OFFICES

FIG. 10 (TOP LEFT): U.S. Embassy, Paris, France. Main entrance.

FIG. 11 (TOP RIGHT): British Embassy, Washington, D.C. Edwin Lutyens (1925–31).

FIG. 12 (MIDDLE): U.S. Legation, Tirana, Albania. Wyeth & Sullivan (1929).

FIG. 13 (BOTTOM): U.S. Ambassador's Residence, Lima, Peru. Paul Franz Jaquet with Leland W. King Jr. for FBO (1945).

FIG. 14 (OPPOSITE, TOP): U.S. Embassy, Rome, Italy (acquired 1946). Formerly known as the Palazzo Margherita. Ambassador's office.

FIGS. 15 & 16 : U.S. Ambassador's Residence, Paris, France (acquired 1948). (OPPOSITE, BOTTOM) Garden entrance. (ABOVE) Interior staircase.

FIG. 17: U.S. Embassy, Canberra, Australia. Chancery (shown), Paul Franz Jaquet for FBO (1946); Annexes, Milton Grigg (1957–60). The office building was modeled on a colonial house.

FIG. 18: Former U.S. Embassy, Tehran, Iran. Ides Van der Gracht for FBO (1948–51). Photograph from October 1976. Appearing to many like a public school, the building was dubbed "Henderson High" after Ambassador Loy Henderson.

FIG. 19: U.S. Embassy, Ankara, Turkey. Eggers & Higgins (1948–53). Photograph from March 1973. A building that resembles Washington landmarks.

FIG. 20: U.S. Embassy, Rio de Janeiro, Brazil. Currently the Consulate General. Harrison & Abramovitz (1948–52). The architects were designing the United Nations headquarters in New York at the same time. The one-story structure in front is the library.

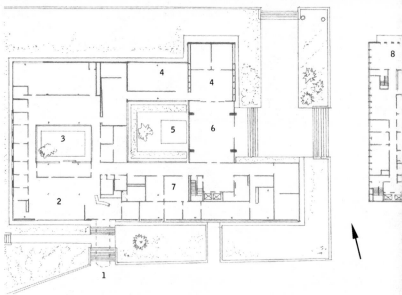

FIGS. 21 & 22: U.S. Embassy, Havana, Cuba. Harrison & Abramovitz (1950–52).
Currently U.S. Interest Section. (TOP) West façade of office tower with consular offices and
consular entrance in one-story wing. (BOTTOM) Plans of first floor (LEFT) and fifth floor
(RIGHT) after drawings in *Progressive Architecture* (1955).

1. ENTRANCE	4. PUBLIC INFORMA-	8. AMBASSADOR'S
2. VISAS	TION SERVICES	OFFICE
3. COURT	5. COURT AND POOL	
	6. ARCADE	
	7. CONSULAR OFFICES	

FIG. 23 (TOP): U.S. Embassy, Madrid, Spain. Garrigues & Middlehurst and Alan Jacobs for FBO (1952–54). Under construction, December 1954. A striking landmark when new, but now surrounded by blocks of modern office towers.

FIG. 24 (BOTTOM): Proposal for the U.S. Embassy, The Hague, Netherlands. Rapson & van der Meulen (1951). Unbuilt. So transparent, Rapson described it as a "nonbuilding."

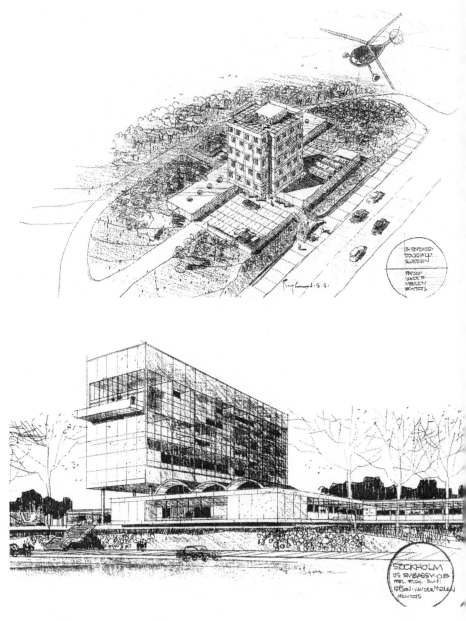

FIGS. 25 & 26: Proposals A (TOP) and B (BOTTOM) for the U.S. Embassy, Stockholm, Sweden. Rapson & van der Meulen (1951).

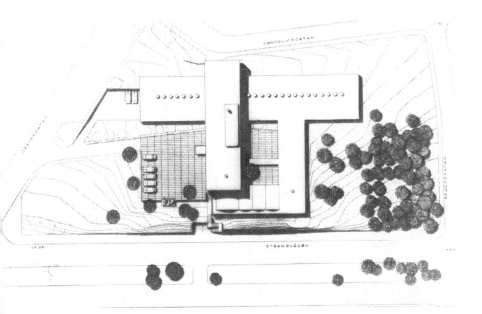

FIGS. 27–30 : U.S. Embassy, Stockholm, Sweden. Rapson & van der Meulen (1951–54). (TOP) Plan from above. (BOTTOM) Façade from southeast. (FOLLOWING PAGE, TOP AND BOTTOM) Interior views with Barcelona chairs and other furnishings by Knoll; and open stairway. Visiting Swedish architects described it as an "architectural Marilyn Monroe."

FIGS. 31–3: U.S. Embassy, Copenhagen, Denmark. Rapson & van der Meulen (1951–54). (PREVIOUS PAGE) Façade. (THIS PAGE, TOP) Proposal (1951). (THIS PAGE, BOTTOM) USIS library. Local approval was given to a modern building only on the condition it fit in with the existing cityscape in terms of setback and overall height.

CHAPTER THREE

Modernism at the State Department

THE STATE DEPARTMENT built its first thoroughly modern embassies in Rio de Janeiro (1948–52) and Havana (1950–52). At the same time, responding to urgent needs for office space and housing in Europe, FBO created regional offices in key European capitals and prepared plans for modern facilities in Madrid, Stockholm, Copenhagen, Oslo, and The Hague, where FBO chief Fritz Larkin had already completed the purchases of prime sites. In the late summer of 1951 the United States signed a peace contract with West Germany and then a peace treaty with Japan. By early 1952, FBO had begun the design and construction of consulates and information centers in Germany and staff housing for American diplomats and consular staff in Tokyo. The Tokyo apartments were among the very first major postwar buildings in Japan and were seen as a gesture of the U.S. peacetime commitment to its former foe. It may be impossible to know the extent to which any or all of these buildings created better diplomats or enhanced diplomacy, but the new architecture attracted attention and tremendously amplified the American presence abroad.

FBO retained Harrison & Abramovitz to design the embassy in Rio de Janeiro in 1948. At the time, Wallace K. Harrison was not only an influential leader among American architects, but also the only one who had served in Washington as a cultural advisor on foreign affairs and had also already completed major design projects in Latin America. Harrison figured prominently in the design of Rockefeller Center, a landmark project of the 1930s, and was responsible for the Trylon and Perisphere, the bold geometrical structures that came to symbolize the New York World's Fair of 1939.

Harrison never attended college, but went to work for a construction firm at a young age. In 1914, he began studies at the Boston Architectural Club, then headed by Henry R. Shepley. His course of self-directed education led him to New York and the firm of McKim, Mead, and White, and then to Paris, where he studied the principles of Beaux-Arts design in preparation for study at the École des Beaux-Arts.[1] Eventually he abandoned plans to pursue the full course at the École in favor of further travel, and returned to the United States where he worked for architects including Bertram Goodhue and Raymond Hood. Through the success of Rockefeller Center, and through his growing relationship with the Rockefeller family, to whom he was related by marriage, Harrison received numerous commissions and became widely known.

In 1945, Harrison formed a partnership with Max Abramovitz, who had started his design career in 1931 as an apprentice in the Harrison office. Harrison also was named to head the cultural affairs division of the Office of Inter-American Affairs in 1945, an office created by President Roosevelt and directed by Nelson Rockefeller. Earlier, as a consultant to Rockefeller, he had designed the Avila Hotel in Caracas (1941). He was also responsible for the U.S. Submarine and Air Base in the Panama Canal Zone (1942) and additional U.S. government facilities at Balboa and Coco Solo in Panama. Like the Caracas hotel, these facilities were notable for their use of materials and local building traditions, and for the careful attention paid to problems posed by the tropical climate.

More recently, Harrison had led the international architectural team that made headlines with the design of the United Nations buildings along New York's East River (1949–52). Harrison & Abramovitz completed all of the working drawings for the project that included an office tower, an assembly hall, and a conference building. The Secretariat tower, which opened in 1950, was a thin rectangular slab thirty-nine stories tall, framed in steel, trimmed in aluminum, and sheathed in green-tinted glass on its east and west sides and Portland stone on its narrow north and south ends. Like a mirror, it reflected the surrounding skyline, the river, and the ever-changing sky. The Conference Building was finished in 1951, and the General Assembly in 1952. The sleek Secretariat, soaring above the curved roofline of the General Assembly below, became a lasting symbol of the fledgling international organization.

Leland King was one of many who admired what Harrison & Abramovitz accomplished at the United Nations. While Larkin traveled the world identifying and acquiring real estate for FBO, King took care of the business of hiring architects and supervising the design work in Washington, and it was in this capacity that he retained Harrison & Abramovitz as a way of bringing attention to the foreign building program. King was familiar with their work, he knew of their Latin American projects and wanted to take advantage of their recent experience there, and he felt he could trust them to handle the Rio project, the largest by FBO since the war. It was King's opinion at that time, and remained his opinion after, that he had the authority to select the architects for FBO projects. His superiors, of course, were in a position to back FBO policy or to veto it, but prior to 1953, King was aware of no outside pressure regarding his policy decisions.

When the firm was hired, however, Nelson Rockefeller was assistant secretary of state for American republic affairs. Did he influence the situation in favor of his friend Harrison? Knowing of the patronage relationship that existed between the two men, one might assume that he did, or that he might have tried to, but Rockefeller's position did not place him above FBO in any administrative capacity, and King asserts that the choice was his own.

The Rio de Janeiro embassy was a twelve-story tower topped with a penthouse loggia (fig. 20). When it was built, it was the tallest and generally most conspicuous building ever constructed by the State Department, and it is no surprise that critics, who knew little or nothing about contemporary Brazilian architecture, associated its design with Madison Avenue and found it hard to think of it as an American embassy. The whole structure, aside from the amoeba-shaped library adjacent to the tower at ground level, had an angular appearance; and even the piers, nonstructural but arranged in a closely spaced line at the base, emphasized the planar quality of the unornamented building. Large round openings in the flat plane that seemed to hover above the top floor caused it to look like a screen more than a traditional roof.

Though located nowhere near the battlegrounds of Europe or the Far East, the FBO project in Brazil made use of foreign credits to pay for its construction. A total of six foreign currencies combined to finance 95 percent of the total cost, and only 5 percent came from American dollar expenditures. The travertine used as cladding on the exterior walls, for example, was purchased with credits in Italy.[2]

In an unusual move, FBO designated three floors of the embassy tower for residential use. Just before the building was completed in 1952, plans changed and one of the three floors was taken over for expanded office space, but two were equipped with eight efficiency apartments each. Although FBO had included a consular residence atop the Naples consulate, this was the first attempt to combine staff housing with designated office space. The apartments were used by the Marines to save the cost of separate quarters and to add protection to the building by having the guards always on site.

Just prior to completion, fire damaged the office building. The fire was caused by careless workmen, and the subcontractor, General Electric, took responsibility for the damage. Congress questioned the cause and cost of the fire, forcing FBO Deputy Director Edward Kerrigan to defend the fire-proof design of the structure. What Kerrigan did not tell the Appropriations Subcommittee, however, was that although the fire was indeed started by a welding rod, the reason it spread all the way to the top of the building in a pipe shaft was that the building lacked the fire stops required of both local construction in Rio and all construction in the United States. Much later, Nelson Kenworthy, an FBO consultant in 1953 and its interim chief in 1954, recalled that the architects considered themselves exempt from the purview of Brazilian building inspectors and "thumbed their noses at these people." "It's damn stupid," Kenworthy said. "Architects' offices are filled with people who don't know up from down." He pointed out that checks are designed as safeguards to prevent foolish or dangerous designs. Diplomatic buildings, he said, ought to meet local building codes. If they are cited for a purely technical violation, then, if needed, they can use State Department authority to circumvent the code, but wherever reasonable, he argued, architects should comply and should want to comply. "Wally's office didn't have to be checked," he said, "and they were not."[3] Repairing the building cost approximately $150,000, and it took many months to replace the damaged elevators in the tower.

The question of whether such buildings needed to meet U.S. safety standards and whether they ought to try to meet local standards remained unresolved and became an issue again in Germany, where architects were permitted to use exposed structural steel beams that would have had to be covered with fire-proofing in the United States. This allowed for design possibilities that could not be explored by architects at home, but also posed some element of danger to the buildings and their occupants.

Although modern in its starkness, the Rio embassy was far from radical architecture in Brazil at that time. With its roots in Europe, the modern movement had spread to Brazil by the 1930s and the influence of Le Corbusier was strongly evident in the work of his disciples Lucio Costa, Oscar Niemeyer, Alfonso Reidy, Carlos Leao, and others already practicing there. The Ministry of Education and Health in Rio, designed by Costa and Niemeyer, et al., was completed in 1937. Its south side was fully glazed, but its north side, which faced the full sun, was covered by a *brise-soleil* (sun screen) of movable louvers, the first of its kind and a bold move to create a building capable of responding to climate and site.[4] Costa and Niemeyer were also responsible for Brazil's contribution to the 1939 New York World's Fair, where they offered a pavilion that seemed to represent the essence of contemporary Brazilian design while presenting the principal elements of the country's modernist architectural vocabulary. These forms included a subtle curved façade, an open ground floor, a second story raised on *pilotis* (stilts), a wide ramp leading to the second floor, and honey-combed louvers for sun control.

What made Brazilian architecture nationally distinct was its lightness (the use of stucco, glass, and tile to achieve an airy effect), its covered walls (protected from the sun by various sorts of screens), its shaded open areas (created by structures raised on stilts), its use of color, its use of reinforced concrete (cheaper and more plentiful than steel), and the overall plasticity of its forms.[5] Interestingly, many of these attributes came to typify American embassy architecture exported to tropical and even to nontropical places as sun control became an ever-present problem—especially for those preoccupied with glass walls—and building on stilts became the fashion. Originally associated with Le Corbusier, such buildings came to be justified by a variety of functional factors, but architectural taste best explains their popularity.

WHILE WORKING ON the Rio project, Harrison & Abramovitz also designed the U.S. embassy in Havana, an eight-story office building on a splendid site overlooking the Gulf of Mexico between the fashionable new apartment buildings lining Calzada Street and the Paseo del Malecón, the seafront boulevard (figs. 21–2). Five factors stand out in the history of this project: its prominent site (a positive diplomatic gesture that pleased both Cuba and the United States); the financial arrangement that made it economical and necessary to import materials from many nations; the unusual structural system, much admired among contemporary architects; the evident attempt to fit the building to the local scene through attention to climate, site, and materials; and the totality of the design, which included the involvement of a well-known landscape architect, Thomas D. Church, and a well-known furniture manufacturer, Hans Knoll. Despite typically uncritical praise from the architectural press, a sixth factor of note was the utter failure of the architecture and the furniture to work as expected.

In 1916, the U.S. government first purchased an embassy residence in Havana, a property prized for its good neighborhood and its distance from the sea. The area declined, however, as "mechanics, tradesmen, and railway employees" rented small dwellings nearby and as other close neighbors came to include a leading Cuban brewery and a slaughterhouse.[6] By 1928, the ambassador had chosen to forego the official residence and rented quarters elsewhere in the city; the chancery, consulate, and other embassy functions had been scattered among rental properties in different parts of Havana. As the area further deteriorated, construction of broad roads near the ocean opened up fashionable new residential sections. In 1938, Larkin urged the purchase of two new parcels—a "desirable site at a proper point in the central business section" for an office building "of the proper type," and a suitable site "in one of the newer and finer residential sections for a new Embassy."[7] He was prepared to spend approximately $700,000 to complete these transactions. Legal restrictions had prevented him from selling the undesirable property, but after the foreign buildings authorization was amended in 1945, he was able to sell the old site and apply the proceeds of the sale to the new transactions. He sold the property for $110,000 in 1952 and purchased the prominent seaside site in the posh new neighborhood where the Cuban government was investing large sums for parks and other amenities in an attempt to attract residences and businesses.

Harrison & Abramovitz expressed the functional division of the embassy in their plan. They housed the consular offices, which needed to be accessible to the public, in a one-story structure facing Calzada Street. That low structure wrapped around the west side of an office tower that extended at right angles from it. In addition to the consular offices, the lower portion also housed the visa section and public information services. Oriented north/south in order to catch the prevailing breezes in winter, the tower slab housed the diplomatic offices and others that required security. It was five stories high and topped with a penthouse that contained conference rooms in the north end overlooking the gulf, and air-conditioning and other mechanical equipment in the south. The ambassador's office was on the fifth floor and was marked by a prominent balcony on the north elevation. While it later became unwise to advertise the location of the ambassador's office, there was no such concern at the time. To protect against storms and rising seas, the entire building was raised three to five feet above sea level on a platform. Its main entrance faced east across a wide plaza designed by the landscape architect Church, who also designed the two interior courtyards.

The first published report on the architecture hailed the "gleaming travertine-and-glass tower" as a "new landmark on Havana's gulf front." In its "Progress Review" of the embassy construction, *Progressive Architecture* explained how the building would be "completely air-conditioned." During the winter months, though, it noted optimistically that "the air-conditioning will be turned off and the building will be cooled by ocean breezes and protected from sun's heat by heat-resistant glass used for the east and west walls." Those were the expectations, but acting FBO chief Kenworthy later recalled that neither the ocean breezes nor interior venetian blinds were able to mitigate what quickly became a climate control disaster: an air-conditioning system that simply could not do its job. The Havana embassy "created one hell of a stir," Kenworthy said. "It was completely unsuitable, an all glass building in the hot sun climate like that."[8]

In its earlier preview of the embassy in 1951, *Progressive Architecture* had rightly observed that "no fins, louvers, overhangs, or other sun control devices were thought necessary." By the time the building opened, it was apparent that the architects had miscalculated the heat load, and special-ists from Carrier were called in to try to make the necessary improvements to the air-conditioning system. Still, as might have been expected, architectural magazines continued to present the new embassy as a design success. *Architectural Forum* mentioned the aluminum venetian blinds only as devices included to "reduce glare and add texture to the façade." In its later review of the building, *Progressive Architecture* praised both the travertine grill for providing sun control to the ground-floor wing of the building, and the "specially designed aluminum blinds with wide louvers," used to "improve outward visibility without inhibiting effective sun control."[9] It did not, however, define the phrase "outward visibility." Is it the way the outside looks from the inside (what people can see when they look out), or is it the way the building appears from the outside to those already outside (the man-on-the-street)? None of the architectural reviews of the new embassy addressed the practical problem of how workers were supposed to create cross-ventilation when window blinds were tightly shut to keep out the sun, or how they were supposed to work with breeze-blown blinds clattering against the window frames.

Although the architects claimed that they sited the building to catch the prevailing breezes, and although they understood that the air-conditioning would operate on a seasonal basis, they simply expected too much from the tinted glass, and probably figured that the cost and trouble of year-round air-conditioning would, if needed, be acceptable to FBO. Ironically, air-conditioning became one of the first features later incorporated into foreign buildings as a security measure. Where opened windows invited access by intruders, made it easier for materials to be moved in or out of a building, and facilitated surveillance, sealed windows reduced risk. But central air-conditioning was the exception, not the norm, in the early days of the building program. A scheme that might have suited Brussels or Reykjavik was not necessarily appropriate to Havana; but this was the first major American office building constructed in a tropical zone, and American architects still had much to learn about heat, light, mechanical systems, the trade-off between internal comfort and external appearance, and ways to handle the opposition between sunshine and symmetry.

FBO was able to make use of $502,000 in foreign currency in Cuba by triangulating the use of credits. The steel came from Belgium and the cement from France; elevators, movable partitions made of extruded plastic, and other special equipment came from England; and furnishings were manufactured for the Havana embassy in Paris. The reinforced concrete frame was clad in rich-looking ivory-colored travertine. Because the marble was imported from Italy and paid for with Italian credits, the only dollar cost to FBO was that of transporting the stone to Cuba. Such arrangements made it possible to finance the building 30 percent through foreign credits, and 70 percent through dollar expenditures.[10] Other materials for the project included heat-resistant window glass, tinted green on all sides like that of the United Nations, and thin slabs of a pinkish-gray coral stone known as jaimanitas. The coral, wood, terrazzo, and other common building materials were purchased locally. The mechanical equipment and aluminum came from the United States.

The project was noteworthy for the design of its structural system and its interiors. Abramovitz conceived of a structural system consisting of 12 inch slabs that spanned the entire 40-foot width of the tower, creating column-free interiors. The slabs were carried by 10 x 24 inch reinforced concrete piers, 5 feet on center. Although there was no absolute need for unobstructed interiors, this structural accomplishment pleased its creators and was widely cited in architectural reviews of the building. The Knoll furnishings were also widely praised in the architectural press.[11]

Hans Knoll had begun his association with FBO by working with Alan Jacobs on the Brussels chancery, and the two may have had other business ties. Kenworthy even wondered whether or not Knoll was "really tied up with the CIA" because his operations seemed to be so ubiquitous at the time.[12] Most likely he was ubiquitous because he knew so many people, but it is not unreasonable to imagine that such individuals could also have been involved in intelligence operations. FBO purchased Knoll furnishings because architects liked them. Because they were manufactured abroad, FBO was able to purchase them with foreign credits, an arrangement that benefited everyone, except, perhaps, American furniture companies. Knoll furnished the sitting areas at Havana with reproductions of Mies van der Rohe's famous Barcelona chair. Other pieces included long, low foam-cushioned sofas, benches, and glass-topped tables. Work areas featured similarly modern pieces that complemented the architecture.

"People considered the furniture very inappropriate," Kenworthy later remarked. He said that when people sat down in the chairs, the chairs broke. "Senior people at the State Department then were fairly conservative," he noted. "They liked traditional things, and they certainly didn't like that!" In the same context, Kenworthy also criticized the way in which architects received government commissions, including fees for interior decoration, and then turned around and brought in people like Knoll, handing the work to them on a "silver platter" without competition. He objected to this "racket that has gone on for years," which he found to be thoroughly "dishonest."[13] The Knoll pieces in Brussels were similarly criticized in Congress. Representatives who visited the Brussels office building in 1953 approved of the "traditional" furnishings used in most offices but objected to the Knoll pieces in the ambassador's suite. The new furnishings, they said, "were impractical and showed poor judgment," and they noted further:

> The stenographic desks had no drawers. There were no front panels in the desks. It would be most difficult to find a chair more uncomfortable than that furnished for the use of the stenographers. Because of the modernistic furniture placed therein the office of the Ambassador lacked the dignity which might be expected.[14]

At the request of the ambassador, who refused to use them, the Knoll furnishings in Brussels were replaced with more traditional pieces. The modern furniture in Havana was more obviously a part of the design unity of the place. Fortunately for the architects of that project the furnishings were not publicly criticized by the ambassador, and investigators from Congress spent their time examining new projects in Europe, not Cuba. At Havana, the Knoll furnishings remained.

Harrison may have been too busy with the United Nations to give either Rio or Havana much time or thought, but his name became linked with both projects, which in turn became associated with the United Nations. In the late 1940s, the United Nations sought to convey an inclusive and optimistic message. Its design team tried to show that a common commitment to the future could unify and strengthen a war-damaged and divided world. Through its stark geometry, its use of glass, steel, and modern metals such as aluminum, and its apparent rejection of place, historical allusion, and even climate as factors influencing design, the UN building became the quintessential expression of modernism—in this case appropriately labeled the "international style"—a meeting place for peoples from around the world, a place that could and would welcome all and proclaim a sense of universal equality. While some saw its grid and the mechanical sameness of its parts as a celebration of bureaucracy, others saw it as a triumph of technology, a suitably anonymous solution to the problem of designing large-scale public architecture in the postwar world. Although the UN was widely admired among architectural modernists, the association between the embassy buildings and the UN later hurt FBO.

•

CONSULATES, SUCH AS THAT designed by Leon J. Stynen for Antwerp (1950), and residential projects, such as the Tokyo apartments designed by Raymond & Rado, were among the most innovative of the foreign buildings designed just after the war. Large office towers, like the embassy in Madrid, however, continued to capture most of the attention from congressmen visiting Europe and those who felt familiar with European capital cities.

In the history of the foreign building program, the U.S. consulate in Antwerp is significant because it was one of the first postwar projects, thoroughly modern, and designed by a foreign architect—Stynen—a Belgian. The four-story structure with glass-walled lobby was inserted with finesse onto a mid-block parcel fronting two streets. Paris regional director Jacobs hired Stynen for the Antwerp project, which was designed and built between 1950 and 1951, and probably completed at about the same time as Rio, prior to Madrid, Stockholm, or Copenhagen.

There was no decision to limit the use of foreign architects until 1954, after Congress began to criticize FBO operations. To the contrary, the practice of hiring local professionals helped FBO see its buildings built. Foreign architects knew the local conditions, understood building codes and other restrictions, knew authorities, were familiar with builders and their capabilities, and, generally speaking, could help FBO win local approval. Moreover, they could be paid in foreign currency, a factor that made their employment particularly attractive. Ironically, when FBO agreed to hire what Congressman Rooney called "high-class" American architects in order to win favor with Congress, many of the architects turned out to be foreign-born, including Walter Gropius, Marcel Breuer, Richard Neutra, and Josep Lluis Sert.[15]

As a small building in a relatively little-known Belgian city, the Antwerp consulate hardly would have been noticed if not for its use of modern materials and its contemporary appearance. *Architectural Forum* included it in its 1953 overview, praising its "clean and sensitive" look. Members of the House Appropriations Committee inspected the project in the same year, however, and objected to its design. They were troubled by the "so-called international architecture," and specifically faulted the design for being "not in keeping with the architecture of the immediate vicinity."[16]

With diplomatic and consular offices scattered throughout the city, State Department operations in Madrid faced what were then considered to be serious security problems.[17] Jacobs was supervising completion of the Antwerp job when King asked him to turn his attention to Madrid. This project followed Havana and expanded upon ideas first explored there. Jacobs hired the firm of Garrigues & Middlehurst as consulting architects and supervised the project from Paris. Designed and built between 1952 and 1954, the project was financed almost completely through foreign credits. The building was unusual in its plan, its structural design, its size, and the impact of its startling new look (fig. 23).

Because both the existing residence and office quarters were rented and needed to be replaced, FBO decided on a plan that combined office and residence. Unlike Naples, where a consular residence sat atop a five-story block, for Madrid the architects decided to separate the two functions almost completely on the ground, with the residential quarters adjoining the rear of an eight-story concrete office tower. Attached to the other side of the tower, as at Havana, was a single-story structure wrapped around an interior courtyard. With a separate entrance off the main street, and totally separated from the residential area, this section housed all visa and public information offices to which the public needed ready access.

As Deputy Under Secretary of State Carlisle Humelsine described to the Senate Foreign Relations Committee, the Madrid embassy office building faced one street, a main thoroughfare, and the ambassador's residence faced another, but the two were connected in a unique attempt to create two separate structures that used shared facilities. "For instance, instead of putting an elaborate dining room in the residence of the Ambassador," Humelsine noted, "we put a dining room in that could be used by the Ambassador when he has to have a function, and it also can be used for other purposes of the Embassy, and we have tried to, by putting the two buildings close together like that, functionalize the requirements."[18]

Despite the old and dilapidated condition of the existing ambassador's residence—not to mention its uncertain rental status—the ambassador expressed no interest in moving into the new and modern residence as its completion neared. When Humelsine's comments were made in 1952, the plans still called for the dual project. But with a recalcitrant ambassador, FBO decided to convert the adjoining structure into a USIS facility rather than a residence. The information program had been spread about in various old properties acquired in connection with the settlement of German reparations. Subsequent ambassador Anthony Biddle decided to reconvert the space back into a residence, but he died before he could move in. His successor did move in, followed by Biddle's nephew, Angier Biddle Duke, who used the new residence as his ambassadorial home. Duke enjoyed the proximity of the two buildings, and commended the whole project for its fine plan.[19]

According to Jacobs, the Madrid design was based upon Havana, where the structural design featured a clear span from one wall to the other. "King was enamored of this sort of block, a structure with no columns," Jacobs declared.[20] He said that there was no need to span the space in a way that structurally necessitated a tall, narrow, rectangular slab bearing no relationship to its place. Others, including congressmen and diplomats, echoed this sentiment. Ambassador John Jova described the impact of the Madrid embassy as "sensational." Editorials called it a crime to put a modern building there.[21]

The early rearrangement of function and the conversion of the residence to office use led to many of the costly changes cited in House appropriations hearings in 1954, when subcommittee members also objected to the architecture itself. In a far-ranging investigation into the operations of FBO, three subcommittee members had visited posts around the world in the fall of 1953. The three, Frank T. Bow (R-Ohio), Sam Coon (R-Ore.), and Prince H. Preston Jr. (D-Ga.), issued a report that was used two years later to push the blame for waste onto the State Department and to show that congressional travel saved taxpayers more money than it cost. Referring to the Madrid embassy, then under construction, the report stated: "Here again the so-called International type of architecture is being used. Considerable resentment was found among the people of Spain regarding the type of building being constructed."[22]

While there were modern public buildings in Rio and many new hotels and apartments under construction in Havana, Madrid was not a place where people were used to seeing towers finished in exposed concrete. At eight stories, the Madrid embassy was modest compared to new office buildings in New York, but in Madrid it was, indeed, a tower. It was not located amidst the old city of palaces and plazas, however, but along the spacious, tree-lined Paseo de la Castellana, one of the radial roads along which the city had been expanding since the turn of the century. When it was built, it stood out as a stark, modernist statement, but those who designed it knew that the city would soon surround it with comparable new buildings—and that is precisely what happened. Today, ringed by high fences, the embassy still looks surprisingly contemporary, but the Castellana now is lined with mirrored office towers and fanciful architecture that makes the U.S. embassy seem dignified, even dull, by comparison.

Ralph Rapson was teaching architecture as a member of the MIT faculty when a call from his friend Hans Knoll took him to Washington to meet Larkin and King in 1951. Knoll was in Washington trying to sell his furniture to FBO when he learned of upcoming jobs in several Scandinavian countries. He alerted Rapson to the situation and Rapson responded quickly, arriving at FBO with his portfolio in hand. He had recently collaborated on the design for the Eastgate Apartments (1949), a 360-unit complex in Cambridge already recognized for the ingenuity of an alternate-floor elevator system that reduced corridor space, provided cross-ventilation to all units, and gave everyone a large glass-walled living room with a view of the Charles River. Architects cited Eastgate (at 100 Memorial Drive) as one of the most significant postwar American buildings to date.[23]

King asked Rapson if he thought he could handle the proposed FBO work, embassies in Stockholm, Copenhagen, Oslo, and The Hague, and Rapson replied that he could. The two agreed that Rapson would go to

Europe and associate himself with local architects—who would be more knowledgeable about local conditions, materials, zoning, and other essential matters—and that he would be paid directly by FBO on a fee and percentage basis. It was an appealing arrangement. Rapson telephoned his former partner John van der Meulen in Chicago, asked him to join him as a partner as soon as possible, and left for the Netherlands. There, he established an office in a back room of the U.S. embassy in The Hague and promptly began work on an array of projects for which there were virtually no programs, no set budgets, no precedents (known to those involved), and over which there was little overall supervision.

To his brief but eventful career at FBO, Rapson brought a strong background in modern design theory. Born in 1914, he graduated from the University of Michigan in 1938 and went on to study urban and regional planning under Eliel Saarinen at Cranbrook Academy for two years. At Cranbrook he collaborated with Eero Saarinen, Charles Eames, Ben Baldwin, and Harry Weese, and came to admire the functional precision of the work of Le Corbusier, Mies van der Rohe, and Alvar Aalto. In 1942 he became head of the architectural workshop at the New Bauhaus (later the Chicago Institute of Design), directed by László Moholy-Nagy, who had created the famed *Vorkurs* course at the German Bauhaus. By the time Rapson joined the faculty at MIT in 1946, he was well versed in new building technologies and the aesthetics of modernism. Furthermore, as Jacobs later noted, Rapson had an extraordinary talent for drawing rapidly and beautifully. Van der Meulen was a classmate of Rapson's at the University of Michigan. After practicing briefly in Grand Rapids, Michigan, he served in the U.S. Army and returned after the war to join Rapson in practice and to teach architecture and design at the Chicago Institute of Design. Although van der Meulen's wife was about to give birth, the couple packed up and headed for The Hague to join the Rapsons. The architects worked as partners, with Rapson as the design architect and spokesman for the team.

At once, Rapson and van der Meulen began working on a design for an embassy office building for The Hague, the first of a series of projects for FBO. The scale of these projects was considerably smaller than that of Rio, Havana, or Madrid because of design controls that existed in Stockholm and Copenhagen. Without those controls, their buildings would also have been towers. As it was, the tallest project they built was the four-story embassy in Stockholm, a scheme that was reduced from preliminary designs that showed six or seven stories. Nearly all of their projects were raised on stilts, as if suspended, often appearing to hover above a single-story wing slid beneath a more massive structure—creating a visual ambiguity, the sort of relationship that intrigued Le Corbusier and that many modernists then sought to explore. They also relied, far more than Harrison & Abramovitz, on glass as the medium by which to enclose space. This was perhaps a curious response to the problem of designing for northern latitudes, where sun is so rare and precious throughout the long winters, but where large windows add to dampness and heat loss, give office workers a view of omnipresent darkness, and create spaces that when illuminated from within look like fishbowls to those outside.

It is no surprise to learn that Rapson was unfamiliar with prior FBO work and by his own account unmindful of the symbolic associations inherent in such projects. He and van der Meulen tried to provide functional office buildings to a client who had plenty of accessible funds and only a vague idea of how to spend them. Rapson cannot recall seeing photographs of Rio, for example, nor did FBO make any effort to acquaint him or other architects with previous or contemporary projects. By themselves, the two architects developed the programs, consulting with local embassy personnel as they went along, and settled matters of urban design with local authorities. "Theoretically, we were supposed to send the stuff back here to D.C.," Rapson later remarked, "but that was so slow that by the time it came back, we were well beyond them."

Rapson's design for The Hague called for a three-story glass-walled building raised above a recessed lobby on stilts (fig. 24). The most remarkable aspect of his scheme was its openness; FBO had no guidelines regarding such matters at that time. Indeed, it would have provided virtually no privacy for its staff. Furthermore, it was a time when architects believed that space should flow freely between interiors and exteriors, when walls represented the past that modernism had rejected. What is also striking about Rapson's design is the juxtaposition of the sleek, modern building with the small and elegant eighteenth-century landmarks that lined the historic square along the Lange Voorhout. "I thought it wrong to place an overly modern building into this traditional setting," Rapson later remarked. "I tried to dissolve the façade," he said, "to treat it as a transparent—almost a nonbuilding—which would not compete with the traditional façades."

Pushed by the urgency of the needs in Stockholm and Copenhagen, the project for The Hague was set aside, and Rapson and van der Meulen moved their small office to Stockholm, where they set themselves up in the architectural office of Anders Tengbom, who spoke English and had a well-established practice. They brought several local architects from Denmark to assist on the Copenhagen project, and went to work on the two embassy office buildings. Basically, Rapson did the design work and van der Meulen handled structural details, including windows, doors, and railings. The local architects turned the designs into working drawings suitable for bidding by local contractors.

FBO had purchased a rocky site in Stockholm on a hill in a park-like enclave recently reserved for diplomatic structures just outside of the downtown area. Though it was Rapson's impression that embassy property was a "sovereign sort of place" where architects could "do anything they damn well pleased," he found that the architect and city planner Sven Markelius closely controlled Stockholm's urban design and that local design review was enforced most of the time, even for embassies. Known to architects in the United States because of his collaboration on the United Nations design, Markelius represented "sort of a god" to Rapson. "Everything in Stockholm went through that man," Rapson said, noting that any proposed building for the city had to be fitted onto a room-size model in Markelius's office and studied before it could be built.[24]

Rapson and van der Meulen made a number of preliminary drawings of the proposed embassy (figs. 25–6). The diversity of their studies shows that they had no preconceived idea of what an embassy should look like and no particular rationale for the variously arranged functions within the building. One project that may have inspired them was Le Corbusier's Villa Stein (1926–27), and another was Pietro Belluschi's recently completed Equitable Building (1948). For Stockholm, the early drawings show a five-story square office block set astride two asymmetrical one-story wings, one of which is topped by a series of barrel vaults and the other by a row of round skylights. Like other architectural details that became popular in the early 1950s, barrel vaults appealed to architects because they added a vaguely exotic air to new buildings and also because new concrete technology permitted variously configured rooflines. At Stockholm, the barrel vaults had no special historical association. A revised scheme added another story to the tower block, a vaulted rooftop loggia, glass walls, and balconies. Through its revisions, the design evolved to a more severe rectangular tower, faced almost entirely of glass on at least one side. In other undated preliminary schemes, the architects examined additional possibilities that included an arc-shaped tower reminiscent of buildings seen in Paris and numerous resort hotels.

"Mind you, none of these [embassy jobs] had programs," Rapson later remarked. "We had virtually no controls on us regarding design." Though there may have been no design directives from FBO in Washington, or even from FBO in The Hague, where there was a regional office, Rapson did run into design direction from the "bull-headed Swedes," who insisted on changes, starting with the overall height. Markelius wanted to preserve the residential character of the Djurgarden neighborhood and did not want the building to dominate its surroundings. Because the site was on the highest ground in the area, Rapson had to lower the tower to three stories and extend the ground floor to cover a greater portion of its site. Other suggested changes prompted Rapson to declare: "It's an American building, and we're going to do it our way even if we make mistakes."[25] He may have been exasperated with some of the changes he was asked to consider, but the planning proceeded rapidly, and within a matter of months the new embassy was under construction (figs. 27–8).

The Stockholm design reflected an aesthetic preoccupation with spatial volume and balance as well as functional needs. Consular and public information services were located in the single-story portion that wrapped around two landscaped garden courts and connected to the upper portion via the shared lobby. This portion also included the visa section, educational and economic sections, administrative offices, a small gallery leading to a large auditorium, and a cafeteria. Accessible from the spacious lobby for receptions and public gatherings, the auditorium could seat eighty people for films and lectures, and, when combined with the cafeteria, could seat 160. This feature proved especially useful over time. Through floor-to-ceiling glass walls, the garden court was visible beyond the lobby, which was furnished with the Barcelona chairs, benches, and tables typical of the Knoll workshop. Glass walls also revealed a dramatic main staircase rising from the ground floor to the top of the three-story office block (figs. 29–30). During construction, the staircase caused a crisis when the ambassador saw it and demanded a change to a more traditional design. FBO halted construction and even Secretary of State Dulles had to enter the fray before the issue was settled and the project was able to proceed as designed.

Political, military, and communications functions, as well as the ambassador's offices, were located in an office block designed to float visually above the lower structure. The architects themselves pointed out that the spatial separation of the building into an upper mass over a lower one "acknowledged the hierarchy of things" and conveyed some concern for security. Public spaces were supposedly "segregated from the rest of the Embassy," but the open staircase and the location of lobby elevators, which were then unguarded, indicate that the segregation was more conceptual than actual.[26] Before terror posed a threat, at a time when fire, theft, and espionage were the key security concerns, there was no reason to design more cautiously and every reason to celebrate new ideas and new technology.

Built on a frame of reinforced concrete, the Stockholm embassy had circular columns that were set back from the walls and supported the structure's main beams. Where it had definable walls, they were faced in thin sheets of granite. Elsewhere, it was enclosed in a glass and aluminum "skin" divided between floors and along edges by granite bands. The heating and ventilating systems were designed to maximize interior flexibility and to bring washed and heated air to all offices. Sited on a rocky ridge, the embassy was accessible by car from a drive that led up to a large entrance court, and by foot from the road and bus stop below by way of a stairway that pierced the wall of rock. To accommodate possible expansion, the architects positioned the structure so that the north wing could be extended to the east.

The situation in Copenhagen differed from Stockholm in that the Copenhagen site was far smaller and more constrained. The embassy had to fit into a busy streetscape, adjacent to the large home that served as the residence for the American ambassador, and amidst other classical buildings. According to the *Architectural Review*:

> The city plan called for a building in traditional style to accord with the Canadian Embassy next door and to the War College beyond, but approval was given to a more contemporary design on condition that the existing cornice-line was maintained and that the main block was set back 23 feet.[27]

Rapson and van der Meulen would have liked to have gone up two or more floors, but they could not. As a result of the constraints, Rapson says he "sort of shoe-horned the thing into the site." Early sketches show a building seven stories high, topped by a roof garden and a penthouse. As built, the embassy is only three stories high (figs. 31–3).

As at Stockholm, the architects created the illusion of one building "floating" above another at Copenhagen, and placed the public portion of the building on the ground floor with a separate entrance to the auditorium and library through a side garden. All ground floor offices, including consular and visa offices, press, and information, were accessible through the main lobby, which led also to the ambassador's offices, the political section, and offices for military and other attachés on the two floors above. Also like Stockholm, the building had a reinforced concrete frame and a lobby featuring a dramatic open staircase and modern furnishings designed in the United States and manufactured in Denmark. All of the sealed double-glass windows, except those on the north side, had aluminum venetian blinds. The architects designed the building structurally so it could be expanded with a third floor. Given the proliferation of Foreign Operations Administration offices, larger and longer-lasting than anticipated, space in the Copenhagen embassy was tight from the outset. The constraints of its site meant that it lacked the spacious reception facilities of Stockholm, but in solving the problem of accommodating so much in such a small space while not appearing to overpower the site, the architects succeeded admirably.

There were as many opinions on these buildings as there were critics. Ides Van der Gracht ran the FBO regional office in The Hague and supervised the construction in Stockholm and Copenhagen. He wrote to King in 1954 to say that Markelius had studied the Stockholm embassy in detail and declared it to be "the best office building in Stockholm"—an assessment that must have truly pleased Rapson, if anyone thought to tell him. When 350 Swedish artists and architects visited the building, as Van der Gracht noted, "not a few looked as though they were really seeing a sort of architectural Marilyn Monroe for the first time....Shook 'em a bit." Even those who were disturbed by the size and modernity of the building conceded that "the trend was in that direction and would certainly not revert to the style of the wealthy individual houses built in the thirties." Though Embassy personnel were initially hostile to the new Stockholm building, they also came to like it as a pleasant, comfortable, and operationally efficient workplace. Van der Gracht proudly stated: "One of the main things to my mind is that it *works* as an Embassy."[28] Not only the Swedes and those who worked in the building appreciated it, but its fans also included visiting American architects and architects from England, New Zealand, and Finland. In its 1953 overview of State Department projects, *Architectural Forum* cited the Stockholm embassy as "one of the handsomest of the new FBO structures," and the AIA awarded it a First Honor Award in 1955.[29]

The *New York Times* presented the Copenhagen embassy with an ambiguously enthusiastic headline: "Modernistic U.S. Embassy in Denmark is a Sensation." "The Danish public is somewhat stunned....[they]are skeptical about the resistance of the light, glass structure to the damp, grim Danish winters," it reported, but it went on to add that "all the modernists in Copenhagen are delighted by the $1,000,000 structure."[30] The embassy was awarded the Danish Medal for Good Design from the Danish government in 1955.

In his 1954 letter to King, Van der Gracht cited press comment that ranged from reports that described the embassy as "sterile," likened it to "a giant Hollywood magnate's villa," and cited its "melancholy undertakers' interiors," to those that praised the elegance of its "restrained interiors" and called it "one of the most beautiful, functional buildings in Copenhagen." "Ambassador [Robert D.] Coe, who is hardly a radical," he wrote, "takes immense interest in the building and has come really to like it." Overall, he wrote, "I think there is no doubt that the buildings [Stockholm and Copenhagen] are a success." He went on to observe:

> Certainly they are regarded as the "last word" for the time being; only last night, the British PAO [Public Affairs Officer] told me...the Stockholm building [had been described] to him as "undoubtedly the best modern

building in northern Europe." For better or worse, they are thought of as "typically American." To what extent we shall be able to carry on from there remains to be seen.[31]

Rapson and van der Meulen moved to Paris when Jacobs invited them to join the U.S. team there. They set up an office in the embassy and began work on Jacobs' pet project—a proposed large new office building for three thousand people that would have necessitated the demolition of an entire city block, including historic landmarks in the heart of the city. Rapson and van der Meulen's preliminary drawings show variations on the theme of high-rise, glass and steel boxes (fig. 34). One scheme features a pair of eleven-story towers straight out of Le Corbusier's Ville Radieuse. Rapson became good friends with Le Corbusier while in Paris and visited the master's buildings with him. At the time, Rapson was sincerely committed to Le Corbusier's ideals.

The same influence is apparent in apartments that Rapson and van der Meulen designed for FBO in 1952. The need for housing was urgent as American numbers swelled in Paris. Not only was the embassy taking on an expanded role, but Paris was also the headquarters for various reconstruction efforts and defense alliances, such as NATO. FBO selected two suburban sites, one at Boulogne-sur-Seine, the other at Neuilly-sur-Seine, and the architects prepared plans for cubes containing two- and three-bedroom and studio apartments. For the sake of economy, the plans for the cubes were identical, as were the materials, which were largely local. Each floor held four apartments arranged so each had a balcony and two exposures for cross ventilation. There were no basements. The studio apartments were on the ground level with service quarters and lobbies. With all of the corridors, elevators, and stairs in the core, the perimeter was open for more flexible and spacious room plans. Rapson remarked that the design was an effort to "break down the usual inbred American foreign compound character that generally surrounds American developments of this type."[32] It is not clear specifically how he addressed this goal, but the small apartment buildings were comfortable and well-liked when they were completed in 1954. A related scheme of paired squares led to the scheme for Le Havre, where he and van der Meulen designed the U.S. consulate and a staff apartment building in 1952.

Despite months of work and extensive planning, many of Rapson and van der Meulen's projects for FBO were never built. Projects for Oslo (fig. 35), Athens, and The Hague were suspended abruptly after the 1952 presidential election. Ultimately all three high-profile embassies went to better known architects—Oslo to Eero Saarinen in 1955, Athens to Walter Gropius in 1956, and The Hague to Marcel Breuer also in 1956. Rapson later noted that he was "bitterly disappointed" by Breuer's building, which he described as a "monster." He was "crushed" at losing the Athens commission because he thought the design was the best of those he had done for FBO, and also because Gropius's later design was "absolutely identical" to his.[33]

Political upheaval in Washington caused FBO to halt work on embassies in Athens and Oslo and staff apartments in Marseille and Dakar. At the same time, MIT asked Rapson to return from leave or forfeit his teaching position. He headed back to Cambridge. Within the year, he moved back to his native Midwest to head the School of Architecture at the University of Minnesota.

The freedom that Rapson and van der Meulen enjoyed between 1951 and 1954 is an interesting and important part of their contribution to the history of diplomatic architecture. Detailed specifications did not emanate from Washington to shape their design efforts, most of which reflected their enthusiasm for the international style, nor did carefully constructed budgets hamper their style. The relative looseness of the arrangements came back to haunt FBO when Congress began to scrutinize its operations more closely. But for a time, at least, the building program in Europe was characterized by its lack of external constraint, and like the buildings themselves, by its remarkable openness. Morale was high as teams of architects from Sweden, Denmark, Greece, France, Norway, and the Netherlands joined with the Americans to work together on the various projects, debating design philosophy and also world politics. (The Scandinavians particularly disdained the American involvement in Korea, Rapson later recalled.)

Another reason the work of Rapson and van der Meulen is so crucial to this history is that they came to the projects with few preconceptions. By his own account, Rapson said that they were unaware of the symbolic connotations that came to be associated with embassy jobs after architects recognized the commissions as "real plums," and started "knocking themselves out to do unique statements," or "ego trips." He recalled that he and van der Meulen tried to treat the embassy projects as "ordinary" modern office buildings, not monumental statements. They were naive, perhaps, in this assumption, but their genuine effort to create buildings that conveyed "the notion that the United States is an open, dynamic and cooperative modern country" was widely appreciated. Only later, when precedents were established, and when prominent American architects saw the prestige value in embassy projects, did many begin to provide more sophisticated and elaborate explanations for their designs—explanations that did not necessarily make the schemes better understood or appreciated. Speaking with his typical candor, Rapson later remarked, "I didn't know much about embassies, it was my first trip to Europe."[34] Two innocents abroad—the perfect pair to launch the official American effort to rebuild Europe.

CHAPTER FOUR

America Exports Democracy

IN THE IMMEDIATE postwar years the United States faced the task of building strong and lasting alliances while counterbalancing Soviet interests and communist-led gains. In the territory of its former foes, Japan and Germany, the United States faced the added challenge of aiding political, economic, and social reconstruction upon a democratic model. The State Department increased the number and size of its embassies and consulates in part to meet the needs of American military men and women and their families stationed abroad—with enlarged offices for passport, visa and immigration, and public health service operations, for example—and also in part to provide space for the administration of new programs, ranging from those that offered immediate hunger relief to those that supplied long-term economic assistance and training. The department was responsible for providing office space and housing not only for its own Foreign Service officers, but also for all senior officers of other departments accredited to foreign governments through American embassies. Thus, the relatively small FBO building program was part of a larger effort aimed at committing American resources to reconstruction, as well as visibly strengthening the American presence abroad.

While embassies may be the most prominent foreign buildings, other types of buildings have also played significant diplomatic roles. Such was the case in Japan, where the first postwar U.S. buildings, Perry House (1952) and Harris House (1953), contained not offices, but apartments. In Germany, the United States launched a program to build seven consulates, nineteen staff apartment buildings, and an array of libraries and information centers in 1952. Amidst widespread ruin in both war-torn countries, the American buildings would have stood out for their newness alone, but they were not just new, they were modern and thus afforded a strong contrast to anything they replaced and everything else nearby.

When General Douglas MacArthur drove into Tokyo just days after Japan's formal surrender in September 1945, there were few structures still standing in the war-torn city. Even the American embassy had been badly damaged by a bomb that crashed through its roof. The general found the embassy residence flooded with water, its furnishings ruined, and its gardens destroyed. Nonetheless, he made it his home and immediately set about the task of making it habitable. As earlier noted, the Tokyo embassy buildings were part of the compound designed by the architects Antonin Raymond and H. Van Buren Magonigle in the late 1920s. Raymond had established his Tokyo office in 1919, and during the prewar years his practice had flourished. He designed houses, embassies, and industrial buildings, including the Dunlop Rubber factory in Kobe (1930) and the Otis Elevator factory in Tokyo (1932). Both were designed to withstand typhoons and earthquakes, and both also withstood air attacks and survived the war intact.[1]

For his office headquarters, MacArthur did not choose to work out of the two-story chancery, but chose instead a six-story office building located at a symbolically significant spot across the moat from the Imperial Palace. Known as the Dai-Seimei Building, it was soon dubbed the "Dai Ichi" ("Number One") in recognition of MacArthur's all-powerful role as head of the occupation. It provided MacArthur with the opportunity to travel at least twice daily across town, back and forth to work and to lunch at home, a ceremonial processional that allowed him to see the city and its people, and more importantly, to be seen. As biographer William Manchester has noted, largely as a result of MacArthur's efforts to understand the Japanese, American GIs were welcomed where they might have been feared and resisted.[2]

By the time Tokyo's weather turned cold in 1945, the Americans had requisitioned nearly all of the steam-heated buildings from the meager supply of standing structures. Among those acquired were two remarkable modern houses designed in the 1930s and situated on a hilltop in central Tokyo. One was the Ishibashi residence, which still serves as a residence for the American embassy's deputy chief of mission. The other was the Kawasaki residence designed by Raymond for Morinosuke Kawasaki in 1933.[3] With ribbon windows, *pilotis*, roof terraces, and white planar surfaces, both closely resembled villas by Le Corbusier. The Ishibashi residence was built in 1937 for Ishibashi Shojiro, then chairman of the Bridgestone Tire Company. According to the U.S. Embassy, the house was designed by Japanese architect Hideo Hirata, who was raised in the United States and studied architecture at Cornell.[4] It closely resembles Raymond's work.

Though military occupation was historically associated with building desecration, events in Japan took a seemingly unprecedented turn. Two of the first postwar buildings in Tokyo were American projects that were conspicuous, but warmly received. Both were designed by Raymond in partnership with Ladislav Rado. One was the Reader's Digest Building (1949), the first major postwar building in Japan and winner of the Architectural Institute of Japan's annual prize in 1951.[5] While they worked on the Reader's Digest job, Raymond and Rado were also working for FBO designing the second new American project, staff apartments for American embassy personnel.

As the American military presence in Japan grew, so too did the size of the overall embassy staff and associated agencies. The Americans badly needed housing in Tokyo for high echelon diplomats and advisors, as well as for clerks, administrative staff, and others, many of whom had families with them. The American Embassy appealed to the State Department for additional housing. The first step toward providing this was acquisition of an 11-acre site, a steep, flat-topped hill in Tokyo purchased from the Mitsui family by FBO. The second step was selecting architects capable of working within the constraints of a situation in which materials were limited and costly but highly skilled labor was plentiful and inexpensive.

Assistant FBO director Leland King headed up FBO's Washington office during Fritz Larkin's frequent departures, and as chief architect, he also handled design decisions. Just when King was thinking about an architect for the Tokyo job, Rado arrived at his office looking for work for the firm that he had recently formed with Raymond. Like his eccentric partner, but twenty years younger, Rado was born in Czechoslovakia and trained at the Prague Polytechnic. In 1931, he established a practice in Prague. When Walter Gropius saw pictures of Rado's early work in 1939, he invited him to join his advanced class at Harvard's Graduate School of Design. Rado leaped at the opportunity. Later he claimed it saved his life, as he escaped only months before the Nazis invaded Prague. He arrived in Cambridge, Massachusetts, speaking almost no English, "a lost soul," by his own description. But Gropius and his circle provided for him, and soon he was thriving as the fifth member of a group he called the "Guard of Four," which consisted of Sigfried Giedion, Marcel Breuer, Josef Albers, and Gropius, whom he described as "the theoretician of the industrial age of architecture."[6]

After taking his master's degree from Harvard in 1940, Rado worked for the designer Norman Bel Geddes in New York. There he met Raymond, who had come to the United States from Japan for the duration of the war. Raymond had returned via Pondicherry, India, where he designed the dormitories at the famed Sri Aurobindo Ashram. In India, he paid particular attention to the problems created by heat and glare, and designed buildings noteworthy for their high vaulted ceilings and louvered façades. Though Raymond has received little critical attention from architectural historians, those who have commented on his work often lump it all together and simply label it "international style." This is an error. Above all, Raymond was interested in context, and there are few who have so successfully understood and interpreted cultural preferences or the varying dictates of climate as he did.[7] During the war years, Raymond practiced out of New York and maintained a design studio in New Hope, Pennsylvania, but his practice failed to thrive. The first project he shared with Rado was one in Guam that was never built. For some time after the two architects formed their partnership, they had virtually no work at all. Making matters worse, Raymond had a terrible reputation not unlike that of his mentor, Frank Lloyd Wright. "He had a very large and excessive ego," said Rado, who observed that Raymond was uncommonly rude and "liked to push people around." "He thought he was God," Rado noted with a mixture of good-humored annoyance and admiration.[8] Given the personalities, few friends thought that the two architects would be able to work together, but they remained partners for thirty years—until Raymond's death in 1976 at the age of eighty-eight.

Rado knew from experience about Raymond's volatile outbursts. Once, when making a presentation to the owner of Best & Co. in New York, for example, the prospective client suggested that he, too, had some ideas about architecture. "Raymond immediately hit the ceiling," Rado recalls, and he declared, "You have nothing to say about it, we are the masters, we are the architects!" Minutes later, Raymond walked out and the meeting ended. Later he apologized to Rado, asking "Why the hell didn't you kick me under the table?" Rado replied that it would not have helped. Understandably, Rado was glad to be able to visit King alone. Anxious to re-establish his Tokyo practice after the war, Raymond had headed back to Japan in 1947, leaving Rado in charge of the New York office.[9]

King was familiar with Raymond's prior FBO work when Rado presented the firm's qualifications to him at the State Department in 1949. "It helped," Rado said, "that we had the nucleus of an office in Japan and Raymond had the experience of long years working in Japan and building in Japan, so I think that was a big plus."[10] These factors convinced King to hire the firm to design the housing for the embassy in Tokyo.

Initial plans called for a number of separate private residences for the American Foreign Service staff, but the project evolved into a sixty-unit apartment building sited on the crest of the hill. The architects proposed a six-story apartment building topped with a seventh-floor penthouse. King approved the design on the basis of a rough sketch in which Rado showed how and why he wanted to use a plan consisting of alternating open and closed corridors providing cross-ventilation and wide, open views through floor-to-ceiling glass window-walls. The general contractor was Ohbayashi-Gumi, Ltd., the same firm that built the first American embassy in 1931. When the apartment building was completed in July 1952, it was named to honor Commodore Matthew Perry, the American naval officer who opened Japan to commerce with the West (fig. 36). Its success led King to ask the architects for a second building in 1952. Slightly smaller (eight bays instead of ten), but otherwise a replica of the first, it was built on an adjacent site, completed in August 1953, and named for Townsend Harris, the first American consul in Japan.

The architects created adaptable interiors for which they also provided furnishings. To build in flexibility for families of various sizes, they installed partition walls that could be removed to provide larger-sized units. The efficiency apartments, as well as the duplexes above, all boasted south-facing terraces separated from one another by thin, painted panels. The balconies and fixed horizontal metal louvers shaded the terraces. The units were also furnished with semi-sheer white floor-to-ceiling curtains. On the penthouse level, there was a laundry and a roof garden. The ground floor featured a foyer and a large common room/lounge. The basement housed heating and mechanical equipment and storage. In countries where service was a customary part of life, and particularly where large numbers of people needed work, Foreign Service families typically retained servants. Japan was certainly such a place when these buildings were built. Raymond & Rado designed direct access to the kitchens off the open corridor so that servants could come and go from apartments without disturbing the occupants. Separate living quarters for servants were provided on the site as well.

Once the apartments were under construction, Rado visited King to appeal for custom furnishings. "I said the rooms were not very large, and the view to the south side was all glass," Rado later recalled, "and you know I hate to even think that the tenants will come in with their huge ugly couches and beds and clog up the rooms, which will look like hell."[11] Raymond knew good carpenters, furniture makers, and weavers in Japan. Because he could pay for everything with counterpart funds or credits, King readily agreed to the plan; and the architects proceeded to design chairs, tables, beds, rugs, and curtains scaled to the size of the apartments. The fit of the furniture, which was both spare and delicate in the Japanese tradition, added further to the effect of the whole (fig. 37). In addition, the custom furnishings assured the architects that the view from the outside would be uniform and, to their thinking, appropriate.

The furnishings were clearly designed for aesthetic pleasure more than physical comfort. American Foreign Service officers found the apartments much too small and resented the fact that their own belongings did not fit into the new units. They were particularly critical of the small beds, well-suited to the Japanese, perhaps, but not to taller Americans. What the architects regarded as "efficient" and "functional" struck many users as just the opposite. The dimensions of the rooms had been partly dictated by economic considerations, but also by Raymond's sincere appreciation of Japanese aesthetics. Like Wright, he translated his appreciation into spaces that he, not his clients, controlled. No doubt he thought that Americans would, could, and should want to live this way in Japan. He underestimated the extent to which Americans wanted to create "American homes" for themselves in Tokyo and elsewhere overseas. Embassy personnel did appreciate the gardens and the landscaped grounds, however, even then a luxury in downtown Tokyo, but they much preferred the apartments in Grew House, a far less inventive apartment block built nearby by FBO in 1965.

If the Raymond & Rado buildings did not totally meet the needs or expectations of Americans living in them, they did have a significant influence on young Japanese architects faced with the dilemma of reconciling traditional design values with modernized construction. Perry House was the first multistory reinforced concrete building in Tokyo, where builders customarily used concrete-covered light steel frames. They had not yet begun to use reinforced concrete as in the United States, nor had they learned of its effectiveness in providing seismic protection for relatively tall buildings. Structural engineer Paul Weidlinger assisted Raymond in creating a floor system supported by the through party walls, a system of cantilevered box frames that resisted both the lateral forces and longitudinal vibrations associated with earthquake shock. These attributes generated interest among local architects as well as professionals in the United States. Tatsuya Okura, the Kyoto architect who designed the U.S. consulate in Osaka (1981), is one who recalls the great excitement at the time of the opening of the American apartment building. Okura later trained at Harvard's Graduate School of Design and worked for The Architects Collaborative (TAC) in Cambridge and Athens before establishing his own practice in Kyoto. Other young Japanese architects were similarly intrigued by what they saw.[12] *U.S. News & World Report* praised Perry House as an "ultramodern" apartment building and featured it in its issue of 19 March 1954, and *Architectural Record* published its floor plans and photographs soon after. Backed by the patronage of his two American clients, Reader's Digest and the U.S. State Department, Raymond reestablished his reputation in Tokyo. The success of the two projects was pivotal to his career and to that of his partner, Rado.[13] Indirectly, the buildings can be seen as logical expressions of MacArthur's firm but deferential attitude, an attitude that created goodwill and smoothed the difficult postwar transition.

•

REACTING TO WAR damage and economic collapse in Germany and to President Truman's call for massive economic assistance, Congress enacted the Marshall Plan in 1948. As in Japan, the American presence in Germany was substantial and U.S. officials operated out of requisitioned houses, apartments, and office buildings. There was an urgent need, however, to return requisitioned property to the Germans, whose housing and overall building shortage was severe. In 1949 the German landscape remained littered with ruin. Touring Hamburg that year as director of the State Department's Policy Planning Staff, George Kennan saw "sweeping devastation, down to the ground, mile after mile." He noted that the attack that had killed seventy-five thousand persons there had taken place in 1943, but that six years later, over three thousand bodies still lay buried in the debris.[14]

Just after the end of the Allied airlift and the Soviet blockade of Berlin in 1949, the State Department assumed the U.S. Defense Department's responsibility for the occupation organization in Germany. The U.S. military government in Germany was replaced by the Office of the U.S. High Commissioner to Germany (HICOG), established by executive order. HICOG officials determined that the government would save money by building its own housing and office space, and began its building program by retaining German architect Otto Apel to design its headquarters building in Bonn. HICOG also began to build staff housing that included a complex of five hundred apartment units in Frankfurt, occupied by U.S. government personnel in October 1950.

The HICOG building program shifted course when President Truman signed a peace contract ending the state of war and the Allied occupation in 1951. As the United States moved toward normal diplomatic relations with the new federated German government, the State Department assumed the responsibility for supervising construction in Germany and supplying the program with architectural and engineering services. An October 1953 deadline to vacate all requisitioned property added exigency to the situation. The department proposed a $19 million building program aimed at supplying needed American facilities while strengthening the local German economy, stimulating cultural exchange, and boosting the local construction industry. It assigned the task of supervising existing projects and the new work to FBO.

Larkin retired as FBO director in 1952 and King, his assistant and chief architect, took over the helm—but not before they both visited New York to examine Lever House, just completed and already hailed as a modern landmark. Its architect was Gordon Bunshaft of Skidmore, Owings & Merrill (SOM). King was interested in retaining SOM for the immense building program proposed for Germany. According to Larkin's son, Lawrence, his father objected strongly to the choice of SOM. "They don't design buildings," the elder Larkin declared, "just boxes!"[15] But the firm was one of the few American design firms that was large and diversified enough to establish and run a foreign office in the early 1950s. It also had government building experience, having successfully completed several large-scale defense-related projects during the war. Bunshaft was an architect whose work was identified with America—more precisely with corporate America. King saw the use of the Bauhaus idiom, transformed into an American icon, as a fitting goodwill gesture toward Germany. He set up a collaboration between the already retained Apel firm and SOM, with Bunshaft as the partner in charge of design. Apel was retained to produce working drawings, specifications, and estimates, and SOM was commissioned for architectural and engineering services. As proposed, the program was expected to cost about DM80 million, roughly $19 million, which would have meant a fee in the vicinity of $200,000 for SOM.[16] King argued that SOM was uniquely qualified for the huge commission; when later questioned about the high cost of the work, he admitted that one of the reasons SOM underestimated construction costs so badly was that it had no prior experience with projects such as these.

King associated his program with SOM as a way of putting FBO into the architectural spotlight. He wanted the same sort of new and eye-catching look that Lever president Charles Luckman wanted for his Manhattan headquarters. According to architectural historian Carol Krinsky, Luckman had asked Bunshaft for "something that looked new, clean (in keeping with Lever's products), spectacular, and American," and he was pleased with the result.[17] With Harrison & Abramovitz already involved in the FBO building program, King was ready to push for further newness and more publicity. Giving Bunshaft the German commission guaranteed coverage in *Architectural Forum* and other leading design publications. In 1952, moreover, the association between SOM and Lever House, like the one between Harrison & Abramovitz and the United Nations Secretariat, seemed to be an asset to the FBO program.

Soon after receiving the FBO commission, SOM set up a satellite office just outside of Bonn at Bad Godesberg, where Apel was proceeding with work for HICOG. SOM's project manager in Germany was David Hughes, and his senior designer was Natalie de Blois. Local architects also contributed to the collaboration. Bunshaft's contribution to individual projects varied. Some of his designs were significantly modified prior to construction, and some were never built. What he did provide was a common theme for all of the buildings.

Three factors determined the pattern of U.S. property holding in the Federal Republic. One was the "long-held, postwar hope of a reunified Germany." Written into West German law, the commitment to reunification meant that Berlin had to be regarded as the eventual capital, and official buildings in Bonn had to be regarded as temporary. According to a State Department report, "if we had built too many structures that appeared permanent, or had given the impression that we regarded Bonn as a permanent capital, we would have offended many Germans who would have seen these as signs that we were 'giving up' on reunification."[18] The other two factors were the federal character of the new West German state and the tremendous American troop presence in Germany, particularly in the south. Taken together, these circumstances led the U.S. to build not only in Bonn, but also in regional centers, foci of German political and administrative activity.

The original building program in Germany called for forty buildings including seven consular office buildings, seven houses for the chiefs of mission, six information centers, temporary headquarters for the newly established Voice of America in Munich, and 275 apartment units in nineteen apartment buildings. The housing alone was budgeted at $7.7 million.

Prior to World War II, the United States had maintained consulates in Bremen, Cologne, Frankfurt, Hamburg, Munich, and Stuttgart, and also in Breslau and Dresden, both of which fell within the Soviet zone after the war. As part of the program, the State Department planned new consulate buildings for Bremen, Bremerhaven, Düsseldorf, Frankfurt, Munich, and Stuttgart; an annex in Hamburg; and staff apartments in all of these locations and also in Berlin and Cologne. Together these would house the consular staffs and Americans serving in Germany in other official capacities. The building program also called for the construction of six new information centers (in Berlin, Cologne, Frankfurt, Hamburg, Munich, and Stuttgart) to be called America Houses. The Amerika Haus program, as it was known in Germany, provided centers to be operated by the United States Information Service for the purpose of disseminating American culture abroad, a mission assigned to the State Department by the newly enacted Smith-Mundt Act.[19]

The five German consulates (in Bremen, Düsseldorf, Frankfurt, Stuttgart, and Munich) were united by a common architectural language. Like Lever House, the consulates all consisted of glass-enclosed office blocks raised on stilts over glass-walled lobbies and open plazas. Plans for all except Stuttgart consisted of rectangles intersecting at right angles, a scheme that provided for a functional separation that also satisfied the demands of the program. The scheme also set up a cross-axis that added counterbalance to the overall design and created outdoor courtyard spaces that then became part of the architecture. Much as sculpture defines the space in which it is displayed, the architecture became part of the surrounding landscape. As art, the plans captured the spatial qualities of constructions and paintings by Gerrit Rietveld and Theo van Doesburg, and as architecture, they expanded upon themes explored by Le Corbusier, Mies, and particularly Gropius, who had designed the glass-walled Bauhaus at Dessau (1926).

The first consulate was built in Bremen, the next in Düsseldorf; both were completed by 1955 (fig. 38). Like the others, these two were designed to embody the principles of an ideal consulate building with one section exclusively devoted to internal operations and another separate but connected section used for support services and/or accessible to the public. For both, the footprint of the building was a T with its stem off-center. The space created by the two perpendicular rectangles and the street became an open, but landscape-bounded court integral to the plan of the building. Both were organized to house relatively large-scale business operations that required little public access. While nearly contemporaneous projects in Stockholm and Copenhagen incorporated large auditoriums, libraries, and other public-access spaces associated with USIS, the German consulates lacked these amenities because USIS operated its program in Germany out of separate facilities.

As a result of being closer to a sizable concentration of American troops and their dependents, Frankfurt had a more complicated program than the earlier two German consulates (figs. 39–40). The architects emphasized the separation of functions by grouping public-access spaces around the lobby of a one-story structure shaped like a square doughnut. Visa operations were situated to the left of the entrance, passport offices to the right, and a large public health unit and a mail room beyond. The ground floor was slipped beneath a glass-walled mezzanine and three stories of offices above. The mezzanine was recessed beneath the tower and ringed by white concrete stilts that supported the three stories above. The overall effect was as if the architects had taken the entire front portion of the Bremen consulate, including its stilts, and placed it on top of another low building. The low building itself seemed to hover just slightly above the ground. Wide cantilevered steps led to the single entrance, situated typically off-center. Beyond the entrance lobby was an outdoor courtyard. More a contemplative space than a functional one, the courtyard was designed as a void rather than an outdoor room. The architects planned it to accommodate a large piece of sculpture and a single backless bench instead of chairs and tables or other outdoor furniture that might have invited use.

The Munich plan also consisted of two parts—a three-story box over a one-story portion that extended out from below. A single entrance and reception area led to visa offices in the low wing and administrative offices above. Both parts of the combined building overlooked landscaped lawns, originally bordered by public sidewalks and open to the street. Stuttgart differed from the others because its plan was simpler and also because it was symmetrical. For Stuttgart, where the program was more limited, the plan consisted of a single, two-story rectangular block raised over a glass-enclosed ground floor (figs. 41–3).

Designs for all of the consulates were extraordinary for the refinement of the architectural detailing, the dramatic use of modern materials, modern art, and modern furnishings, and the way in which the buildings stood out amidst the older environs. This was particularly apparent at Bremen and Düsseldorf, the first two projects and those most closely associated with Bunshaft. Using stark, modern materials and the repetitive geometry of flat, unornamented façades, the architect distanced both from their immediate surroundings. For windows, he chose a single-glazed casement type with steel frames, hinged to permit simultaneous lowering and swinging outward, and he mounted them above light colored travertine-faced panels. In opting for a glass exterior, he paid no particular attention to the demands of the climate or to the cost of fuel (coke) for heat. The buildings were not air-conditioned.

The façades at Bremen and Düsseldorf were divided horizontally into six bands defined by rows of windows and vertically into seven intervals defined by straight linear elements connected to the supporting *pilotis* below. Every aspect of the Düsseldorf building, for example, from its neatly expressed edges and corners, to the differentiation of the clear glass spandrel panels that mark the interior staircase, to the asymmetrical placement of its entrance canopy, showed an exquisite sense of proportion and a talent for expressing nonstatic balance and measured, but not monotonous, rhythm. Both inside and outside, the white painted structural steel frames gave the whole the crisp definition that its architects so admired.

At Frankfurt and Stuttgart the same basic modular elements were arranged with less finesse. The Frankfurt façade, for example, was a grid of white-trimmed, aluminum-framed windows paired with rows of similarly trimmed dark gray glass panels. Without any overall vertical articulation, both façades lacked the animation of the earlier projects. Both read more like pieces cut arbitrarily from an infinitely big piece of plaid fabric than like carefully composed designs. The unbroken curtain wall grid, the lack of corner definition, the evenly spaced columns aligned with nothing above, and the centered entrance made Stuttgart's design seem even clumsier than the others, although its theme was essentially the same. Poorly chosen proportions produced a static effect at Munich. While there were seven bays of six windows each at Düsseldorf, there were eight bays each consisting of four windows at Munich. However it is presented, a four-to-eight ratio lacks the dynamic potential of six-to-seven, and an even number of bays reduces the visual impact of an asymmetrical plan.

At Frankfurt, as at Munich, the original SOM scheme was revised due to changes in the program, the scarcity of certain materials, and spiraling costs. Comparison of Bunshaft's early renderings and the completed Frankfurt consulate shows that he originally designed the tower block with five floors of offices, not three. In addition, he designed the ends of the tower to be windowless as at the UN Secretariat. When the scheme was revised, windows were added to the end walls giving the entire block a continuous, flat modular surface. It is no surprise that Bunshaft later claimed authorship of the first projects, Bremen and Düsseldorf, only.[20]

SOM furnished most of the lobbies and entrance halls with modern pieces, including glass-topped tables and reproductions of Mies's Barcelona chair manufactured by Knoll, and finished the lobbies with marble and other rich-looking materials. Lobbies at Bremen and Düsseldorf featured open steel staircases with wide steps of pre-fabricated black terrazzo, and bright blue walls contrasted with adjacent walls of cream-colored marble. The architects also selected art that was distinctly modern to complement the architecture. For the outdoor court at Frankfurt, they selected a large Calder stabile—smaller than the "more formidable" version originally proposed, but nonetheless bold and stark.[21] For outdoor plazas at Bremen, Düsseldorf, and Munich, they selected specially commissioned sculptures by Harry Bertoia (fig. 44).

While up-to-date in fashion, the waiting areas, where people often had to sit for hours for appointments or for papers to be processed, were neither cozy nor comfortable, nor were they intended to be (fig. 45). The openness of the plan and the glass walls, though explained as a means of making the buildings seem inviting, produced exposed spaces that might easily have intimidated foreigners who approached the buildings with private personal business. But such openness was precisely what Bunshaft was trying to exploit as a design device and as a technological achievement. As architecture, the lobbies were intended to startle, maybe even amaze, visitors who had never before pulled open a transparent door or sat in a wall-less room.

By and large, the Knoll furnishings at Frankfurt, Havana, and Brussels, as well as the custom-designed pieces for the apartments at Tokyo, were the exceptions, not the rule. Today, for example, visitors to the Munich consulate cannot help but notice the discrepancy between the lasting modernity of the exterior architecture and the ordinary look of the desks, chairs, and conference tables within. Distressing as it might have been to many architects, standard government office furniture and traditionally-styled reproductions were the norm.

More than any other figure, Anita Moeller Laird was responsible for the interior design of America's foreign buildings. From 1949 until her retirement in 1972, Laird headed FBO's interior design group, which was responsible for the furnishing of nearly all FBO projects, including office buildings, ambassadorial residences, and staff housing. Trained at the Parsons School of Design in New York, she worked with architects and with individual ambassadors to select appropriate furniture, carpeting, draperies, upholstery fabrics, and wall coverings for embassy use. During the years when foreign credits were available, Laird purchased china from Germany, crystal from Czechoslovakia, and silver from Peru, and commissioned foreign-made copies of American furnishings under special agreements with various manufacturers.[22] If modern pieces were not always favored, the reasons had to do with overall considerations of economy—it was far more economical to buy pieces that could be widely used than items that were individually customized—and with input from ambassadors (and their spouses) who generally preferred the look and comfort of traditional interiors. The interior design program was surprising in the extent to which it permitted new ambassadors to influence design choices. An ambassador's strong preference for wood, for example, caused Marcel Breuer to specify teak in place of previously selected stainless steel handrails in the embassy at The Hague, completed in 1959. Costly choices were and still are provided to individuals who may live and work for less than a year or two at a given post.

THE FORMALITY OF the SOM plans allowed each building to appropriate ambient space as part of its design. Neither Bunshaft nor his colleagues saw any need to relate the consulates to surrounding buildings, or even to established streets. Instead, by siting each consulate in its own park-like setting, they made it clear that each modern building was recognized as a unique architectural creation standing apart from anything that existed nearby.

If Bunshaft was a top choice for an architect identified with an "American" look, he was not as good a candidate for projects that were supposed to be contextually unobtrusive. Lever House, for example, was a glass-enclosed volume, set back on a plaza and raised on stilts. Much of its visual impact on Park Avenue derived from its contrast with its older and less conspicuous neighbors. Though trained in the tradition of the École des Beaux-Arts and graduated from MIT while the program there was still tradition-oriented, Bunshaft took an early interest in the work and writings of Le Corbusier and Mies. Like theirs, his architecture was intended to be assertive and to stand as a rebuke to the historicist eclecticism that preceded it. In language written into amendments to the Foreign Service Buildings Act in 1952, Congress had called upon FBO to provide architecture "designed to be as distinctively American as possible without clashing with the surrounding buildings." Anywhere it appeared, SOM's architecture was bound to clash with its surroundings. That is what happened at Munich, and this is why the SOM design ran into serious local opposition.

The Munich site overlooked the city's beloved Englischer Garten and was also directly across the street from the Prinz Karl Palais (1805), an elegant and widely admired landmark. Local officials who reviewed the SOM presentation were shocked at its arrogance. SOM's biggest mistake, according to former U.S. Consul General Robert Harlan, was assuming that city officials would be impressed by "a building so purely functional that it would work [as] well in Alaska."[23] Outraged and insulted by this claim, and the implication that a building right for a city that prized its medieval and baroque architecture could be equally right on America's arctic frontier, the city rejected the SOM scheme. After a fact-finding visit to Munich in 1954, Henry Shepley reported to FBO that SOM had made no effort to consult with planning officials or with the mayor before presenting plans to them for approval. "The plans went against their traditions and policy," Shepley noted, "and Bunshaft would not make any concessions." In his report on the situation, Shepley went on to say:

> The Mayor then hired a German Architect, Sep Ruf, to draw up a compromise scheme. This scheme went extraordinarily well for them and was quite a handsome building—more suitable in appearance than Bunshaft's, I think, less commercial. It was so like Bunshaft's that it could have been agreed to quite easily except that the Germans, especially Stadtrat Fischer, the Planning Commissioner was, in his turn, so arrogant and uncompromising in his attitude that our Deputy Commissioner, who had come down from Bonn to negotiate a compromise, walked out of the meeting in disgust.[24]

FBO lost valuable time and the Munich project was delayed as officials tried to undo the damage. Ruf told consular officers that if FBO hired him, they would have no more problems. Bonn architect Otto Apel also wanted the job. Shepley advised that neither could be trusted, and urged FBO to hire an American architect who was "flexible and not too stuffy," someone adept at negotiation as well as design. He pointed out, however, that the Ruf compromise plan was "so good and so nearly what Bunshaft had planned" that there was good reason to try to use it and to allow FBO to proceed with working drawings. That is precisely what happened. As a result of the delays, however, the project was not completed until 1958, well after the others. As Robert Harlan later noted, "One lesson we learned in Munich was the importance of paying attention to cultural sensitivities of local authorities."[25] Retrofitted for security, the consulate is not the spatially open building that it once was, (and its architects would cringe at the sight of the air-conditioners later installed in some windows), but the well-maintained building remains a landmark in the architectural history of the postwar era.

Partly because of the way in which the consulates called attention to themselves, and particularly because of the unusual amount of glass they required, the new American buildings ran into unanticipated trouble. Not only did they attract vandalism that proved to be a costly nuisance to the State Department, but they were expensive and difficult to heat and cool. According to Harlan, the glass walls at Frankfurt seemed to invite rock-throwing incidents. From the outset, he said, many hundreds of windows and glass panels were smashed—even when no special grievance was involved. Not only did this present a maintenance problem, but the overall appearance of the building was affected when FBO was unable to replace all the broken glass panels with the same color glass.

Using glass as he did, Bunshaft not only showed little interest in the architectural uniqueness of cities such as Munich, but also little interest in climate. Munich is mild and sunny compared to Bremen, which is located on the Weser River just thirty miles from the North Sea. Bunshaft's prototype was a building with walls almost entirely made of panes of single-glazed glass. Moreover, it was raised on stilts. With cold air trapped under the building, and with no basement beneath it, the design maximized the heating load, and likewise, the cost of heating.

Apparently FBO never questioned the wisdom of all the glass, but scarcity and cost did force cuts in the use of steel. Bunshaft had planned a structural system based upon the use of specially treated exposed steel, a building material not available to him in the United States because its use violated U.S. fire codes. When the first bids were analyzed, FBO realized that to keep the program close to budget they would have to minimize its use of structural steel. By the time Bunshaft came to design the consulate for Frankfurt, he had to turn to a reinforced concrete frame instead of a steel skeleton. Of the consulates, only Bremen and Düsseldorf featured the steel structure that Bunshaft originally envisioned. The steel work was unusual enough to warrant enthusiastic mention in *Architectural Forum*, which described a no-rust German treatment by which the steel was "first welded, then sand-blasted, then acid-etched, then zinc-coated and finally given three coats of paint."[26] The America Houses were also supposed to feature the special steel, but Bunshaft had to abandon his ideal. German steel was in short supply, and its postwar price was rising rapidly. Furthermore, to Bunshaft's surprise and dismay, the Germans were unable to fabricate the steel in the many sizes and shapes available to him in the United States. Unhappy with the results of compromise, he became disenchanted with FBO and its program and made little effort to publicize these works. Nonetheless, German architects bestowed a design award on the American consulate in Bremen in 1974, citing it for its powerful influence on postwar German architecture.

Largely as a result of concern for appearances and a perceived need for discretion, plans to build housing for Americans in Germany and plans for new information centers provoked sharp debate in Congress. Just after SOM began planning the new projects, negative reports about HICOG's new Bonn headquarters reached Washington. The wrath of the critics fell on FBO, which had by then taken over supervision of the HICOG building program. Members of Congress were disturbed by rumors that newly built American apartments in Germany were too expensive and luxurious for their intended use and labeled the new German apartments "palaces."[27] Much of the criticism was on target. In the rush to provide needed facilities, HICOG had been both wasteful and inefficient. It is easy to understand, for example, why critics were distressed by reports that high quality weather-stripping was used not only on exterior doors, but also on the interior doors of bathrooms.

Writers such as C. L. Sulzberger had already expressed the fear that lavish living or the display of too much affluence might compromise the U.S. mission aimed at German reconstruction. Writing after a visit in 1949, he said, "Obviously, the Americans in Germany are living a far more luxurious life than most of them would be accustomed to in their own country." He went on to state:

> It is a super-Westchester existence. The Germans must resent this. The unconscious arrogance of such a victorious occupation army must be building up fires of resentment, and this is tactlessness in the highest degree. There is so much destruction in German cities, housing is such a serious problem, there are so many millions of destitute refugees that one cannot help but feel that a more modest and more austere mode of American life would, to say the least, be in better taste.[28]

In response to criticism, the House Committee on Government Operations established the Special Subcommittee Investigating the German Consulate/America House Program, chaired by Congressman William E. Miller (R-N.Y.). Beginning in February 1953, the subcommittee held hearings not questioning the strategic need for the program, but rather its cost and its management. The subcommittee brought in investigators from the Bureau of the Budget and together they scrutinized plans for the SOM-designed staff apartments in Bremen. Using often convoluted reasoning that compared the unit cost of apartments in an eight-unit building in Germany to the unit cost of much larger projects in the United States, including a 581-unit building in New York City, subcommittee members declared that the unit costs in Germany were too high. They did not question the need for the housing, but they did question the size of the units, the number of bedrooms and bathrooms, and the need for certain features, such as spaces identified by the architects as "dining room terraces." Beyond all else, they were outraged by the provision of a maid's room for each apartment. As part of an overall condemnation of waste and elitism, they asked why diplomats needed to entertain as they did, and why they needed maids to assist them. Members of Congress knew that it was customary for Foreign Service families to have a service staff drawn from the local population and knew also that it was not unusual to provide housing for the household staff, particularly where there was a desperate housing shortage, as in Germany. That notwithstanding, men in Congress purported to be appalled by the notion that American Foreign Service wives needed household help.

FBO agreed to cut accommodations for maids by fifty percent in future projects. Moreover, FBO also cut the number of two-bedroom family apartments by 50 percent, substituting one-bedroom units on all future projects, and cut the number of bathrooms in the family apartments. Glenn G. Wolfe, executive director of HICOG, testified that he reluctantly agreed to make the cuts knowing that it meant "that the time is going to come when we are going to put families of two or three children in one-bedroom apartments."[29] Also, the architects were advised to stop using the phrase "dining room terraces."

Congressional critics also wondered why the architects chose to use so much glass in a cold and gloomy place such as Bremen. They were not persuaded by architects' arguments that the glass was used to let in the sunlight and lighten the heat load in the dark season. It seemed obvious to everyone that the glass walls were going to require more heat than ordinary masonry walls in the winter, not less. At the same hearing, James Riddleberger, director of the State Department's Bureau of German Affairs, offered his opinion that Germans liked glass and preferred the new architecture to the "baroque or old German type." But subcommittee members wanted to know how it could already be the preferred type if no precedent existed in Germany, as King had suggested when he tried to explain why the architects were unable to estimate the costs with accuracy. The project in Bremen was the only SOM-designed apartment project that was built.

Between 1946 and 1950, HICOG opened and operated 153 America Houses in Germany. All operated out of requisitioned space. From the outset, HICOG planned to turn them over to be run by German civic organizations and gradually it was doing so. There were forty-two centers in 1953, when the State Department announced plans to build six new centers in Cologne, Frankfurt, Hamburg, Stuttgart, Munich, and Berlin. Each America House was to include a library stocked with books and periodicals about the United States, its history, and its democratic government. Each also included an auditorium and an exhibition hall where Germans could meet with Americans, study English, read American newspapers, and see American films. In 1952 alone, German America Houses counted fourteen million visitors.

As part of their investigation into the management of the U.S. building program in Germany, in 1953 members of the House Special Subcommittee also interrogated State Department officials on the American House program. In testimony, department officials declared that the purpose of the centers was to explain the United States and its democratic institutions to the Germans and to counteract increased Soviet influence in Germany. The Soviet government had already begun to establish its own information centers, known as Houses of Culture. U.S. officials were worried about the high-profile Soviet propaganda effort and how it might undermine the mission to build a democratic government in West Germany.

Bunshaft literally took the theme of the glass house and expanded upon it to accommodate the USIS program. His prototype design for all of the new America Houses consisted of two rectangular units connected by a glazed entrance hall. One unit, containing the library and reading rooms, was to be made of glass and steel, and the other unit, containing the auditorium and exhibition space, was to be made of brick. Like exhibition structures, such as Mies's Barcelona Pavilion, the America Houses were designed for display purposes. Both the buildings and their contents were open to view—even the visitors, whose privacy was not recognized as a priority (fig. 46).

Critical testimony did not focus on the appropriateness of the architecture, but rather on the semantic distinction between "information" and "propaganda." The State Department made every effort to describe its program as an information program, even though Germany was recognized as "a propaganda battlefield" at the time.[30] At the opening of a requisitioned America House in Stuttgart in 1950, for example, High Commissioner John

McCloy made a point of dissociating the America House program from propaganda. In remarks included in the 1953 testimony, he declared:

> The Amerika Haus is not a house of propaganda. It is a house for free men and free women to exchange views, to learn and to reach understanding. Above all, it is a house for the young...I do hope that you will be able to discern from your visits to the Amerika Haus some of the vast energy and thought which the United States represents today. It is here that you may gain a conception of what a youthful nation can accomplish in the way of living peaceably with it neighbors under a constitutional system, a system which permits the fullest expansion of the economy, the science, and the religion of the country, all without suppression of personal liberty.[31]

Intent distinguishes information from propaganda. When it is designed to be provocative or subversive, information is described as propaganda. Questions by members of Congress reflected an uneasiness with the idea that the rightness of American democracy was anything but self-evident. They did not see the need for the America Houses as information centers, but they did want to make sure that the United States was not out-maneuvered by the Soviets.

The State Department used anxiety about Soviet intentions to bolster its building program. German affairs expert Riddleberger told the subcommittee that he had visited a Soviet House of Culture in Berlin, and he described it as a "showplace." He noted that it was "extravagantly done" to make "a certain impression on the Germans." By way of emphasizing the more modest character of the American equivalent, FBO director King added the fact that the Soviet center was 350 percent of the size of the proposed American center. Testifying before the House Government Operations Subcommittee, State Department and HICOG officials were not asking for new funds; they were defending their program against charges of waste and mismanagement. Naturally, they claimed that Soviet propaganda threatened U.S. interests. They may have exaggerated the perceived propaganda threat to augment their case, but the threat was nonetheless real.

More than the other new buildings designed by SOM in Germany, the America Houses were conspicuous as political statements because they were so simple and straightforward, specifically designed to "sell" America to the postwar Germans. Though there was no official State Department policy to use modern architecture as a way of amplifying or underscoring the American message, the selection of SOM by King certainly addressed that goal.

At a time when the USSR was housing itself abroad in classically detailed masonry buildings that looked to the distant past for inspiration, the United States offered a striking contrast—radically modern buildings of steel and glass. Raised on stilts above glazed open spaces, the consulates seemed to float in space. The overall American presence in Germany was regarded as temporary. Either consciously or unconsciously, American architects created impermanent-looking structures. More importantly, they gave the American presence in Germany an architectural identity that was notably forward-looking.

Partly as a result of disagreements among the architects, FBO, local officials, and others; partly as a result of inflation, rapidly rising costs, and changing priorities; and largely as a result of congressional oversight, FBO built only a handful of the forty buildings originally projected for Germany. Still, the program was historically significant for what it tried to accomplish—using modern architecture to tell the German people about the United States. In an article published in the *Journal of the American Institute of Architects* in 1950, Hugo Leipziger-Pearce even suggested that architecture had a use as a political weapon and that Germany was the "testing ground" where "East-West ideological controversies" faced each other politically and culturally.[32] State Department critics were uncertain about the need for so many new facilities and did not recognize modern architecture as a diplomatic asset. SOM had barely prepared its preliminary plans when King was ousted as head of FBO and the program was reorganized. At the department, there was no conscious effort to derail the SOM commission, but neither was there any shared enthusiasm for it.

To the few Germans who might have been able to recall the efforts of the prewar avant-garde, the modern architecture exported from America to Germany in the early postwar years was not the same as that which had been launched in Germany in the 1920s and exported to America before the war, though it might have looked similar. The early modern masters, notably Gropius and others associated with the German Bauhaus between the wars, fervently believed that modern architecture was part of an upheaval that would lead to economic, social, and political betterment. Their interest in mass production and functional expression was inextricably linked to the socialist-oriented political agenda associated with the Bauhaus.

When America became the locus of architectural innovation, and the transplanted Germans, joined by men like Harrison and Bunshaft, led the vanguard of what became the postwar modern movement, the socialist agenda was noticeably absent. A specific commitment to an egalitarian society was replaced by a more general commitment to democracy, and the political agenda was replaced by one that was almost exclusively artistic.[33] Outwardly, the architecture looked the same, but to those who claimed to

understand it, its meaning had changed. Modernism now represented capitalism—corporate capitalism—not socialism. Moreover, it was architecture
that both the Nazis and the Soviets under Stalin had condemned and rejected. For that reason alone, it conveyed exactly the right sort of American
message. And for that reason, too, American architects were eager, maybe
even too eager, to redefine modernism in Germany.

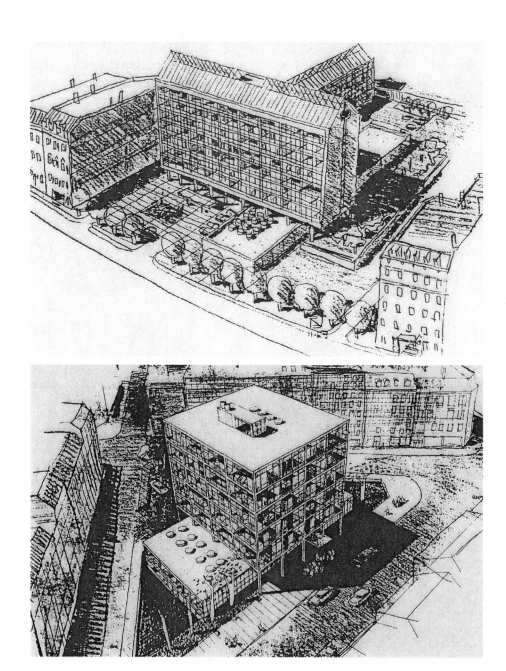

FIG. 34 (TOP): Proposal for U.S. Embassy, Paris, France. Rapson & van der Meulen (1952). Unbuilt.

FIG. 35 (BOTTOM): Proposal for U.S. Embassy, Oslo, Norway. Rapson & van der Meulen (1951). Unbuilt.

FIGS. 36 & 37: U.S. Embassy staff apartments
(Perry House), Tokyo, Japan. Raymond & Rado
(1949–52). Demolished and replaced by Mitsui
apartments designed by Harry Weese. (ABOVE)
Façade. (RIGHT) Interior with custom
furnishings.

FIG. 38 (BELOW): U.S. Consulate, Düsseldorf,
Germany. Gordon Bunshaft for Skidmore,
Owings & Merrill (1952–53).

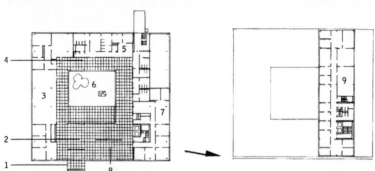

FIGS. 39 & 40 : U.S. Consulate General, Frankfurt, Germany. Skidmore, Owings & Merrill with Apel (1952–54). (TOP) Night view. (BOTTOM) Plans after drawings in *Bauen + Wohnen* (1956).

1. ENTRANCE	4. IMMIGRATION WAITING	7. PASSPORT OFFICES
2. VISA WAITING AREA	AREA	8. RECEPTION
3. VISAS	5. PUBLIC HEALTH SERVICE	9. OFFICES
	6. COURT	

FIG. 41 (TOP LEFT): Former U.S. Consulate, Stuttgart, Germany. Skidmore, Owings & Merrill with Apel (1952–55).

FIGS. 42 & 43 : U.S. Consulate General, Munich, Germany. Skidmore, Owings & Merrill with Sep Ruf (1952–55). (TOP RIGHT) Façade. (BOTTOM) Gold-trimmed ground-floor windows in 1992.

FIGS. 44 & 45 : U.S. Consulate General, Munich, Germany. (ABOVE) Sculpture by Harry Bertoia. (LEFT) Visa office waiting room in 1992.

FIG. 46 (BELOW): Proposal for America House, Frankfurt, Germany. Gordon Bunshaft for Skidmore, Owings & Merrill (1952). Unbuilt. Expanding on the theme of the glass house, the information center was designed to "sell America."

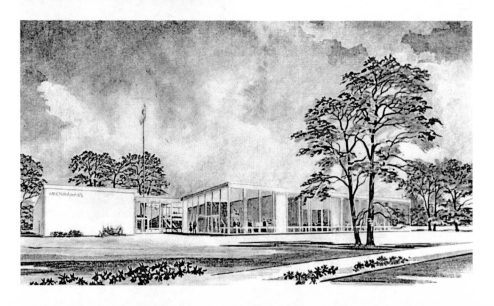

FIG. 47 (TOP): Apostolic Nunciature, Washington, D.C. Frederick V. Murphy (1938–39). A "Renaissance Palace" on Embassy Row.

FIG. 48 (BOTTOM): U.S. Embassy, Jakarta, Indonesia. Raymond & Rado (1953–58). Indonesian president Sukarno wanted a tower.

FIG. 49: U.S. Consulate General, Hong Kong. Wurster, Bernardi & Emmons (1954–57).

FIG. 50 (PREVIOUS PAGE, TOP): Proposal for U.S. Embassy, Amman, Jordan. Paul Rudolph (1954). Unbuilt. Revised five times, this scheme failed to impress AAC members.

FIG. 51 (PREVIOUS PAGE, MIDDLE): U.S. Ambassador's Residence, Tegucigalpa, Honduras. Michael Hare (1954–58). FBO asked the architect to add a "picture window" to capture the breathtaking view, but he refused.

FIG. 52 (PREVIOUS PAGE, BOTTOM): Proposal for U.S. Consulate, São Paulo, Brazil. Mies van der Rohe (1958). Unbuilt.

FIG. 53 (ABOVE): U.S. Embassy, New Delhi, India. Edward Durell Stone (1954–59). The deceptively grand glass box wrapped in a white sunscreen is only two stories tall.

FIG. 54 (TOP): Eastern Airlines Terminal, Logan Airport, Boston. Minoru Yamasaki (1967–69). Model.

FIG. 55 (BOTTOM): Proposal for U.S. Embassy, Bangkok, Thailand. John Carl Warnecke (1957). Model, unbuilt. Widely praised for its resemblance to a Thai pagoda.

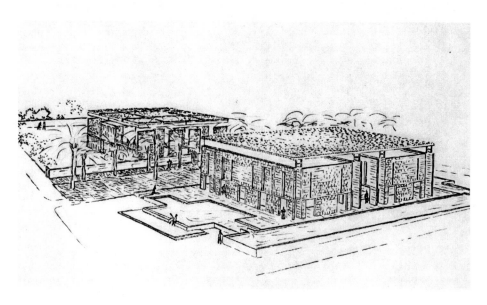

FIG. 56 (TOP): Proposal for U.S. Consulate General, Luanda, Angola. Louis Kahn (1960). Unbuilt.

FIG. 57 (BOTTOM): Proposal for U.S. Embassy, Beirut, Lebanon. Ralph Rapson (1953). Unbuilt.

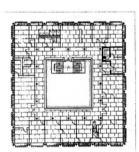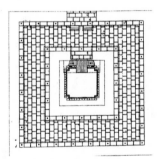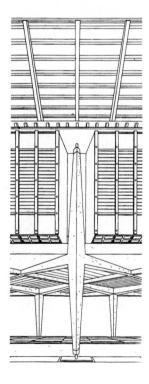

FIGS. 58–60: Former U.S. Embassy, Accra, Ghana.
Harry Weese (1956–59). (TOP) Façade. (ABOVE)
Ground floor and first floor plans. (RIGHT) Detail of
tapered concrete pier. Weese claimed the inspiration for
the piers to be African spears.

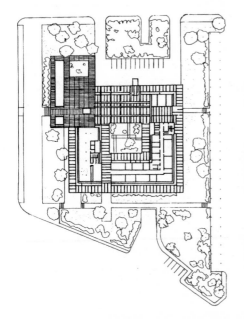

FIGS. 61 & 62: U.S. Embassy, Athens, Greece. Walter Gropius, The Architects Collaborative (1956–59). (TOP LEFT) Ground floor/site plan after drawing in *Architectural Forum* (1961). (TOP RIGHT) Aerial photograph from 1980 with main entrance at front left.

FIG. 63 (BOTTOM): Former U.S. Embassy, Lima, Peru. Keyes & Lethbridge (1956–59). Built on a busy downtown street, this embassy had to be replaced by a less accessible building in the 1990s.

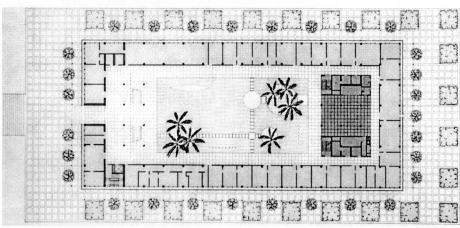

FIGS. 64 & 65: U.S. Embassy, New Delhi, India. (TOP) Courtyard with tropical water garden. (BOTTOM) Courtyard plan.

FIG. 66 (LEFT): U.S. Embassy, Athens, Greece. Courtyard.

FIG. 67 (BELOW RIGHT): U.S. Embassy, Mexico City, Mexico. Southwestern Architects (1957–61). Courtyard.

FIG. 68 (BELOW LEFT): U.S. Embassy, Oslo, Norway. Eero Saarinen (1955–59). Courtyard with teak panels.

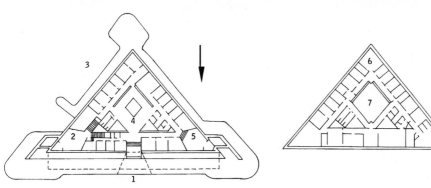

FIGS. 69 & 70: U.S. Embassy, Oslo, Norway. (TOP) Façade with (former) USIS entrance in center and main entrance under canopy at right. Saarinen selected a granite aggregate that has weathered to black. The trim is white. (BOTTOM LEFT AND BOTTOM RIGHT) Ground floor plan and typical floor plan, after drawings in *Architectural Forum* (1959).

1. ENTRANCE	6. ADMINISTRATIVE
2. USIS LOBBY	OFFICES
3. PARKING	7. COVERED COURT
4. LOBBY & RECEPTION COURT	
5. CONSULATE LOBBY	

CHAPTER FIVE

Modern Architecture
under Fire

THE YEAR 1952 marked a watershed in the history of the foreign building program. Things were going well at FBO. In January of that year, the peripatetic and powerful Fritz Larkin retired at the age of seventy and was succeeded as chief by his assistant, Leland King. After fifteen years as head of FBO, Larkin was described as a "legend in the Foreign Service," and was hailed by his colleagues for leaving behind "a heritage at every post around the world." Speaking on behalf of the State Department, Deputy Under Secretary Humelsine praised Larkin and also King for all that they had done to make "our Missions and our offices overseas infinitely more representative of this nation's greatness and position in the world."[1]

Alert to political events that could affect his program, King had little reason to sense that it was at a turning point in 1952. Solidly backed by the Truman administration as well as by the Democratic leadership in Congress, FBO and its worldwide building program enjoyed strong support at the beginning of that year. Some heated opposition to the program and its use of foreign credits did emerge when the House debated amendments to the Foreign Service Buildings Act in March, but King won a major legislative victory when Congress approved his request for $90 million in credits to finance an ambitious program that included construction of eighty-five office buildings, fourteen embassy and legation residences, 245 officers' residences, 568 units of staff housing, and fifty-four attachés' residences.[2] By summer, he had hired Skidmore, Owings & Merrill for the German program, he had increased the size and scope of his Paris regional office, and he had again retained Raymond & Rado, this time to design a new embassy in Jakarta. Personally, he continued to negotiate with the Duke of Westminster, directing the difficult and meticulous process of acquiring 999-year leases to parcels on the west side of London's Grosvenor Square for the eventual construction of an embassy there. The U.S. government, like other foreign governments, could not own land in London, where land was commonly leased for varying periods of time. Thus it was necessary to acquire long-term leases for the land on which construction was planned. Also in 1952, FBO completed new construction at Rio de Janeiro, Havana, and Addis Ababa, and renovations to properties at Zagreb, Belgrade, Dublin, and Aden. Other projects proceeded in Ankara, Naples, Madrid, Managua, Jeddah, Dhahran, and Bangkok. King retained Eero Saarinen to design a new embassy for Helsinki, and Rapson & van der Meulen continued work on embassy designs for Stockholm, Copenhagen, Oslo, The Hague, and projects in Le Havre, Neuilly, and Boulogne.

When Stalin repossessed the Red Square building used as an embassy by the United States, King arranged to lease and rehabilitate a recently completed apartment block known as the Tschaikovsky Building for offices and staff housing. As in London, the United States could not own property in Moscow; it had to rent the space from the Soviet government, which supplied construction and maintenance services through the state-operated agency known as Burobin. King had the structure stripped to its bare walls and rebuilt by the Russians to American specifications. This arrangement gave the United States needed space, but allowed the Soviet government to control or monitor that space—a situation that the United States would later regret. At the time, however, the knowledge that offices were bugged did not concern Ambassador George Kennan. When King offered to shield Kennan's office with lead, the ambassador protested. He argued, according to King, that the bug permitted him a direct line into the Kremlin.

Amendments to the Foreign Service Building Act in 1952 brought FBO the added authorization of credits expected to cover the costs of the program for at least five years. The new amendments expanded FBO's mandate and prompted procedural changes. For the first time, FBO could spend its appropriated funds for alterations, repairs, and furnishings following the initial provision of such items, for example, and it could rent and insure objects of art. In order to further the use of credits, the amendments exempted FBO from a new requirement that purchases be manufactured in the United States, and it permitted a more flexible arrangement in the determination of professional fees for architects and engineers working abroad.[3] However, none of these changes figured prominently in debate on the bill. They were insignificant compared to two issues that really did shape that debate: the further use of credits and a new concern with security.

While the success of the 1952 legislation was evidence of support for the mission to provide suitable office space and living quarters for Americans abroad, that support was based principally on a bipartisan enthusiasm for the notion of recovering foreign credits by any means possible. Above all, it was the assertion that "the building program can be financed by a further authorization of foreign credits without cost to the American taxpayer" that propelled the legislation through Congress and secured its passage.[4]

Deputy Under Secretary of State Carlisle Humelsine told the Senate Foreign Relations Committee that there was roughly $750 million worth of credits available in 1952.[5] Others set the amount at $900 million. No one in Congress wanted to let that sum slip away—even if that meant spending it on State Department construction. In the House report on the proposed 1952 amendments, the Committee on Foreign Affairs presented the situation as an urgent one, citing as a principal legislative objective not only the provision of diplomatic housing and office space, but also the maximum recovery of foreign credits. "These sums, it must be stressed, can never be converted into dollars," the report stated. "If they are not used in the country of origin, they are lost to the United States."[6] The report reviewed the facts concerning new construction in Rio and Havana and emphasized that even in countries where no credits existed such funds were available for use by transfer.

Congressmen who opposed the administration's conduct of foreign policy and those who mistrusted the State Department, thinking that it had grown too fast since the war, nevertheless agreed that the foreign building program deserved support if it helped the United States recover credits owed to it by foreign governments. Politicians were drawn to the idea of using credits by the notion that such funds did not represent tax dollars. Supporters of the bill also argued persuasively that inflation was eating up the value of the credits. Amendments attached to the authorization bill were designed to make it easier for FBO to buy materials and services abroad. Credit availability varied by country and agreements had to be negotiated with each country concerning the use of such funds. In Germany, for instance, credits totaled $69,606,217 from the sale of surplus property.[7] Furthermore, in addition to the $90 million in credits authorized in the legislation, FBO was also able to draw on the sum of $14 million in dollars that remained from the $15 million 1946 authorization. To the maximum extent possible, FBO wanted to be able to pay all of its contractors in foreign currency and to purchase or fabricate construction materials locally. Some furnishings, like those in Tokyo, were custom-made nearby. While this permitted FBO to operate using credits, it meant that the range of choice was more limited than it would have been if all materials had been purchased and shipped from the United States. It also meant that congressmen were bound to find fault with the program when they realized that FBO was purchasing building materials, china, crystal, and furniture from foreign vendors when these large contracts could have been going to their own constituents.

Actually, opposition to the program's use of credits emerged before the 1952 amendments were even passed. Declaring that Congress had been "completely hoodwinked" by language in the authorization bill, Rep. Thomas B. Curtis (R-Mo.) told his House colleagues in April that the proposed building program would not only cost the American taxpayers current dollars, but it would also cost much more over time than any of its supporters admitted or knew. Like others who opposed the bill, he rebutted claims that all of the credits would be forever lost if not used for foreign buildings.[8] California Republican John Phillips, for one, had already argued that Congress never intended for foreign credits to be spent on anything other than building up the industries of foreign nations and strengthening their economies, and Democrat William C. Lantaff (Fla.) had denounced the "elaborate building program" and asked why Congress couldn't use such credits to purchase strategic materials or to pay American troops stationed overseas instead.[9] Speaking before the House the day after it voted to approve the bill by a two-to-one margin, an outraged Curtis objected that no one had studied key questions pertaining to the bill, and he condemned it as evidence of waste and inefficiency. "Are we spreading American democracy by building palaces for the representatives of this democracy in these countries?" he asked in a fifteen-minute speech that referred four times to "palaces," and concluded, "I hope the Senate will go into this matter thoroughly, so we will not have to go back into our districts to explain why there is no money for flood control, for example, but plenty for building castles in Spain."[10] While such doubts persisted, they did not grow into widespread opposition to the building program in early 1952. The Senate added its approval in May, and the new authorization bill was enacted into law.

New findings on the need for increased embassy security also bolstered the building program in 1952. Until World War II, nearly all references to security with regard to diplomatic facilities had to do with concerns about theft, burglary, unauthorized entry, and, above all, fire. But with the Cold War came new threats. Prompted by increased concerns about foreign governments spying on Americans, the rapidly rising use of electronic equipment, and the increased quantity of sensitive information to be processed and stored at embassies, the Senate authorized an investigation headed by Senators Theodore Francis Green (D-R.I.) and Henry Cabot Lodge (R-Mass.). They submitted a report in 1950 and their findings were incorporated into the 1952 foreign buildings legislation. The investigators concluded, for example, that government ownership of foreign property greatly reduced the overall security risk. "For security reasons," their report notes, "it is desirable that the United States should own rather than lease its buildings abroad."[11] In a hearing on the FBO program Green stated, "Senator Lodge and I went into it quite fully and we find it is very dangerous, this hiring [renting] of buildings. We find that all the walls are wired for listening purposes...and the only way we can be sure they are not is by owning them. I don't know then if we can be sure, unless we supervise the construction."[12]

Supporting their conclusion, the senators cited unsatisfactory arrangements that existed at numerous posts. They called for ownership to permit the special construction required for the security of sensitive areas such as code and cryptographic rooms and to permit the installation of air-conditioning where windows needed to be kept closed to protect specialized equipment. Citing the situation in Bern, for example, where the United States had six separate buildings, Tehran, where it had three, and Stockholm, where it had four, their report also urged the State Department to unite its various offices in each city, often scattered in different locations, into a single "consolidated" office building.

Endorsed by the Senate and the House, the policy promoting property ownership presented a major policy mandate to the State Department. It justified the expenditure of funds on new construction, even where U.S. facilities already existed, and gave FBO a powerful argument to support its $90 million budget request. In defense of the 1952 foreign buildings bill, FBO and its congressional supporters argued disingenuously that consolidation would lead to overall savings resulting from a reduced staff size and the elimination of rental costs.[13] They also argued that consolidation would result in an overall reduction in maintenance and administrative costs, though anyone who examined the projected building program could see that the new buildings were being designed in response to expanding rather than shrinking staffs, and that the cost of maintenance could only be expected to climb.

FBO embarked on its program in 1952 backed by what appeared to be strong congressional endorsement—even if Congress reduced its annual appropriation for fiscal 1953 from an expected $20 million to $6.5 million. (The State Department had to request annual appropriations from previously authorized funds. Congress often provided less than the department wanted or expected.) Most of those who supported the legislation did so to recoup credits and to increase security, not out of a commitment to the building program, its administration, or its architecture.

But following the November election that put Eisenhower in the White House and brought John Foster Dulles to Foggy Bottom as secretary of state, FBO found itself in a particularly vulnerable position. Austerity was suddenly the watchword of the day. Dulles began his tenure in 1953 with a major reduction in force and a rearrangement of the offices in his department. The Republicans had not only won the presidency for the first time in twenty-three years, but had also narrowly won control of both houses of Congress. Cruel claims by Senator McCarthy became issues in the election, as Eisenhower focused on the communist threat and the need for the United States to respond to it. McCarthy's anticommunist witch-hunt and his tactic of making unsubstantiated but ruinous accusations reached deep into the State Department, with devastating impact on the Foreign Service in particular. George F. Kennan, removed from his post as U.S. ambassador in Moscow by Dulles, left the State Department after twenty-seven years of service. Kennan later noted that "the housecleaning conducted by Mr. Dulles's minions as a means of placating congressional vindictiveness had been thorough and sweeping."[14]

Even before the election, King felt the pressure of congressional scrutiny. At the first sign of trouble, when he learned that questions were being asked about the high cost of the new German housing, for example, he began to make cuts in his program to forestall accusations of waste. Then, in hearings before the Senate Foreign Relations Committee, Senator Green asked Deputy Under Secretary Humelsine whether or not FBO had any written policy concerning the planning and design of its embassies, and Humelsine admitted that nothing of the sort existed. Green criticized the location of the ambassador's residence far outside New Zealand's capital, Wellington, for example, and urged both King and Humelsine to come up with a more explicit policy regarding the location and accessibility of U.S. embassies in foreign capitals.[15] The specifics of Green's concern are less important than their overall thrust, aimed at trying to pin down FBO on matters of policy. Never had issues such as location, architect selection, or architecture been codified. Although an office within the government bureaucracy, FBO was not confined by rules and regulations at every turn. It was more like a small fiefdom under the semi-autocratic control of one man (originally, Larkin) who was in a position to make his own decisions. The request for a written policy on embassy location was a small step in the direction of trying to impose limits on FBO's autonomy, limits more explicitly demanded after the November election.

After that election King sensed the new political atmosphere, but he still had little reason to doubt the viability of his program or his continued ability to direct it. Drawing upon seemingly unlimited supplies of foreign credits and fettered by little oversight review, FBO continued to move ahead, buying land, leasing space, and planning bold new buildings. Undoubtedly there had been waste in the past. The ready availability of credits had contributed to a lax attitude toward economy. Newly elected or re-elected congressmen were always eager to target waste and inefficiency and to condemn it. In addition, Larkin had made many enemies over the years, and they, too, were eager to retaliate against FBO for unrenovated offices, broken air-conditioners, unfilled swimming pools, uncomfortable modern chairs, and the like. The fact that King lacked the network of political connections that had always shielded Larkin from his enemies did not worry him, sincerely convinced as he was that his program and its architecture were essentially "apolitical."

Within a matter of months, FBO found itself mired in a series of investigations—investigations that scrutinized its management, its personnel, its budget, and even the look of its architecture. Abetted by widespread fears about security and aided by disgruntled employees, congressional and budget investigators also questioned King's integrity and sought to expose mismanagement and malfeasance in his performance. Newly appointed State Department officials called in outside consultants to examine FBO and faulted recent projects in Rio, Havana, and Madrid for being architecturally inappropriate. The officials objected to the modern architecture for its perceived luxury, cost, and what they considered to be its negative associations.

One of the associations that was most damaging was the frequent comparison between the new embassy buildings and the recently completed United Nations headquarters. Both the Secretariat and the General Assembly shocked the public and members of the design community, including noted architects such as Rudolf M. Schindler, Bruce Goff, and Pietro Belluschi, who expressed dismay at the skyscraper Secretariat. They wondered whether or not its design signaled an architectural endpoint rather than a new beginning. Paul Rudolph minced no words when he condemned the new General Assembly building for bringing "the so-called International Style close to bankruptcy."[16] Though much smaller in size, the embassy towers in Rio, Havana, and Madrid were often compared to the slab-like Secretariat and described also as examples of the "international style." Many who objected to the UN as an international organization had similar misgivings about architecture labeled "international style." They somehow associated the architecture with a political perspective known as "internationalism" and feared foreign involvement that might compromise U.S. interests.

Criticism of the "so-called International Style" came just when SOM was completing working drawings for all of the new consulates and America Houses in Germany, just when Saarinen had completed a preliminary design for the embassy in Helsinki, and just after King had entered into discussions with Edward Durell Stone for the design of an embassy in New Delhi. The architectural profession voiced subtle opposition to the building program as well, not so much because of its architecture, but out of professional envy. Harrison & Abramovitz had completed two FBO commissions, and SOM had an apparent monopoly on all of the work in Germany. As Belluschi later noted, other architects wanted a piece of the action.[17]

These assaults severely disrupted the building program, hampered its daily operations, and eventually led to a suspension of new construction. Despite support from his architects and well-known design critics, King would fall victim to Dulles's purge. Modern architecture, however, survived King at FBO. Identified by that time with democracy, modernism thrived in the Dulles years as the official architecture of the foreign building program.

Soon after arriving at the State Department in January 1953, Dulles appointed Donold B. Lourie as under secretary for administration and directed Lourie to impose economy on the department. Described by Dulles as "one of the most competent executives in the country," Lourie was president of the board of the Quaker Oats Company when Dulles tapped him for the new job. Lourie was assisted by Edward T. "Tom" Wailes, who replaced Humelsine as assistant secretary for administration in March. Wailes was a career Foreign Service officer who had served in Western Europe, North Africa, and Canada. He was assigned to the Inspection Corps in 1948 and named chief inspector in June 1952. Lourie reported to Dulles, Wailes reported to Lourie, and King reported to Wailes. Summing up the position of his department and the administration, Dulles said, "The desire of this administration is to be frugal, to balance the budget, and to trim our expenditures accordingly." He boasted to Congress that after only one month on the job, Lourie had already cut 1,066 jobs, "a very substantial saving in terms of dollars."[18] He directed Lourie to make further cuts, and those cuts followed.

After critics condemned the lavishness of the first HICOG buildings, for which FBO had no direct responsibility, King had cautioned SOM to avoid evidence of extravagance in their designs for new housing. He stressed the need for economy and announced that "Variety for variety's sake is out," a statement that suggests design innovation as a goal once might have been "in."[19] The newly appointed Lourie was interested in more than the appearance of economy. He ordered cuts that specifically reduced the German program budget by $2,475,580, and then, after further review, by $3,192,962 more. The Bureau of the Budget followed with another cut of $5,676,458, and the overall budget for the German building program, originally set at $19 million, was reduced by more than half, to $7,655,000. It is no wonder that designs were modified, projects shelved, and architects and diplomats disillusioned as the department cut the program in size and scope.

By the time the projected $15 million Truman budget for FBO went to the House Appropriations Committee on 18 March 1953, it had been reduced to a mere $5 million. Naturally this meant that some projects had to be suspended and others simply dropped. Projects in Lima, Montreal, Marseille, Cairo, and Alexandria, for example, were deleted from the program. Sums remained for a new office building, residence, and staff housing in New Delhi ($1 million); an office building in Tegucigalpa ($300,000); consulates along the U.S. border in Mexico ($650,000); an embassy annex in Helsinki (the Saarinen project, budgeted at $600,000); the consulate in Le Havre ($150,000); and an office building in Port of Spain ($80,000 to complete the project).

To meet staff reduction guidelines, King also had to eliminate the positions of two staff architects. Frank Harrison was first in line to be cut, but when King fired him, or attempted to fire him, his case was quickly taken up by another staffer, Alan C. Donaldson, who precipitated a damaging grievance action against King on behalf of Harrison. Donaldson's "whispered" charges of "maladministration and corruption" followed King everywhere. As King describes it, Donaldson also persuaded a gullible congressman, Rep. R. Walter Riehlman (R-N.Y.), to write to Dulles warning him of possible embarrassment by FBO, pending the outcome of ongoing investigations.[20] Donaldson's vendetta also played into the hands of the malevolent Robert W. S. "Scott" McLeod, who was recognized even then as McCarthy's "stooge" in the State Department. McLeod, already experienced as a communist-hunter, was brought into the State Department to set up a security service, to pry into the personal lives of employees in order to assess "loyalty," and to rid the department of "risks." In addition to rooting out suspected communists, he was especially interested in eliminating suspected homosexuals, nymphomaniacs, and others whom he considered to be dangerous or simply too liberal. He joined the department as administrator of the Bureau of Security and Consular Affairs and set his sights on the Foreign Service. "Within a few weeks of his arrival," as Leonard Mosley has written, "he had shattered what morale was left in the department after Foster Dulles's opening address to the staff. His operatives broke open desks, read private letters, listened in on conversations and telephones, and tailed employees after hours."[21] As this sad episode in State Department history unfolded, by his silence Dulles permitted many prominent careers to be hurt or destroyed. In addition to the celebrated diplomats George Kennan and Charles "Chip" Bohlen, others, like King, also felt deserted by Dulles and, in King's own words, "thrown to the wolves."[22] Donaldson was rewarded for his "cooperation" when McLeod promoted him to chief of the Office of American Interests Abroad. McLeod himself eventually became U.S. ambassador to Ireland.

Throughout the winter and early spring of 1953, King was repeatedly called before Congress to answer various charges, including a dubious accusation that he personally profited from departmental real estate transactions in London. Many of the questions directed at FBO seemed designed not so much to elicit information as to harass and intimidate King and his staff.

Though King may have felt as if he had no allies, he did have supporters. Prominent among them was John Rooney, one of the most powerful congressmen on the Hill. First a member and then chairman of the Subcommittee on the State and Justice Departments, the Judiciary and Related Federal Agencies of the House Appropriations Committee, Democrat Rooney exercised tight control over the State Department's annual budget almost continuously from 1944 through 1975. Even if funds had been previously authorized, Rooney's committee could refuse to appropriate them or reduce the amount of the annual budget request. To Rooney, control of the State Department budget represented a way of increasing his own importance and influencing foreign policy. Though his influence was somewhat diminished while the Republicans controlled Congress (1953–54), Rooney wielded great clout. For years he had been a crony of Larkin's, someone who traveled with him when he visited foreign posts, taking along an entourage that often included his wife and assorted congressional aides. The overseas visits involved some fact-finding, but mostly entertainment—including fine food, fine wines, and occasional visits to pet projects. Every year, for example, to secure votes in his multicultural Brooklyn district, Rooney liked to stop in the "three I's," Israel, Italy, and Ireland. He expected to be welcomed and feted by American officials wherever he went and Larkin did his best to make that happen.[23] Though he was a man known to hate waste and had little use for Foreign Service officers, whom he publicly disdained, Rooney stood up for King and FBO.

As King was grilled by unfriendly questions from Republican committee members, Rooney interjected the following on 25 March 1953:

> I want to make an observation, such as I very seldom do. There have been quite a number of investigations of the Foreign Buildings Office, and quite a bit of attendant publicity with regard to it. I have known Mr. King's predecessor, Fritz Larkin, ever since I have been a member of this committee, and I have known Mr. King all during that time. I have never known two finer public servants than these two gentlemen who have been handling these operations and funds. They are men of the highest integrity and great ability and they have administered this program with practically little or no cost to the American taxpayer, because all these dollars that are appropriated in connection with foreign buildings operation are merely counterpart funds out of the Treasury. Mr. King has my confidence. That is all I have to say, Mr. Chairman.[24]

Prince H. Preston Jr., Rooney's Democratic colleague from Georgia, concurred with his support. The Republicans were enjoying their new-found, but brief, control of Congress, however, and congressional sentiment went the other way.

In June, when hearings on the German construction program resumed,

King showed that he had cut the cost of the consular buildings by 29 percent, eliminated all houses for ranking officers and cut all of the America Houses from the program. He had also reduced the specifications for new apartments based on directives from the Bureau of the Budget and the Housing and Home Finance Agency, both of which had illogically applied standards developed for subsidized, low-cost housing in the United States to staff housing for Foreign Service officers abroad. King told the subcommittee members that the resultant housing would be inadequate for consuls general, public affairs officers, and all high ranking personnel, who would be forced to find appropriate housing for themselves in a tight housing market.[25] He pointed out that the principal aim of the program had been to prevent Americans from taking up available housing and inflating local rents. But waste-hunters, focusing only on the bottom line, had no interest in that argument.

It was not long before journalists and other critics began to grasp the implications of overall cost-cutting at the State Department. In a scathing editorial, the *New York Times* warned on 10 June 1953 that recent appropriations cuts threatened to reduce the Foreign Service below the danger point and cripple American diplomacy. Referring to news from Mexico City that the U.S. embassy staff there had been cut by 25 percent, the editorial noted that plans to implement similar cuts around the world would force United States foreign policy to "operate with one hand tied behind its back." The editors continued:

> The reductions in the State Department budget made in the name of economy surely constitute one of the major pieces of folly of the present Congress. It is hard to avoid the suspicion that this is a punitive move as well as an economic one. There are too many influential members of Congress who have talked of "cookie pushers" and "striped pants" in the past not to make it clear that some of them are taking a shortsighted method of revenge. There is also a strong feeling which Senator McCarthy made vocal that anyone who carried out policies under Secretary Acheson must be suspect if not subversive.[26]

Furthermore, the editorial observed that embassies cannot function without all of the Foreign Service personnel, political officers, labor and commercial attachés, agricultural and financial experts, public relations officers, and others essential to their mission. "One wonders whether the Congressmen who voted the cuts," it asked, "stopped to think that the United States is the most powerful nation in the world and that we are facing a crucial struggle with the Communists. Many consulates will have to be closed as we reach the peak of responsibility as a World Power." Whether or not critics accepted the need for large and diversified embassy staffs, they could plainly see that the cuts would hamper diplomacy. It was a classic "baby and bath water" situation in which economy was the top priority and cost-cutters sacrificed programs, regardless of the future costs—economic, political, or military— of such moves. No one seemed to be considering whether or not established goals should be maintained, how to assess the merits of programs being slashed, or how to determine diplomatic priorities. This is not to say that all established programs were sacrosanct, but rather to suggest that, at the very least, critics wanted Dulles and his group to evaluate the policy implications of their cuts, along with the dollar savings.

Troubled by charges that his cuts were arbitrary and anxious to improve FBO rather than destroy it, Under Secretary Lourie called in outside consultants in June 1953. He turned to Webster B. Todd and Nelson A. Kenworthy to examine foreign building operations and advise him on a course of action. Todd was president of Todd & Brown, Inc. and Todd Associates of New York, firms that specialized in engineering, design, and construction management, and Kenworthy was his executive vice president. Todd & Brown was best known for supervising the restoration of Williamsburg (1928–32) and for supervising the construction, operation, maintenance, and management of Rockefeller Center, Inc. (1932–42). Kenworthy, a licensed engineer, was involved in the construction of Williamsburg and Rockefeller Center, and managed the operating department of Rockefeller Center from 1933 to 1942, when he joined the Marines. His military duties included planning air station and air base facilities for the Navy. After the war, he rejoined Todd in New York. Lourie, Todd, and Kenworthy were also former classmates at Princeton.

Todd and Kenworthy made two short visits to Washington to acquaint themselves with the operations of FBO and reported back to Lourie, but not before a crisis enveloped King and his program just prior to the Fourth of July weekend. As King recalls it, on Thursday, 2 July, Assistant Secretary Wailes called a meeting "and gave me a verbal fiat to discontinue 'modern' architecture in favor of Georgian."[27] King was stunned when Wailes told him to use an Italianate palazzo housing the Vatican's diplomatic delegation in Washington as the ideal embassy type. Officially known at the time as the Apostolic Delegation, but popularly called the "Vatican Embassy," the building still stands directly across from the Naval Observatory compound, now also home to the vice president, on Washington's Embassy Row. (Since 1984, when diplomatic relations were established, the building has been officially called the Apostolic Nunciature.) King was especially confused, since nothing about the suggested model could be described as "Georgian." Washington architect Frederick V. Murphy designed the building for the Vatican in 1938 and clearly modeled it after a Renaissance palace (fig. 47).

Despite the risks, King bravely defended his program and its use of modern architecture. Privately, he branded Wailes's suggestion "stupidity." Publicly, in notes directed to Wailes, he made the following nine points: twenty-two projects valued at about $9 million would be affected by the order to change from "conservatively modern" to "one of the traditional styles," and nearly all of the architects engaged on those projects would resign rather than change; little of consequence in the United States or abroad had been built in the previous decade except in the contemporary style, mainly for reasons of economy and technological necessity; "Even among the more conservative art circles," he said, "the modern 'style' is considered as well established as any style of the past"; no school or society had given an architectural award to a building in the traditional style during the past twenty years; there was no reason to confuse quality contemporary architecture with that which was merely experimental or esoteric; recognized leaders in the architectural profession would never work for a client who dictated design; FBO's policy of retaining private architectural and engineering firms had been widely lauded among professionals and had saved the government money; Congress showed its support for such a policy in its recent recommendation directing the Public Buildings Administration to retain "competitively independent architects" for all of its buildings; and articles about FBO in *Life* and *Architectural Forum* produced no criticism of the "modern" architecture. "Considering the widespread, and even proprietary interest on the part of the public in Federal buildings," King wrote, "I submit that this is a truly remarkable endorsement."[28]

Summing up his position for Wailes, King stated that "the Department should conform to this world-wide contemporary trend, in which the United States is the undisputed leader, if its buildings are to be truly representative of the progressive and characteristic way of American life."[29] For those who were still apprehensive about the architecture, he added his recommendation for a design review board made up of prominent architects as well as representatives of the department and the public.

King met with Wailes and his budget officer, Edward B. Wilber, on 9 July and wrote again to them the next day with further recommendations for a review panel, which he desperately hoped would validate his design policy and protect him from design interference. He thought that if all major projects were submitted to a "carefully selected cross-section of professional and lay opinion," problems related to design would be solved. For the panel he recommended membership consisting of a representative from the AIA, to be selected by the AIA president; a representative from the State Department, to be selected by Lourie and Wailes; the FBO director; and a representative from the National Commission of Fine Arts (NCFA)—possibly David Finley, Joseph Hudnut, or Pietro Belluschi. At the time, Finley was NCFA chairman and director of the National Gallery of Art, Hudnut was an NCFA commissioner and dean of Harvard's Graduate School of Design, and Belluschi was an NCFA commissioner and dean of the School of Architecture at MIT.[30]

Days later, Todd submitted a long letter to Lourie outlining his recommendations, which included the same idea of an architectural advisory panel.[31] He praised FBO for saving taxpayers' money by using "frozen" foreign credits, and he praised the earlier buildings for their architecture which appeared "appropriate for the respective locations" with due consideration to the surrounding architecture. But, speaking for himself and Kenworthy, he said that "the more recent buildings have gone somewhat overboard on what is described in the FBO booklet as 'international modern'....The appropriateness of it, in some of the recent instances, is open to strong criticism." FBO lacked adequate direction, he said, and needed clarification of its architectural policy. Was that policy aimed at crusading for "international modern," he asked, or providing requisite and adequate facilities, appropriately designed to fit in their sites and create good will? He also noted that FBO's owner-client relationship with the State Department was a source of confusion and needed clarification.

Kenworthy's recommendations were simple and surprisingly noncritical: make it clear that FBO serves the State Department; revise architectural policy to emphasize good will of other nations and efficiency of layout, not style; create some sort of honorary panel composed of people appointed by foreign governments to advise on architectural fit; create a small, "well-balanced" advisory panel of American architects to advise on policy; create a small, honorary panel of outstanding interior decorators; and prepare and maintain a complete manual of FBO policies and standards. Todd also understood that Lourie would be appointing a new head of FBO. The new man, he said, should agree to support departmental policy, should be an administrator with some construction and/or architectural experience, and ideally should come from within the department, not from outside.

After he received Todd's letter, Lourie asked his two consultants to make additional recommendations for follow-up, but they had little more to offer regarding implementation. According to Kenworthy, he was not sure what they were going to do about implementation, and "by the time I woke up, I was it!"[32] For nine months beginning in September 1953 he found himself in charge of the reorganization as acting director of FBO—drafting a new (actually first) official design policy, deciding what to do about the array of suspended projects, establishing a management system, and moving quickly to select members of a blue-ribbon architectural advisory panel.

Some of King's ideas may have been implemented, but his efforts to protect himself failed. He was devastated when Wailes called him in that summer and, as King put it, "fired" him. The tragedy in this story is that King felt personally victimized by the series of events in 1953 and never recognized that the political situation made his removal not only likely, but probably inevitable. Larkin, by retiring when he did, maintaining his close alliance with Rooney, and continuing to work behind the scenes as a consultant, slipped out of the limelight and avoided King's fate.

King's reputation for toughness won him few friends at FBO and even fewer within the Foreign Service. James Johnstone, who later served as FBO director, discounted the suggestion that King was fired by foes whose grievance was really with the much feared Fritz Larkin. "If an ambassador wanted something, anything, furniture, and if he got along with Fritz Larkin, he got it; if Fritz Larkin didn't like him, he didn't get it," Johnstone recalled. As a result, Larkin had plenty of enemies. But King did too. Johnstone described him as Larkin's "alter ego," a man who "thought he was much more important than he was."[33] To Paul Serey, a former deputy director of FBO, King was someone known to be "brusque."[34] Others, however, were far more favorable in their assessments. Architect Ladislav Rado, for one, described King as "one of my favorite professional associations," and he lauded him for *not* being a bureaucrat. In the end, that probably cost him his job, but it also made it possible for him to accomplish what he did at FBO. Rado praised King for his commitment to modern architecture when it would have been comparatively easy to move in another direction. "Lee King's courageous reversal of a policy of pseudo-colonial buildings to creative demonstrations of U.S. know-how is of historic significance to the advancement of modern architecture," Rado wrote.[35]

Why was King able to build modern buildings when other government programs were bound to tradition? King later answered the question himself:

> The overriding reason lay in the almost total absence of directives or restraints in the operation from the Department of State, the various interested Congressional committees or the media. This freedom to act, backed up by an organizational autonomy and independent appropriations was not enjoyed by many government agencies....This freedom from bureaucracy lasted from 1941 to mid-1953 when Assistant Secretary Wailes sought to bring the program more under the control of the Foreign Service.[36]

He could have added that Congress, too, sought to expand its authority over the program beginning in 1953.

When he left FBO, King was praised by AIA executive director Edmund R. Purves for his contribution to modern architecture and, of course, for his patronage of private firms. *Progressive Architecture* echoed this praise in an article by Frederick Gutheim, who described FBO as "the best architectural program ever put together in a government agency." Gutheim, who was assistant executive director of the AIA at the time, lamented FBO's ruined state in November 1953. He lauded FBO's Paris regional director Jacobs for his "extraordinary job" in Europe, and cited Bunshaft and Rapson for their fine work, "infinitely superior," he said, to work in other public building programs.[37] As spokesman for the AIA, Gutheim asserted that "important public buildings, in this case embassies, should be designed by architects in private practice." He also worried that King would be replaced by a timid, compromise-oriented administrative type. Arguing that great public architecture requires boldness, he regretted that no one "of the caliber of Leland W. King" would likely get the job.[38] It was an endorsement that King appreciated.

Linking his own fate to that of others accused and professionally ruined by Senator McCarthy, King later claimed that "It was architecture not communism that was the victim in my case."[39] It is not odd that King recalls the events of that period as tragic even if subsequent findings cleared him and his office of charges of fraud and wrong-doing. As it turned out, the principal victim was not the architecture, but King himself, and more specifically his freewheeling management of the foreign building program. Neither he nor the architecture was ever accused of communist leanings, but in the housecleaning that followed the Eisenhower election, he was clearly viewed as a carry-over from the Truman days and someone whose time was up. The architecture was accused only of being "inappropriate," not corrupting or subversive. Given strong support from the architectural profession, the open-minded attitude of Nelson Kenworthy, King's temporary successor, and the fact that the building program had assumed something of a life of its own, Wailes's directive to "go Georgian" was ignored, and the architecture remained modern.

DESPITE THE CHARGES of mismanagement and waste, highlighted already in testimony before the Miller subcommittee, Kenworthy's principal task at FBO was to reorganize the office around a new architectural policy. He had to satisfy men like Wailes, whose preference for traditional design was known; but aside from matters of personal preference, he also had to consider the larger issues of architecture in relation to public diplomacy. His October reorganization plan had two key parts: to revise architectural policy; and to establish an honorary panel to advise on architectural design. It is clear from his early notes on the panel that Kenworthy envisioned it as a sort of forum for the exchange of possibly opposing ideas, not as a rubber stamp. Like King, he recommended the inclusion of at least one non-architect, a State Department official on the panel to provide a voice for client interests. A panel consisting of three prominent architects and one Foreign Service officer, however, was not exactly an open forum, nor one designed to elicit a wide range of critical opinion. If the members were prominent enough, though, it would provide the State Department with a barrier of protection against unwanted criticism. After all, if prominent outside "experts" approved of a design, presumably they would also have to bear responsibility for its propriety. If they thought it proper, then who could argue? It was an often-used trick, creating a review panel to distance an agency from its critics; but at the same time it represented an honest effort to try to come to a better understanding of what sort of architecture might create international "goodwill." Precedents for such design review panels already existed in Washington—the Fine Arts Commission and the Joint Committee for the National Capital were two.

A year later, a bipartisan congressional committee traveled to Europe and the Far East and then submitted a report on foreign buildings to a subcommittee of the House Committee on Appropriations. Members of the investigating committee were Republicans Frank T. Bow (Ohio) and Sam Coon (Ore.), and Democrat Preston (Ga.). Although their report was not formally presented until 29 January 1954, they made their trip in September 1953. During the brief period of Republican majority (1953–54, the first session of Eisenhower's term), Cliff Clevenger (R-Ohio) served as chairman of the House Appropriations Subcommittee, temporarily replacing Brooklyn Democrat Rooney. In a move that expressed dissatisfaction with the building program, the subcommittee refused to appropriate any funds for foreign buildings for fiscal year 1954. The investigative report, known as the *Bow Report*, added to concern about the program. Its stinging criticism left its mark on subsequent architectural policy endorsed by FBO.

The *Bow Report* was replete with references to "the so-called international type of architecture" and its numerous failings, including, above all, that such architecture was in and of itself simply "too elaborate" and too conspicuous to be suitable for American foreign buildings.[40] The report reviewed recently completed or almost completed projects in Brussels, Antwerp, Madrid, and Tokyo. (The investigators did not visit Havana or Rio, which they would certainly have added to their list if they had seen them.) The embassy office building in Brussels, the congressmen said, was not in keeping with its surroundings, and the "modernistic furniture" placed in the ambassador's office there "lacked the dignity which might be expected." The

Antwerp consulate, they said, was another example of the "so-called international architecture," one that was similarly "not in keeping with the architecture of the immediate vicinity." Likewise, they faulted the embassy office building and residence in Madrid for architecture that they claimed provoked resentment among the people of Spain, a claim for which they provided no evidence. While praising the staff apartments in Tokyo for *not* being too "luxurious," they still criticized the project. It could have been built at far less cost, they suggested, if "more conventional designs" had been used.

Shortsighted in its view of future representational needs, ignoring the ready availability of precious properties after the war—worth procuring even at the risk of ending up with a surfeit—and adamant in its view that the State Department should not purchase or hold real estate for speculative purposes, the *Bow Report* also condemned FBO for purchasing older properties that appeared to be too elaborate for America's no-nonsense needs. A magnificent Roman villa surrounded by six acres of gardens was purchased by FBO in 1948 for a mere $149,071 in foreign credits. Since the property was being occupied by a low-level Foreign Service officer when investigators visited, the report found it to be "altogether too pretentious" for its use, and urged FBO to dispose of it at once.

The report's assessment of the recently purchased Rothschild residence in Paris was even harsher. After recounting the curious history of its purchase, the report described the noble mansion as "completely worthless for any practical purpose," and again urged FBO to be rid of it as soon as possible. Ignoring its prominent location and repelled by its apparent grandeur, the congressional investigators and those from GAO concluded: "This building must be completely torn down, and another building built, if the property is to be of any useful value to the United States."[41] They saw no reason why American diplomats needed to live in such a "show place," and went so far as to suggest that Americans of all diplomatic ranks should live modestly and, above all, without pretension.

Additionally, the *Bow Report* rightly pointed out that the use of foreign credits in Paris, as elsewhere, had resulted in purchases that would eventually prove costly for American taxpayers to maintain and operate. The credit windfall only facilitated the purchase of such properties, not their maintenance over time, a cost that had to be met by further appropriations.

Kenworthy was aware of the Bow investigation when he drafted FBO's first proposed architectural policy in October 1953. The notions that American buildings should avoid being conspicuous, that they should appear unpretentious, that they should fit in well with their surroundings, that they should be practical, and that they should be admired by their hosts were all woven into his statement and further amplified by his later revisions. The full text of his first draft read:

> The policy shall be to provide requisite and adequate facilities in an architectural style and form which will create goodwill by intelligent appreciation, recognition and use of the architecture appropriate to the site and country. Major emphasis should be placed on the creation of goodwill in the respective countries by design of buildings of distinguished architectural quality rather than adherence to any given style of architecture. Designs shall adhere to established good practice and, to the extent practical, use construction techniques, materials and equipment of proven merit and reliability.[42]

Soon after, Kenworthy revised the first sentence:

> The policy shall be to provide requisite and adequate facilities in an architectural style and form which are distinguished, will reflect credit on the United States, and increase goodwill by intelligent appreciation, recognition, and use of the architecture appropriate to the site and country.[43]

It was not enough to be friendly; the buildings had to be impressive as well. He feared that the architects might balk at the requirement for adherence to proven techniques and materials, but he wanted to "prevent repetition of some of the recent design *faux pas* and to definitely establish that FBO is not an architectural research laboratory."[44] What sorts of things were considered to be *faux pas* and why? Building an all-glass building in the hot sun of Cuba and filling it with Knoll's "inappropriate" and uncomfortable furnishings was, to Kenworthy, a mistake, as was selecting those same furnishings for Brussels. Installing a nonfunctioning air-conditioning system in Havana was another; failing to comply with local building codes in Rio, another still. Indeed there were many other moves that prompted harsh but understandable criticism of FBO. When he presented his proposed policy statement to the new Architectural Advisory Committee in January 1954, Kenworthy added one more recommendation: "Buildings shall be dignified and economical to build, operate, and maintain."

Defending his proposals, Kenworthy stressed the importance of being open-minded about architecture. "We are neither committed to glass fish bowls, nor to Georgian tradition," he assured wary congressmen.[45] If the aim of the policy was to deflect congressional criticism, why did the State Department eschew sedate buildings designed in a traditional style in favor of conspicuous buildings in the modern idiom? Because in terms of the building program, as King had earlier noted, modern architecture was already recognized as an American asset abroad. Thus Kenworthy agreed to allow for the possibility of "fish bowls," but convinced his congressional critics that the new architectural policy would ensure against future embarrassment. And why did the policy ignore reference to permanence or monumentality, qualities that might have conveyed American strength and power? Because contemporary self-consciousness made expressions of grandiosity seem out of place, and because modern architecture was, by definition, less solid than spatial, and less massive than planar. If some of the new buildings later appeared insubstantial, it is no surprise. In the 1950s, most modern architects were intentionally exploring ways to stress space and deny mass. Brutal or consciously monumental concrete buildings would have served the purposes of the program no better than models based on recycled tradition. The new design policy directed them to use architecture to express respect rather than dominance.

Kenworthy's statement was the first official pronouncement on embassy design, and it defined the embassy as a building intended to please its foreign hosts rather than its domestic critics. Kenworthy was of course aware that many in Congress, like Bow and his colleagues, objected to the modern look of recent buildings. "I would have to say I think a great deal of the criticism ...was because things really didn't work very well, weren't too functional," Kenworthy suggested, "and a great deal of it was opposition to modern design." He continued:

> It's a question of how much of it was modern and how much was modernistic, if you make that distinction. I do. I have nothing against modern design, *per se*. To me it's not a question of whether it's modern design, traditional, or whatever, it's a question of whether it's good design.[46]

To better acquaint himself with FBO projects and to prepare for testimony on FBO appropriations, Kenworthy toured overseas posts in December 1953. He was surprised and dismayed to learn that FBO had been hiring architects for major projects and giving them only general requirements, but no written program. That he vowed to change. He expected the buildings he visited to work well. Most architects, he said, worked backwards; he thought that buildings should be designed from the inside out. In Helsinki, for example, he examined Saarinen's plans for a new embassy office building and he found them lacking. "Unfortunately, a lot of these people think every time you design something, it has to be original and new," he said, referring to Saarinen. The Helsinki project was one that he dropped from the FBO program, but nearly all of the others already in the pipeline received a green light to proceed. These included plans for a Jakarta office building by Raymond &

Rado, a consular office building and staff housing in Leopoldville by Weed, Russell, Johnson Associates, and a consular office building in Port of Spain by local architects Mence & Moore.

Kenworthy did make one additional change in the program, and that was to veto extensive rehabilitation plans scheduled for the embassy residence in London. Instead, he brought in Perry, Shaw & Hepburn for limited renovations. The London building was a palatial house in Regent's Park, the former residence of the heiress Barbara Hutton, who had given the property to the U.S. government as a gift after the war. It replaced J. P. Morgan's London house as the official residence of the American ambassador, and the former residence at 13/14 Prince's Gate was sold in 1956 for $138,198.[47] The Regent's Park house had been used as a military club for some time and needed extensive attention in order to resume its use as a residence. In Kenworthy's opinion, however, the house did not need to be totally pulled apart and put back together again. He declared it to be a "perfectly decent place," and said it was presumptuous to try to rebuild it. All the ambassador wanted, he noted, was to have his private quarters slightly modified—a dining room for his family and kitchen improvements that would permit catering. Kenworthy was familiar with William Perry's work—he and Perry worked together on the restoration of Williamsburg, and he knew that Perry "perfectly understood" the Georgian building.

•

IN HIS QUEST for prominent experts for the advisory panel, Kenworthy turned to the American Institute of Architects for advice. The AIA was the premier professional organization representing American architects and their professional aspirations. Headquartered in Washington, it was well positioned to lobby for legislation that protected and enhanced the profession, and it was long associated with efforts to encourage the federal government to retain architects in private practice over staff architects for government buildings, arguing that private firms provided higher quality work at less cost than government-employed architects. When the AIA sponsored the first Washington exhibition of FBO's recent architecture in February 1954, the purpose was to make it clear to all concerned that the profession wanted to see more government work by its members.

AIA officials urged Kenworthy to contact Ralph Walker for assistance in forming a committee. Walker, a graduate of MIT, had served as president of the AIA from 1949 to 1951. He was a partner in the New York firm of Voorhees, Walker, Foley & Smith and a Fellow of the AIA. Acting on behalf of Kenworthy, Walker proceeded to contact Henry Shepley and

Pietro Belluschi. Educated at Harvard and the École des Beaux Arts, Shepley was also widely respected as a leader in the profession. An AIA Fellow, he was a senior member of the Boston firm of Shepley Bulfinch Richardson and Abbott, a member of the National Academy of Design and the Boston Society of Architects, and recipient of the Gold Medal of Honor of the Architectural League of New York. He had served as an architectural advisor to the Treasury Department, the Federal Works Agency, and the Fine Arts Commission, and had been associated for years with the development of the Harvard University campus in Cambridge. Belluschi was the most avant-garde of the three, best known for the Equitable Savings and Loan Association Building (1948) in Portland, Oregon, already a modern landmark. Educated in Italy and at Cornell, Belluschi practiced architecture in Portland until 1942, when he moved to Cambridge as dean of the School of Architecture and Planning at MIT. Kenworthy recommended the three architects to Wailes. They were supposed to represent a spectrum of approaches to design, ranging from conservative/traditional to contemporary/modern. As alternates, he recommended John Root, George Howe, and William Wurster, but Wailes approved the first three.

To chair the panel, Kenworthy recommended Col. Harry A. McBride, a former Foreign Service officer and assistant secretary of state who served as administrator of the National Gallery of Art from 1939 until 1953. McBride had a cosmopolitan education and a varied career in government. He entered the Foreign Service at the age of twenty-one, and was posted first to Dresden, then to Spain, Switzerland, Belgian Congo, England, Liberia, and Poland. He returned to the United States to serve as assistant chief of the Foreign Service Buildings Office in 1930–31. That was soon after Congress passed the Foreign Service Buildings Act, when the new office was at the height of its prewar prominence. He became assistant to Secretaries Stimson and Hull and was appointed consul general of the Foreign Service in 1936. Then, in 1938, he moved on to become administrator of the newly established National Gallery of Art, where he served on the committee that supervised the construction of the gallery building at the foot of Capitol Hill. After the museum's opening in 1941, McBride took charge of its administration and the protection of its works of art. During the war, he served on the General Staff in Africa and in Europe, and he accompanied Secretary Hull to Moscow in 1943. He retired from his post at the Gallery in 1953.

In early January 1954, Secretary Dulles formally invited each man to join the committee, known at its inception as the Architectural Advisory Committee (AAC). No official document created the AAC, but the original intention was to appoint four members, each for a fixed term of two years.[48] With a series of press releases, the State Department announced the formation of its new committee, which met for the first time on 21 January 1954 to take a loyalty oath and meet with State Department officials. The AAC was charged with the task of recommending "the most appropriate style of architecture" for prospective projects, reviewing the quality and fitness of designs, and providing both majority and minority views where "unanimity of opinion" was lacking.[49] At its first meeting, the group reviewed work in progress in Port of Spain and Beirut and a proposed consulate general office building for Hong Kong.

At the same meeting, Belluschi agreed to draft a written statement of general philosophy to guide the panel's work.[50] His memorandum endorsed Kenworthy's policy statement and added his own philosophy on the importance of local history, the exploration of newness, and the need to focus attention on the "American" identity of the work. Seeing this as an opportunity to display high American cultural achievements abroad, he wrote:

> To the sensitive and imaginative designer it will be an invitation to give serious study to local conditions of climate and site, to understand and sympathize with local customs and people, and to grasp the historical meaning of the particular environment in which the new building must be set. He will do so with a free mind without being dictated by obsolete or sterile formulae or clichés, be they old or new; he will avoid being either bizarre or fashionable, yet he will not fear using new techniques or new methods should these constitute real advance in architectural thinking.
>
> It is hoped that the selected architects will think of style not in its narrower meaning but as a quality to be imparted to the building, a quality reflecting deep understanding of conditions and people. His directness and freshness of approach will thus have a distinguishable American flavor.
>
> The committee feels that if the above philosophy is adhered to, we need not fear criticism; on the other hand, if we act timidly, solely in the hope of avoiding any and all criticism from whatever quarters, we shall surely end up in dull compromises with the result that we shall have nothing but undistinguished buildings to represent us abroad. We would thereby have forfeited our opportunity to display the high American cultural achievements in the field of architecture generally recognized by architects of the more advanced nations of the world.[51]

Although Belluschi's full statement opens with an expression of support for Kenworthy's newly drafted policy, it departs in emphasis by making no effort to underscore practicality, and no reference to function or economy. In addition, it is conspicuous in its focus on recognition of architects by other architects. He does not mention the broader constituency for these public buildings, and, more importantly, offers no clue as to how an architect might reconcile the apparently conflicting directives to reflect both the local and the American scenes. Belluschi's words, cited in various journals and reviews, became closely associated with the building program.

The publicity surrounding the inauguration of the AAC confused many writers, who later made the mistake of assuming that the entire FBO building program and its use of modern architecture began in 1954 with Belluschi's "manifesto." After the 1953 reorganization at FBO, politics prevented anyone from crediting King with the modern look of American buildings, and, as acting director, Kenworthy maintained a low profile. The *Boston Globe*, for example, erroneously reported:

> The State Department began using the architectural genius of the country only in 1954 when government planners in the Foreign Buildings Office found themselves swamped by the expanded building program. Previously, all architectural work had been done by government blue-printers in the conventional style.[52]

Time magazine and the *New York Times* similarly suggested that FBO introduced its first modern architecture in 1954.[53] Some publications, including *Time*, credited FBO director William Hughes with the "bold decision" to give the United States a new diplomatic face, but Hughes did not even join FBO until after the policy was drafted and the review panel formed. What changed in 1954 was not the program, but its administration.

Of all those who played a role in the U.S. building program, none worked harder to promote it and to protect its integrity than the first members of the AAC. All participated actively in frequent meetings and all maintained interest and enthusiasm in the program well beyond their initial two-year terms. Walker, in fact, was the only one who actually served just two years. The others extended their terms to allow for a staggered rotation. Shepley served for three years, and Belluschi served for three and a half.

Despite periods during which few or no projects were being built, the AAC existed for fifty years. Officially renamed the Architectural Advisory Panel (AAP) in 1957, known as the Architectural Consultants between 1967 and 1971, and after that as the Architectural Advisory Board (AAB), it continued to review most new embassy plans and provide design advice to the State Department until 2004 when its role was eliminated as part of a reorganization of the overall building program. The architecture of new embassies changed almost beyond recognition during that same period.

CHAPTER SIX

Power Shifts

WHILE SOME IN CONGRESS saw the building program as a means to recoup America's "frozen" assets abroad and strongly endorsed it, congressional criticism grew steadily during the 1950s as Congress vied with the State Department and the White House for increased authority in international affairs. Those who claimed to represent "average" Americans, and were themselves often of modest means, took pleasure in sparring with State Department officials whom they identified as part of a privileged "elite." Described by former ambassador Ronald Palmer as a dispute involving issues of class, this quarrel was certainly part of a larger struggle over the distribution of power and it figured significantly in the ensuing history of the program.[1]

Congress's interest in enlarging its own sphere of influence and asking new questions regarding America's increased international commitments strongly affected the foreign building program during the Eisenhower years. In particular, rivalry between Congress and the executive departments intensified after the Democrats regained control of Congress in 1954. Increased staffing requirements at posts abroad and interagency competition for funds and facilities also affected the building program. Nongovernmental groups entered the political fray, too, seeking to protect and strengthen their own interests. Naturally, architects vied for access to the program, and they were among its strongest advocates in a struggle that included an array of relatively powerless partisans and a few staunch and influential critics. The two congressmen most notable for their influence were John Rooney and Wayne Hays, bitter rivals. The ongoing struggle for political power, fueled also by the decreasing availability of foreign credits and changing conditions overseas, caused the foreign building program to falter in the late 1950s and early 1960s when its funding was halted and new construction ceased. A new authorization in 1963 permitted FBO to move ahead once again, but by then Hays had managed to gain significant control of the program. Although the architectural review panel functioned continuously, and although new projects were built, only after Hays left Congress and only after the country had begun the task of recovery from the Vietnam War in the late 1970s did the embassy building program regain its architectural prominence—with a different sort of architecture than that which drew so much attention in the 1950s.

The Foreign Service had grown from 750 officers before World War II to more than three thousand by 1950. As Graham H. Stuart noted in his 1952 overview of American diplomatic and consular practice, Foreign Service officers were exasperated after years of being shut out of policymaking that affected their living and working conditions abroad.[2] The rapid increase in staff size also fueled tensions. Fritz Larkin had always made decisions according to his own agenda during his long tenure as head of FBO. His job was not to please the Foreign Service, but rather the key members of Congress who controlled his appropriations. When congressional investigators toured foreign posts in 1953, they heard complaints about poor quarters and inadequate living allowances, but they dismissed most of the criticism as being without merit and managed to convey the impression that those who complained somehow lacked "sincerity" and/or "patriotism."[3] Given the fact that Foreign Service officers were not encouraged to share grievances with outside critics, it is perhaps surprising that the congressmen heard any complaints at all. But angry or discomfited ambassadors did complain about conditions abroad, prompting Washington newspaper reports about dilapidated American facilities in Manila, Moscow, Tehran, and Baghdad. In Manila, one paper reported, Americans were still living in Quonset huts erected as emergency housing after the war.[4] When Loy Henderson was ambassador to Iran, his official residence in Tehran was condemned because of the danger that it might collapse; while Waldemar Gallman was ambassador to Iraq, his Iraqi landlord refused to make necessary repairs to his rented residence in Baghdad. In both instances, the State Department moved ahead quickly with plans to build appropriate new U.S.-owned facilities, but even with a well-financed building program the department could not remedy all of the problems.

Changing diplomatic practice and the rapid influx of aid workers and other newcomers at posts abroad also heightened stress within the State Department. McCarthy-era investigations had naturally produced demoralization within the department. Conflicts had also arisen between the career Foreign Service and the career civil service. The need to staff new overseas programs with teams of specially-trained professionals challenged the club-like atmosphere of the Foreign Service and lessened the primacy of traditional diplomats, who had created what they considered to be "a pretty good club" for themselves.[5] They were not exactly pleased to share space and resources with the ordinary American civil servants whose postwar influx expanded embassy staffs abroad. They also resented the shift from foreign policy focused on diplomatic practice to one keyed to the delivery of aid, both military and nonmilitary. And they further resented their own weakened position within the State Department, which had treated them with deference for so long. With efforts underway to make diplomatic service more "democratic" and less exclusive, the traditionalists feared the loss of long-shared prerogatives. Moreover, they resented criticism from congressmen whose knowledge of foreign affairs, it seemed, was limited to what they had learned at official receptions and on travel junkets.

Enmity between congressional critics and the Foreign Service added more friction to the inherently adversarial relationship between Congress and the State Department. Congressional resentment of the Foreign Service and its spokesmen and allies spilled over into resentment of FBO, which became a convenient target for criticism. Critics took special pleasure in denouncing the building program for supposed frills and niceties, such as maids' rooms, dining rooms, swimming pools, and other features such as air-conditioning and entertainment allowances—all of which were important, if not essential, to diplomatic life overseas but considered extravagant or unacceptable to popular taste at home.

During the 1950s, "traditionalists" comprised the most identifiable group serving abroad in the State Department. They were linked by educational credentials and by their membership in what columnist Joseph Alsop dubbed the "WASP ascendancy."[6] The key State Department officials who appeared before Congress on behalf of FBO, the men who presented the budget requests, endured the cross-examinations and tried to make the case for the building program—Loy Henderson, Isaac W. Carpenter Jr., and William Hughes—all shared this background of accomplishment and perceived privilege, although Carpenter and Hughes were not career diplomats.

A former ambassador to India and to Iran, a diplomat, and a distinguished Foreign Service insider, Loy Henderson became deputy under secretary of state for administration when President Eisenhower brought him back to Washington from Tehran in 1955. His new duties included administration of the foreign building program, a program he knew well and in which he had already shown a strong interest. Henderson grew up on a farm in Arkansas, graduated from Northwestern University in 1915, and had just entered law school when the United States entered World War I. He served abroad with the Red Cross and then entered the Foreign Service in 1922, becoming vice consul in Dublin. To his dismay, he found that the consulate at Dublin was located over a saloon. During the visa season, he said, "Crowds were so great wanting visas that the stairs would be packed all the way to the street...

because there was no room upstairs." Once the United States established diplomatic relations with Ireland, Henderson made it his business to vacate the saloon structure and secure a "decent" embassy building.[7]

From Ireland, Henderson moved first to Latvia, where he was responsible for establishing the American legation in Riga, and then to Russia, where he helped organize the new American mission in Moscow. When he became minister to Iraq in 1943, he faulted facilities at the rented embassy, which he described as a "very poor imitation" of the White House. While he was in Baghdad, he managed to introduce air-conditioning and made plans to relocate the embassy to what was hoped to be a better site. In 1948, President Truman named him ambassador to India. There, too, he found inadequate accommodations. American diplomatic facilities in New Delhi consisted of unconnected old rented buildings, one of which was a former palace. All of the spaces were crowded and hot. Henderson secured a prime site for a new embassy in New Delhi, then moved on to become ambassador to Iran in 1951. In Tehran, the newly completed U.S. chancery became known as "Henderson High," a name which pleased him. Though undistinguished in appearance, the new red brick chancery worked well even if "it did not fit in with the architecture in Iran at all," a matter he thought was important.[8] When he recommended a new residence to replace the crumbling one there, he was very specific in the sort of architecture he wanted and the way in which he wanted the new building to take advantage of the site with its mountain views.

Henderson's assistant, Isaac W. Carpenter, was a wealthy businessman, not a seasoned diplomat. A Dartmouth graduate who attended Harvard Business School before completing his military service in World War I, Carpenter was chairman of the board of his family's paper company when he took a leave of absence to serve as assistant secretary of state for administration and personnel. He succeeded Edward T. Wailes, who became ambassador to the Union of South Africa in 1954.[9]

William Hughes joined FBO as director in May 1954 as part of Kenworthy's reorganization. Hughes came to FBO from the International Boundary-Water Commission where he had served as budget finance officer. He had no background in construction or design, but some experience in mid-level management. With a B.A. in business administration from Baylor and an M.B.A. from Harvard, he served as comptroller of Gallaudet College and as an administrative officer at the Institute of Inter-American Affairs in Honduras and Brazil, and then embarked on a civil service career, not a Foreign Service career, with the State Department. He was assistant chief of the Division of Foreign Service Planning and deputy executive director of the Office of American Republic Affairs. To those who brought him to

FBO, he seemed suited to run the building program. He reported directly to Carpenter, who in turn reported to Henderson.

Henderson was held in high esteem by almost everyone, including State Department foes. He had both a strong interest in maintaining the dignity of the American presence abroad and a strong commitment to tradition. Behind the scenes, he urged Hughes to pursue moderation in design. Publicly his most visible role was to defend the building program before Congress and to support Hughes in his skirmishes on the Hill.

To the sons of immigrants, farmers, and factory workers who had worked their way up the political ladder to positions of power in Congress, American diplomats often seemed "foreign." Further, for many it was politically expedient to picture the diplomatic world as alien and elite. Though widely respected on the Hill, Loy Henderson and his State Department colleagues found themselves lampooned by men such as John Rooney, whose subcommittee—the House Appropriations Committee's Subcommittee on Departments of State, Justice and Judiciary and Related Agencies—determined how much money the State Department could have for embassy construction, housing, and even for overseas entertainment. The son of Irish immigrants, Rooney liked to ridicule the "striped pants" elite at State and denounced requests for additional living allowances in 1955 as "booze allowances for cookie pushers."[10] Much of his rhetoric was aimed at cutting waste and maintaining the support of his Brooklyn constituency. His jibes at the State Department did not signify a total disregard for diplomatic necessity, but rather a real antipathy toward privilege. Nevertheless, he loved foreign travel and expected to be entertained in style when he visited U.S. embassies abroad. While he was on his junkets, State Department officials saw to it that he enjoyed all of the perquisites of his position.[11] But when he returned home he routinely condemned State Department inefficiency and waste.

Rooney knew how to bully and cajole FBO into making cuts that played well in headlines in his home district. His subcommittee hearings were replete with questions about the necessity for new buildings and fine things. In order to maintain a reputation for parsimony, Rooney insisted upon the opportunity to pare down any budget, including the FBO budget, that came before him. His special talents lay in line-by-line scrutiny of budget statements and intimidation of executive agency witnesses. Not surprisingly, many at the State Department came to see him as an "ogre," and few saw that much of what he did was for effect. Despite the superficial animosity, Henderson described Rooney as a personal friend, noting that both understood what the other was trying to do. Acknowledging that Congress made it hard for FBO to fulfill its mission, Henderson later added philosophically, "That's what

they're supposed to do, that's their job to keep us from spending too much."
Still, he declared that cuts in foreign buildings were simply unacceptable if
it meant that the State Department could not produce and maintain buildings "that would be representative of the United States and if we were to be
respected abroad."[12]

Rooney's position of power was significantly strengthened in 1955
when FBO had to begin asking for increased dollar appropriations to supplement its credit funds. Rooney had been generous to Larkin when the funds
were credits, but he was less magnanimous when it came to what he called
"the taxpayers' cash money."[13] Until 1975, when he retired from the House,
Rooney reviewed all FBO appropriations—often making cuts and voicing
his own opinions on particular projects. He also arranged for a series of continuing resolutions whereby his old friend Fritz Larkin was able to remain on
the payroll as a consultant for years.

The other principal combatant in the tug-of-war between Congress and
the State Department was Wayne Hays, Democrat from Ohio. A farmer's
son, Hays was elected to Congress in 1948 and soon began his climb to
power as a member of the House Foreign Affairs Committee, a committee that he joined in 1955. By 1957, he was chairman of its Subcommittee
on State Department Organization and Foreign Operations. Without his
approval, the State Department could not build new embassies. And by the
late 1950s all new construction did in fact cease while Hays and Hughes
locked horns in a power struggle ostensibly related to the proposed design
for the new embassy in Dublin.

Keenly aware of the power of the Senate Foreign Relations Committee,
Hays hoped to use his influence to build his subcommittee into a body of
comparable prominence. As he increased his influence on the Hill, he
increased his influence over the State Department and FBO, and indirectly,
his influence over foreign policy. He tested his strength in negotiations over
proposed projects for new African capitals, and even earlier, in the battle
over Dublin—a battle which pitted him not only against the entire State
Department, but the White House, too. By 1961, Hays had acquired veto
power over projects in the FBO program. Like Rooney, Hays held hearings
that taxed the patience of State Department witnesses. Like Rooney, he generally left State Department officials with less than they needed or wanted.
And like Rooney, Hays was called an "ogre" by those officials.[14]

The two congressmen were political enemies for whom the building program represented contested turf. They disagreed over the disposition of particular properties and also over matters of policy. For example, Rooney and
his colleague Frank Bow condemned the department for buying the former
Rothschild residence in Paris, even though they knew that the purchase was

made with credits that effectively cost the taxpayers nothing. In 1957, they rejected the idea that the historic property was worth renovating as a home for the ambassador and urged FBO to get rid of it. FBO had already initiated planning for a large consolidated office building in Paris. When Hughes suggested to Hays in 1959 that FBO might sell or demolish the property, possibly to make way for the new American office building, Hays was outraged. Arguing rightly that Parisians would never allow such a building to be razed, and insisting that it should be re-used as a residence, Hays made it clear to Hughes that plans for the renovation should proceed.[15] Hays's enthusiasm for the Paris property stemmed in part from a personal interest in it (to the amusement of his critics, he imagined himself as a sometime ambassador) and even more from his eagerness to oppose Rooney.

Another key issue that divided the two congressmen was whether or not FBO had an obligation to make maximum use of products made in America. Claiming that there was no good reason to use "hard dollars" for the purchase of rugs, furniture, and other supplies that could be purchased abroad using foreign credits, Rooney told Hughes to buy as much as possible abroad. Hays took the opposite view, urging Hughes to "buy American!"[16] He agreed that it made no sense when FBO ordered bricks made in Virginia for the new embassy annex in Canberra and then sent them all the way to Australia to match Australian bricks used earlier in the construction of the embassy. But he insisted that many other products could and should be bought in the United States as a way of boosting American business, even if the cost of such purchases *exceeded* the cost of buying abroad.[17] Hays had his own constituents in mind when he made certain suggestions, and in this case, he was anxious to promote the interests of china and glass manufacturers in Ohio. Caught between the two congressmen, FBO officials agreed to buy American products exclusively only if they were ordered to do so by Congress. As a result, the authorization legislation approved in 1963 reversed the exemption granted in 1952 and required FBO to make maximum use of American-made products at its posts abroad.

As part of their efforts to strengthen their own power, both Hays and Rooney placed allies in influential positions within the State Department. Rooney's influence reached directly into the department after he secured a job for his protégé William Crockett, a man he first met in Rome, when Crockett was working for Ambassador Clare Boothe Luce as a counselor for administration at the embassy. Crockett was not a career Foreign Service officer, a fact that endeared him to Rooney and even more so to Rooney's ever-present aide, Jay Howe, a man known to despise the Foreign Service. The indomitable Luce thought she was being poisoned by paint chips that fell from the ceiling over her ambassadorial bed and onto her breakfast tray.

She detested Rooney, blamed him for poor conditions at the embassy and residence, and lectured him on inadequacies there. A wealthy woman with extravagant tastes, she criticized Rooney for his tight-fisted control of the special fund used to finance diplomatic "emergencies." Rooney retaliated by refusing to show up at an official luncheon with her after all of her invited guests had assembled. During that trip, Crockett and his wife entertained Rooney and made a good impression on him. By way of thanks, Rooney helped him to become the department's deputy assistant secretary for budget and finance in 1958.

When President John F. Kennedy was elected in 1960, he decided to fill all of the major ambassadorial posts, including the European posts, with career Foreign Service officers, as opposed to wealthy campaign contributors, for whom the most costly posts, such as Rome and London, had been generally reserved. Kennedy and his advisors understood that most career officers could not afford the high costs of entertaining the visitors who flocked to these posts combined with the overall expense of representation. According to Crockett, they turned to Rooney and asked him "to do something that would make such assignments possible." Rooney told them that the matter could be handled by increasing the embassy "emergency" fund, but insisted "that he wouldn't trust anybody to handle that fund except Bill Crockett." Though almost no one knew Crockett, and he had never even met Secretary of State Dean Rusk prior to his appointment, he was quietly named assistant secretary of state for administration in 1961. Soon after, Attorney General Robert Kennedy called him to his Justice Department office—where Crockett found himself confronted by a big dog. "Kennedy didn't look up," Crockett recalls, "but feeling my presence, said, 'Just step over him.' So I stepped over the dog and approached his desk. He asked me to sit down. Almost without looking up he said that we needed to get some things straight." Kennedy declared:

> I don't know how you got your job, or how you think you got your job. But I can tell you where your loyalties lie. You work for my brother, the President of the United States, and you do whatever he says. Your job in the State Department is to make sure that all the personnel in the Department understand that they work for the President and that they are to be loyal to him. So now you know what your job is![18]

Kennedy was not done. "Do you know how to do your job?" he asked. Crockett hesitated. "You kick people in the ass so hard that teeth will rattle in all the embassies. That's what you will do. That is how to get your job done!" With that, the interview was over. When Crockett later received calls periodically "ordering" him to do certain things, he complied. He was asked to find jobs for former Kennedy campaign workers, for example, and also to provide funds for counterinsurgency efforts directed, he said, by Robert Kennedy.[19]

In order to enable certain ambassadors to afford diplomatic appointments, Crockett supplemented their salaries and allowances with grants from the "Confidential Funds" that could be used for any legal purpose, often for food, clothing, and gifts. "I went to the Director of IRS to talk about the tax consequences of these grants," Crockett said, and "we got a letter from him excluding these grants from taxable income." It was a good program, he felt, and permitted "a number of Foreign Service officers to accept appointments which they could not have otherwise afforded." The funds were also used to pay for presidential trips, since regular embassy budgets could not cover the cost of hosting a guest such as Lyndon Johnson. Funds were used to rent private backup planes for contingency travel and even to buy American flags to be waved by welcoming crowds. Neither Crockett nor his colleagues discussed these special funds widely "in order to maintain the confidentiality of the program and the 'Confidential Funds' appropriation as a whole."[20]

By 1963, Crockett had also befriended Hays, who came to like him despite his closeness to Rooney. With the support of Hays, Crockett managed to move up to become the deputy under secretary for administration, a position that he admittedly coveted.[21] Often Crockett found himself trying to satisfy Rooney or Hays, sometimes both. When Hays asked him to travel with him instead of Rooney at a time when Rooney had already scheduled a trip, Crockett did the only politically correct thing—he had a doctor declare him too ill to travel with either.

Hays dabbled in State Department personnel matters even more than Rooney did and he particularly disliked Hughes.[22] When Hughes appeared before Hays in 1959 asking for funds for Dublin and the entire capital program, Hays had already declared him to be intolerable and had demanded Henderson remove him. By threatening to hold up funds for FBO, Hays forced the department to fire Hughes. Soon after, Henderson offered the FBO position to James Johnstone, a relaxed and optimistic Foreign Service officer who believed that there was "absolutely no reason why Congress should not know all about the foreign buildings," and no reason why advice from Congress was all bad or necessarily tainted.[23] This open-minded attitude was threatening to his superior, Bill Crockett, who liked to think that he controlled access to key congressmen. Crockett became jealous of Johnstone and *his* relationship with Hays and Rooney, his cordial relations with Frank Bow, the ranking Republican on Rooney's committee, and his friendship with Frances Bolton, the representative from Cleveland known as the "dean of the Republicans." Bolton enjoyed the wide respect of her colleagues, and given her senior position, she was uniquely able to contradict Hays without irritating him. The ambitious Crockett was annoyed that Bolton liked Johnstone and that Johnstone talked directly with her without going through him. According to Johnstone, Crockett "jettisoned" him in 1965 and sent him off to become consul general in Frankfurt because he thought Johnstone was after his job.[24]

With Johnstone gone, Crockett personally named his replacement, hand-picked by Hays: Ralph Scarritt, a Foreign Service officer whom Hays had met for the first time just weeks before on a visit to Mexico City. "He was the last Foreign Service officer on foreign soil that he had seen, and that's why the name came to him," Johnstone later commented.[25] Thus Scarritt, who also owed his position to Hays, became the FBO director (see Appendix A).

Next, in a move that ultimately contributed to his own political demise, Hays installed his longtime friend Orlan Clemmer Ralston (known as "Clem") as Scarritt's deputy. Ralston, like Hays, was a native of Flushing, Ohio. There, he had managed a department store, the store in which Hays had leased space for his first congressional office in 1948. Though eventually named a Foreign Service Reserve officer, he had never served in the Foreign Service, nor had he any known experience related to construction or architecture when he assumed his post under Scarritt. His duties then were more or less ceremonial, which was fortunate, since colleagues described him as thoroughly unprofessional, a man who kept no regular hours and had no interest in other administrative necessities.[26] Even Hays admitted that he closely monitored Ralston's activities at the State Department because, he said, "he's from Ohio and I want to make sure he doesn't embarrass me."[27] The ill-equipped Ralston eventually took over as acting director of FBO in 1973, replacing Scarritt's successor, Ernest "Jud" Warlow. The following year Ralston became deputy assistant secretary of state for foreign buildings, a position which he held until 1977. While Ralston was at FBO, Hays directed contracts to friends and constituents.

The real differences between Hays and Hughes had to do with power, not taste. Hays's major accomplishments included a two-year authorization limit giving his committee the opportunity to monitor FBO's funding and planning every other year, as opposed to every five or ten years. With this device, he gained virtual veto power over individual building projects. Moreover, through his actions he succeeded in preventing his nemesis Rooney from acquiring control of the program through Rooney's annual review of the State Department's appropriations request. Hays's two-year review requirement was a severe blow to a program that depended upon long-term planning and the commitment of funds to design and construction projects that often spanned many years.[28]

Failing to understand the fact that political necessity prompted Congress to find and eliminate "waste" in the federal budget, failing to appreciate that all federal policies and programs were ultimately political products, and confusing cooperation with contrition, many State Department officials showed a political naiveté that did not help them on the Hill. As Crockett and Johnstone found out, any accommodation to congressional wishes, any effort to create a more cooperative atmosphere between the department and its "foes" on the Hill, was viewed with suspicion within the department. On leaving his post at FBO, for example, Hughes insulted his successor Johnstone by suggesting he was a "patsy" for being willing to work closely with Congress. "Anyone who gets along with Mr. Hays and his committee," Hughes remarked bitterly, "will be brown-nosing him."[29]

With its separate allocation, the FBO budget was an easy target for congressional critics. Legislators in search of "safe" places to cut the federal budget found attractive and vulnerable targets in FBO, AID, and USIA because the budget for each was considered apart from the overall departmental request. Decisions about the design, construction, and leasing of office and residential space represented part of a larger foreign policy initiative from which Congress, particularly House members, felt excluded. Debate over proposed budgets for foreign aid (through the Agency for International Development, or AID), information dissemination (USIA), and foreign buildings offered a logical opportunity for critical evaluation of Administration policy and a chance to shape that policy. Thus, for example, Hays's Foreign Affairs subcommittee met for a total of nine days over a period of seven months in 1959 to assess a request for new authorizations for FBO. Hearings conducted in 1962 for the same purpose included eight days of testimony. Again in 1963, Hays held hearings that heard seven days of testimony. As chairman, he was in a position to question State Department witnesses about all aspects of the building program. He also demanded an immense amount of data showing the past and proposed distribution of funds on a worldwide, project-by-project basis. To some extent his examinations were designed to intimidate the department, but many of the questions he asked were reasonable and necessary. From a political standpoint, it was especially easy to cut away at the FBO budget because the faraway projects seemed remote, if not irrelevant, to American taxpayers. Congressmen could wave the flag, cut the budget, and never risk hurting loyal voters who were skeptical about foreigners, foreign places, and Americans who preferred living abroad to living "at home."

Debate over the building program was also part of a larger debate over foreign commitments. The debate between politicians who championed higher military spending and involvement in foreign affairs and those who favored a balanced budget or more emphasis on domestic programs led to questions about the usefulness of aid, the need for foreign obligations, and the efficacy of international organizations, including the United Nations.

Kicked about like a political football, the foreign building program showed signs of injury. In 1959 all new capital projects were postponed, and a year later FBO ran out of capital funds. The impressive building program seemed headed for ruin. After a two-year hiatus, Congress seemed ready to approve a new authorization in 1962, when local opposition to the location of foreign chanceries in residential neighborhoods of Washington, D.C., caused yet another year's delay. The program was not rescued until 1963, after congressional approval of a new two-year authorization totaling $49,824,000, a compromise struck by Senator J. William Fulbright, chairman of the Senate Foreign Relations Committee, and Hays, the new House power broker.

THE BUILDING PROGRAM had its foes, but architects were not among them. Architects saw the program as a means to showcase modern architecture and increase recognition of their profession. Their approval gave the program added credibility, deflected public criticism, and conveyed the misleading but useful impression that a government-sponsored building program could be apolitical. Popular publications such as *Time* and *Life* featured articles that helped to create popular awareness of modernism. They applauded the use of modern architecture and focused on it as a direct and deliberate challenge to the recycled classicism favored by the Soviets. Architects and architectural writers, although a small group in size and absolute influence, added their voices to those calling for better foreign buildings and praising FBO for its innovative policy of hiring private-sector firms. Architects viewed the embassy commissions as "plums" and often agreed to work without profit, sometimes even at a loss, just to participate in the widely publicized program. Their hope that quality design could build international understanding or would win respect for the United States may have been self-serving at times and naively optimistic, but the physical presence of new American buildings was, indeed, a clear indication of an America actively engaged abroad.

Even among leading architects, however, there was no consensus on modernism, the meaning of history, the importance of context, and ways to avoid artistic sensationalism. Addressing the AIA national convention in 1954, for example, Paul Rudolph condemned the monotony of modern architecture, ridiculed the arbitrary use of *pilotis* and the overabundance of glass, and questioned the rightness of a building unrelated to its neighbors.

Rudolph had studied under Gropius at Harvard, and though he was only thirty-six years old, he was already recognized as a spokesman for the profession. He censured architects for producing "too many goldfish bowls, too few caves." Others who addressed the same convention crowd included Eero Saarinen, Josep Lluis Sert, William Wurster, and Ralph Walker.[30]

At what *Architectural Record* referred to as "the best-listened-to of all the sessions," Sert condemned the new architecture for producing "clichés of an appalling poverty" and called upon architects to design buildings that fit into their sites harmoniously. Wurster called for greater emphasis on history. And former AIA national president Ralph Walker, recently appointed to the AAC, also underscored the importance of history as a source of inspiration. Walker described as folly any effort to design for a particular moment in time. He said that such effort was bound to result in design that soon becomes "affected, shallow and too often a copied stereotype." Each of these convention speakers also played a subsequent role in the FBO program. Sert designed the embassy in Baghdad; Wurster designed the consulate general in Hong Kong and served on the AAP; Saarinen designed the embassies in Oslo and London and also served on the AAP; Rudolph designed an embassy for Amman (never built); and Walker was a key member of the first AAC. Their remarks, heard at the profession's national convention and featured in one of its leading publications, represented ideas circulating among architects at that time. In fact, along with its article on the AIA convention titled "The Changing Philosophy of Architecture," *Architectural Record* included a bibliography of other related articles by notable architects and defenders of modernism, including Joseph Hudnut, Sigfried Giedion, Frank Lloyd Wright, Lewis Mumford, and Pietro Belluschi. Of the more than twenty articles listed, nearly all had been published since 1951 as part of a renewed debate on the merits of modernism.

Like the Foreign Service, the relatively small group that headed the architectural profession in the early 1950s operated to some extent like a private club. Prominent members of the profession had trained at Ivy League schools, mostly Harvard and Yale, but also at MIT and Berkeley; and they knew each other through training, teaching, or professional association. Of the five architects who addressed the AIA in 1954, for example, Rudolph graduated from Harvard's Graduate School of Design and later became chairman of the School of Architecture at Yale; Saarinen graduated from Yale and worked for MIT beginning in 1953; Sert taught at Yale and became dean of the GSD at Harvard in 1953; Wurster graduated from Berkeley, studied at Harvard, became dean of MIT's School of Architecture and Planning, then dean of Berkeley's College of Environmental Design in 1950; Walker graduated from MIT. The most prominent architects practiced in New York,

Boston, Chicago, or San Francisco, and their work was featured in exhibitions in New York and in a handful of architectural journals published there. Drawn to a field that offered relatively small financial rewards, they were often financially independent—or at least seemed to be—and they rarely, if ever, ran for public office or spoke out on major political or social issues. Even among those who emigrated to the United States before and during the war, some to escape tyranny and persecution and some simply to find better work, few involved themselves in foreign affairs or in policy matters unrelated to their own profession.[31]

Partly through the use of a specialized language and partly through a tendency to confine debate within the field, architects reinforced the exclusivity of their calling and made it difficult for non-architects to venture opinions on their projects. Working for FBO, private-sector architects almost never had to speak to anyone but other architects on the FBO staff. State Department spokesmen presented their schemes to Congress when such presentations were called for; architects never appeared at hearings themselves, although their names were often mentioned and their designs discussed. It is no wonder that they thought the program was apolitical: they rarely participated directly in the political process. Instead, they preferred to think of themselves as artists, and, given the self-selection that exists among those who enter the profession, to a large extent they *were* artists. And as artists are wont to do, they preferred to depend upon the largesse of a wealthy patron, FBO, rather than to cultivate the public awareness that might build a much broader constituency for their work.

By emphasizing its exclusivity, the architectural profession reinforced the notion that its members were experts uniquely qualified to assist and direct the architectural dimension of the foreign building program. At their best, architects worked closely with the AAC to try to do what Kenworthy and Belluschi asked them to do: they examined foreign sites; suggested economical adaptations of construction technology; tried to understand local sensibilities; and tried to convey something of American optimism in their designs and choices of decoration. Projects such as those in Karachi, Athens, Tangier, London, and Accra, designed by old "stars" such as Neutra and Gropius, and young "stars" such as Hugh Stubbins, Saarinen, and Weese, created lasting landmarks that were admired, if also criticized, both by architects and non-architects. At their worst, architects ignored the State Department, although it was their client, and acted in ways that caused others to describe them as "difficult." Rudolph, for one, had a hard time trying to design within the constraints of the program at Amman. Others showed a curious disregard for the needs of people who had to work or live in the foreign buildings. Michael Hare, for example, totally ignored or misunderstood the climate in

Tegucigalpa and designed an embassy residence at which the ambassador and his family and staff were routinely soaked by driving rains as they scurried across open walkways. Worse still, the Honduran site had been selected for its breathtaking view, but Hare's design blocked the view and the architect refused to add a window when asked to do so. These are examples of projects on which architects created problems for themselves by assuming the role of the artist/genius, the stereotype depicted by Ayn Rand in her 1943 novel *The Fountainhead*. Many other architects were less flamboyant and far more willing to work within the program's constraints, but the temptation to use embassy commissions as "signature" pieces was hard to avoid.

CHAPTER SEVEN

The Architectural Advisory Committee

AFTER TAKING CARE of initial formalities and defining its role, FBO's newly appointed Architectural Advisory Committee began reviewing existing projects, and started the process of selecting new architects. By March 1954, FBO had already awarded contracts to its first group of architects, and by early summer, under the direction of newly installed director William Hughes, the committee was in the process of reviewing plans for new projects in Hong Kong, Asunción, Kobe, Lagos, Leopoldville, and Tegucigalpa. There was a need to move ahead quickly with the program, and everyone understood the urgency of acting while funds were in hand.

Architects embarked upon each project with virtually no idea of what was expected of them. Aside from the generally worded policy statement, FBO provided them with a program that outlined the various functional needs, but little else. They saw no casebook of previous embassy projects around the world, nor did any such reference exist. Whatever information architects gleaned about past or concurrent efforts was anecdotal, most of it learned in the course of meeting with FBO staff. It was not a subject that had been studied by anyone, either within FBO or without.

Ralph Walker, Henry Shepley, and Pietro Belluschi felt strongly about maintaining a hands-off attitude toward architectural choice, but they were thorough and often surprisingly critical in their effort to bring schemes into line with the newly stated design policy. Their successors on the AAC faced the same problem of wanting to generate suitable architecture, but not wanting to be didactic or artistically restrictive. All found it easier to pinpoint problems with a design than to make detailed specifications beforehand; it was easier, for example, to tell an architect to make his scheme "less spectacular" than it was to explain to him at the outset how he might achieve "dignity."

The AAC met frequently between 1954 and 1956, the formative period of the reorganized program. The committee established its own working rules and procedures guided by Nelson Kenworthy's policy statement and by Belluschi's much-publicized design guidelines. At the first meetings, members proposed limits that they wanted to impose upon their involvement in the overall design process. They decided, for example, not to recommend a "set style for a given location," despite a request for such guidance from State Department officials.[1] Members agreed to give consulting architects free rein in terms of expression and to evaluate the projects only on a case-by-case basis using the new design policy as a guide. The architect members also maintained that they would not substitute their own skills for those of consulting architects. If there was dissatisfaction with a given design, for example, they said they would not step in as designers to offer alternative solutions.

One of the first projects they reviewed was a design prepared by a Lebanese architect for a proposed embassy in Beirut, a scheme that reminded committee members of prior projects in Rio, Havana, and Madrid. There was disagreement as to whether or not it was appropriate, and discussion followed about various alternatives. This prompted members to conclude that they were beginning to function in the role of the architect. Instead, they recommended selection of a new architect and a "fresh start."[2] (Eventually, in 1957, FBO retained Ralph Rapson to design the Beirut embassy, but the project was suspended during the Lebanese civil war in 1958. In 1971, FBO retained McCue, Boone & Tomsick to design the embassy; again the project was suspended amidst civil war and was never built.)

AAC members reiterated the "hands-off" philosophy in May 1955 when, they said, Richard Neutra "attempted to obtain the personal views of the Committee concerning the design of the Karachi office building prior to undertaking his first sketches."[3] They refused to share their views with Neutra at that time, but when they reviewed the firm's first studies in August, they offered a scathing critique, objecting to the plan and the design. Minutes of the meeting show that:

> The Committee expressed its feeling that the design was rather disunited and required organizing, that it gave the impression of being a commercial enterprise similar to a mail order business rather than the dignity necessary for a U.S. Embassy. The Committee particularly mentioned the entrance as being transitory and Hollywoodish and suggested that it be restudied and made less spectacular.[4]

They did not hesitate to tell the architect what was good about his scheme (little, they thought) and what needed to be changed, but they did not call for a new architect. They told Neutra's partner, Robert Alexander, that the building's main office corridor was too long and too narrow, for example. They also urged that the building be set back further on its site, called for better landscaping, and asked Alexander to consolidate garage, parking lots, and shops under a plaza and around a court. Further, they told him that his scheme over-emphasized the barrel-vaulted storage warehouse, which was not, after all, supposed to be the focal point of the project. Alexander left the meeting with instructions to restudy the program and return with a new *parti* (plan) along the lines suggested.[5]

Similarly when Chloethiel Woodard Smith presented a site plan and overall *parti* for Asunción in early in 1955, members made it clear to her that the scheme needed to be modified to meet the requirements of the program. Too much terracing of the graded site, they said, would lead to excessive costs and would not be sanctioned. They also criticized the scheme for exceeding the gross floor area of the program and asked her to bring it within size and cost guidelines that she had been given. They questioned her closely on her choice of materials and her intention to use marble cladding, advised her on structural revisions to the roof, told her to screen the roof openings against animals and birds, and suggested that she line forms with brick or tile to prevent fungus growth on the concrete.[6]

At the suggestion of the first AAC, FBO adopted a "hire American" policy for all major new projects.[7] Though Congress did not demand a stop to the practice of hiring foreign architects, the State Department sensed the political importance of commissioning Americans. Through its lobbying effort, the AIA also created the impression that Americans could do a better design job than foreigners and that architects in private practice could out-perform government designers. The American architectural community applauded the new hiring policy, although many of those hired ironically turned out to be adopted Americans, European immigrants who moved to the United States before and during World War II.

The AAC proposed two other new policies: that architects be paid a fee for preliminary work to protect against termination, and that architects be sent to foreign sites for "firsthand observation" prior to beginning work. Early in the program, architects designed buildings for sites that they had never seen. Neither Raymond nor Rado had visited Jakarta when they designed the embassy there in 1953, although they had sent an assistant to assess the site; the AAC was determined to avoid that situation in the future. Brief site visits, however, often provided inadequate information. Staff at the New Delhi embassy joked, for example, that Edward Durell Stone must have visited India during winter or a drought to have so badly miscalculated the impact of wind-driven rain on his building and its occupants. Screened but not enclosed from the elements, the building's courtyard was often soaked by monsoon rains.

Members of the AAC claimed no special expertise in geography, history, or international relations, and members certainly did not visit all of the sites that they were called upon to evaluate. The State Department did send Shepley and Belluschi to India to assess the situation in New Delhi. As part of that fact-finding mission, the two architects also visited Amman, Baghdad, Beirut, Karachi, London, and Rome to meet with local architects and contractors and to learn more about conditions that affected the FBO program. On behalf of the department, Walker also traveled to London, The Hague, and Dublin. Subsequent AAC members, however, did not travel regularly to visit sites. Only design architects visited the sites and generally only once prior to the start of a project.

The AAC understood that FBO's staff would be responsible for the functional assessment of the new buildings and that serious security matters and structural issues would be assessed by experts, including Army engineers. Function and appearance were often hard to separate, however, and AAC members quickly found themselves analyzing practical problems as well as aesthetics. They played no role once the projects moved from design to construction, and none of the architects could do much about situations where construction supervision was inadequate. Neutra's partner Alexander complained loudly to FBO that the concrete mix at Karachi was being watered down by the local contractor. He even warned of a possible building collapse (which, fortunately, never occurred), but he could do nothing to correct the problem because his firm had no contract to provide supervision and his complaints were dismissed. Years later, William Metcalf's alarm over inadequate construction supervision at the residence in Giza (Cairo) was similarly dismissed; due to the shoddy construction there, a fine project had to be abandoned.[8]

BEFORE CONSIDERING NEW WORK, the AAC began its duties by reviewing existing FBO commissions. Aside from the Saarinen project in Helsinki, suspended in its preliminary stages, there were six ongoing projects in early 1954: two for which FBO had retained private American firms—staff housing in Manila (Gardiner A. Dailey) and an embassy in Jakarta (Raymond & Rado); two by FBO in-house architects—a consulate and apartments in Leopoldville and staff housing in Bangkok; and two by foreign architects— embassies in Port of Spain (Mence & Moore) and Beirut (Makdisi). Nearly a dozen foreign architects were working for FBO at the time.[9] Of the ongoing projects, the AAC urged extensive revisions to four and rejected two— Beirut and Leopoldville—as unacceptable. The AAC found the scheme for consular offices and staff housing in Leopoldville "ungracious and uninviting" and declared the overall design inappropriate for the tropics.[10] They urged FBO to hire a new architect for that project, and within months FBO awarded the contract to Weed, Russell, Johnson Associates of Miami. The AAC also found many problems with the proposal by Mence & Moore for Port of Spain. When Belluschi saw the sketches, he was appalled. "I will not hide from you my sense of shock at the lack of competency shown by these sketches," he wrote to Hughes. "Perhaps the first sketches submitted by the architects were a rehash of what must be prevalent in Trinidad." Shepley found them "immaturely conceived and uncoordinated."[11] Disappointment with the quality of this work made AAC members more convinced of the rightness of the new hire-American policy.

Ironically, the move to hire only Americans added to the direct cost of the building program since FBO had been able to pay foreign-based architects with foreign currency in place of new tax dollars. The policy shift, however, did not prevent American firms from hiring local architects to assist with working drawings or to provide useful site-specific knowledge. Waiving the chance to hire local architects as principals, FBO passed up a major opportunity to invest in local talent, but that was not its priority. No single factor contributed more to the American flavor of the foreign buildings than the fact that they were designed by Americans—as a matter of policy.

Criticism of plans for staff housing in Manila and Bangkok focused on questions about practical matters such as laundry, garbage, storage, and the availability of hot water. The AAC concluded that the local custom of employing servants necessitated larger kitchens and additional exits at these posts. Otherwise servants would have to carry laundry and garbage through living spaces while families entertained or slept. After reviewing the Manila project four times, the AAC also urged FBO to increase the allowable size of bedrooms and living rooms, to add a servants' toilet on each floor, and to provide storage areas for baby carriages and bicycles. Both projects prompted the AAC to ask formally for a revision in the Bureau of Budget's building standards, which were then used as specifications for all federally-funded housing. As the AAC pointed out, standards that applied to domestic housing simply did not suit housing abroad, particularly housing in tropical regions. It urged an increase in space and argued that such an increase was "necessary because of fundamental differences in requirements resulting from climate, customs, living conditions, and greater dependability [sic] upon native help in lieu of the services and appliances generally available in the United States."[12]

While honest concern for local customs and sensibilities did indeed prompt many of these suggestions, other factors were equally significant. The AAC frowned upon the sight of hanging laundry, for example, and urged Dailey to provide indoor drying facilities at the Manila apartments "to prevent and preclude possibility of laundry being hung outside where it would be objectionable." Objectionable to whom? Surely not to local people who knew no other method of drying clothes. Architects who visited foreign places and paid attention to what they saw were naturally most likely to understand and appreciate local customs, finding charm where others saw only vulgarity. For instance, when San Francisco architect William Wurster visited Hong Kong as he prepared to design the consulate general there in 1954, the festive atmosphere delighted him, and he was particularly impressed by the laundry which he saw hanging across the streets on poles. The drying clothes reminded Wurster of floating banners, and he urged other architects to make the most of such displays.[13] Not everyone shared that view. In banning outdoor laundry at Manila, AAC members disregarded the fact that laundry does not dry properly hanging indoors in hot and humid places and also ignored the added cost of electricity and maintenance associated with mechanical drying. Clearly, theirs was an aesthetic objection. Such clashes between the practical and the artistic were not uncommon in AAC deliberations.

The Jakarta embassy project illustrates a different sort of clash—a clash between the practical and the political. Indonesian president Sukarno strongly objected to Raymond & Rado's first scheme. Evidence suggests that Sukarno, adept at playing off East against West, had hoped that the United States would build a high-rise tower, something suitably impressive to symbolize the importance of his capital city. Moreover, he wanted the building to dramatize his own importance and underscore the U.S. commitment to him, as opposed to his guerrilla foes.

The first scheme featured an unimposing two-story building with sunshades over the front-facing windows, fixed louvers over windows on the sunnier side, and a simple *porte cochère* (a covered space adjoining a building's entry) in front of an entrance set back from the street on a circular driveway. The relatively small building did not satisfy the Indonesian president. Cables crossed the ocean carrying complaints and veiled political threats as the job was suspended. Sukarno wanted assurances about the retention of a handsome rain tree on the property, he wanted the building set back further to accentuate its prominence, and he wanted a building designed specifically for the local climate rather than one designed, as he suggested this had been, for a cool climate with sunshades appended. He also wanted a much taller building that would set the tone for development around its site, the corner of a prominent downtown square.[14]

The AAC decided that the building was adequate as it was designed. To allow the Indonesians to avoid embarrassment, members agreed to ask the architects to redesign the entrance and add a small reflecting pool to make the whole appear "more impressive."[15] Not only did the AAC members defend the building's suitability to its climate and site, which, incidentally, none of the principals had visited, but they also defended its scale and character, and pointed out, "that having once built a tall building in an area surrounded by low buildings (as we did in Havana), the mistake should not be repeated." A stern cable signed by Secretary of State Dulles urged the Embassy to get Sukarno to agree right away to the design modifications or else to expect retaliation against his diplomats in Washington.[16] The architects made the requested modifications, and Sukarno agreed to accept them. Already delayed well over a year, the sorely needed project proceeded at last (fig. 48).

To the front of the embassy, the architects added a scallop-shaped, thin-shell *porte-cochère* designed by engineer Paul Weidlinger and two decorative screens—one made of thin slabs of white marble and another made of dark blue painted iron. On the iron screen, under the canopy roof and behind the pool, they hung a large replica of the Great Seal of the United States, the national symbol displayed with varying prominence on most embassies. "I am not real proud of it," Rado later remarked about the Jakarta project. He was troubled by the idea of using decorative devices to "dress up" his small building. He was pleased, however, that Sukarno "swallowed it."[17] When *Architectural Forum* featured the embassy in its December 1957 issue, it criticized the architects for overlooking the unusual indigenous architecture, including the "astonishing 'buffalo horn' roof profiles," as inspiration. But since the architects were trying to provide economical and efficient office space, their preference for what the magazine called "international tropical" was sensible, and their willingness to accommodate local inclinations was pragmatic. In the history of the building program, architects willing to compromise in order to expedite the construction of a badly needed facility are relatively rare. But such compromise is often commendable and ought not be unilaterally dismissed by critics as "selling out."

The Jakarta embassy was important because it showed the State Department that it could use the AAC effectively as an expert body whose decision was essentially beyond reproach. Sukarno was informed that the "experts" approved of the design. As the minutes show, FBO modified the design only to provide the Indonesians with a political face saver.

AS PART OF ITS FIRST DUTIES, the AAC outlined general procedures for nominating architects and for reviewing their work, although both procedures were only vaguely defined. Members examined brochures submitted to FBO by interested architects, requested lists from friends and colleagues, and exchanged names among themselves. In recommending architects to FBO, the AAC stepped in to fill a role formerly assumed by FBO director and chief architect Leland King. When Rep. Thomas J. Dodd (D-Conn.) queried King in 1953 about how he had come to select Skidmore, Owings & Merrill to design the German consular buildings, King vaguely answered that there were eighteen hundred qualified firms in the United States, never actually saying that he had reviewed the credentials of all (or any) of those firms. Thirty years later, FBO director William Slayton echoed this response when he described the same selection process. Profiles of "some 800" firms were listed in a computer file distributed to each member of the advisory committee, he noted, without specifically saying that the files were actually reviewed.[18] Though Slayton conveyed the idea of a selection process that was technical, rigorous, and somehow objective, the process remained necessarily subjective.

In 1953, congressmen demanded a better-defined selection system, and envious architects clamored for better access to the prestigious government work. In the reorganization, what changed was not how selections were made, but who made them. Both before and after the AAC was established, the professional network that existed among architects was the principal source of architects' names. It is particularly apt to refer to this as "the old boys' network" as there were few women practicing architecture in the 1950s and even fewer elected to Congress or holding top positions in executive departments. While they were occasionally charged with responsibility for representational duties at posts abroad, women had little input into the building program. Architects Chloethiel Woodard Smith (Asunción) and Victorine Homsey (Tehran) were the only women who participated in design deliberations as principals between 1954 and 1976. Two other women played an important role in congressional debate on the subject of foreign buildings: Edna F. Kelly (D-N.Y.) and Frances P. Bolton (R-Ohio). Bolton's sensible questions and astute observations stand out markedly in the proceedings of the Hays subcommittee. Her prescient interest in Africa (she personally paid for a committee study mission to Africa) and her commonsense attitude toward household management were invaluable assets in debate over new construction, particularly housing. Her comments suggest that other knowledgeable men *and* women who could afford to be candid in their views (as she could) would have been welcome assets to these deliberations.

FBO notified the AAC in January 1954 that the department wanted to move ahead quickly with ten new projects. The agenda for that year included office buildings in Lagos, Dakar, Hong Kong, Nagoya, and Tegucigalpa; offices and apartments in Fukuoka, Kobe, Juarez, and Asunción; and a residence in Tangier.[19] Of these, all proceeded except Juarez and Dakar. If project architects thought that they were dealing with imposing or large projects, they were mistaken. All of these projects were modest in size, most averaging about 10,000 square feet. These were not opportunities to reinvent the Lever House.

Limited by a cutback in its annual appropriation, FBO proposed only those new projects that could be paid for with available funds and put off until 1955 and later other equally pressing projects. The 1955 agenda included office buildings in Port-au-Prince (12,000 square feet, maximum), The Hague (37,500 square feet, maximum), and the largest of the proposed projects, New Delhi (50,000 square feet, maximum).

As they compiled lists and exchanged the names of architects, AAC members began the task of pairing names with the jobs on the FBO agenda. In addition to architects already known to them, the AAC reviewed lists maintained by FBO and later even solicited names from architectural editors. When congressmen inquired as to how their constituents might qualify for consideration, they were advised that the selection process was apolitical and that it was handled by experts. Interested architects were told to submit brochures to FBO. There were more than sixty on file when the AAC began its duties, but the AAC only occasionally devoted meeting time to reviewing the brochures on hand. It is apparent from a review of members' notes and letters that most of the names came from their own contacts and familiarity with the profession. They were attracted to current "stars" and what they expected to be the next generation of leaders. When Eustis Dearborn, a little-known Stamford, Connecticut, architect wrote to Shepley in 1955 asking him to consider his firm for an FBO job, his chances of being selected were slim.[20]

The AAC was looking for architects known by their experience or reputations as likely to come up with imaginative schemes, architects whose prominence and flair would add luster to the overall building program. They were anxious to include men like Neutra, and later Gropius and Breuer, hoping they would create original and provocative designs that would bring notice to the program at home and abroad. Even the name of Frank Lloyd Wright, whose career was in eclipse at that time, appears on a number of lists, though it seems that he was never seriously considered for a commission. In 1958, Shepley wrote to Hughes saying that he was willing to take a chance on Wright, but a month later, after seeing Wright's designs for the University of Baghdad, he changed his mind and wrote again to Hughes to withdraw his earlier suggestion, saying, "I think he has 'had it.'"[21]

The AAC was also willing to take risks with younger people, architects who had never before completed major commercial or institutional projects. Paul Rudolph had designed and built only vacation houses in Florida when the AAC picked him to design the embassy in Amman in 1954. Minoru Yamasaki, Hugh Stubbins, and Chloethiel Woodard Smith were all in their early forties and just at the beginning of prominent architectural careers when they won similar commissions. Architects most adept at creating distinguished small buildings were often those involved in residential work; hence the AAC was willing to consider men such as Rudolph, or later, John Johansen. Inexperience showed, however, and valuable time and money were wasted as some of the architects wrestled with the demands of the program.

Relevant expertise was certainly another selection criterion. Though Smith was young and relatively inexperienced, she knew more about South America than most other American architects, having lived and worked in Bolivia when her husband, Bromley K. Smith, a Foreign Service officer, was posted there in 1944. Her work in La Paz brought her honors from the local architectural community and led to her appointment in 1948 as chairman of the AIA Committee on Pan-American Affairs. As Bolivia borders Paraguay, it made sense for the AAC to select Smith to design the embassy in Asunción.

AAC members considered ethnicity when pairing architects with host countries, selecting, for example, Americans of Japanese ancestry for projects in Japan: Minoru Yamasaki in Kobe (1954), and George T. Rockrise in Fukuoka (1958).[22] Yamasaki designed mostly houses until he won commissions for the St. Louis Airport and the Kobe consulate. The airport job, completed in 1956, brought his young firm Hellmuth, Yamasaki & Leinweber numerous awards and established its international reputation just as the Kobe project reached completion.

The names of Yamasaki and Rockrise, along with that of George Matsumoto, appear together on several of the early AAC lists. One list even contains a pencil note that says "1/2 Jap." next to Rockrise's name. This would indicate some intention to pair these architects with projects located in Japan on the theory that they might bring a special sensitivity to the task of designing buildings there. Later, AAC members paired Argentine-American architect Eduardo Catalano with the chancery project in Buenos Aires (1970), and African-American architect Robert Madison with the chancery project in Dakar (awarded first in 1965 and renewed in 1972), although no official policy guided this effort.

AAC members had agreed at their first meeting that they would not actually pick architects; realizing that they could only suggest names anyhow, they made lists that they shared among themselves and then turned over to FBO with specific recommendations. Shepley's personal papers contain a number of lists, some with annotations by himself and some by his assistant, Jean Paul Carlhian. His records also contain lists by Belluschi and others.

On one list, compiled prior to March 1954, Shepley lists twenty-seven architects. Those whose names are marked with checks include Paul Rudolph, Hugh Stubbins, Morris Ketchum, Carl Koch, Marcel Breuer, Walter Gropius, Holabird & Root, Josep Lluis Sert, Edward Durell Stone, Robert Hutchins, Vernon De Mars, Roland Wank, Walter Kilham Jr., and Henry Hill. Of those fourteen, eleven subsequently received FBO contracts. Others whose names are marked with X's include: Ludwig Mies van der Rohe, I. M. Pei, Frank Lloyd Wright, Philip Johnson, Carl Feiss, George F. Keck, Lorimer Rich, and Charles Eames. Mies and Pei also subsequently received contracts. From a list of forty-two potential architects compiled by Belluschi sometime early in 1954, twenty-eight eventually received FBO commissions (see Appendix B).

At a time when the AAC members only knew the agenda for 1954 and 1955 (a total of thirteen projects), its members had generated much longer lists of possible architects. Belluschi's potential candidates eventually received contracts for a total of twenty-nine FBO projects. Aside from Louis Kahn's contract for the Luanda consulate, which he received in 1959, all of the others were awarded between 1954 and 1957, a period during which FBO awarded a total of fifty new design contracts. If 56 percent of the contracts awarded over the next four years were assigned to architects whose names were suggested in the first weeks of 1954, it is apparent that architects were selected primarily for *who* they were, rather than for what they might be expected to accomplish at a specific site with a particular design problem. This means that the selection process, though tailored to the projects to some extent, largely consisted of identifying those architects who were already widely admired and thought to "deserve" an FBO commission. Architects were in effect selected before the projects were even identified.

As they reviewed the lists of names, the AAC members made tentative assignments to projects, generally including at least two choices for each job. Shepley's working list, for example, reveals that Stone was his first choice for New Delhi, Neutra his second. For Asunción, he listed Sert first and Neutra again second. For Tangier, Rudolph is listed first, with Koch the number two choice. Weed is listed as first choice for both Leopoldville and Lagos, and the firm of Hare & Hatch, partners who subsequently split into two firms, is linked with Tegucigalpa. For Beirut, the list shows Ernest Kump as first choice and Gropius as second. Rudolph is number one for Amman, as is Hutchins for Dakar. There is no indication of which jobs are housing and which are office buildings on these preliminary rosters. Lists compiled later in the program include such information, plus the location of each architect's practice, data supposedly considered by FBO.

By early March, the AAC made its first official selection, recommending William Wurster for the consulate general in Hong Kong (fig. 49). Wurster was a partner in Wurster, Bernardi & Emmons and dean of the College of Environmental Design at Berkeley. He had worked in the office of John Lyon Reid in San Francisco and also in the Delano & Aldrich office in New York. Prior to 1954 he had designed mostly houses. His work had been featured in *House Beautiful* and *Architectural Forum*, and he was already known as an architect whose work reflected the character of its locale. He was no extremist, but he was certainly a committed modernist. All said, he was precisely the sort of well-connected professional that the AAC might have been expected to select.

By the end of that month, FBO had awarded five new architectural and engineering contracts, including a contract to Michael Hare for the design of an embassy and a separate residence in Tegucigalpa, contracts to Weed, Russell, Johnson Associates for the design of consular offices and staff housing in Leopoldville and Lagos, and a contract to Edward Durell Stone for New Delhi. Wurster signed his contract on 11 March and returned on 16 June with his first presentation. Thereafter, the others began to present their schemes, and additional contracts were awarded to Rudolph, Yamasaki, Moore & Hutchins, Stubbins, and Smith. By the end of 1954, FBO had retained nine firms for a total of ten new projects, and a new phase of the program was well underway.

Although it was created by the State Department, the AAC did not turn into a rubber stamp for FBO. And though architects saw it as a means to boost the careers of colleagues, it did not turn into a professional grandstand either. The advisory architects generally supported project architects, preferring to help them rework and revise schemes rather than hire replacements. In order to protect the artistic independence of their professional colleagues, they often found themselves in the uncomfortable position of defending work about which they had serious misgivings, but they were not reluctant to criticize the work of project architects during review sessions; indeed, they leveled harsh criticism at those whose work they deemed inadequate.

Beleaguered with troubles, Rudolph's Amman embassy project illustrates how far the AAC was willing to go in defense of artistic freedom, but also how difficult it was to work with architects who seemed unable or unwilling to meet program requirements. Artistic differences also arose at Tegucigalpa, where architect Michael Hare tried to defend his own artistry, but the AAC refused to be drawn into a squabble that pitted artistic expression against professional obligation. Both examples show how the AAC functioned and how its members defined their purview.

Paul Rudolph studied under Gropius and Breuer at Harvard, and appeared on numerous AAC selection lists. Evidently the architects on the AAC recognized the talents of the young architect who had already won several major design awards and had recently joined the design faculty at Yale. When the AAC tapped Rudolph for Amman his design repertoire consisted almost exclusively of imaginary projects and beach cottages, including his "Umbrella House" in Florida (1953). The Amman commission was his first major multipurpose office building.

The Amman site was an urban square bounded by wide streets. The scheme that Rudolph presented in August 1954 and later revised showed a rectangular two-story building with a nine-bay façade topped by an umbrella roof created out of a series of low or flattened barrel vaults supported on exterior columns (fig. 50). With no air-conditioning, it was supposed to be kept cool by its open roof, its thick masonry walls, and the placement of its tiny, recessed windows. The whole structure was raised on a low podium and accessible at its entrance by a double flight of stairs. In his rendering, Rudolph tried to show that his arched bays fit well with the local surrounding architecture. Unfortunately, critics were not impressed by his effort.

AAC chairman Col. Harry McBride vociferously opposed the design. His objections carried added weight not only because he was chairman, but also because they mirrored views held by other State Department officials and by potential critics on Capitol Hill. From the outset, McBride thought that the design was not suitable as an American embassy. As originally drafted, minutes of the August meeting indicated that the *parti* and scheme were "approved enthusiastically" by the committee. But at McBride's insistence the minutes were revised and that comment was deleted and replaced with the words "considered interesting."[23] Even the architect members who tried to show enthusiasm for the scheme found problems with its umbrella roof; criticized the interior for its overall darkness; asked the architect to revise the design of the entrance, window openings, and column spacing; and told him to restudy all of the interior stairs and exits to meet security and fire regulations that had been largely ignored.

Following the presentation in Washington, Walker and Shepley were so troubled by the design that Walker wrote directly to Rudolph to ask more questions about the proposal. Since the AAC minutes show so little of the back and forth that accompanies the review process and the personalities of the individual participants, Walker's letter is remarkable for what it reveals about both. His own ever-present concern about "stunt" architecture is the principal focus. He opened his letter with words of encouragement, admitting, however, that the scheme seemed "experimental," one thing that the program was supposed to avoid. His comments help to explain McBride's consternation:

> I got from Colonel McBride just the kind of reaction you might encounter from people who do not admire modern architecture merely because it is

new, especially in its delineation, and who sometimes feel at a loss to understand it. Therefore he is quite worried about the quality of design. I assured
him that I though the design was very fine, and while definitely an experiment I thought it could be developed into something that would be greatly
admired and [meet] the needs of the Mission at Amman.[24]

In the same letter, Walker suggested that Rudolph flatten the arc of the
ribs supporting the umbrella roof and asked him to consider how his small,
recessed windows were going to be washed, adding sensibly, "I believe that
an American Embassy should be clean looking in every aspect, not only
philosophically but it should be easy to maintain." He criticized the second
story projection for its "unpleasant bumpy appearance," which he urged
the architect to handle with more finesse. As to the building's relationship
to its surroundings, Walker said, "I can understand your delight in having
a tradition where two floors do not actually coincide as a starting point for
creating an interesting building," but he cautioned Rudolph, noting, "Again,
I think an American Embassy should be housed in a building which is very
monumental, and I say your design can so develop, but I think it should be
done in such a way that it will not look like a stunt." Writing with an almost
professorial tone, Walker reassured the young architect, saying, "Your mind
is naturally critical and I think if you can look at this design with a possible future feeling for it, and I know how difficult that is, the design will
become disciplined into something all of us will like much better." Then, in
a comment that sums up the pitfalls of aping local motifs, he added, "Henry
Shepley wondered whether you were not out-Arabing the Arabs."

In closing, Walker urged Rudolph to "always remember that you are the
architect and in the long run it is your judgment which has to be satisfied as
well as that of your client," and he emphasized that his criticism was intended to be "friendly," not harsh. The reminder that he was the architect was his
way of saying that he and the AAC recognized the primacy of his position as
the consulting architect and that they would bend as far as possible to defend
his judgment. Walker shared his letter with McBride, Shepley, and Belluschi.
While the evidence in the minutes suggests that McBride was Rudolph's lone
opponent, Walker's letter indicates that the others shared at least some of
McBride's reservations.

The AAC reviewed the Amman design five times. Each time the archi-
tect promised further study. Late in November, Belluschi agreed to contact
Rudolph to try to resolve outstanding differences. Belluschi reported back to
FBO asking for more space and more money for the building in order to give
Rudolph the chance to make his design successful.[25] Walker also reassured

Rudolph, gently trying to coax him into modifications, but affirming his own commitment to the architect's artistic independence.

The architects may have had misgivings about Rudolph's work, but only McBride openly objected to the architecture. He classified the proposal as "an architectural experiment," something precluded by the new design policy, and declared simply that the design was "not dignified, distinguished or appropriate for an American Embassy."[26] Citing the dissension among AAC members, FBO director Hughes wrote to the architect to express his dismay at the scheme, which he thought resembled "a fort, an outpost of the foreign legion." Like the earlier letter from Walker, Hughes's letter reveals the review process to be far more critical and delicate than is conveyed in the politeness of the official minutes. He may have been flattering Rudolph when he told him that the advisory architects found his latest drawings "brilliant and outstanding," but he was quite direct in letting him know that the architect members had agreed that they could only defend a design from outside criticism if it showed "dignity and character," qualities that the design supposedly lacked.[27]

Hughes was clear in reiterating McBride's opposition and added his own observation that the perspective renderings gave the impression of a stockade. Hughes went on to rebuke Rudolph for continuing to ignore various program requirements, such as placement of adjoining offices, and for insufficient study of practical requirements, such as "stairs, toilets, incinerator, chimney, location and swing of doors, etc." Other problems included the fact that the ambassador's office was "remote and buried" within the building. Also, the ambassador's office was supposed to be adjacent to the Political Section, not the Economic Section; all rooms were supposed to have doors; partitions were supposed to run to the ceiling; and too many exterior doors compromised the building's security. For fire protection, stairs were supposed to be enclosed and one stair had to exit directly to the outside; the open well through the second floor was not permitted, sprinklers were needed in the garage, and other fire protection and prevention features were supposed to conform to U.S. standards, which they did not. The proposed scheme was also approximately one-third larger than it was supposed to be.

The AAC architects made every effort to defend the design and the capability of the architect, reluctantly approving the scheme in January 1955 (in McBride's absence). But delays over design differences had already taken a toll on the project. Political turmoil eventually caused the United States to revise its priorities for Jordan, and the project was sidelined. So when *Architectural Forum* noted only that it was "suspended indefinitely because of Middle East unrest," the magazine was being kind to the architect.[28] The Jordan project illustrates the difficulties faced by the AAC when its architect members tried to defend a colleague. It shows, also, the importance of having a nonarchitect on the panel—someone unburdened by professional loyalties who could declare, when necessary, that the emperor was indeed naked.

Michael M. Hare was another architect who clashed with FBO over program requirements. Unlike Rudolph's Amman project, Hare's two Tegucigalpa projects were built, but the architect's failure to understand local conditions seriously compromised his completed work. Furthermore, Hare lacked Rudolph's credentials and reputation. While Rudolph managed to maintain strong support from architects on the AAC despite serious problems with his designs, Hare found no such support when he appealed to his professional colleagues for help in resolving his differences with FBO. Partially because of the way he approached them, and partially because of his own obstinacy, the advisory architects told Hare to abide by the wishes of his client and did nothing to support his aesthetic grievance.

Hare had graduated from Yale, studied architecture in Paris, and received his architectural degree from Columbia in 1935. Until just before he won the Tegucigalpa commission from FBO in 1954, he had been in partnership with Donald E. Hatch, who had an office in New York and had also opened an office in Caracas right after the war. Together, Hare and Hatch designed a number of buildings in Venezuela in the early 1950s, including a major hotel in 1953. Thus they were well-positioned to vie for State Department work in South America. AAC members considered both architects for commissions. FBO retained Hare early in 1954 for a chancery and a residence in Tegucigalpa, and Hatch won commissions for chanceries in Port-au-Prince (1955) and Caracas (1957).

Founded in the sixteenth century, Tegucigalpa is located at an altitude of 3,300 feet in a region known for its silver and gold mines. In presenting Hare's designs in 1955, *Architectural Record* described the climate as "ideal."[29] Obviously, the architect thought so too, because what he provided were two buildings wrapped in partially screened walkways and surrounded by open verandas. Both buildings are distinguished by their use of local brick, stone, and wrought iron, their high ceilings, their reinforced concrete construction, and their sharply sloping roofs. The embassy and the residence were sited separately. The office building was located downtown, while the residence was outside of the city on a hillside site chosen for its fine view of the Honduran landscape below (fig. 51). The AAC complimented Hare on his *partis*, and approved both schemes asking for only a few minor changes.

The project proceeded uneventfully until Hughes instructed the architect to make one change in the east wall of the ambassador's library at the residence—the addition of a window "to take advantage of the wonderful view from that room." Hughes made it clear that he wanted "a large picture window." When Hare was not forthcoming with the requested drawings, Hughes had his own architects prepare a sketch and sent it to Hare. The very day on which he received Hughes's letter, Hare sent him an angry telegram refusing to make the change and demanding a ruling from the AAC. Further, he accused Hughes of undermining the "principle inherent in retaining private architects" and of attempting to destroy his architecture. He followed the telegram with a longer letter in which he outlined his objections in more detail and deepened his own predicament by telling Hughes:

> I am positive that this idea did not originate in your office because it would be clear to any architect of sensibility that the introduction of such a feature is strictly a vulgarity which has no place in a building which purports to represent the best of the United States. In effect we would be taking a symbol of suburbia and inserting it in a representational building. There is no objection to the basic idea underlying a picture window. What is objectionable is the debasement of the idea.[30]

Hare also sent a letter to Shepley sharing his predicament and begging Shepley to intervene "in the interest of the profession." Hare knew that the AAC had no authority, and he knew also that he had no right to go over Hughes's head, so he advised Shepley to proceed with discretion. Shepley's response was brief and to the point:

> I got your letter and the material you sent me. The window does damage but your client is evidently determined to have it, and it appears has been for some time. His is a legitimate point—cannot be disregarded. If you will look at the situation objectively, you will realize that your sending a telegram of the kind that you did has made it impossible for any of us to plead your cause. I am sorry but you will have to solve this one yourself, and I do not think it should be impossible.[31]

Writing again to Shepley, Hare attributed his brash telegram to his temporary "state of shock," and then launched into another curious argument about cutting down a rare and beautiful shade tree that would obscure the view from the proposed new window. Then he threatened to write an open letter to the architectural publications if the State Department failed to show him deference. Defiantly he wrote, "I think there is an important principle involved when the Department makes decisions involving aesthetics and issues change orders without prior consultation with the architect."[32] The department had tried to consult with him, but he had wanted no compromise.

This incident illustrates the gap that existed between some architects and the government client in terms of expectations and needs, both aesthetic and practical. Members of the AAC could do nothing to assist an angry young architect who allowed himself to go into shock over one window. When Shepley sent copies of Hare's letters to Belluschi, he added a note that said "[Hare] will get nowhere writing letters full of architectural jargon."[33]

Other architects were also dismayed when program changes affected their designs. For many, the embassies they designed for FBO were their first major multipurpose office building projects. Some proudly listed their work for the State Department in subsequent biographical listings, and some omitted it. I. M. Pei, for one, disowned his FBO work over design differences that emerged as changes were made to the program for the embassy in Montevideo (1960).

There was much more wrong at Tegucigalpa than a single misplaced window, however. It seems that the architect had paid little heed to the FBO design guidelines, and it also seems that the AAC was insufficiently familiar with the site to know what would work there. In 1958 Louisa Willauer, wife of the American ambassador, wrote to Shepley—who she thought would lend a sympathetic ear—concerning conditions at the post:

> As far as [the residence] as a whole is concerned, I do not believe you were told that it rains six months out of the year in Tegucigalpa or you would not have approved a building in which one cannot walk from the bedrooms to the other parts of the house without being drenched by rain and blown by wind. And I do not think you could have known that the building site had been chosen because of its view when you approved a twenty-foot wall directly in front blocking off that view. By the way, the view was blocked off from every room in the house except the breakfast room.[34]

Willauer cited other inconveniences: bathroom doors that could not be opened when two beds were placed in the bedrooms; no lights in the bathrooms. She objected to having only one linen closet (located in the dining room) and noted that although there were five master bedrooms, "there was no place inside the house where a table and chairs could be placed for the servants to eat." She added also that when two cars were parked side-by-side in the two-car garage, no one could get in or out of either of them. Further, she made the important observation that despite FBO's claim that economy dictated all of the apparent deficiencies, the cost of maintaining the poorly planned and needlessly extravagant residence forced the State Department to raise the local expense allowance dramatically.

Aesthetic decisions of the sort that Hare fought over, Willauer continued, ignored the functional needs of Foreign Service personnel. In consideration of the local climate and the lack of recreational and entertainment facilities in Tegucigalpa, for example, the post had requested a small swimming pool, which would have cost several thousand dollars at most. Instead, FBO approved construction of a $10,000 lily pond. The economic excuse, Willauer pointed out, was being falsely employed.

Despite all of the sensible comments in the Willauer letter, when Hughes received a copy from Shepley he dismissed the ambassador's wife as a nuisance. Once the buildings were built, criticism of them was criticism of FBO. The identity of the individual architects more or less faded out of the picture. Even on Capitol Hill, the harsh assessment of many new buildings almost never led to direct criticism of individual architects, and few people, aside from those who read architectural publications, were even aware of the names. Hughes was not interested in criticism that could affect his budget, and by the time that Shepley learned of the problems at Tegucigalpa, his AAC term was long behind him.

RICHARD M. BENNETT REPLACED Walker on the AAC in March 1956. Bennett was a partner in the Chicago firm of Loebl, Schlossman & Bennett, and at forty-seven he was younger than the others. He had taught architecture at Pratt, Vassar, and Yale, and served as chairman of Yale's Department of Architecture in the mid-1940s. A graduate of the Harvard GSD, he had been appointed an AIA Fellow in 1946 and was active in AIA affairs. Bennett was Edward Durell Stone's first employee, with whom he worked on sketches for the Museum of Modern Art (1939), and he became widely known when he won first prize with Caleb Hornbostel in the competition for an art building at Wheaton College in 1938. Although that project was never built, the competition was a key event in Bennett's career. Jurors selected the Bennett design over entries by Gropius and Breuer, Bunshaft, Neutra, Stubbins, Howe, and others, they said, because it fit better into the picturesque New England countryside.[35] For a program that ostensibly prized context, Bennett was a fine choice.

Early in September 1956, Belluschi and Shepley asked FBO director Hughes about the possibility of adding Eero Saarinen to the AAC panel. Hughes expressed his willingness to pursue the nomination and told the architects that he would check further in the department.[36] He wrote to Deputy Under Secretary Loy Henderson recommending Saarinen as "one of the foremost modern architects in America" and asked for approval. Hughes acknowledged that Saarinen was working for FBO on two commissions (London and Oslo), but assured Henderson that neither project was likely to come before the panel officially again. Henderson, however, rejected the Saarinen nomination, saying that as long as the architect was engaged in FBO work, he could not serve on the advisory committee. As alternatives he suggested architects who had nothing in common with Saarinen— James Kellum Smith, a partner in the New York firm of McKim, Mead, and White, designer of the Wharton School of Finance and Management at the University of Pennsylvania, and president of the American Academy in Rome; others affiliated with Harbeson, Hough, Livingston & Larson of Philadelphia; and Eggers & Higgins of New York. He cited these men "for their good taste and concern for traditional American values."[37] Henderson's assistant I. W. Carpenter later explained that Henderson actually rejected Saarinen "because of his modernistic viewpoint."[38]

Henderson made it clear that he wanted someone who thought along traditional lines. In response to his directive, FBO turned to Edgar I. Williams. Like Walker and Belluschi, Williams had MIT ties. He graduated from MIT in 1908, received his architectural degree from the school in 1909, and studied for three additional years at the American Academy in Rome, after winning its first Prix de Rome in 1909. He taught at MIT, opened his New York practice in 1920, and was for many years consulting architect to the New York Public Library.[39] He was president of the National Academy of Design, the Architectural League of New York, and the Municipal Art Society. He was already in his seventies when named to the AAC.

Henderson and other State Department officials thought of Williams as a traditionalist when they named him to replace Shepley, but Williams himself disputed that notion. "No architecture is good if it is not contemporary," he wrote in a letter to Hughes, "but being contemporary does not necessarily make it good. I suspect it was expected of me to be the conservative on your committee—perhaps, even that my architectural diet consisted largely of dentils and accanthus [sic]. It has been too boring to try to combat such a foolish thought."[40] While Williams was on the panel, FBO retained Milton Grigg to add two office annexes to the embassy in Canberra, a red-brick "colonial" building much admired by Representative Rooney. But during Williams's tenure, FBO also retained Mies and younger modernists such as Edward Larrabee Barnes and John Carl Warnecke. Mies designed a stark modern glass box as a consulate for São Paulo, but the project was never built (fig. 52). Likewise, the Warnecke project, an embassy for Bangkok, remained paper-only. Barnes designed a handsome consulate in Tabriz that adapted local architectural themes to modern use. It was realized, although later abandoned amidst the Iranian revolution.

In a debate with Philip Johnson in 1950, Williams presented the case for what he called "traditional" architecture. He defined traditional as

> The sense that the spirit of the people of a locale, deriving its character from the traditions of the people above all other considerations, gives life, interest and vitality to the architecture of the locale....This thought is opposed to the view that the architecture should be international in character. Between the international concept and the egotistic personal concept of architecture, both of which I believe represent the so-called modern point of view, there is great confusion. I find it paradoxical that those who speak contemptuously of eclecticism and advocate originality are quite ready to snatch up the clichés of contemporary Brazilian, French or other distant architecture.[41]

For a program that aimed to combine modern building technology with local tradition, Williams added a useful perspective. He replaced Shepley in January 1957. That month also, Hughes announced that the advisory group, formerly known as the "Architectural Advisory Committee," would be officially known henceforth as the "Architectural Advisory Panel" (AAP). Williams served on the AAP from 1957 to 1959.

Once Williams had joined the panel, Henderson asked Hughes to think about Harrie T. Lindeberg, the antithesis of a modernist, as a possible replacement for Belluschi, whose extended term was set to expire in June 1957. Hughes replied by asking for Saarinen again. Henderson's assistant, Carpenter, advised Hughes to submit at least two additional names along with Saarinen's. As part of his strategy to secure the job for Saarinen, Hughes submitted two names that Henderson was not likely to approve: traditionalist Thomas H. Locraft and modernist Percival Goodman. Locraft practiced in Washington with Frederick V. Murphy and was chairman of the architecture department at Catholic University. Goodman practiced in New York City and taught city planning and design at Columbia. He was best known for his design of Jewish synagogues.[42] Henderson made the expected move and approved Saarinen. After three and a half years representing the most modern viewpoint on the AAP, Belluschi resigned in June. Saarinen joined Bennett and Williams as a panel member in July 1957 and served through June 1960. Subsequent panelists included Berkeley dean William Wurster, Roy F. Larson, MIT dean Lawrence B. Anderson, and Washington University (St. Louis) dean Joseph R. Passonneau (see Appendix C). Due to the slowdown in the capital program, there were fewer projects to review in the 1960s than before. During the slow periods when the AAP did not meet or met infrequently, terms were extended.

Anderson, for one, served on the committee for ten years.

Distinguished architects continued to replace each other on the AAP and there were few gaps between their appointments, but the situation with the chairman's position was different. Largely due to the presence of McBride, early meetings included lively debate on matters of taste. Because of the tendency among the collected architects to treat McBride as if he were invisible, the nonarchitect chairman often had trouble getting the others to take his views seriously. Even the press release that announced the formation of the advisory group made no effort to convey his knowledge of art and architecture, his extensive familiarity with conditions at U.S. posts abroad, and his experience in building design and management.[43] Clearly, the architects did not care to acknowledge that McBride's expertise, that of a nonarchitect, was as valuable to the department as their own.

FBO anticipated that the committee's opinions would be unanimous and that its own staff would likewise concur with the decisions. Official minutes tried to find common ground among the participants and almost never identified individual opinions.[44] As the panel's nonarchitect, McBride became a conduit for dissenting views. He had an ally in Hughes, who shared his doubts about Amman and other projects, and his concerns often coincided with those of Henderson. Having a member of the panel who was willing to resist the pressure to concur with "experts" made the entire advisory committee more valuable to the State Department. Overall, McBride was the very sort of widely traveled and broadly experienced "lay" person whose views most benefited FBO. Certainly none of the architects had traveled as extensively, nor had any supervised a major government construction project as he had. But he was not an architect. Despite his knowledge, the architects managed to depict him as an outsider.

When McBride retired from the advisory committee in 1956, there was confusion about how to replace him. After a brief gap, during which there was no official chairman, the State Department named Raymond Hare, director general of the foreign service, in June 1956. Hare attended only a few meetings and departed from Washington soon afterward to resume his diplomatic duties as U.S. ambassador to Egypt. His absence created a gap that troubled no one. A year later the department filled the gap by naming Ambassador Joseph C. Satterthwaite to replace Hare. Satterthwaite had succeeded Hare as director general of the Foreign Service and remained on the panel until early 1959. Thus, a short-lived tradition was established for the director general, while on assignment in Washington, to serve as chairman of the advisory panel (see Appendix D). Over time, it became more difficult to fill the chairman's position from the high-ranking Foreign Service officers on temporary assignment in Washington, and the position slipped in importance. When Kenworthy selected McBride in 1953 as chairman, he said:

> Apart from his intimate knowledge of the State Department and the Foreign Service, Colonel McBride is well known and respected for his administrative ability and understanding of art matters. With Colonel McBride as chairman, the three architectural members would be on an equal basis in discussions.[45]

But that "equal basis" never became a reality. In fact, the rationale for the presence of a nonarchitect on the panel was lost upon those running the program within a few years. By the time that Assistant Secretary of State William Crockett appointed himself chairman of the advisory panel in 1961, few people remembered that the chairman was originally intended to be a knowledgeable nonarchitect, not a political insider. After 1967, when Crockett's tenure ended, the chairman's job more or less disappeared and the architects solidified their control over design review while also separating themselves further from the political process.

THE AAC MET thirteen times in 1954 and reviewed plans for twelve new projects, including eight embassy office buildings. At the same time, it recommended architects for the new jobs. The AAC met ten times in 1955 to review plans for eight projects, including six embassies (see Appendix E). One reason that the panel met fewer times in 1955 was that its members traveled that spring and summer to visit prospective sites. In 1956, the AAC met twelve times and reviewed plans for fifteen projects, ten of which were embassies. Members also served on the seven-man jury that judged the London competition in February. In the fall of 1956, FBO signed contracts with nine additional architects recommended by the panel. That year marked the high point of the building program in terms of total work under construction and under review. The AAC met nearly as many times as it did during its first year, but considered even more projects.

The embassies reviewed in 1956 included those in Accra (Harry Weese), Saigon (Curtis & Davis), London (competition winner Eero Saarinen), Manila (Alfred L. Aydelott), Ciudad Trujillo (Rogers, Taliaferro & Lamb),

Athens (Walter Gropius, TAC), Rabat (Ketchum, Gina & Sharp), Lima (Keyes & Lethbridge), Helsinki (Harwell Harris), and The Hague, (the same project as 1955, but with a new architect, Marcel Breuer). The three consulates were Nagoya (Alexander Smith Cochran), Basra (Harris Armstrong), and Tangier (a different project from the 1954 legation, but the same architect, Hugh Stubbins). The Saigon project was delayed many years, and the annex in Ciudad Trujillo was never built. Plans for the Helsinki office annex, a project first awarded to Saarinen and then to Harris, were again suspended. The others were built. Two other significant 1956 projects were staff housing in Belgrade by Carl Koch and the ambassador's residence in Tehran by Samuel and Victorine Homsey.

The advisory group, renamed AAP, met eleven times in 1957 and reviewed fourteen projects. Nine were new embassies: Bangkok (John Carl Warnecke), Beirut (Ralph Rapson), Algiers (John Lyon Reid), Taipei (Anderson, Beckwith & Haible and Campbell & Aldrich), Caracas (Don Hatch), Dublin (John Johansen), Mexico City (Southwestern Architects), Singapore (Jones & Emmons), and Warsaw (Welton Becket Associates). Nearly half of the projects reviewed in 1957 were eventually suspended, in most cases for lack of funds. Political unrest was another factor that affected plans. Rapson's 1957 design for Beirut, for example, was shelved after U.S. Marines landed in Lebanon in 1958 to prop up a regime engulfed in civil war. Difficulties in site acquisition caused delays that eventually led to cancellation of Warnecke's project in Bangkok. The number of new projects plummeted in 1958 and the panel met only four times. That year, the AAP reviewed designs for only one embassy, in Kabul (Kilham & O'Connor), and four consulates: Fukuoka (George T. Rockrise and Clark & Beuttler), São Paulo (Mies van der Rohe), Tabriz (Edward Larrabee Barnes), and Rotterdam (Victor Christ-Janer). Of those, Rotterdam and São Paulo were suspended, and Kabul was delayed and then turned over to another architectural firm. By 1958, the heyday of new construction had passed. The following year showed a further dip. The AAP met just five times in 1959 and reviewed plans for two new embassies, Ottawa (Harold Spitznagel and W. E. Bentzinger) and Mogadishu (Diegert and Yerkes), and a consulate in Palermo (Mario Ciampi)—but all were suspended. During 1956, however, FBO was busy with new work; expecting much more of the same, the advisory architects met frequently and reviewed many new projects. No one anticipated the delays, cancellations, and other problems that lay ahead.

CHAPTER EIGHT

The Program at Its Peak

THE PERIOD EXTENDING from 1954 through 1960 was the heyday of the American foreign building program. Those years were historically distinct from those before and after, so there is reason to examine as a group the embassies designed during that time. The program actually peaked between 1954 and 1957, if judged by the number of times the architectural advisors met and the number of new projects they reviewed. FBO was able to expand its operations until 1957 without seeking a new authorization or drawing upon new tax dollars. After 1958, shrinking funds, increased political interest and intervention, and changing world events led to a sharp decrease in the number of new projects and to far less frequent advisory committee meetings. However, many of the buildings commissioned in 1954 and 1955 were reaching completion in and around 1959 and 1960, creating the impression that the program was still thriving. American newspapers celebrated the opening of new embassies around the world, and architectural journals praised the significance of FBO commissions and the creativity of the architects.

Although membership on the AAC changed, the outlook of the advisory panel remained largely consistent throughout the period, guided as it was by the design policy outlined by Nelson Kenworthy in 1954 and subsequently reinterpreted by Pietro Belluschi. That policy shaped the State Department's architectural thinking until 1961, when political events prompted a reorganization at FBO and a new and more cautious statement of design policy.

Predictably, architects tried to use embassy commissions as a way of calling attention to their own inventiveness and artistic individuality. An architectural *tour de force* such as the New Delhi embassy by Edward Durell Stone attracted the most attention and drew the strongest support from AAC members (fig. 53). If there was one blind spot in the design vision at that time it was that architects seemed to think that a good design had to be at least somewhat bombastic; it was difficult for many to design buildings that were both beautiful and quiet. Furthermore, there was a tendency to look at embassies as if they were pavilions at world's fairs or airline terminals instead of distinguished-looking office buildings. This meant that embassy architecture shared a design vocabulary with structures intended for far different purposes, and it also meant that embassies became testing grounds for new design ideas. Minoru Yamasaki's design for the Eastern Airlines Terminal at Boston's Logan Airport (1967–69) bears a striking resemblance, for example, to prominent embassies from a decade earlier (fig. 54).

Everyone associated with the foreign building program understood that the State Department wanted its new architecture to convey the image of a young, vigorous, and forward-looking nation. Negative reaction to early postwar buildings had prompted a call for dignity and an avoidance of ostentation. In his 1954 statement, however, Belluschi offered little or no guidance on how to create a new image that combined dignity and tradition with a touch of exuberance and innovation, an image that joined elegance and optimism but managed to avoid looking lavish or materialistic. In fact, he offered no comment on the two most obvious problems faced by architects—how the new buildings should look and how they should be organized. Why? The advisory architects did not want to become involved in a debate over what the department referred to as "style," and they wanted to leave plan-related matters, such as program needs and functional arrangements, to be handled by the FBO staff.

In keeping with the departmental directive to promote international goodwill, the Belluschi statement called upon architects to pay special attention to local conditions and customs in an effort to grasp the meaning of particular environments. Where possible, Belluschi said, they should utilize new technology. He also urged them to use their talents to convey what he described as "a distinguishable American flavor," but he offered no clue as to how that might be achieved and made no effort to explain what might define architecture as uniquely "American."

Many architects responded to the new design directive by focusing on the exotic—much like the editors of *National Geographic*. The intentional vagueness of Belluschi's directive to create "American" landmarks, the clear message to explore the uniqueness of foreign places, and the impulse of architects to impress one another with work that was unusual and personal gave designers the chance to pursue new themes. They assumed that the State Department could best meet its goal of pleasing its foreign hosts by creating buildings that mirrored local design traditions, even if those traditions had nothing to do with office buildings, large or small. This assumption is controversial today, a time when culture critics battle over issues of authenticity and the appropriation of heritage, but it was not seriously questioned in the 1950s. Those architects who went the farthest in search of novelty to create a new and imaginative image for the United States, those whose work bordered on what may be called theme architecture, received the most attention—even some whose projects were never built. The foremost example was Stone's embassy in New Delhi, but there were others. Harry Weese's design for Accra featured a glass box raised on stilts and wrapped in wooden shutters. Though impractical, it was built and celebrated for its inventive design, hailed by its hosts as a symbol of U.S. commitment to Ghana, the first of the former African colonies to win independence in the 1950s. John Carl Warnecke's proposed embassy for Bangkok was widely publicized in architectural journals and praised for its resemblance to a Thai pagoda, and Louis Kahn's fort-like design for Luanda was widely known and admired, although neither project was built (figs. 55–6).

Although the new projects varied widely in location, climate, seismic conditions, accessibility, and the availability of materials, many shared a common design vocabulary. Despite the temperature extremes at many sites, a surprisingly large number of new embassies featured glass walls—New Delhi, Athens, and Manila, for example. To protect the glass walls from the tropical sun, most were shielded by exterior shades, including fixed and movable fins, wooden grilles and shutters, and variously designed masonry screens—a veritable encyclopedia of sun control devices created at a time when mechanical cooling was unavailable or undependable at many posts, and when few foreign buildings were fully air-conditioned. Wrapped in teak grilles, the consulate in Basra by Harris Armstrong had relatively few windows and was air-conditioned from the start, but the much larger New Delhi embassy had glass walls and was only partially air-conditioned.

Like the glass walls, *pilotis* were another hallmark of modernism, popular among architects even if they created wasted space and later posed a security hazard. Projects built at Accra, Athens, Karachi, Singapore, and Tangier, and others designed for Bangkok and Beirut (fig. 57), featured stilts either fully or partially supporting the buildings. At Mexico City, wide arches supported the building above. Such projects featured first floors either recessed, as at Tangier, where the ground floor was enclosed in glass, or eliminated entirely, as at Accra, where there is no ground floor and the entrance level consisted only of an open staircase leading to the offices above (figs. 58–60). Other common elements at Accra, Karachi, Tangier, Amman, Baghdad, and Tabriz included variously designed vaults, covered walkways, screened openings, and shutters—all linked to vernacular traditions.

Most of the embassies from the 1950s were located in downtown areas, generally near other government and diplomatic buildings in the capital cities, on sites purchased by FBO after World War II. In some instances, FBO received properties as outright gifts from foreign governments, and sometimes, as in Athens, the properties were acquired by exchange (figs. 61–2). In other instances, FBO was directed to a particular site by local authorities trying to develop diplomatic enclaves and new parts of older cities, such as New Delhi and Baghdad, or enclaves in entirely new cities, such as Islamabad and Brasilia. Wherever possible, though, FBO chose prominent sites that were accessible to the general public and also convenient for American businessmen, government officials, and diplomats. Thus, the London embassy fronts onto Grosvenor Square, The Hague embassy faces a small historic open space, and the Oslo embassy overlooks the grounds of the royal palace at the center of downtown. One of the criticisms of the Dublin project in 1959 was that the United States had given up a small but prominently located property on historic Merrion Square for a new site far from the historic core.

Plans varied with the size and configuration of sites, and also with program requirements. Nevertheless, many of the new buildings shared two basic plan formulas: blocks with offices situated on either side of a central corridor, and courtyard plans with perimeter offices. Vincent Kling designed both an office block and adjacent auditorium set back on a wide plaza at Quito, and Keyes & Lethbridge designed a similarly configured block at Lima. The Lima scheme faces a busy street on the front, but overlooks its own enclosed plaza at the rear (fig. 63). Numerous projects featured central courts, these being either totally open to the sky (as at Accra, Athens, Mexico City, and Rabat), partially open to the sky (New Delhi), or covered or enclosed (Basra, Dublin, Manila, and Oslo) (figs. 64–8). The court at New Delhi contained a tropical garden. At Dublin, clerestory windows above the court brought sunlight into the building's interior, and the circular space also provided an area that could be used for receptions and other entertainment needs. The triangular plan at Oslo, more or less dictated by the triangular site, produced some awkward corner spaces and oddly-configured offices, but the diamond-shaped interior court was useful for entertainment (figs. 69–70). Neither in Dublin nor in Oslo were the sites big enough to accommodate an outdoor plaza or garden. With an L-shaped plan, Marcel Breuer provided space for a small manicured lawn at The Hague (figs. 71–2). In Kobe, Minoru Yamasaki incorporated an elaborate traditional Japanese garden designed by landscape architect Ken Nakajima. Although much of the formal entertaining associated with diplomacy generally occurred at the residence of the ambassador, new office buildings were also increasingly called upon to host events that required flexible open spaces.

Architects needed to provide separation between public and private (or nonpublic) spaces within each office building. At many sites, the lobby area was open to the public, and public-oriented functions adjoined the lobby. Offices requiring limited access were stacked above, accessible via an elevator or stairs situated beyond a reception desk or checkpoint. The need to separate functions produced plans in which USIS offices, libraries, and auditoriums, for example, had separate entrances often set off to the side of the main embassy entrance. Breuer designed dual entrances for The Hague and divided his building into two connected but visually distinct blocks. At London and Oslo, Eero Saarinen provided three entrances—an entrance for consular offices on one side, one for USIS on the other, and a main entrance for other embassy business in the center.

Embassies in Oslo and The Hague bordered public sidewalks and had to fit in with an existing cityscape, but elsewhere projects were designed as compounds set apart from their surroundings by walls, fences, and open space. A distinctive lava-stone wall surrounded the consular compound at Kobe. To protect the enclosed buildings and gardens from frequent floods, Yamasaki drew upon local Japanese tradition and raised the structures up on pedestals about 2 feet high. The wall served as a dike when its rubber-sealed wooden gates were closed. In interviews, Yamasaki suggested that the wall provided the compound with necessary security in addition to flood protection.

Like Kobe, compounds at New Delhi, Tabriz, and Tangier included office buildings and residences. Josep Lluis Sert's extensive Baghdad compound was located outside of the old city, on the banks of the Tigris River adjacent to the royal palace, a prized location when the site was purchased in 1946. Previously, diplomatic offices were housed in rented space, but as the Iraqi landlord continually raised the rent and the State Department recognized the benefits of ownership, the mission was moved to new facilities, which included a three-story embassy office building, an ambassador's residence, staff apartments, garages, and storage warehouses. The Baghdad compound was the model for later projects, such as Mogadishu and Islamabad, where Americans lived and worked in a single "protected" place. Although members of Congress objected to what they called "ghetto" living by Americans abroad, arguing that Americans should not be isolated from local life, the State Department favored compounds for economy and efficiency, and later for security.

The Great Seal and the American flag were the two national symbols used by architects to identify embassy buildings. They also variously interpreted the American eagle, which is part of the seal, to add emphasis and a visual accent to the highly symbolic buildings. As further identification, the words "Embassy of the United States of America" were carved into architectural elements, etched into glass, or printed somehow on the buildings—sometimes subtly by the entrance, sometimes more boldly above it. The ways in which architects chose to use the seal varied depending on the design and on their own preferences. Often the seal was displayed almost discreetly by the main entrance, but some architects, including Stone and Gropius, enlarged the image of the seal and used it as a major decorative device over a main doorway (figs. 73–4).

The great eagle mounted five floors above the ground in London was unique. Earlier schemes, such as Brussels, had incorporated the eagle motif into embassy identification plaques or signs, but Saarinen was the first to use the eagle as a separate sculptural element. No one other than Saarinen ever tried anything as provocative or tried to explore the use of American political symbols to the same extent. The London eagle caused much consternation, but from a design standpoint, it is an eye-catching focal point on a façade that spans a whole city block. John Johansen later mounted a smaller but even more stylized golden eagle above the entrance to the Dublin embassy (figs. 75–7).

The largest and most dramatic use of the entire Great Seal was the giant replica above the main entrance to the New Delhi embassy. It is a full story high and fills the entire width of the entrance bay. Stone designed the abstracted version of the seal as the focal point of his entrance. Gropius did the same thing at Athens, but the impact of the device is less dramatic there, where the architecture itself is more distracting. At Jakarta, a seal adds decoration to the architecture and provides information about the identity of the building. At New Delhi and Accra, where the replica is much larger, it indicates the location of the main entrance and also works as an architectural element, providing focus, animation, and contrast.

Every embassy also featured a prominently placed flagpole and an American flag waving above. Where poles were mounted on embassy roofs, as at London, Oslo, and Quito, the flag became a locator and a signal of the American presence. The sight of the American flag waving in a foreign city can have a powerful impact on citizens of host countries as well as Americans. Before American embassies became targets of attack at the time of the Vietnam War, there was little concern for perimeter security and no need to downplay the presence of an embassy. Architects did not pursue patriotic themes or motifs drawn from American history. There were no busts of the Founding Fathers, for example, no likenesses of George Washington or Abraham Lincoln, no replicas of the Bill of Rights or the Liberty Bell, nor did postwar embassies resemble well-known American landmarks such as Monticello or the White House.

Because the State Department gave the highest priority to the needs of hardship posts, those where the climate was most challenging and decent facilities were scarcest, many of the new embassy projects between 1954 and 1957 were destined for tropical or subtropical locations. Air-conditioning was a luxury at most posts, and electricity was both costly and undependable. As a result, architects had to devise ways to shield their buildings from intense sunlight, glare, and high daytime temperatures without relying on mechanical cooling.

Architects also faced other climatic factors including low night-time temperatures, extremes of humidity and aridity, driving rains, and strong winds. Although located on the banks of the Tigris River and bisected by an irrigation canal, the Baghdad site, for example, was hot, dry, and dusty. Like sites in New Delhi, Amman, Tangier, Athens, Quito, and Asunción, it was subject to intense sunlight and extremes of temperature. The only local foliage at the site in Baghdad consisted of a number of beautiful old palm trees, trees that contained colonies of wood-eating ants. Voracious wood-eating termites also posed a problem in Accra, where wood was naturally cheap and plentiful but rarely used for major construction projects. Other environmental hazards included torrential rains in Tegucigalpa, flooding in Kobe, and earthquakes in Athens, Karachi, Jakarta, Port-au-Prince, Nagoya, Accra, and Quito. Though far less of a problem for architects, the dampness and omnipresent gloom associated with northern winters were also considerations in cities such as London, The Hague, and Oslo.

Throughout history, buildings have featured screens as decorative and functional elements. Magnificently colored and carved screens fill arched openings in the thick walls of the Alhambra in Granada, and elaborate wooden and stone grillwork occupies open bays at mosques throughout the Moslem world. Such screens, which are not glass-filled, continue to provide filtered light, shade, and privacy, to permit breezes to penetrate interior spaces, and to allow heat to escape. In the twentieth century, architects have turned to screens and other surface modifications less for climate control than to add texture and color to their façades, to adjust relationships of scale, to pick up local themes or make use of local materials, and to reconcile the glass exterior with its site. After all, modernism first emerged in Europe, where the climate is temperate. Modernists, including Le Corbusier, Gropius, Breuer, and Mies, advanced a new philosophy of architecture, a philosophy that emphasized function as an abstract idea and looked to new materials, such as plate glass, as a way of defining new relationships between buildings and nature. In its rejection of history, modernism seemed to embody the present while anticipating the future, and in its rejection of added ornament, it seemed to be functional.

Breuer went so far as to declare the sun control device such an important element of architecture that "it may develop into as characteristic a form as the Doric column."[1] He claimed that the glass curtain wall offered the greatest hope for people to enjoy the winter sun and the other splendors of nature. Like so many modernists, Breuer associated the glass curtain wall with the concept of openness, and was convinced that openness was essential, even if it meant that the curtain wall had to be mediated by a mesh of concrete or metal designed to obscure nature, not reveal it.

When exported or imported to tropical or semi-tropical places, the modernist vocabulary had to be expanded in order to work well. Before the days of thermopane, when costly and often energy-inefficient air-conditioning forced architects to consider the effects of the sun's rays, the *brise-soleil* was the most conspicuous architectural adaptation to climate. Architects turned to screens and louvers, some mechanically controlled, as ways of adapting the beloved glass box. At Nagoya, for example, Cochran, Stephenson & Wing used wooden louvers to shield the east and west elevations of the consulate building from the sun, and similarly at Fukuoka, George T. Rockrise shaded only the sunny side of his consulate building with horizontal louvers (figs. 78–9).

The proliferation of the glass curtain wall in the face of severe tropical climate conditions illustrates just how entrenched was the modernist commitment to this device. To shade or shield these glass walls, architects were forced to use screens or louvers, which they argued—somewhat disingenuously—were designed to provide site-specific climate control. Thus, the *brise-soleil* became the defining cliché of the embassy building program in the 1950s; nearly all architects participating during this period used it in some form. The screen designed by Edward Durell Stone for New Delhi was made of a concrete and marble aggregate (fig. 80). At Manila, Alfred Aydelott used precast concrete, fabricated, he said, to resemble a curtain of laced bamboo (fig. 81). Josep Lluis Sert's design for Baghdad featured both screens and wooden shutters (fig. 82); Harris Armstrong's design for Basra featured grilles of teak; and for Accra Harry Weese designed louvers made of mahogany. At Leopoldville, Weed, Russell, Johnson used decorative pierced panels to partially screen the consulate building, and at Kobe, where sun was not a problem, Minoru Yamasaki used translucent fiberglass panels hung from a delicate bronze grid to create an allusion to traditional Japanese *shoji* screens (figs. 83–4). The screen proposed by Curtis & Davis for Saigon consisted of white terra-cotta flue sections arranged in rectangular bays to envelope the building.

The AAC quizzed many architects on details of how their screens were to be put together and hung. Members advised Aydelott, for example, to

refine his screen design in order to make it more effective and more likely to serve its intended purpose. Walker was particularly concerned about
how the covered glass would be washed, and he advised architects to allow
enough space to permit window-washing.

Other sun screens included ceramic tiles at Athens and Quito, fixed
or movable fins at Jakarta, Karachi, and Asunción, and wooden louvers
at Nagoya, Basra, and Singapore. Don Hatch's vertical louvers at Port-au-
Prince (1955) were made of colored metal (fig. 85), while Weese's louvers at
Accra were constructed of varnished mahogany, chemically treated to repel
hungry termites. Sert's brightly colored shutters at Baghdad were handmade
of imported teak. Stone's precast screen in New Delhi was similarly handmade, as were the gilded aluminum studs used as accents across its surface.

Fundamental flaws in designs that relied upon screens were that screens
actually provided only incidental protection from the sun; the desired openness of glass was lost when the glass was covered; screens created interiors
that were closed-in, not open, sometimes even claustrophobic; and closed
louvers blocked ventilation. Walker focused on these flaws when he noted
that architecture that responded to climate had no need for exterior grilles.
He compared louvers to prison bars and criticized lazy architects who used
louvers only to create gloomy interiors.[2] As an advisor to FBO, he approved
of designs that featured screens when the screens contributed to the overall
design in terms of theme, for example, but he was skeptical of claims that
screens and louvers were themselves necessary to the modernist vocabulary
and even more skeptical of assertions that they provided climate control, as
claimed.

The ubiquitous use of screens had more to do with architectural fashion than climate control. At Tangier, for example, Hugh Stubbins employed
screens mainly to create an animated architecture (fig. 86). Stubbins has
compared the Tangier screen to one he designed soon after for the Loeb
Drama Center in Cambridge, Massachusetts. His idea, he says, was to provide some daytime privacy and to allow the building to glow from within at
night. Yamasaki featured an aluminum screen on the Reynolds Aluminum
building in Detroit not so much to screen out the sun as to showcase his
client's principal product, aluminum.[3] Architects were experimenting with
glass walls and screens at home just as they were abroad. Their intent was
generally to reduce scale, provide surface texture, and add visual drama.

Guided by architects' assertions, however, most critics supposed that
the exterior screens really screened the buildings from sun. *Architectural
Forum* praised Stone's New Delhi grille, for example, for its sun-screening
function. According to *Forum*, the grille elements were "worth their weight
in air-conditioning equipment, taking the edge off the fierce glare of India's

summer sun." While the journal noted that the wall behind the grille was "largely glass," it did not question the idea of using such a glass wall in the first place. *Forum* also praised the design of the central court at New Delhi, a space, it said, that would "be roofed over by suspended strings of aluminum discs, making a dappled shade." Neither *Forum* nor others who commended Stone's design for its presumed adaptation to climate observed that the sun's impact was magnified by the glass walls, nor did they note the fact that the open courtyard and corridors allowed both heat and humidity to build up inside the building, compromising the comfort of those moving in and out of the closed, air-conditioned offices that ringed the central space. *Forum* described the aluminum mesh that was hung above the courtyard, but did not comment on the rain-soaked interiors that often resulted. Furthermore, it went so far as to describe the cast terrazzo screen as a security device "intended to baffle burglars," a claim that had no basis in fact.[4] Despite the building's ultimate shortcomings with regard to climate control, the screen worked well as an overall decorative device, giving the relatively small two-story building the appearance of a much more imposing structure. In photographs, for instance, it looks strikingly similar to the John F. Kennedy Center for the Performing Arts in Washington, a later and vastly larger Stone project.

Any or all of the architects could have chosen to use small recessed windows punched into thick and well-insulated walls instead of glass walls covered by screens, but few did. One exception was Paul Rudolph, who presented a scheme for Amman with small, slit-shaped windows deeply recessed into masonry walls. With irony that is only apparent today, FBO director Hughes admonished Rudolph to revise the scheme and come up with one that looked "less like a fort and more like an embassy."[5] Though the design might have been appreciated ten or fifteen years later, in 1955 FBO wanted to see a more symbolically open building, even if it meant one less attuned to climate.

Looking out from offices in numerous new embassy buildings, people's views were obscured by the screens (fig. 87). In cities such as Port-au-Prince and Singapore, screens or fins were barriers between office workers and the cities beyond. The aluminum louvers at Singapore, which were anodized to resemble teak, were placed at one-foot intervals along the exterior of the embassy building so that people in the building could look straight out from the offices, but not from side to side. To outsiders, perhaps, the glass-walled buildings were conceptually open, but to those on the inside, the screened offices often seemed confining and the screens actually prevented easy escape in cases of emergency.

The wooden jalousies at Accra, for example, were hand-operated, and had to be cranked open and closed by the embassy's maintenance staff. According to Shirley Temple Black, who served as U.S. ambassador to Ghana from 1974 to 1976, occupants were instructed to smash through the heavy shutters with axes in case of fire, a task that Black said she would have been unable to perform. To her and to others, the elegant wooden screens created a "fire-trap."[6] The building had just a single entrance that also served as its single exit, a significant danger in case of fire or unwanted intrusion.

Screens added to the difficulty of building maintenance and created nuisance problems by providing nesting places for birds. Additionally, screens often made interior light control more difficult, not less, and without shades or heavy curtains, they provided little privacy. C. L. Sulzberger described Gropius's Athens embassy as a "goldfish bowl"; by 1965 the Russians had trained their telescopes on its glass walls, forcing the embassy to keep its venetian blinds drawn day and night.[7]

As early as 1957, members of the newly dubbed Architectural Advisory Panel voiced concerns about all-glass buildings. They cited Welton Becket's scheme for an embassy in Warsaw not only as a security problem, but as architecturally inappropriate. They further noted that it would have required the sort of precision craftsmanship that did not exist in Poland at that time. Panelists also questioned "the wisdom of a glass structure in Mexico City for aesthetic reasons and also because of the impracticality of operation caused by sun problems." They doubted whether "the dignity proper to an embassy can be achieved through the use of glass and metal as an exterior treatment," and suggested masonry in lieu of glass. John Johansen first presented a scheme for Dublin at about the same time, mid-1957. The panel repeatedly sent him back to his drawing board to reconsider his design, which was based on a concrete skeleton with glass infill. After five presentations, panelists rejected his design for being "out of character for Dublin." They said, "The building lacked solidity, which was considered more important in Dublin than a glass cage type of design." The following year, considering a presentation on a proposed embassy office building for Taipei, panelists did not simply question the use of glass walls, they questioned the "contradiction between the building being all glass yet being a completely barred secure structure."[8]

By the early 1960s, the State Department recognized that screens, rather than protecting against intruders, often did just the opposite. The screen at Quito, for example, had to be modified to prevent trespassers from scaling the façade (fig. 88). As FBO stopped approving new projects that featured screens, architects could no longer experiment with glass boxes.

Architects also experimented with designs featuring wall set-backs and roof overhangs to protect their buildings, and used umbrella roofs designed to shield flat roofs from direct sun by providing a second, raised roof slightly higher than the first. Each floor of Sert's embassy at Baghdad was stepped back beneath the floor above to provide shade below. For both the office building and the residence, he designed angled umbrella roofs (fig 89). The roof over the ambassador's residence, painted blue on its underside, was high enough to permit use of the lower roof as a terrace. Weese, Gropius, Smith, and Rudolph also designed double roofs (fig. 90).

Some architects designed elaborate entrances that offered protection from sun and rain, as at Port-au-Prince, where cars could actually drive right up to the building under an extended *porte cochère*. For Karachi, architects Richard Neutra and Robert Alexander proposed a dramatic entrance canopy suspended by cables, but the AAC criticized it for being too showy.[9] As completed, the canopy seems to have little to do with the weather, and much more to do with announcing the presence of the embassy, much as a marquee announces the presence of a theater (figs. 91–2). FBO tried to save money by not installing the vertical louvers on the ribbon windows on the east side of the Karachi building, but the offices were unbearably hot until they were added. These adjustable louvers, like those at Jakarta and Port-au-Prince, actually did protect against the sun and helped to make the building comfortable. But unlike many of the other projects, Karachi was not a glass box, and its architects did try to pay attention to the local climate, even if their efforts were initially undermined by others.

LOOKING FOR WAYS to link their work to locale, architects searched for themes and historical references that they could incorporate into their embassy designs. Because this effort seemed to violate a principal tenet of modernism, the prohibition against borrowing from the past, architectural critics were harsh in their criticism of modern buildings that appeared to have taken their inspiration from older monuments. Writing in 1961, Vincent Scully condemned the screen wall as "superficial decoration." Five years later, John Jacobus ridiculed the "notorious" screen devices of Stone and others as "quaint and even foolish," claiming that they were trite and lacked dignity.[10] Jacobus linked the grille with the idea of a commercial style and went so far as to read into Stone's design a smug display of the affluent society imposing itself on a pre-industrial society, an inappropriate choice for embassy design. By contrast, in the New Delhi embassy's neat white grilles, thin slab-like roof, narrow golden columns, and pedestal base, the popular press saw a fanciful pavilion somehow linked to Indian architectural tradition.

Yamasaki, too, made good use of historical reference. His authentic Japanese garden at Kobe paid homage to a beloved tradition of the host country. In Athens, Gropius claimed the Parthenon as his inspiration. But a Parthenon of steel and glass? A Parthenon whose most striking feature was its great, extended roof? Did the architecture of the new embassy have anything to do with the Athenian landmark, or was the architect merely making an association to boost appreciation for his design? Few people would have noted the parallels between the two buildings if Gropius had not specifically mentioned them himself. Unquestionably, efforts to flatter local sensibilities and efforts to link designs to well-known foreign landmarks led to contrived explanations, and sometimes also to contrived designs.

Gropius argued that modernism was a vehicle for regional expression. It provided architects with the raw materials, he said, steel or concrete skeletons, ribbon windows, cantilevered slabs or hovering wings on stilts, "with which regionally different architectural manifestations can be created." Writing in 1943, he had rejected the notion of styles and condemned the phrase "international style," because, as he noted, "It is not a style, because it is still in flux, nor is it international, because its tendency is the opposite—namely, to find regional, indigenous expression derived from the environment, the climate, the landscape, the habits of the people."[11]

When Gropius took on the Athens commission, he was obligated to study and incorporate something of the local architectural tradition. In their earlier scheme, Ralph Rapson and John van der Meulen had used a "square doughnut plan," a design based on a steel skeleton and a simple glass box raised on stilts. Gropius wrote to Rapson asking for his sketches and Rapson sent them, if reluctantly.[12] Gropius then used the same plan but suspended his glass wall from concrete girders supported by a massive portico of marble-clad columns. This, he *said*, linked his embassy to its environment, specifically to the Parthenon. The AAC, which then consisted of Pietro Belluschi, Henry Shepley, Richard Bennett, and Raymond Hare, questioned Gropius's "complicated and confused" plan, which reminded no one of the plan of the Parthenon or any other Greek landmark. Though the roof extended beyond the glass wall, it was pierced with large cut-outs and provided little sun or glare protection to the offices. The AAC advised the architect that the overhang made the whole structure seem "colossal, raw-boned, and forbidding" and said that his design lacked "delicacy." They urged him to restudy the solution and subsequently approved a revised version.[13]

It is hard to know what Gropius really meant when he wrote in the early 1940s that modern architecture could be tailored to regional differences. Confronted with the problem himself in 1956, he came up with a display building that critics today might describe as an example of theme architecture wrapped around a functional core—the sort of buildings seen at world's fairs. Panelists applauded the theme, but found the performance lacking.

Although FBO sent each architect to visit the site of his proposed embassy to try to grasp the historical meaning of the place, many architects concluded that there was no local architecture capable of providing inspiration or suitable as a model for an up-to-date office building. Robert Beatty said this about Niamey in 1964, for example. In the capital of Niger, conditions were so poor that there was only one paved road. Though the road ran past the embassy site, transportation was difficult and Beatty could see that it would be hard just trying to bring in supplies, not to mention assembling them.

The inaccessibility of Asunción similarly challenged architect Chloethiel Woodard Smith. Located just south of the Tropic of Capricorn, approximately 700 miles west of São Paulo, the Paraguayan capital was not accessible by road and was noted for its extreme and sudden changes of weather. Building materials could be delivered only by air or by shallow barge via the Paraná River, which empties into the ocean at Buenos Aires, 1,000 miles to the south. Though she specified a reinforced concrete frame, Smith built interior partitions of native brick and exterior walls of stucco on brick in an attempt to maximize the use of local materials.

Likewise, in Lagos and Leopoldville American architects found no local architecture and no history that they considered useful to their needs. Sometimes architects reached this conclusion simply because they considered such faraway places alien. More often, development differed completely from what they knew in the United States or there was no history of building large-scale government and commercial structures, leaving architects without precedent in either case.

Another problem, of course, was how to incorporate historical references in countries where embassies were sited in areas detached from a definable past or undergoing rapid change. And yet another problem was deciding whether to draw on precedent associated with colonial regimes in newly independent nations. The French had built the most impressive non-religious buildings in Saigon, for example, but were their public buildings appropriate as models for American buildings?

John Carl Warnecke studied vernacular themes with care as he prepared his design for Bangkok. In explaining his design, he cited hospitals, royal palaces, and also religious architecture he saw in Thailand for his inspiration. What he proposed was a whimsical four-story building made up of open verandas and terraces rimmed with decorative railings (fig. 55). The building stood on stilts, or rather on piles, and was to be surrounded by a lotus-shaped lake, known in Thailand as a *klong*. Warnecke recalls that he saw the Broadway production of *The King and I,* the romantic story of Anna and the King of Siam, just before he visited Thailand. The play had a "powerful" impact on him, he says, and though he was not interested in creating anything "Hollywoody," the effect of the musical stayed with him as he toured Bangkok and developed his *parti* for the embassy.[14]

Where architectural features such as barrel vaults were commonplace as in Moslem countries, architects incorporated them into their designs. Neutra & Alexander devised a distinctive vaulted roofline for Karachi (fig. 93). In his first design for the Tangier legation, Stubbins also created a vaulted arcade to mirror local tradition (fig. 94). At Tabriz, Edward Larrabee Barnes used even more elaborate vaults to define the profile of the consulate and its residence (fig. 95). At Baghdad, Sert used the barrel vault as a motif on the staff apartments that were built as part of the embassy compound, and Rudolph used the same low-vaulted roof to give his Amman design a local flavor (fig. 50).

Harry Weese's reference to local custom in Accra was perhaps the most irreverent and also, perhaps, the hardest to believe. He declared that his design for a single-story structure raised above ground level on a concrete frame was inspired by towering African anthills and by an inverted chieftain's hut. He also claimed the idea for his tapered concrete piers came from tapered African spears (fig. 60). Was it flattering or insulting when he said the embassy was inspired by huts and anthills? Should an embassy be inspired by spears? Was Weese just groping for ways to link his design to the FBO guidelines? Does it make sense to try to explain a modern office building in terms of small and unrelated indigenous structures?

Weese may have exaggerated his experience in Ghana in order to explain his work, but the truth is that he created a handsome and widely admired embassy building that needed no literal explanation. Historian Ron Robin believes that schemes such as Weese's "trivialized African culture and tribal lore while dismissing the unique political aspirations of individual nations."[15] As Robin suggests, the architect's comments sound insensitive by today's standards. But it remains unclear how the actual architecture dismissed Ghana's collective "political aspirations." Though functionally flawed, Weese's design was imaginative and certainly not tied to colonial tradition. While his *words* may have trivialized African culture, his architecture did not.

Evaluating Morris Ketchum's design for Rabat, the AAC praised the design for its attention to native influence, and for its lively use of color and materials. "No one seeing this building," the minutes said, "could accuse the United States of being a war-like country when it builds Embassies with this character."[16] To those unfamiliar with the history of FBO design policy, this may seem like a curious assertion, coming as it does amidst a detailed presentation of an architectural *parti*. But what links the concern for "native" influence with the desire to appear peace-loving is the architectural policy aimed at creating goodwill through inviting architecture.

The idea that goodwill could be achieved through a flattering architectural evocation of local custom was merely speculation, but it had evolved in response to prior criticism of American buildings that seemed out of place. Perhaps this notion represented an obsessive self-consciousness on the part of Americans, a discomfort with Great Power status, and a preoccupation with modesty and frugality as the only appropriate expressions of a democracy. Perhaps it indicated a lack of interest in American history and in iconography that was intrinsically *American*. Whatever its deeper meaning, the policy was a good faith effort to improve American diplomacy, and that meant creating buildings that were reassuring and nonthreatening.

In a major three-part series featuring new work from FBO in 1955, 1956, and 1957, *Architectural Record* focused on the new American architecture as regional expression. The series examined how American architects designed buildings that respected local climate and tradition and still managed to convey an American flavor. Other publications ran articles as well, but *Record*'s editors offered the widest selection of FBO projects. Carefully withholding any statement of "universal approbation" for the designs, they hailed the AAC as an example of what all government agencies might try to emulate and cited the importance of giving commissions to architectural innovators. The editorial message clearly suggested that the new emphasis on regional expression offered "break-through" architects a chance "to lay aside their more egocentric preoccupations," a chance to concentrate on what their buildings "say" to people who use them, not just on what they mean to other architects.[17]

Record's endorsement of regionalism reflected a growing awareness that much modern architecture was ultimately nonfunctional and represented a denial of place. Its editors realized that the FBO program and Belluschi's often quoted policy statement represented an effort by professionals to right some of the wrongs created when architects used small glass houses or large factories as prototypes for apartments, hospitals, and office buildings, when they recycled schemes designed for northern Europe to the tropics, and when they favored design elements like flat roofs that made no practical sense where there was any sizable snowfall or heavy rain. Nonfunctional though they were, such elements had taken on ideological connotations for modernists and had come, in part, to define their work.

The "international style" was a title that suited the modern movement well—not so much because the architecture had its origins in Europe and was then transplanted to other parts of the world, but because as it was introduced in new locales it was barely translated to reflect or respect vernacular styles, local building customs, or climate. It was "international" in the sense that architects assumed that the same basic formulae could be applied anywhere.

The same concerns voiced by *Record*'s editors in 1957 were more forcefully expressed by Ralph Walker as early as 1951, when he was AIA president and published a provocative two-part essay in the *Journal of the American Institute of Architects*. Walker's premise was that the machine aesthetic had impoverished society and the architecture that it produced, and that as long as architectural education promoted theory at the expense of practical knowledge, schools would not produce clear-headed and capable architects. "Design problems always should be based on actual sites— *which can be seen* by the student," he wrote, "and the problem studied always from actual climate and living potentials." Proper use of nature, he said, would lead to "an architecture without the use of the *brise-soleil*." He called for a rejection of the machine as the master and urged architects to invest their efforts in understanding real, not theoretical, design conditions. In conclusion, Walker blasted the legacy of the European architects who, he claimed, brought to the United States nothing but what he termed negativism, neurosis, and nihilism.[18]

Not surprisingly, Walker's essay prompted a sharp response from Gropius, then chairman of the architecture department at the Harvard Graduate School of Design. Gropius was shocked to read Walker's words, and he wrote to him demanding an explanation on behalf of himself and other European immigrant architects, including Ludwig Mies van der Rohe, Richard Neutra, Ivan Chermayeff, and Marcel Breuer, to each of whom he sent copies of his letter. Walker replied with a long typed letter in which he reiterated his previously stated themes and expanded upon them. The decline of European civilization, he said, was linked to the spread of negativist totalitarianism, a movement that promoted the "engineer-aesthetic," the development of "the cell man," loss of human dignity, political and social irresponsibility, and materialism—all of which represented the antithesis of what was needed to enrich American life. He specifically criticized the Congrès Internationaux d'Architecture Moderne (CIAM) for being dogmatic, for encouraging a false intellectualism, and for fostering a nihilism that was alien to American values. Gropius, Le Corbusier, and Sert were leaders of the CIAM movement, which advocated the unity of design and planning, and the primacy of theory. Despite his apparent rage, Walker assured Gropius that he intended no personal insult and quarreled only with his philosophy.

Walker's words were clearly intended as a rebuke to Gropius and, to some extent, all those who had recently arrived in the United States and risen rapidly to positions of prominence in practice and teaching. Most of them came from Germany and had prior association with the Bauhaus. This is not to say that Walker rebuked modern architecture, but he refused to see it as a European derivative. Furthermore, he rejected what he called "a kindergarten approach to design": solutions that were esoteric, self-referential, and not simply open, but to him, empty.

Belluschi fundamentally agreed with Walker. He had also written that society had become "conditioned by the machine," that architecture had lost touch with climate and context, and that the modern architect had to "come to terms with his environment."[19] Although he celebrated what he described as the slaying of the "Beaux-Arts dragon," he lamented modern architecture's loss of emotional value and its dogmatic intolerance for "symbols and forms of the past." While Walker expressed concern for the "cell man," the product of a monotonous, machine-oriented aesthetic, Belluschi looked forward to the making of the "complete man," a product of science and intellect, but also a product of good sense and feeling. The idea of "internationalism" could never be modern, Belluschi said, as long as it tried to be nothing but a "style" and ignored nature. As early as 1941, Belluschi was urging fellow architects to attend to climate, local materials, and the human response to both, themes that he restated in the FBO guidelines. Belluschi himself had left a successful practice in the Pacific Northwest to take over as dean at MIT in 1951 specifically because he wanted to redirect architectural education away from theory and toward what he considered to be more humanistic concerns.[20]

Shepley, too, shared a concern for finding ways to make modern buildings that were workable, as opposed to being simply fashionable or doctrinaire. Though Shepley's Boston firm was best known for its long association with the traditional look of the Harvard campus, Shepley was seriously interested in modern architecture. According to Shepley's long-time colleague Jean Paul Carlhian, Shepley invited Gropius to his office to look over plans for the B. B. Chemical Company building in Cambridge (1938), a building he was proud to call "modern," a project noteworthy for its use of glass block and ribbon windows. Gropius looked at the plans but said nothing—a reaction that pained Shepley.[21] As long as the architecture was sympathetic to its surroundings and as long as its goal was not simply to startle, Shepley had no quarrel with newness. But like Walker and Belluschi, he saw no use for "passing fashions," or what he called "experimental" architecture that aged poorly and was soon outmoded.

Walker's hostility to Gropius was a matter of public record, yet Gropius and many of his former students and colleagues were listed as AAC choices or had already been selected for commissions. Walker raised doubts about the selection of Rudolph, Gropius's pupil, and about Yamasaki, too. Only after Walker's term expired—five weeks after, to be precise—did Gropius win a contract from FBO. But if Walker had strong doubts about these men, and if the others shared his doubts, why did the AAC select them at all? If Walker and his AAC colleagues shared a common view regarding the limits of modernism, why were they prepared to select men like Neutra and Breuer, or even Saarinen and Sert? The answer to that question seems to be that the three architects on the panel wanted above all to promote the interests of the profession, and they felt an obligation to go along with the much-admired idols and the rising stars in the profession.

Addressing Shepley, Belluschi, and Bennett in 1956, Walker lamented that "the great names" had produced poorer work than those he called the "youngsters," and he went on to decry "the stunt" as architecture that lacked dignity. "Granting the possibility for a difference of opinion," he said, "there is no true reason why architects who are the acknowledged cultists of the ugly should be employed so that they may convincingly fail in furthering our friendly approach to foreign relations." He advised his former colleagues to "keep looking over the names of the young and pick them rather than the old and the stupid," adding "the latter may *even* include you and me."[22]

To Walker, Belluschi and Shepley, the design review of the FBO projects represented a unique opportunity to direct architects away from the abstraction associated with the "international style" and toward more contextual solutions that they hoped could build goodwill for the United States. But by early 1959, Saarinen, by then an AAP member, declared that the group was "close to the bottom of the barrel" in terms of finding new architects. He suggested "repeat performances," as one way of dealing with what he saw as the paucity of qualified candidates.[23] Shepley, though retired from the panel, wrote to Hughes expressing the same views. He suggested that Yamasaki, who had already designed a consulate, "be promoted to an Embassy." He made the same suggestion about Edward Larrabee Barnes. As for "new" talent, he suggested another look at Paul Rudolph, the recently appointed dean of the Yale Architectural School whose Amman embassy was never built; at I. M. Pei, who had recently established an independent practice; and at Philip Johnson. "When you start repeating," he told Hughes, "you might consider [Wallace K.] Harrison and [Gordon] Bunshaft [of SOM]. They have learned a lesson by seeing what we have done in our program and will, I think, profit by it."[24]

It is hard to believe that architectural talent could have been so scarce—a sorry comment on architectural education or else a reflection of elitist snobbism. The problem may have had less to do with a dearth of talent than uncertainty about the commissions themselves and what they were supposed to represent. As FBO and its advisory panel worked to match architects with embassy projects, the building program ran into roadblocks that made much of the panel's effort superfluous. The program would soon shrink in size and scope, but not before architects asserted themselves with bold designs, and not before an array of new embassy buildings opened for business.

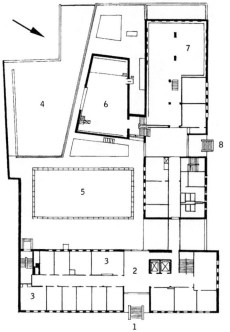

FIGS. 71 & 72: U.S. Embassy, The Hague, Netherlands. Marcel Breuer (1956–59). (ABOVE) Auditorium from rear. (LEFT) Ground floor plan after drawing in *BOUW* (1959).

1. MAIN ENTRANCE
2. MAIN LOBBY
3. OFFICES
4. DRIVEWAY TO GARAGE
5. GARDEN
6. AUDITORIUM
7. LIBRARY
8. USIS ENTRANCE

FIG. 73 (OPPOSITE): U.S. Embassy, New Delhi, India. Edward Durell Stone (1954–59). Entrance. According to tradition, the eagle looks to its right and holds an olive branch and arrows in its talons.

FIG. 74 (ABOVE): U.S. Embassy, Athens, Greece. Walter Gropius, The Architects Collaborative (1956–59). Entrance. Gropius compared his building to the Parthenon.

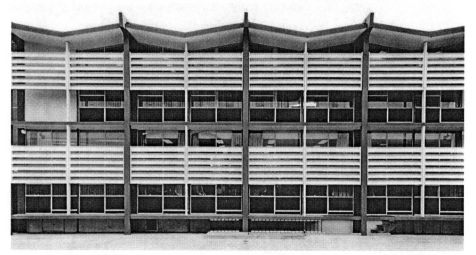

FIG. 75 (OPPOSITE, TOP LEFT): U.S. Embassy, Brussels, Belgium. Alan Jacobs for FBO (Paris) (1948–49). Eagle.

FIG. 76 (OPPOSITE, TOP RIGHT): U.S. Embassy, Dublin, Ireland. John M. Johansen (1957–64). Entrance with eagle in 1992.

FIG. 77 (OPPOSITE, BOTTOM): U.S. Embassy, London, England. Eero Saarinen (1956–59). The controversial 35-foot eagle is by sculptor Theodore Roszak (1958). Roszak's bird looks to its left; neither olive branches nor arrows are clearly depicted.

FIGS. 78 & 79: U.S. Consulate, Fukuoka, Japan. G. T. Rockrise with Clark & Beuttler (1958–60). (THIS PAGE, TOP) Entrance with water garden. (THIS PAGE, BOTTOM) Rear with horizontal louvers for sun protection.

FIG. 80. (OPPOSITE): U.S. Embassy, New Delhi, India. Exterior with *brise-soleil*. Columns are covered in gold leaf. Paving stones are from the River Ganges.

FIG. 81 (TOP): U.S. Embassy, Manila, Philippines. Alfred Aydelott (1956–59). South side, rear. The concrete screen was compared to a laced bamboo curtain.

FIG. 82 (BOTTOM): Former U.S. Embassy, Baghdad, Iraq. Josep Lluis Sert (Sert, Jackson & Gourley) (1955–59).

FIG. 83 (TOP LEFT): U.S. Embassy, Kinshasa, Congo. (Formerly U.S. Consulate General, Leopoldville, Belgian Congo.) Weed, Russell, Johnson Assoc. (1954–58).

FIG. 84 (TOP RIGHT): U.S. Consulate, Kobe, Japan. Hellmuth, Yamasaki, Leinweber (1954–58). Sold and replaced with consulate in Osaka.

FIG. 85 (MIDDLE LEFT): U.S. Embassy, Port-au-Prince, Haiti. Don Hatch (1955–59).

FIG. 86 (MIDDLE RIGHT): U.S. Consulate General, Tangier, Morocco. Hugh Stubbins (1956–59). Main entrance, east façade. Photograph from 1974.

FIG. 87 (BOTTOM): U.S. Embassy, New Delhi, India. Office interior.

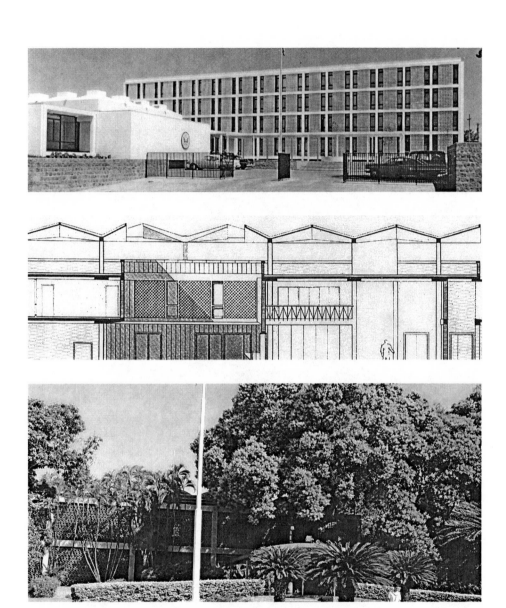

FIG. 88 (TOP): U.S. Embassy, Quito, Ecuador. Vincent Kling (1955–59).

FIG. 89 (MIDDLE): Proposal for U.S. Ambassador's Residence, embassy compound, Baghdad, Iraq. Sert designed a double roof to shield the building from the hot sun.

FIG. 90 (BOTTOM): U.S. Embassy, Asunción, Paraguay. Keyes, Smith & Satterlee (1954–60).

FIGS. 91–3 (OPPOSITE): U.S. Consulate General, Karachi, Pakistan. The U.S. Embassy until the capital moved to Islamabad. Neutra & Alexander (1955–59). (TOP) Main entrance and front façade. (BOTTOM LEFT) Detail of louver-covered ribbon windows at rear. (BOTTOM RIGHT) Overview with adjacent warehouse.

FIG. 94 (TOP): Proposal for U.S. Legation, Tangier, Morocco. Hugh Stubbins (1954). Unbuilt. Stubbins redesigned the building when the program changed.

FIG. 95 (BOTTOM): Former U.S. Consulate General, Tabriz, Iran. Edward Larrabee Barnes (1958–65). Construction of vaulted ceilings.

FIG. 96 (TOP): Former U.S. Embassy, London, England (on east side of Grosvenor Square). Leased in 1937, purchased in 1947, and later sold. Currently the Canadian embassy.

FIG. 97 (MIDDLE): Proposed U.S. Embassy, London, England. Competition entry by Minoru Yamasaki (1956). Unbuilt.

FIG. 98 (BOTTOM): Proposed U.S. Embassy, London, England. Competition entry by Josep Lluis Sert (1956). Unbuilt. The rendering contrasts a British Rolls-Royce and an American Thunderbird (note the reversed juxtaposition in figure 99).

FIGS. 99–103: U.S. Embassy, London, England. Eero Saarinen (1956–60). (PREVIOUS PAGE, TOP) Façade as seen from the north side of Grosvenor Square. (PREVIOUS PAGE, BOTTOM) USIS library, custom-designed table and chairs with view of the square beyond. (THIS PAGE, TOP) USIS library, showing "diagrid" ceiling construction. (THIS PAGE, BOTTOM LEFT) Façade. (THIS PAGE, BOTTOM RIGHT) Sidewalk view.

FIGS. 104–7: U.S. Embassy, The Hague, Netherlands. Marcel Breuer (1956–59). (TOP) Exterior from across Korte Voorhout showing former side entrance. (BOTTOM LEFT) Window detail. (BOTTOM CENTER) Conference room with trapezoid-shaped windows. (BOTTOM RIGHT) Main entrance facing historic square.

FIG. 108 (TOP): Congressman John Rooney (pointing to globe) and members of the House Appropriations Committee with Inspector General Gerald Drew (standing to Rooney's right), meet on inspection tour of Europe (c. 1962).

FIG. 109 (BOTTOM): Proposal for U.S. Embassy, Dublin, Ireland. John M. Johansen (1957). Double-twist scheme, one of the designs presented to President Kennedy.

CHAPTER NINE

Architects Assert Themselves

THE ARCHITECTURAL ADVISORY COMMITTEE chose architects who added prominence to the State Department's building program, sometimes pushing them to tailor their work to FBO design guidelines but more often allowing them wide latitude. To the maximum extent possible, the AAC deferred to the architects it selected. Those who were most enterprising used FBO commissions to experiment with new ideas and materials and to assert themselves architecturally. Less because of the embassies themselves and more because individual architects benefited from the prestigious association with State Department patronage, these projects furthered careers and actually created international reputations for a number of architects. Four case studies illustrate how the design review process worked at FBO.

NEARLY EVERYONE WHO VISITS the U.S. embassy in New Delhi comes away praising it, and it has to be the most popular, certainly the most widely recognized, of U.S. embassies. Why has this building captured the imaginations of so many? The principal reasons are twofold. The first has to do with international relations and India's importance to the United States in the 1950s; and the second with the architecture itself—how Edward Durell Stone seemed to satisfy the design requirements of the FBO building program, creating a memorable landmark hailed as a diplomatic coup for the United States in the process.

India's place as a pivot point in the Cold War power struggle between the United States and the Soviet Union along with its status as leader of the nonaligned nations put it high on the U.S. foreign policy agenda as a nation to nurture in the 1950s. At that time, American foreign policy was based upon the premise that international communism represented the number one threat to world peace; Indian Prime Minister Jawaharlal Nehru did *not* share that view. The United States sought to minimize Indian ties to the Soviet Union to prevent India from falling to communism and to contain Communist China. It also wanted improved relations with all of South

Asia as a means of stabilizing that region and strengthening its Western ties. At a time when differences between the United States and India seemed to be widening, not shrinking, India posed difficult problems for U.S. policy-makers.[1]

Despite strong congressional opposition to aiding any nation not firm-ly committed to the fight against communism, in order to battle the Cold War, in India and elsewhere, the United States embarked upon an economic assistance program proposed by President Truman in 1949. Dubbed the "Point Four" program, it was administered by the Technical Cooperation Administration set up in the State Department in 1950 and staffed by newly recruited technical and economic advisers who were sent abroad to assist local efforts at economic betterment. In 1951, Truman appointed Chester Bowles as American ambassador to India, making him responsible for the new U.S. program that focused on regional development.

New Delhi was a busy and energetic place when Bowles, a former advertising executive from New York, arrived there. As his biographer Howard Schaffer describes him, Bowles was an idealist and a committed liberal who believed that aid could lead to understanding and that under-standing would produce lasting goodwill among nations. Moreover, at a time when all of the American aid to India represented only a tiny fraction of the military and economic aid going to Western Europe and the Far East, Bowles was firmly committed to emphasizing India's strategic importance to the United States. As Schaffer notes, members of Congress objected to Nehru's closeness to the Soviets, to strong anti-Western feelings in India— especially obvious after the outbreak of the Korean War—and to proclama-tions linking colonialism, racism, and U.S. imperialism. Later, Secretary of State Dulles would object to aiding any nonaligned nation and refused to expand funding along the lines suggested by his predecessor, Dean Acheson. But Bowles was optimistic when he arrived in New Delhi in 1951—before the Eisenhower election, while Acheson was still secretary of state.

Everything he had learned in business, Bowles applied to his new career as a diplomat. Although he served in his post only until President Eisenhower took office, Bowles dramatically expanded the size and scope of the U.S. mission. The Point Four program alone brought 115 Americans to India. Keenly aware of the power of media to create a positive image, Bowles strengthened the USIS mission and the Voice of America, expand-ed student grants, opened new libraries, and made inexpensive American books widely available. He urged his staff to study Hindi, and by his own example encouraged them to get out of the embassy and visit other parts of the country, other cities, and the countryside. Back in the United States, he applied the same energy and enthusiasm to acquaint Americans with India and thereby better understand its economic potential and strategic importance. Other men, better known than Bowles, also contributed to India's growing prominence in the United States. Harvard economist John Kenneth Galbraith, for one, had a much publicized tenure as ambassador to India (1961–63), and when First Lady Jacqueline Kennedy visited the new embassy and toured it with him in March 1962, the press coverage was extensive. Photographs of the embassy appeared in newspapers and mass-circulation magazines, not just architectural journals.

Loy Henderson preceded Bowles as ambassador to India and entered into negotiations to purchase the land for the new U.S. compound in New Delhi even before the expansion of the mission there, when it was already apparent that the United States needed better facilities. When Henderson arrived in New Delhi, the U.S. mission was spread between two houses, one a former palace, the other a more modest structure located nearby. Servants lived in crowded little houses behind the larger building, the chancery. According to Henderson, the chancery was hot and very crowded, with no air-conditioning, only fans to provide a semblance of comfort. Built to be staffed by dozens of servants, the palace was ill-equipped for American representational needs. As Henderson noted, Americans had only a small staff for such purposes. Furthermore, the properties were leased and the leases were soon due to expire. What Henderson wanted was an "embassy in India that would be worthwhile, a credit to us and a credit to India."[2]

Though surrounded by the remnants of centuries of history, New Delhi was a new and grandly conceived city, completed in 1929 and formally opened in 1931. Intended as a showcase for the Raj, it became instead the capital of the new Indian democracy, established in 1947. Indian authorities sought to locate new embassies together in an international enclave and opened up a new part of the city for that purpose. They gave first choice to the British and offered the Americans second choice in selecting an embassy site. As ambassador, Henderson selected 13 acres that he described as "beautiful." In its typically short-sighted fashion, the State Department rejected his appeal to buy the land when it first became available. Henderson explained the situation to Indian officials, and they graciously agreed to hold the parcel for the United States. Just before he left India for Iran in 1951, he was able to persuade the department to purchase the parcel. By 1953, with the mission already greatly expanded by the economic assistance program, with Indian awareness of the United States heightened by Bowles's efforts, with American awareness of India steadily increasing through public interest in Nehru and his variable East/West leanings, and with local building leases about to expire, FBO put New Delhi at the top of its list of construction priorities.

Leland King entered into a hand-shake agreement with Stone to design a new embassy office building in New Delhi during the summer of 1953.[3] But site acquisition was delayed; Stone did not yet have a contract when King was fired and replaced temporarily as FBO director that summer. King's successor, Nelson Kenworthy, put negotiations with the architect on hold and suspended other ongoing projects in order to reassess FBO priorities.

Kenworthy and Stone knew each other from Stone's early working days in New York. Stone had participated in the design of Radio City Music Hall at Rockefeller Center, a project managed by Kenworthy and his firm Todd & Brown, Inc. When Stone lost his job after the first phase of the Rockefeller Center construction, Kenworthy had personally hired him to design his own office there for fifty dollars. During the intervening years, Stone's career had its ups and downs. When Kenworthy ran into him outside of King's FBO office in July 1953, it was at a low. Alan Jacobs and Hans Knoll had brought him back from Paris, where he was living on a houseboat on the Seine, reportedly drinking a lot and designing little.[4] The two friends made and carried out a plan to sober him up and bring him to Washington to meet King.

As a public official, Kenworthy did not think he could recommend someone so troubled for the New Delhi commission. He turned the question of what to do with Stone over to the newly appointed AAC. But Stone had friends on that committee: he knew both Henry Shepley and also Ralph Walker from his student days at the Boston Architectural Club; moreover, Shepley had given him his first job. To no one's surprise, Shepley came to his defense and advised Kenworthy and the others that Stone had reformed. He offered to take personal responsibility for Stone's performance and for completion of the job. After Shepley vouched for Stone, the others concurred. Setting aside his own doubts, Kenworthy offered the New Delhi commission to Stone in what amounted to an endorsement of the architect and modern architecture, together. Stone signed a contract on 26 March 1954, wrote to Shepley to thank him for the job, which he described as "a busman's holiday," and flew off to India in April.[5]

When Stone had visited Washington, D.C., as an eighteen-year-old, he was struck by the city's grand civic architecture. Paul Cret's Pan American Union Building made such an enormous impression on the young Stone that he wrote in his autobiography about "its garden court lush with tropical vegetation, birds, fountains and brilliant colored tile" and described the experience of visiting the building as "the moment of truth" that convinced him to become an architect.[6] It is no wonder that years later he should design a similarly evocative court in New Delhi, a court constructed around a water garden filled with fountains, tropical plants, fish, and even birds. It is no wonder that he took an interest in Indian temples and monuments, both elegant and grand, and incorporated much of what he saw into his embassy design.

Stone's prior work included the Museum of Modern Art with Philip Goodwin (1939) and the El Panama Hotel in Panama City (1946). The hotel gave him experience with problems associated with heat gain and glare and the opportunity to experiment with sunscreens even before he visited India. Divorced in 1950, virtually unemployed, Stone had remarried in 1954. He was romantically optimistic as he headed for New Delhi that year with his new wife, hoping to come up with a design idea big enough to resurrect his career.

After two weeks in India and three months of work, Stone presented a preliminary scheme to the AAC on 19 August 1954. Inspired, he said, by the Taj Mahal, the sketches presented a low box wrapped in a white sunscreen. His plan took the shape of a rectangular doughnut, with the main entrance placed on the short end of the rectangle, a move that minimized the mass of the two-story building as seen from its approach drive. Stone raised the box above the ground on a low platform that housed a lower-level service floor and a garage. The flat roof, with round cut-outs at the edge, extended well beyond the screened walls, which obscured the scale of the building and gave it the appearance of a temple-like pavilion. The roof was supported by slender columns covered in gold leaf. Stone later added gold-colored anodized aluminum balls to enliven the cast white terrazzo screen. Similar gold details on Saarinen's embassy in London were later ridiculed as tasteless and gaudy, but critics applauded Stone's use of gold, most likely because India was seen as an "exotic" place where such display was acceptable (figs. 53, 87).

Like other architects who used umbrella roofs to reduce heat gain, Stone added a second roof above the first to promote air circulation and minimize accumulated heat. Arranged around the perimeter of the court, the offices were air-conditioned, but the court was not. Instead, it was shaded by an aluminum screen hung on cables and engineered to deflect sun and direct rain water into the pool and away from the office corridors. He used rounded stones from the River Ganges for paving the entrance forecourt, and hung a giant replica of the Great Seal of the United States over the dramatically recessed entrance (figs. 73, 80).

The AAC urged Stone to study the project further after reviewing his first presentation. He returned in September with an improved scheme that they liked better. A subordinate returned once more in October with additional revisions. The October meeting was attended only by Walker and

Colonel McBride, who found the building "interesting," an adjective generally used in the official minutes to disguise disagreement. A month later, I. W. Carpenter, assistant secretary of state for administration, showed up at the next AAC meeting to express the department's "interest" in the project. Carpenter spoke on behalf of his boss, Loy Henderson, now deputy under secretary of state for administration. Given his history at the post, Henderson had a special interest in New Delhi, and as Carpenter's presence was a departure from typical procedure, it would be fair to conclude that his "interest" was a reflection of Henderson's concern.

Five months after McBride expressed strong reservations about a proposed legation design for Tangier, and two months after the committee deadlocked over objections to a design for Amman, there were serious doubts about New Delhi. At its March 1955 meeting the AAC could not reach unanimous approval of the Stone scheme. Although FBO director William Hughes felt that it was not always practical to demand unanimous approval of any one design, he shared reservations about the Stone project. Carpenter arranged for Hughes and the AAC to meet with Henderson on 29 March. At that meeting, Henderson expressed his opinion that new embassies "should be designed in keeping with local architectural standards, not necessarily modern to the extent they might be termed freakish or of design representing temporary fads."[7] Given the prominence of the project, he wanted AAC members to be more familiar with the site before making a final decision. Therefore, he approved plans for the first such fact-finding trip, and Shepley and Belluschi set off on a trip that took them to seven capitals between 26 April and 15 May 1955.

Once they saw the New Delhi site, the two architects said, they were convinced of the rightness of Stone's design. The just completed Papal Nuncio's palace nearby was "heavy neo-Venetian and very dull," Shepley noted in his report, and he described the neighboring Russian embassy as "an undistinguished modernistic building."[8] All the new buildings there were "contemporary" in look. "Some are fairly good," he said, "but our [proposed] Embassy is superior to any that we saw." In particular, the two architects admired the Taj Mahal and other Indian monuments. Shepley noted that the pierced masonry screens of brick or stone and the overhanging roof slabs of other older buildings offered good protection from the sun and heat.

Upon their return to Washington, they reported their full approval to Carpenter and staunchly defended the scheme after that. They felt certain that Stone had abstracted "the best from local tradition and created a truly modern Embassy of great distinction in the American spirit." The following month *Architectural Forum* featured Stone's scheme in a six-page pictorial spread that opened with a full-page photograph of the Taj Mahal facing a view of the embassy model. Excitement about the proposed design soon became widespread among professionals.[9]

Although U.S. Ambassador John Sherman Cooper (1955–56) returned from India in July 1956 and tried to convince the State Department that Stone's design was "unsuitable," AAC members stated emphatically that it was ideal and reiterated their conviction that it would turn out to be a great American building. Architects on the advisory committee went so far as to predict that the embassy "would become the outstanding architectural achievement of the century."[10]

Stone had to devise a building system capable of being executed by local laborers. During the four years of construction, as many as eighteen hundred Indian workers lived on the site. They fabricated building materials, produced the concrete and marble aggregate sunscreen out of 1-foot square molds, polished the aluminum, and applied the gold leaf. The general contractor was Sardar Mohan Singh, described by Stone as a patriarchal religious leader with millions of Sikh followers and a savvy businessman who held India's Coca-Cola franchise.[11] Stone was impressed by the craftsmanship of the Indian laborers.

When the embassy was dedicated on 3 January 1959, it made news both in India and the United States. Ambassador Ellsworth Bunker, who officially opened the new embassy, recalled later "what a great impression that building…made on all who saw it."[12] The *New York Times* informed its readers that the new embassy was "probably the most elegant in the world," and that Prime Minister Nehru hailed the building and its American architect. "I was enchanted by the building," Nehru reportedly said. "I think it is a very beautiful structure and a very attractive combination of typically Indian motifs with [the] latest modern technology." Guided by press releases from the embassy, the *Times* praised Stone for blending ancient Mogul grandeur and contemporary American design, likened the embassy to the Taj Mahal, and praised the State Department for its enlightened new design policy, which recognized how important it was for American buildings overseas "to be in harmony with the cultural, architectural and climatic conditions."[13] The press seemed especially fascinated by the allusion to the Taj Mahal, a landmark familiar to many Americans. Writers seemed confused about it, though, describing it as an ancient temple, not a seventeenth-century tomb. No one seemed bothered by the fact that it was an office building modeled after a Muslim memorial. Stone was certainly not worried about such matters, nor was he greatly concerned about the functionality of the office building or the residence that he designed as part of the same compound in 1957.

The biggest problem with the chancery proved to be the open court-yard—which felt like a steam-bath or a shower to those coming and going out of the air-conditioned offices (figs. 64–5, 87). It was lovely to look at, but hard to maintain. Open to the elements, it amplified India's cruel summer heat and winter wetness. Some claimed that staff members suffered from colds all year round as a result of the temperature changes. Others complained about being splashed by rain that failed to fall directly into the decorative pool and spattered all around. Leaks also proved to be a problem. Another conspicuous difficulty lay with the acoustics in the residence. Since its walls were partitions made of open grill-work, there was no privacy; conversations were audible all over the residence. This was obviously not practical for discussions of confidential matters.

But as might be expected, the architectural journals touched only on the positive in their reviews. *Architectural Record* lauded the embassy for its "shimmering dignity," praised it for combining "Eastern and Western skills," and described it "as a symbol of friendship and good will." *Architectural Forum* seized the opportunity to condemn typical government architecture and praised Stone's project as "a vivid example of what can be achieved by junking old governmental building styles and replacing them with inventive design." According to *Forum*, until the State Department unveiled its new program, "the American Government—like most other governments—had housed itself abroad almost exclusively in muscular, monumental buildings designed in one or another of the heavy authoritarian stereotypes." It was Stone, *Forum* said, who "decided to substitute grace for grandiose tradition." Suddenly, Stone was dubbed a diplomat, the man who knew how to "represent this country's democratic vitality and romance, its pleasures as well as its power, its strength, all *without* ponderous weight."[14]

If Stone had ended his design career at that high moment, or perhaps four years later after he designed the United States Pavilion for the Brussels World's Fair (1958), he would be remembered today as a hero. His work was prominently featured in architectural publications and he was recognized outside of architectural circles as a celebrity, a star in a profession that boasts few. Even Frank Lloyd Wright said that he loved the New Delhi embassy. Wright called it "one of the finest buildings of the last hundred years and the only Embassy to do credit to the United States," an unexpected compliment that particularly endeared him to Stone.[15] New Delhi reestablished Stone's reputation as a leading modernist and opened the door to dozens of major commissions. More than a decade before the opening of Washington's Kennedy Center, Stone was well known and widely admired. By repeatedly recycling the New Delhi theme, however, he undermined his assertion that it was uniquely fitted to its place and purpose. The banality of his later work ultimately discredited Stone.

As a deliberate device to advance American interests in the Cold War, the New Delhi embassy was a success, a success that contributed to the prominence of the State Department's foreign building program at its peak. FBO may have had trouble maintaining the New Delhi buildings, and diplomats may have had trouble working in the chancery and living in the residence, but still they admired the project and recognized it as an asset to the American mission. Ambassador Galbraith summed up the situation, observing:

> The Edward Durell Stone buildings in New Delhi...were immediate showpieces, proof for all of quality in American taste. Visitors swarmed the chancery, yearned to see the house—Roosevelt House. Both were marvelously non-functional but so is the Taj Mahal. And to be non-functional is greatly appropriate for an embassy, for so are many of its functions. We cannot in our overseas buildings celebrate our industrial eminence such as it is. But we can try to show our excellence in the arts.[16]

•

EERO SAARINEN WON the commission to design the U.S. embassy in Oslo in June 1955. Unlike many of the other young architects retained by FBO, Saarinen had already collaborated on many large-scale projects, including college dormitories and office buildings. He had just completed the Kresge Auditorium and chapel at MIT when he was tapped by FBO to design the Oslo building.

FBO director Leland King had first hired the Finnish-born Saarinen to design a new chancery for Helsinki, but that project was suspended when King was dismissed late in 1953. As a rising star in the profession, Saarinen was a logical choice for another FBO commission, but which one? With Finland no longer available, the AAC offered Norway as the next best alternative. The Oslo site was prominently located on a major street across from the gardens of the royal palace. It was a small, triangular-shaped plot that would have challenged any architect. While working for King in 1952, Rapson and van der Meulen had also proposed several designs for the site (fig. 35). One scheme consisted of a six-story glass cube raised on stilts above a one-story office block below. Saarinen's was not at all the same, though he was likewise constrained by the odd and difficult site.

Saarinen made his first presentation of preliminary drawings and floor plans to the AAC on 10 November 1955. His proposal featured load-bearing wall construction with surfaces made of prefabricated modular stone panels—no stilts and no glass walls. The four-story building was shaped like a triangle to conform to its site, abutting the sidewalk and off-street parking on all sides. Its plan was symmetrical with a central courtyard, skylit from above. The projecting marquee over the main entrance was particularly admired by members of the AAC. Two additional entrances at either corner of the front façade led to consular offices on one side and the USIS offices and library on the other. The rooftop flagpole, suggested by the AAC, added to the central focus.

As originally presented, the color scheme was black and gold. In the end, the black remained, but the gold had to be omitted. The architect had intended to use polished granite pier facings with windows and spandrels conspicuously framed in lustrous bronze, but he agreed, as he later would at London, that a less costly gold-finished anodized aluminum would work as well as bronze. Eventually, he had to settle for even less expensive teak, painted white. As a result, the building never had the dazzle that Saarinen envisioned. Black was an odd choice for a city that spent so much of the year in relative darkness, and when AAC members saw renderings of the scheme, they objected and suggested a lighter palette. But Saarinen maintained his preference for a dark color, and the choice was left up to him. When he found that he could not get granite quarried and cut inexpensively in Norway, he considered using precast frames filled with black glass. Eventually, he selected a green-black granite chip aggregate, which was produced locally, possibly for the first time for use on this project. The aggregate weathered into a dull blackness, not the reflective surface that Saarinen had imagined.

The most dramatic aspect of the Oslo design was the sharply angled triangular plan. On the interior, the plan produced a poor circulation pattern and odd-shaped offices. But the lobby-courtyard, walled with narrow teak fins and natural brick, proved to be a handsome space that worked well for gatherings such as concerts and receptions (fig. 68). More sensible and maybe more dignified-looking than Rapson's proposed glass cube, the new Oslo embassy had an air of permanence, seriousness, and modernity. Standing by itself as a city block, it took on a certain prominence in a cityscape that boasted few modern buildings. Nothing about the design suggested Norwegian tradition or any particular concern for climate, nor did it convey anything uniquely American, aside from the fact that the building's materials took advantage of a new stone composition technology. Saarinen presented this project to the AAC once in November and again in March 1956. There was great respect for his talent among members of the AAC and general agreement that the design met FBO requirements; it was approved after just the two presentations.

LONDON WAS CONSIDERED the most important project on the FBO agenda in 1955, important enough to warrant a trip by Ralph Walker, who was sent by FBO to assess the embassy site there. Walker reported that the problem at London was preservation of the scale and quality of a historic district. Dismayed by the "new so-called modern abortions" he saw in London's Berkeley Square, he called upon his AAC colleagues to recognize the patterns of proportion that characterized eighteenth- and nineteenth-century squares and urged selection of designs that aimed for harmony above all else. Local authorities in Baghdad had retained the world's foremost modernists to design large-scale major public projects in the 1950s hoping that the modern architecture would come to symbolize a new and progressive Iraq, and leaders in other developing nations similarly favored the newest of new architecture as a sign of commercial prosperity. But Walker thought the key to successful urban design in European cities lay not in conspicuous newness, but rather in the opposite direction. "Steel and glass," he wrote, "seem all too inappropriate, all too temporary and, moreover, all too impersonal. There is need for a new monumentality, quiet and restrained, without any sense of the stunt."[18]

The United States had been associated with London's Mayfair district and specifically with Grosvenor Square since John Adams arrived in London in 1785 as the first American minister to Great Britain. Adams rented a red-brick house (No. 9) that still stands at the northeast corner of the square. Although the legation did not remain on the square, it remained in the area. In 1913, in the days when the American ambassador still had to find and pay for his own lodging, Walter Hines Page again rented a house on the square, this time at No. 6.

When the British government completed construction of its grand new embassy/residence in Washington (1931), the Lutyens-designed edifice was hailed as the ultimate in embassy architecture (fig. 11). Members of the House Foreign Affairs Committee described the new British Embassy as the finest in the world, and the Foreign Service Buildings Commission stepped up its effort to secure a comparable property for the United States in London, the only major foreign capital that lacked a government-owned embassy at that time. FSBC chairman Rep. Stephen Porter looked first at property around Trafalgar Square. "Every American wants to see Trafalgar Square when he goes to London," Porter declared, "and as a matter of pride we would like to have a building there."[19] But no deal was struck, and the FSBC concentrated on furnishing the former J. P. Morgan residence, donated to the State Department in 1921, and on securing leased office space in a newly constructed seven-story office building on the east side of Grosvenor

Square (fig. 96). The United States rented several floors in the new building for a period of ten years and moved in late in 1937. Later, when General Eisenhower arrived in London during World War II, he also set up his head-quarters on Grosvenor Square, opposite the embassy offices on the west side of the square. In 1947, officials erected a statue of Franklin Roosevelt on the north side of the park. By then, the area was known locally as "Little America." The Grosvenor Square property now belongs to the sixth duke of Westminster, Gerald Cavendish Grosvenor. The duke is a descendant of Thomas Grosvenor, married in 1677 to a twelve-year-old bride whose dowry included a 300-acre cabbage farm around which the city of London spread and grew.

The square was ringed by Georgian buildings when Adams took up residence at No. 9, but not so a hundred years later. As Fello Atkinson put it, the square "went to pieces in the nineteenth century."[20] Nevertheless, the duke, who owned the property, wanted it to retain its visual unity, its charm, and its value. He commissioned a master plan of elevations to be imposed by covenant on new buildings that would be built around the square's perimeter. The building leased by the United States in 1937 was one of the first projects completed according to the duke's "neo-Georgian" plan, which envisioned Grosvenor Square bordered by similar-looking buildings, offices, hotels, and luxury apartments. Intervening events slowed the prog-ress of the renewal plan, but it remained in effect when the United States began to consider building a new office building along the west side of the square after the war.

Prevented by statute from owning land, the U.S. government could still lease land and own buildings built upon it. In a position to exchange for-eign war debts for valuable real estate, the State Department purchased Nos. 1, 3, and 20 Grosvenor Square in 1947, paying $8,337,280, at the same time signing a ninety-nine-year land lease with the duke's estate. The entire transaction was completed in credits. A year later, in order to provide space for the burgeoning USIS operation, the department purchased No. 5 Grosvenor Square. Although U.S.-controlled, the new property did not ade-quately meet embassy needs. For one thing, residential tenants still occupied apartments in the building and had meals served to them by waiters who passed through the building's public corridors—a curious situation noted by Shepley when he visited there in 1954. The long-range plan, according to former FBO director Leland King, was to sell the newly acquired proper-ties and use the proceeds to help finance the construction of a consolidated office building on a single site nearby.[21]

Thus, in 1950, FBO entered into a series of difficult negotiations with the Grosvenor estate and acquired the west side of Grosvenor Square as an embassy site. The cost was $2,192,003, a sum again entirely derived from credits.[22] Prior to construction, buildings on the site needed to be demolished. Some had already been damaged by wartime bombing. As part of an effort to discredit FBO and King, members of Congress later criticized this transaction, linking it with the 1947 purchase, questioning the financial arrangements, and complaining about the presence of hold-over residential tenants in the U.S. buildings. What they failed to appreciate was the far-sightedness shown by Larkin and King, who acquired the entire side of a historic London square in a deal that cost American taxpayers next to nothing. Even the land lease fee was a bargain—just one peppercorn per year.

Members of the AAC deemed the London project important enough to justify the expense and time of a competition, the first in FBO history. They selected Robert W. McLaughlin Jr., as professional advisor, selected the entrants, agreed upon the format and the program, and announced the competition in the fall of 1955. Formerly a partner in the New York firm of Holden, McLaughlin & Associates, McLaughlin succeeded Sherley Warner Morgan as head of Princeton's architectural program in 1952. The Princeton program was still relatively free of the modernist dogma being taught at Harvard and other leading design schools at the time. McLaughlin had graduated from Princeton and received his M.F.A. there in 1926.[23] After traveling in Italy, France, and England, he returned to New York in 1928 to begin work in the office of H. Van Buren Magonigle and to begin the archeological studies that later became his passion. He opened his own practice in 1931 and became a pioneer in the field of prefabricated housing. He was active in AIA affairs, a member of the executive committee of the Architectural League of New York, and a trustee of the Beaux-Arts Institute of Design.

Surprisingly, pressure to build a "traditional" embassy building in London came more from the American side than from the British. U.S. Ambassador Winthrop W. Aldrich presented the strongest case for the importance of tradition. Aldrich, who returned from London to address a special meeting of the AAC on 5 August 1955, tried to convince the AAC that the new London embassy should not only respect English architectural tradition, but also that its design should be "in the nature of the late eighteenth-century architecture as designed by Nash."[24] Aldrich, whose own Hudson Valley house was modeled after an English country house, was emphatic in his belief that modern architecture would be inappropriate in London. The duke's estate would never condone a contemporary building such as "those being erected along Park Avenue in New York and in the capitals of South American countries," he said referring to SOM's Lever House and to American embassies recently designed by Harrison & Abramovitz in Rio and Havana. Aldrich declared his opposition to a skyscraper and shared Walker's objections to glass and steel.

In what must have been an acrimonious discussion, members of the AAC questioned Aldrich's assertion that the duke's estate would never allow a contemporary building, pointing out that the estate had already sanctioned such buildings in London. Furthermore, they noted that representatives of the Royal Commission of Fine Arts "hoped that American architects would not be influenced by the architecture of Lutyens." Instead, they were looking forward to a design that "would not be stodgy English but purely American...expressive of the best that is being designed in America today."[25] They did share the ambassador's objections to "glass and steel" construction, however, and agreed that a skyscraper would be inappropriate; but they did not want undue restrictions imposed upon architects participating in the competition. In retrospect, it is clear that those responsible for setting up the London competition had no intention of insisting upon a Nash reproduction. But it is also clear that they understood Aldrich's concern for context and incorporated that concern into the competition's program.

The strongest evidence that the committee favored a modern building can be seen in its selection of architects. Only eight firms were invited to participate in the competition: Anderson, Beckwith & Haible; Ernest J. Kump; Eero Saarinen & Associates; Josep Lluis Sert with Huson Jackson and Joseph Zalewski; Edward Durell Stone & Associates; Hugh Stubbins Associates; Wurster, Bernardi & Emmons; and Yamasaki, Leinweber & Associates—all committed modernists. AAC members were already complaining to one another about the absence of notable talent in the profession, but it is still surprising that they turned to men whom FBO had hired before. Except for Anderson, Beckwith & Haible (later awarded the commission for a proposed embassy in Taipei), all of the entrants were already working for FBO on other commissions when they were invited to participate in the competition. Each was paid $4,000 for a design and also to cover travel expenses, as each participant was required to travel to London to inspect the site in person.

The ten-page competition program emphasized context. It advised participants not to try to copy other buildings directly, but to pay careful attention to the historic surroundings.[26] The program called for an office building with a maximum of 150,000 square feet of floor space divided into three areas, each with a separate entrance: the central administrative area, including the ambassador's offices (121,500 sq. ft.); the consular and visa area (15,000 sq. ft.); and offices for the USIS (13,500 sq. ft.). The program outlined specific space requirements for the lobby, the ambassador's office, his staff, the deputy chief of mission, and the political counselor. It noted, for example, that the ambassador's office had to be accessible through public hallways and also through private corridors connected to the offices of the other key officials, that it should not be on the ground floor or on the first floor, and that there should be at least two floors *above* it. The basement was to contain areas for storage, service, and a cafeteria, and the sub-basement was to provide parking for twenty-five cars. The building was not to be air-conditioned, materials were to be procured if possible in England, and the overall height was not to exceed 100 feet. "The building will occupy and will visually establish one side of the Square," the program stated. "Its visual relationship to the other three sides as well as to the surrounding area of London is of the utmost importance." Additionally, the program stipulated that each scheme be capable in doubling in size if future needs called for additional space.[27] Stubbins, for one, took that requirement seriously, but the others, including Saarinen, ignored it.

According to one report, the architects made hasty visits to London during one of the worst winters on record.[28] It is hard to know how much the gloomy, wet scene may have affected subsequent designs, but it is worth noting that Grosvenor Square was in a poor state of repair at that time and would have looked shabby to the American visitors. Railings had been removed and gardens neglected. The competition review was set for 14 February 1956 in Washington. Judges included the three AAC members—Belluschi, Shepley, and Walker—in addition to FBO Director William Hughes, Deputy Under Secretary of State Loy Henderson, Assistant Secretary of State (for Europe) Livingston Merchant, and AIA President George B. Cummings. McLaughlin conducted the jury sessions, but was not himself a juror.

The entries varied widely. Minoru Yamasaki's scheme was perhaps the most eccentric—two connected parallel buildings wrapped in a lacy stone-clad screen with arched openings reminiscent of an English perpendicular Gothic façade. The architect's rendering shows a de-emphasized American flag waving from a short flagpole to the right of the off-center entrance (fig. 97).[29] William Wurster tried to capture what he called London's "violent" contrast in black and white, using white Portland stone and black brick as facing on his seven-story building, which extended the full width of the square. Three flags waved over the off-center entrance like flags over the entrance to a hotel, a perplexing feature given that only the American flag flies above a U.S. embassy. The Anderson, Beckwith & Haible scheme also extended the full width of the square, claiming to be a statement of "architectural tact." Indeed, the design was so tactful that it lacked any semblance of personality and did nothing to proclaim itself an important building. Ernest Kump's design similarly lacked any hint of its special purpose. It featured an enormous five-story portico of projecting columns, wrought-iron balconies, a brick and stone exterior, and glass-walled interior courtyards.

Like his later design for Tangier, Stubbins's proposal featured a building raised on stilts. The most remarkable elements of his scheme were a glass-walled lobby and an open courtyard accessible to pedestrians via an arcade that ran through the main building. According to Stubbins, the courtyard expressed "the traditional accessibility between the two countries." Materials included Portland stone, glass panels detailed in dark gray aluminum, and slabs of pink granite. The entrance was in the center, but the overall plan was asymmetrical. Of all the entries, this design was probably the most animated and certainly the most open. It would have proven the most difficult to secure in later years, but security was not as yet a priority.

Sert's design was less planar than the others. Its boxy volumes defined spaces, including the ambassador's office, consular offices, and facilities for the USIS. Like Saarinen, Sert devised a window pattern that alternated fixed glass with narrow, movable glass panels. His principal building material was dark brick, and for contrast the windows were set in steel frames painted white. More than the others, Sert tried to recreate the alternating rhythm of the townhouses that once stood side by side on the site. Unfortunately, the design lacked unity. While it was dramatic, it must have struck the jurors as disorganized.

In renderings that illustrated each design, the architects took great license, often adding full-grown trees where none existed, or eliminating telephone poles, signs, or even adjacent buildings where such elements seemed to detract from the proposed scheme. Sert's rendering, for example, included two automobiles—the hood of an enormous old Rolls-Royce, cast in shadow, and a white Thunderbird in blazing sunlight just beyond. The American sports car symbolized newness, fashion, and American technological know-how. Through the two cars, the architect commented on the relationship between the two nations, and also on the relationship between the venerable old surroundings and the proposed new embassy building (fig. 98).

Edward Durell Stone's rendering included only a building and atmospherically appropriate trees—no people, and no cars. Stone's was the only design, aside from Saarinen's, to try to grasp the importance of the embassy as a symbol. His scheme, which later became one of his trademark designs, was a seven-story block with a façade of floor-to-ceiling windows set back behind thin columns, topped by a roof loggia and a flat, overhanging roof. The principal building materials were limestone and glass. Like Kump, Stone incorporated black ironwork balcony railings in keeping with the decorative detail of neighboring buildings. Like Saarinen, he composed his scheme symmetrically and did not extend to the edges of the square on its sides. Thus it was set off as a building unto itself, surrounded at its base by parking areas and by trees. Perimeter walls screened it from the square, focusing attention on the centered entrance beneath a large replica of the Great Seal. Stone's plan featured two skylit courtyards landscaped with fountains, trees, and hanging gardens—an "atrium" plan, later popularized by architect John Portman.

Saarinen presented a symmetrical scheme that featured an even larger replica of the Great Seal mounted much more prominently over the entrance. The seal hung just below an elaborate cornice. His five-story building was classically divided into base, middle, and top. To underscore that it was a unique building and not simply an enclosure for the square, Saarinen brought the building in slightly from the edges of the block. Though he avoided a clear distinction between window and wall, his window openings were scaled to the windows of the nearby buildings. He alternated the narrow operable windows with fixed glass panels mounted, like pictures, in flat frames made of Portland stone. The scheme was not particularly eye-catching, but neither was it dull.

When it came time to select a winner, members of the jury found themselves choosing between Stone and Saarinen. Belluschi recalls that "Stone seemed the favorite," but that he ended up voting for the Saarinen design "but not with great enthusiasm."[30] It would be fair to suppose that it was the conspicuousness of Stone's scheme, its 93-foot height for one thing, that proved to be its downfall. But surely other factors entered into the decision, not the least of which was Saarinen's uncanny knack of knowing how to present a winner. With a mixture of envy and admiration, colleagues joked that Saarinen nearly always won competitions because he ignored program requirements and gave the judges what he thought they really wanted to see rendered in the most elegant and attractive fashion. As Stubbins later said:

[Saarinen] was a good friend of mine and we always were going into competitions together, and this guy won them! And what he did was he went against the rules every time. I guess we all should have learned a lesson from that, you don't have to follow rules, all you have to do is do the best job.[31]

At forty-five, Saarinen was already a major figure on the American architectural scene. Son of famed Finnish architect Eliel Saarinen, he had studied sculpture in Paris and architecture at Yale. He joined his father's practice in Ann Arbor in 1936 and collaborated on many major commercial and institutional projects before he launched his own firm in 1950. Although the Grosvenor estate had waived its right to insist upon a "neo-Georgian" building, and although the program made it clear that the sponsors of the competition were not looking for an eclectic reproduction, Saarinen sensed that a compromise was called for. Knowing that three of the seven jury members were State Department officials unlikely to favor a radical scheme, and knowing that the AIA president was likely to be conservative as well, Saarinen took his cue from the surrounding area and designed a "modern" building using "traditional" methods and materials. Robert McLaughlin's son, Robert T. McLaughlin, recalls that his father was the one who "wound up calling the shots" at the jury deliberations, and that "it was on his advice that they selected Eero Saarinen....They wanted to be cautious with a huge national symbol," he said. Stone was named the runner-up, and Saarinen took first prize.[32]

For the scheme that Saarinen proposed (though not the one that was built), he chose Portland stone as his principal building material and bronze for details. Portland stone was widely used in London's public buildings and noted for the varied black and white patterns that it acquired as a result of exposure to the local climate and pollution. He even called attention to the "Englishness" of the project by referring to the design of the exterior wall as "an English pre-cast structural system."[33] Elegant and expensive materials added to the formality and distinction of the design—sand-molded, black oxidized bronze for the cornice and natural bronze for the Great Seal and the "protective" grill at ground-level. Saarinen intended the building to age and blacken from soot like so many other London landmarks, and he imagined that the bronze would add brightness to the darkened façade.

British newspapers covered the competition, and major architectural journals from both countries announced the results and ran pictures of the designs.[34] The *Times* of London cited the winning project as a "welcome acquisition" to the area and noted how well Saarinen had harmonized his design with the existing façades. The paper commended Saarinen for the choice of a "strictly symmetrical" building that retained "the traditional formality of the London Square." Other British publications had a different reaction. The *Architects' Journal* came out and praised the winning entry—not for "fitting in," but for just the opposite. "As the first contemporary building—if in a very restrained way—in this part of Mayfair," the *Journal* said, "it will provide a welcome example for future development in

ARCHITECTS ASSERT THEMSELVES

an area unduly wedded to neo-Georgian commonplaceness." The *Journal* report suggested that a good modern building might jolt the area out of its dull infatuation with the past. American journals reported the competition results with no editorial enthusiasm.

Immediately after the judging, FBO director Hughes congratulated the AAC on the "outstanding success" of the competition. On his return from a late-February trip to London, he happily announced "the ready acceptance of the results by Ambassador Aldrich and the London authorities," an acceptance that he attributed to the "careful preparation of the program, cautious selection of contestants and competent judgment of the drawings."[35] But FBO released little news about the competition and did nothing to publicize the results. This apparent silence surely stemmed from the fact that some members of the jury were profoundly disappointed with the outcome. The jury deliberations, it seems, were marked by serious disagreement. Walker, for one, labeled the competition a failure. In a letter to Shepley and Belluschi he wrote, "I was tremendously upset by the failure of the group of men to realize an opportunity, and I think that failure is inherent in modern architectural philosophy today." In that letter, written just days after the judging took place, he continued, "Pietro often seems to be scornful of aesthetics, or at least my concept of them, but surely the results show a complete lack of understanding of what aesthetic relationships mean." Belluschi's later recollection that he preferred the Stone scheme but voted for the Saarinen proposal with "little enthusiasm," at least suggests that his vote was part of a compromise.[36] According to Walker, nearly all of the competitors entered designs that were completely lacking in taste. In September 1956, perhaps with more than a touch of melodrama, Walker wrote to his former AAC colleagues, "I thought the nadir in American architectural design had been reached in the London competition."[37]

Saarinen's winning scheme was not actually built; largely because of an increased need for space, FBO changed its program after declaring him the winner. Saarinen redesigned the building, adding a lower floor and raising the overall height, making other major changes that included a complete redesign of the structural system. He presented his new plan and design to the AAC on 15 May 1956. The AAC agreed that the new height did not adversely affect the building's relationship to its neighbors and praised the "diagrid" system of crisscrossed supporting beams, evident inside and out, that permitted the main façade to overhang the column line. Saarinen said the metal fasteners trimming the windows and other details would "add sparkle to the façade."[38] To cut the cost of the project, he was forced to abandon his preference for bronze, substituting gold-colored anodized aluminum in its place. (He unsuccessfully attempted to downplay the association between gold and glitz by describing the aluminum detailing as "straw-colored.")

A conspicuous difference between the original and revised schemes was the elimination of the Great Seal and its replacement by the infamous eagle, but there was no mention of the giant eagle motif in the May presentation. In fact, Saarinen did not bring the eagle into the picture until later. Although the cost of the new design was still "considerably over the budget," the AAC approved and commended it as a "real improvement over the competition design"—a comment that suggests again that there was dissatisfaction with that scheme. Saarinen flew to London to make arrangements for construction (fig. 99).

Once the embassy was under construction, sometime late in 1957, Saarinen proposed the addition of the thirty-five-foot-wide eagle, a riveting symbol on the front of the embassy (fig. 77). American sculptor Theodore Roszak created the eagle out of gilded aluminum. His inspiration, he said, was a pre-Independence carved wooden eagle that he had seen in a New England museum. From the outset, the monumental bird raised questions. Saarinen was himself a member of the Architectural Advisory Panel when Hughes asked him to make a special presentation of his scheme to resolve the "eagle" question. Thus wearing two hats at once, Saarinen presented a slide-illustrated talk to his colleagues on the use of the eagle throughout American history and presented his design to the panel, of which he was a member. "At the psychological moment, the façade was uncovered and the committee was given the opportunity to study the size, design, texture and material of the eagle and its relation to the façade," the minutes report.[39] AAP members Edgar Williams, Richard Bennett, and Ambassador Joseph C. Satterthwaite unanimously supported Saarinen, and he proceeded with his plans for the sculpture.

Even before the embassy opened in 1960, critics greeted the building with doubt and scorn. The eagle drew much of the negative attention— it was too loud, too blatant, too oppressive, and too fierce. Some critics worried that the bird was iconographically incorrect—it looked to the left instead of to the right, as was the custom. Missing, too, were the arrows clutched in the left talon and the olive branch in the right, traditional symbols of war and peace. As former ambassador Sargent Shriver later noted, "the eagle drove them crazy!"[40] The *New York Times* reported British concern over whether or not it was "the ideal symbol to brood over a famous square" and cited a young British architect who asked what Americans would think of a thirty-five-foot-long lion atop the British embassy in Washington, or a thirty-five-foot-high hammer and sickle over the Russian?

It also reported British comments that compared the building to "a cigarette factory," and other remarks about its "Hollywood-Broadway influence." Sen. J. William Fulbright complained bitterly about the new building, Sen. Frank Church ridiculed the eagle, and Rep. Wayne Hays called the whole thing a "monstrosity." Usually anxious to look on the bright side of projects and people, Rep. Frances Bolton called the building "an eyesore" and declared it to be "an offense to our whole relationship with London." Hays suggested a big sign saying "EAGLE," because, he said, it looked like a buzzard to him. Others were even less charitable.

Architectural Forum reprinted scathing remarks by British architects and critics, including Peter Smithson, who called for something far more daring and questioned the very idea of wanting to fit in; Reyner Banham, who compared the building to an empty cenotaph and said that it represented "the 'Ballet School' in U.S. architecture;" and R. Furneaux Jordan, who faulted the United States for "exporting prestige in the form of 'glamour,' " for claiming to pay homage to a non-existent Georgian tradition, and for exploiting a "false humility." To Jordan, the "xenophobic" eagle represented "the tragedy of Americanism." The *London Times* reiterated Jordan's contention that the competition wrongly placed its emphasis on finding a design "appropriate" to London, and declared the results to be "lavish," "tawdry," and "superficial." In a published statement, Saarinen defended his work—the plan, the design, and the eagle, which, he said, "is used not in the form of the great seal, but freely and symbolically as it has so often been used in the past."[41]

When the London embassy opened, only a year before his death at the age of fifty-one, Saarinen was working on many very different commissions, including the now famous terminals at Kennedy Airport—for TWA—(1956–62) and at Dulles Airport (1958–63). Just as the sweeping Dulles design came to "symbolize" air travel, Saarinen's Gateway Arch (1959–64) came to "symbolize" St. Louis as the American gateway to the West. In much the same way, the eagle was added to "symbolize" the London embassy, to tell people that it was an embassy, not an ordinary block of offices. Even the trim contributed to this effort, with bright gold stars at the exposed ends of the diagrid.

More than anyone else who analyzed the new embassy, Fello Atkinson seems to have appreciated what Saarinen was trying to do. Writing in the British publication *Architectural Review*, Atkinson praised the metal trim for its richness and for the way it reflected light. The interior, he observed, was probably the most successful part of the building, though it figured relatively little in the competition. He wrote:

From the moment one ascends the steps...one senses all those things which
have made the architect his reputation. Restricted by an almost impossibly
rigid planning problem, unable to gain much spatial variety, he has yet
achieved a fascinating interior....The upper floors consist almost entirely
of small offices. Yet even from these Saarinen has made a quiet, disciplined
elegance out of corridor width, door rhythm and meticulous detailing,
which achieves a separation of walls and ceiling in an almost Japanese way.
Indeed it is the fastidiousness of the detailing—raising standards of finish in
England to a new level—which is the greatest contribution. Such detailing
is not merely concerned with appearance but with the feel and operation of
things. While not in itself architecture it heightens the appreciation of it.[42]

Atkinson went on to explain how Saarinen integrated the diagonal
(structure) and the right angle (plan) in a effort to move beyond the Miesian
grid to a "newer plastic phase." He compared Saarinen's interior to those of
Charles Rennie Mackintosh and Josef Hoffmann, and commended its quiet
elegance as "sheer relief after a decade or so of cheap and dowdy gaudi-
ness." Atkinson's article illustrated hallways, stairways, handrails, ceiling
modules, doors, and doorstays. The interior included steel library tables,
long, low, wall-mounted banquettes, and massive armless swivel chairs
upholstered in leather (figs. 100–1). Some of the custom-designed furniture
was from Knoll and other pieces were by Charles Eames.

When he redesigned the competition entry and raised the building on a
gently sloped pedestal base, Saarinen inadvertently provided a subtle defensive device that separates the building from immediate contact with the sidewalk and passersby (figs. 102–3). In that way, he was ahead of his time. He
erred, however, when he predicted that the building would gradually take
on a rich black luster from pollution, because a new London ordinance cut
acceptable pollution levels just after the new embassy opened. Moreover,
when it became dirty, it was washed. Since 1960, the Grosvenor estate has
completed the rebuilding of the square, now enclosed on three sides by red
brick, faux-Georgian façades. Near the World War II memorial and the statue of Roosevelt stands a statue of General Eisenhower—further evidence of
the symbolic association between the United States and Great Britain.

As Atkinson pointed out, the State Department's directive to its architects to incorporate local themes and to sympathize with local customs and
local history was "praiseworthy but hardly meaningful" in places where
buildings were to be built in areas that were "new or mushrooming with
brash commercial modernism." Furthermore, he noted that the directive
may have caused architects to seek desperately (in their brief but mandatory

exploratory visits) for local gimmicks "to hang on their architecture." In New Delhi, and also at Accra and Athens, architects played with such gimmickry and still managed to design suitable embassies. But London was no place for gimmicks, or as Walker called them, "stunts."

British modernists were less interested in allusions to the past than they were in insights into the future. They considered the "meek-mock-Georgian" façades prescribed by the Grosvenor plan to be inauthentic. They argued the square was in transition, and that its new buildings should not feature false fronts in an effort to recapture a past that was already lost. Efforts to harmonize or fit in with such a plan were fundamentally flawed, they said. From the Americans, they were hoping for something new, even something radical. Since the architectural expectations of such critics were inextricably mixed up with their feelings about the United States and its status as a world power, they were just as bound to be baffled or irritated by something restrained (not architecturally inventive enough) as by something strong and assertive (too imperialistic or aggressive-looking). There is no way to separate aesthetic judgment from political outlook where the object to be judged is itself a political statement. That so many British critics were disappointed when the big new American embassy opened in 1960 should have surprised no one.

UNDER THE AEGIS OF FBO, three separate architects prepared designs for a new embassy in The Hague (Den Haag). Rapson and van der Meulen prepared a design in 1951, William Gehron prepared another in 1955, and in 1956 Marcel Breuer designed the building that was ultimately built. After the two false starts, FBO turned to Breuer as an architect who could add real "class" to the State Department's architectural roster, and his scheme was approved almost automatically. The embassy was built in 1958 and dedicated on 4 July 1959.

While Amsterdam is the Dutch capital, The Hague is the seat of the Dutch government and the location of foreign missions to that nation. The Hague is also home to the International Court of Justice and the Peace Palace, the city's best-known landmark. When John Adams sailed to England to establish diplomatic ties between the United States and Great Britain in 1785, he had already been to Holland to establish formal diplomatic relations between the United States and the Netherlands. Adams arrived in The Hague as America's first minister plenipotentiary in 1782. Soon after, the Dutch state formally recognized the independence of the United States and sent its first minister plenipotentiary to establish a reciprocal diplomatic mission in the American capital, then located in Philadelphia. Since

Adams's day, the American mission has been located at various sites within The Hague.

An amalgam of seventeenth-, eighteenth-, and nineteenth-century architecture, The Hague is noted for its spacious parks and charming squares lined with solidly built brick and masonry buildings designed with large windows to capture the precious northern daylight. Sober or serious as a group, many older buildings feature exuberant design touches around rooflines, doorways, and balconies. Despite a strong attachment to the past, Dutch architects were leaders in the evolution of architectural modernism, and there was nothing intrinsically radical about the idea of building a modern-looking embassy office building in The Hague in the mid-1950s. The Dutch were concerned less with issues of style, *per se*, than with the contextual limits imposed by the embassy site and the quality of the proposed design.

Located on the corner of an old square, the site became available for purchase under tragic circumstances. Trying to destroy the emplacement from which the Germans were launching V1 and V2 rockets at London, British RAF planes accidentally bombed the square on 3 March 1945.[43] Damage from the bombing was extensive—tearing a hole in the city's fabric and claiming many lives. More than five hundred civilians were killed in the attack, the second worst bombing raid in The Netherlands, after Rotterdam. (The RAF admitted the error, but no real explanation was ever offered.) Using foreign credits, the State Department purchased the vacant site just after the war. Some local residents were offended when the Americans selected the site; years later, many still view the spot with sadness. It is hard to know whether or not the unfortunate association colored local feeling towards the new American embassy, but the building did produce bitter debate over architecture and context and provoked protest from its Dutch hosts.[44]

After the war it was clear to all that new buildings would someday be built near the intersection of the Lange Voorhout and Korte Voorhout where the site was located. But what was not at all apparent was the Dutch citizens' desire to see the area restored. When Ralph Rapson first examined the site in 1951, he was most impressed by the swath of emptiness where the bombs had fallen. Faced with the task of designing a new American embassy on the site, Rapson was more interested in creating something new and forward-looking than something traditional. There was no program for the proposed building and only a rough budget; payment was to come from credits. As Rapson recalls it, FBO provided him with no design guidance, and neither he nor his partner John van der Meulen gave any thought to the significance of the embassy as a symbolic building. What they designed was a three-story glass box raised on *pilotis* (fig. 24). While the design may have called attention to itself because it was so unlike surrounding buildings, it is apparent from Rapson's later comments that he and his partner thought of it more as a utilitarian office building, even as a sort of background statement, than as a building designed to startle or shock. For reasons having little to do with the architecture, however, FBO shelved the Rapson and van der Meulen proposal when the State Department reorganized FBO late in 1953.

When the AAC convened in 1954, members discussed the possibility of holding design competitions for The Hague and London. The Hague was one of the most significant projects on the FBO agenda, nearly as large in size as projects in New Delhi and Hong Kong. FBO estimated its budget at $1 million. The only project on the 1955 agenda with a bigger budget was London, budgeted at $3 million. But The Hague competition idea was quickly discarded and AAC members began the process of selecting an architect. As a first step, Shepley visited the Dutch site and reported back that there were design restrictions on the adjacent square. He cautioned his colleagues that any proposal would eventually have to be approved by a local commission of fine arts. In his notes of his visit, he did not mention the bombing accident or anything about the destruction of historic buildings along the square or nearby. He did note, however that the architecture of the Hague was "very robust." "Frank Lloyd Wright buildings would go well there," he declared. He was also impressed with the lavish care of lawns and gardens. He recommended that landscaping be incorporated into the design of the new building.[45]

A year later, Walker reiterated Shepley's concern about context after he also visited the site for FBO. "I wandered all over the square, sat in a cafe, and drank in the quality of peaceful charm as well as the good Dutch beer," he wrote in his August 1955 report to his colleagues. "A good part of a delightful morning so employed," he went on to say, "led me finally to wonder at the outrageous willingness to force an unfriendly result." He referred to the earlier glass box by Rapson and van der Meulen as "unsuitable," and "stupid." He also made several other important observations concerning a possible design. First, he commented on how new buildings he saw in England and in Holland had "the appearance of early obsolescence....Exposed concrete near the sea," he pointed out, "seems to disintegrate badly." And second, he pointed out that new concrete, steel, and glass buildings required refurbishing more often than older styles in order to remain "shipshape." This was especially relevant to the foreign building program, he said, because Congress could never grasp conditions abroad and the State Department was unlikely to have sufficient funds to maintain its buildings properly.[46]

AAC members recommended the firm of Holabird, Root & Burgee as their first choice for the job. Instead, FBO offered the job to their second choice, New York architect William Gehron. Gehron was best known for his campus buildings at West Point and Denison University, and for government buildings, military bases, and war memorials. A 1912 graduate of Carnegie Tech, he was sixty-eight years old in 1955, and recognized by his peers as a capable professional, though certainly not a leading modernist. Compared to the others nominated by the AAC, he was an improbable choice for an embassy project.

Gehron did not appear in Washington himself because he was ill. When his partner, Gilbert L. Seltzer, presented preliminary sketches to the AAC on 12 December 1955, the committee was sorely disappointed. Members told the architect that the *parti* and designs were simply "not suitable." They asked him to return with a new design more compatible with nearby eighteenth century landmarks. Seltzer returned in January with a new model, but the committee was even more dismayed by his second presentation. Minutes show that they found the design "dull, unimaginative, and uninspired." They decided that the situation called for a new architect and "a fresh start." FBO director Hughes concurred with the AAC recommendation and wrote to Gehron who replied with a thoughtful and thorough defense of his design. Admitting that he was handicapped by illness, however, he resigned.[47]

The enthusiasm with which the AAC greeted Gehron's resignation suggests that they were glad to be rid of him. Other architects had presented revised schemes to the committee, and a number were even asked to begin anew, but no other architect was so unceremoniously terminated. Rudolph appeared five times before the panel, and despite doubts about his design and strong opposition from McBride, the architects on the panel continued to express confidence in him. The AAC severely criticized Neutra & Alexander's first Karachi presentation, saying that it "gave the impression of being a commercial enterprise similar to a mail order business." They demanded a new *parti*, but did not discuss replacing the architect.[48] And Stone's New Delhi project was under review for seven months with no move to hire a new architect. Gehron's dismissal came about at least in part due to the availability of Marcel Breuer as a replacement.

Walker's AAC term ended in December 1955, a month before Gehron was forced to quit. Walker's antipathy to the work of Gropius and Breuer was well known. As long as he served on the AAC, Walker would have opposed the selection of either man; but after he resigned from the AAC, new possibilities opened up. By 22 March 1956, FBO had entered into a contract with Gropius for the design of the embassy office building in

Athens, and just three weeks later Breuer signed a contract for the building in The Hague.

Despite what Walker thought of the former Bauhaus masters, they had arrived in the United States to a thunderous welcome from the academic community, many of whom were Americans insecure about their own architectural history, and viewed the European modernists as heroes. The Hungarian-born Breuer joined the faculty at Harvard's Graduate School of Design in 1937 as an associate professor of architecture under Gropius. He remained at the GSD and practiced architecture in Cambridge until 1946 when he moved to New York and set up an office there. Aside from one project in Ontario and another in Minnesota, until the mid-1950s nearly all of his U.S. work was located in and around the New York/New England area, and much of it was residential. Then, in 1952, he began a collaboration with Pier Luigi Nervi and Bernard Zehrfuss for the UNESCO headquarters building in Paris. UNESCO's bold, Y-shaped concrete structure later became his trademark. With offices in New York and Paris, he was well positioned to win another European commission in 1953—the De Bijenkorf department store in Rotterdam. Then, while at work on the Rotterdam project, he secured the FBO commission. He welcomed the prominent project and the chance to design an "American" building in Europe. He signed the contract with FBO in mid-April and was already in Washington in mid-May making his first and *only* presentation to the AAC.[49]

By the time Breuer began work on the embassy project, many of the partially-destroyed townhouses on the square had already been restored. A large, new building for the Dutch Ministry of Education had been built on the Korte Voorhout on the opposite side of the street from the proposed embassy. But much of the land along the Korte Voorhout was still vacant and scheduled for redevelopment. Breuer looked to the future of the area in justifying his design, arguing that the many other large buildings to come would create a new scale for the area. With this in mind, he focused on the side street and its inevitable development, largely ignoring the historic buildings nearby.

What he designed was a four-story building made up of two blocks connected by a glass hall. The load-bearing walls were sheathed in panels of striated imported limestone. Joined at right angles, the two blocks enclosed a garden and a flat green lawn not visible from the street. Both blocks were raised slightly over a recessed base so that they seemed to hover over the sidewalk, creating a tension between the masonry mass above and the thin shadow of space beneath (fig. 104). The smaller block faced front onto the square and contained the entrance hall, the ambassador's office (with its own balcony), political offices, and other offices requiring controlled access.

The larger block, behind, contained support facilities including USIS offices, auditorium, and library. Both the front and the side featured prominent two-story entrances with flag poles above. As at London and Oslo, separate entrances facilitated direct public access to the building.

The design bore a striking resemblance to the De Bijenkorf project. Both buildings were alike in their massing of form and in their attention to surface pattern and geometry. While the hexagon was the basic module for the De Bijenkorf, the trapezoid was the module for the embassy. If the hexagon was appropriate for the De Bijenkorf because it resembled a honeycomb (*bijenkorf* is the Dutch word for "beehive"), there was no particular rationale for the use of the trapezoid at the embassy. But nearly every architectural element in the embassy was somehow trapezoidal. The auditorium was shaped like a trapezoid, piers in the library were shaped like trapezoids, even conference room tables and doorknobs were shaped like trapezoids. Window modules that looked to some like bowling ten-pins or coffins, looked to Breuer like double trapezoids (figs. 71–2, 105–7).

Breuer treated the embassy like a piece of sculpture, and the small monumental building did achieve the intimacy and craft-quality of an art object, both of which were absent in later Breuer projects built larger in size and scale. By staggering the window placement and by not arranging the openings in continuous rows, and also by adding staggered rows of slit-like windows on the side, he created a wonderfully plastic surface that changed dramatically as light shifted across it. The exterior granite sheathing, cut into thinner trapezoids between the windows and rectangles above and below them, further emphasized the block-like quality of the walls. The embassy was even more highly finished on the inside, where walls were covered with tiles of rough-cut white crystalline marble imported from the south of Switzerland, and by contrasting panels of sand-colored aggregate. The floors were made of black slate from Norway. Steel window frames, doors, and metalwork came from England, rugs were imported from India, and the curtains were made in Belgium—all purchased with foreign credits where possible. Breuer specified Burmese teak for paneling in the library, the ambassador's office, the conference room, for hand-railings throughout the building, for the parquet floor in the auditorium, and even for the elevator interiors.

Breuer presented his proposal to the AAC on 15 May 1956, at which time he described how the city's desire to restrict traffic around the small park led him to separate the *parti* into two buildings, and how he had created openness by incorporating vistas through the lobbies and connecting elements. AAC members must have been enthusiastic about what they saw. They even note in the minutes that Breuer's building carefully preserved the scale of the small eighteenth-century opera house nearby—though it must have been almost impossible for them to discern any relationship between the new building and any surrounding structure, including the opera house. Regardless, the AAC approved Breuer's design and recommended that "the architect be complimented on his fine *parti* and for his sensitive approach to the proper design solution."[50] Curiously, no one wondered whether or not the prominent side entrance might be mistaken for the main entrance (as it later was), a criticism that had already been directed at Gehron's plan; and no one suggested that the odd shaped wooden-trimmed windows might chronically leak air and water (as they did and still do). The AAC was not looking for flaws in Breuer's scheme.

Architectural traditionalists in The Hague did not see the embassy as an art object and protested the design. They criticized it for clashing with its environment and for exhibiting only "the material riches" of the United States, though neither the materials nor the architect actually came from America. They felt that Breuer's proposed building was too tall, and that it violated local design control restrictions that required balconies, for example, to be trimmed only with open ironwork. Though only a small group, the protesters managed to publicize their objections; reports of the opposition were even published in the *New York Times*. The *Times* pointed out, however, that the ordinances cited by protesters had been rescinded in 1950, and it went on to note that local opposition was "probably doomed" because plans for the embassy had already been approved by the City Council and town planning authorities. Why did city authorities approve the plans if "the quaint Old World atmosphere" was so important to the place? Dutch critics said that although there were serious doubts about the plans, authorities felt compelled to approve them. Not to have done so, they felt, would have dishonored both the architect and the United States.[51]

When Ralph Walker stopped by the FBO offices in Washington in October 1956 to visit with director Hughes and look over new designs, he examined Breuer's scheme, among others. Writing to his former colleagues after the visit, he commended Sert's design for Baghdad and Stone's design for New Delhi, both of which, he said, would represent the United States well. He expressed some dismay about Saarinen's Oslo job, but thought that Ketchum's work in Rabat was "superb." As for Athens, he felt that Gropius, whom he described as "an architect of small merit," was doing better than he would have expected. But Breuer's project outraged him. "The design for The Hague," he wrote, "takes the cake for pure unadulterated and vulgar ugliness." He leveled a scathing critique of the architecture, stating:

It would seem to flow from what the Scotch call a *"disjaskit"* mind. After looking at it a second time I believe the French would do a better job in verbal expression and I remarked to myself, *"C'est formidable, quelle merde!"* If all three of you were so intrigued with coffin shapes and really unpleasant windows why not make the catastrophe complete and insist that the whole building be covered alike. At least a unity in brutality would be achieved. Did anyone ever see a more unfriendly entrance for supposed friends of the U.S. to enter into. The whole thing fits into a quiet charming square and is related to the little opera house in much the same way as is a gold tooth glittering in a Japanese grin. The brutal self-assertion of a designer's ego has never been more in evidence.[52]

Other critics were less damning, but the overriding sentiment expressed in the Dutch press was one of disappointment—disappointment that an architect of Breuer's stature had foisted such a bad building upon such a special place. What is most interesting about the overall criticism is that it was aimed less at the State Department or the United States government than at the architect, who was seen by many as a European, rather than an American, artist. Writing in *BOUW*, J. J. Vriend saw Breuer's project as a "step backward....Breuer's building truly cannot be called ugly. That is too cheap....We see an originally fully functional architect lose himself in modern 'art for art's sake.'" And he, too, described the trapezoid-shaped windows as bizarre.[53]

Another critic, A. Buffinga, lamented the fact that Breuer fell so short of expectations at The Hague. He faulted Breuer for representing a European point of view instead of an American one and for ignoring FBO guidelines aimed at recognizing and respecting local history and context.[54] To Dutch critics, FBO design policy was an expression of something intrinsically American. The idea of fitting in and reflecting locale, they suggested, was an American idea, not one shared by other nations. In Washington, Americans admired foreign missions distinctively designed or decorated to reflect their home countries; abroad, they wanted their own buildings to "fit in." Breuer was correct in anticipating the large modern buildings that now line the Korte Voorhout. His goal, though, was never simply to fit in. Instead, in the opinion of many, he suffered from the irrepressible impulse to design a personal monument. His selection of "heavy" materials and his emphasis on the mass of the walls, however, did produce an embassy with a pronounced sense of permanence—a precursor to the more highly fortified buildings that followed.

FIGS. 110–3: U.S. Embassy, Dublin, Ireland. John M. Johansen (1957–64). (PREVIOUS PAGE, TOP) Night view at completion of construction in 1964. © Norman McGrath (PREVIOUS PAGE, BOTTOM) Added security barriers and window protection as seen in 1992. (THIS PAGE, TOP) Interior court. © Norman McGrath, Department of State (THIS PAGE, BOTTOM) Ambassador's office.

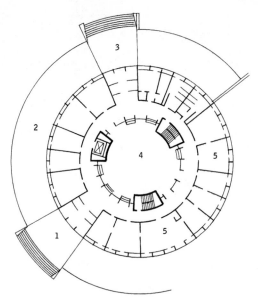

FIGS. 114 & 115: U.S. Embassy, Dublin, Ireland. (TOP) Aerial view showing moat and former USIS entrance. (BOTTOM) Plan after drawing in *Architectural Forum* (1964).

1. FORMER USIS ENTRANCE	4. LOBBY
2. DRY MOAT	5. OFFICES
3. MAIN ENTRANCE	

FIG. 116 (ABOVE): Congressman Wayne L. Hays (far right) with colleagues from the House Foreign Affairs Subcommittee on State Department Organization and Foreign Operations, members of the Architectural Advisory Panel, and State Department officials on the roof terrace at the State Department prior to luncheon, 9 May 1963. Left to right: William H. Orrick (deputy under secretary of state for administration), E. Ross Adair (R-Ind.), William Wurster (AAP), Lawrence Anderson (AAP), Dean Rusk (secretary of state), Edna F. Kelly (D-N.Y.), Roy F. Larson (AAP), John S. Monagan (D-Conn.), and Hays (D-Ohio).

FIG. 117 (NEXT PAGE, TOP): U.S. Embassy, Niamey, Niger. Robert Beatty (1964–70).

FIG. 118 (NEXT PAGE, MIDDLE): U.S. Embassy, Wellington, New Zealand. Robert Beatty (1972–77). Front elevation, looking south from Tinakori Hill.

FIG. 119 (NEXT PAGE, BOTTOM): Proposal for U.S. Embassy, Belgrade, Yugoslavia. Raymond & Rado (1971). Unbuilt.

FIG. 120 (TOP LEFT): U.S. Embassy, Colombo, Sri Lanka. Victor Lundy (1961–85).

FIG. 121 (TOP RIGHT): U.S. Embassy, Dakar, Senegal. Madison & Madison, International (1972–77).

FIG. 122 (BOTTOM): U.S. Embassy, Brasilia, Brazil. Henningson, Durham & Richardson (1971–72).

FIG. 123 (TOP): U.S. Embassy, Madrid, Spain. Guards at gate (1991).

FIG. 124 (BOTTOM): U.S. Embassy, Jakarta, Indonesia. Protesters scale fence (1994).

FIG. 125: Former U.S. Embassy, Accra, Ghana. Architect Harry Weese in courtyard on inspection trip in 1978. Deemed an asset in the 1950s, the building's openness posed a security hazard by the late 1970s. Weese returned to assess whether the building could be upgraded to meet new requirements, but found the obstacles insurmountable. The embassy was forced to relocate.

FIG. 126 (TOP): U.S. Embassy, Lisbon, Portugal. Frederick Bassetti (1978–83). Note fencing on widows.

FIG. 127 (BOTTOM): U.S. Embassy, Kuala Lumpur, Malaysia. Hartman-Cox Architects (1980–83). The balcony fronts are actually bullet-proof shields. "It looks friendly," says the architect, "but it's built like a fortress."

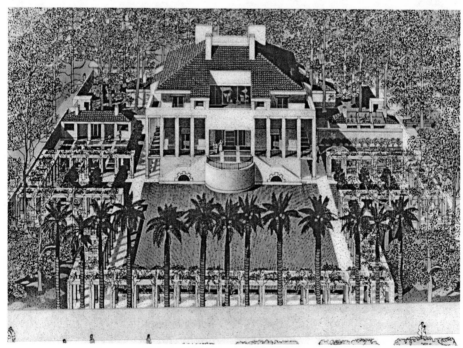

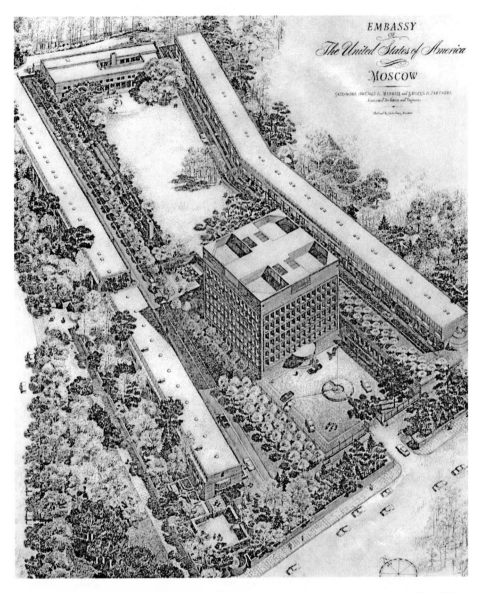

EMBASSY
OF
The United States of America
MOSCOW

SKIDMORE, OWINGS & MERRILL and GRUZEN & PARTNERS
Associated Architects and Engineers

Prepared by Carlos Diniz, Associates

FIG. 128 (OPPOSITE, TOP): U.S. Embassy, Dhaka, Bangladesh. Kallmann, McKinnell & Wood (1983–88).

FIG. 129 (OPPOSITE, BOTTOM): Proposal for U.S. Ambassador's Residence, Giza, Egypt. Metcalf & Associates (1982–86). Property sold after construction scandal.

FIG. 130 (ABOVE): U.S. Embassy compound, Moscow, Russia. Skidmore, Owings & Merrill and Gruzen & Partners (1973–85). Partially completed in 1985; chancery reconstruction completed in 2000.

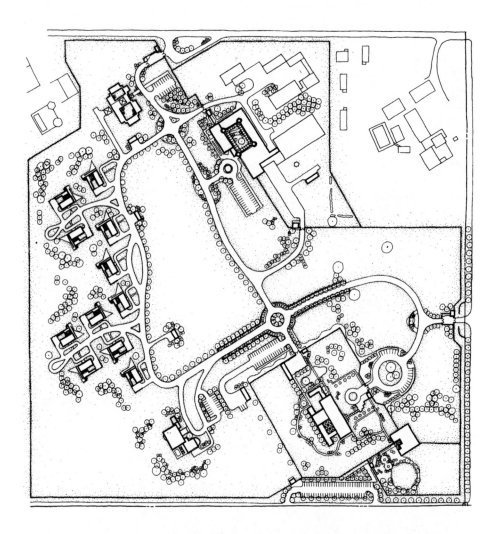

FIGS. 131–4: Former U.S. Embassy, Mogadishu, Somalia. Oudens + Knoop (1984–90). (ABOVE) Site plan; (OPPOSITE, TOP) soldiers guarding main entrance to the compound; (OPPOSITE, BOTTOM LEFT) perimeter wall; (OPPOSITE, BOTTOM RIGHT) American flag by newly built concrete trellis. The compound was attacked by Somali mobs and abandoned in 1991 following a daring rescue of American personnel by Marines and Navy SEALs.

FIG. 135 (TOP): U.S. Embassy compound, Sanaa, Yemen. CRS-Sirrine, Architects (1986–90).

FIG. 136 (BOTTOM): U.S. Embassy compound, Amman, Jordan. Perry, Dean Rogers & Partners (1988–92). Larger than six football fields in area and surrounded by a 9-foot wall.

FIG. 137: U.S. Embassy, Amman, Jordan. Courtyard.

FIG. 138 (TOP): U.S. Embassy, courtyard, Kuwait. RTKL (1992).

FIG. 139 (BOTTOM): U.S. Embassy, Muscat, Oman. Polshek & Partners (1981–89).

CHAPTER TEN

Deadlock Over Dublin

A 1957 YEAR-END special issue of *Life* devoted itself entirely to the theme of "America's World Abroad" and featured renderings and photographs of recent U.S. embassy projects in London, New Delhi, Baghdad, Accra, and Bangkok. The magazine, which emphasized the connection between overseas construction and the nation's tremendous new foreign interests and commitments, appeared concurrently with a New York exhibition on the same theme. Sponsors of the exhibition included the New York chapter of the AIA, the Architectural League of New York, *Life,* and *Architectural Forum,* which also published a ten-page feature article on the State Department's Office of Foreign Buildings Operations and its many works in progress.[1] The AIA had sponsored the first exhibition of FBO work at its national headquarters in Washington in 1954 and continued to back the building program as a showcase for the work of its members. At the AIA's 1957 centennial celebration in Washington, national president Leon Chatelain Jr., presented Deputy Under Secretary of State Loy Henderson with a citation of honor in recognition of FBO's outstanding achievement. Widely praised, the foreign building program had already achieved a high profile and seemed securely established as a component of U.S. foreign policy, but appearances were deceptive. At the same time that it was being celebrated for its success, the program was embroiled in serious trouble.

When Henry Shepley wrote to Under Secretary of State Christian Herter in 1958 citing the acclaim that surrounded the building program, his purpose was to alert Herter to problems that he feared would soon wreck it. Shepley went to Herter, the former Massachusetts governor, because he knew that he would reach the ear of a friend with a known interest in architecture. Shepley wanted him to know that there been attempts to pack the advisory panel with men whom Shepley called "reactionaries," and he cited efforts to undermine FBO by combining it with other government real estate operations thereby reducing its output "to the usual mediocrity of government bureaus."[2] Shepley was reacting in part to rumors that FBO director

William Hughes was plotting to transfer FBO operations (and himself) to the General Services Administration (GSA), the agency responsible for all domestic government real estate operations. Shepley urged Herter to intervene to protect FBO from efforts to compromise its mission. "You would in this way be making the finest kind of contribution to the architecture of this country," he told Herter, who had briefly attended Columbia University's School of Architecture and had also served in the Foreign Service. Shepley pleaded with him to prevent unwitting damage to the program that "has been bringing such kudos to our government."

Shepley was correct in sensing trouble ahead, but he was looking in the wrong direction for the cause. While he and his colleagues lamented the scarcity of qualified architects, lowered design standards, the appointment of diehard conservatives to the Architectural Advisory Panel, and possible administrative reorganization, what they failed to see, and probably only dimly understood, was that pressure from Congress posed the biggest threat to the program. Appearing before the Senate Foreign Relations Committee in 1957, Loy Henderson testified that currently authorized funds would not cover another year of foreign building operations. When FBO director Hughes asked Congress for $100 million to fund a five-year construction program, the request was denied.

By the time that the next session of Congress held hearings on State Department funding, Wayne Hays had become chairman of the House Foreign Affairs Subcommittee. When Hughes appeared before the Hays subcommittee in 1959, FBO had a remaining balance of only $10,095,000—all in local currencies. With its dollar authorization exhausted, it could not pay American architects or builders in American dollars, nor could it pay for elevators, air-conditioners, plumbing supplies, or other products and services purchased in the United States for use abroad. Hughes reduced his 1959 request to $50 million for a two year program.[3] But FBO received no new funds in 1959, nor any in 1960, 1961, or 1962. During these four years, FBO cut back its operations and ceased all new construction, put ongoing projects on hold, and no longer convened the AAP in Washington to review new plans.

FBO was left with three potential funding sources: remaining counterpart funds or credits; monies from the sale of surplus American agricultural products abroad (the "Food for Peace" initiative); and profits from the sale of its existing properties. But even combined, the three sources could not have financed the whole program.[4] Foreign credits were still available, but like dollars, they had to be authorized for State Department use, and Congress was no longer inclined to treat the credits simply as lost assets to be recouped through new construction abroad. Furthermore, 92 percent of the more than $900 million in credits that remained in the Treasury was by then earmarked for military and other restricted use, and what was available could only be used in thirty-three of the eighty countries where the United States maintained representation. FBO could no longer shift credits from one country to another unless both were among the thirty-three; nor could it use Food for Peace funds in those strategically important places. As Hughes indicated in his testimony in 1959, those countries where credits existed did not include any of the newly independent African nations where new projects were urgently needed. Profits from the sale of existing property could only supplement a budget. FBO could never hope to operate on the basis of speculation in real estate.

One key pending project ultimately financed through the sale of surplus property was the embassy in Dublin, a project that was controversial from the outset. Before work even began, Rep. John Rooney poisoned the atmosphere surrounding the project by describing the proposed site and its neighborhood as a "slum" (fig. 108).[5] Always trying to find ways to impress his Brooklyn constituents, many of whom were of Irish ancestry, Rooney frequently visited the Irish capital. His comments may have been only an attempt to tell voters that he had actually been there, but whatever his rationale, the U.S. Embassy in Dublin faced a public relations nightmare trying to soothe local feelings injured by the Rooney remark. Then embassy officials had to convince doubting Dubliners that the United States still intended to build a new building after Hays threatened to cut it from the program. The project took on special significance when President Kennedy's election heralded closer U.S.-Irish relations and the new construction became an even more important diplomatic priority.

The triangular site at the intersection of Elgin and Pembroke roads was purchased in 1955. The Ballsbridge section of Dublin in which the embassy was to be located, an area with some commercial development, was largely filled with the ubiquitous brick row houses that line most of Dublin's residential streets. The site was a considerable distance from the center of the city with its public buildings and tourist attractions, including Georgian landmarks and the stately stone buildings of Trinity College. It was still in town, but a good taxi ride away from the prestigious Merrion Square location where existing U.S. embassy offices were located. Those offices were in two small brick buildings, residences that had been clumsily converted into office space.[6]

When Ralph Walker visited Dublin on behalf of FBO in the summer of 1955, he inspected a number of proposed sites for a new embassy and concluded that the American offices ought to remain on Merrion Square.[7] He was adamant in his opinion that all of the other sites lacked proper distinction, and he pointed out to his FBO colleagues that Merrion Square had a special political importance because it faced the buildings of Parliament. For a number of reasons, including the high cost of property on the square and its architectural restrictions, Walker's advice was rejected and the Ballsbridge site was purchased instead.

Working conditions at the Merrion Square chancery could not have been worse. Writing to President Kennedy in May of 1961, Ambassador Grant Stockdale described the situation as "disgraceful.... In all my experience of previous Federal, State and Municipal buildings, nowhere have I ever witnessed a more deplorable sight than the interior of our Dublin Embassy."[8] Stockdale urgently advised the president to instruct the State Department to expedite construction of the sorely needed embassy. He noted that plans for the new project had existed since 1958, that local officials had "enthusiastically" approved them, and that his infamous predecessor, Ambassador Robert W. S. "Scott" McLeod, had tried without success to move the project along over a period of three years. Stockdale blamed Hays and his subcommittee colleague Edna Kelly for the delay, and he told the president that the Irish people were convinced that the "so-called 'design controversy' " was merely a ruse to conceal American unwillingness to build the new embassy. To be absolutely certain that the president read his letter, Stockdale attached a cover letter to the president's secretary, Evelyn Lincoln, asking her to see that he read it. "I simply cannot overemphasize the importance of getting the United States Embassy building built in Dublin," he wrote.[9]

The "so-called 'design controversy'" involved a design prepared by Connecticut architect John Johansen, who had been retained by FBO late in 1956 to design the embassy. Johansen was a graduate of Harvard College and Harvard's Graduate School of Design. In 1948, after working in New York for Skidmore, Owings & Merrill, he opened his own practice in New Canaan, Connecticut. By 1955 he was a professor of architecture at Yale, and late in 1956, at the age of forty, he won the commission for the Dublin project. "Having designed only houses up to then," he recalled, "I might not have been qualified for this commission, except for the advisory architects, recognizing talent, said to me, 'If you have designed these fine houses, you can design a fine embassy.'" He was selected, he thought, because he was in his "neoclassic phase at the time."[10]

A panel consisting of Henry Shepley, Pietro Belluschi, and Richard Bennett recommended Johansen in November 1956, although Edgar Williams had replaced Shepley by the time that Johansen presented his first proposal in May 1957. It was a skeleton frame and glass structure based on a square plan with an open interior court, a four-story building with the three upper stories treated as a single mass mounted over a ground-floor podium base.[11] AAP members noted that the lobby floor did not provide enough space for required ground-floor offices, that the circulation pattern was "cramped," that the open court was too small to be useful, and that the dual corridors on upper floors wasted space. Further, they felt that the long cantilevers and heavy columns on the exterior "would create a heavy scale effect," and that the "over-all glass infilling of the bays" and "curved ceilings" suggested "an alien importation" (a spaceship, perhaps). They asked the architect to return with revisions.

A month later Johansen came back with revised drawings and a scale model. Minutes show that "the details of the façade still left much to be desired," and "the plan seemed to have been sacrificed for the aesthetics." Again, panel members reminded the architect about the need for more ground-floor offices to accommodate consular and information activities. They also suggested reducing the number of entrances to improve security. Johansen defended the *parti*, explaining that various building restrictions and the odd shape of the site made it impossible to reconfigure the plan. Minutes of the meeting include rare attributed comments in which Belluschi voiced particular dismay with the scheme and Hughes "expressed his own opinion that the design was not suitable...and was not compatible with the architecture of the neighborhood." In remarks that were later struck from the record, Hughes even accused Johansen of copying the design "from the modernistic bus terminal" recently built in Dublin. After a meeting in executive session, Hughes informed Johansen that AAP members could not bring themselves to approve his design. In an unusual move, they recommended "that the architect should 'shelve the entire plan and design' and submit an entirely new approach to the problem."[12]

In September, Johansen returned with a second design, a hexagonal scheme. The AAP agreed that the two-story building was better planned than the earlier one, but seriously questioned the projecting balconies and vertical fins on the exterior, wondering why so much sun protection was needed in Dublin. Johansen replied that those elements "were to give a sculptural richness to the façades," and that neither was designed to provide shade. He asked for permission to develop yet another alternative design, and though panel members were hesitant, they allowed him to proceed.

How to avoid an "exhibition-type" appearance and how to convey "dignity" were questions that troubled Shepley, Belluschi, and Bennett as well as Johansen. Also in 1957, the AAP faulted a proposed design for Mexico City by Southwestern Architects that they said lacked "the dignity proper to an embassy," and a proposal for Warsaw by Becket Associates that resembled "an exhibition type structure." They asked the architects to strive for "a character of dignity and repose that would be more diplomatically representative of the United States."[13]

By the time Johansen returned with his fourth presentation, now a three-story version of the hexagonal scheme, Saarinen had replaced Belluschi on the AAP. The architects on the panel seemed at a loss at how to assess the new proposal, describing it with inconclusive expressions such as: "not yet arrived," "could be good or bad," "sincere striving but controversial," and "poetic but confused."[14] Hughes was more specific in his assessment. Dublin was still an eighteenth-century city, he told the group, and he "considered it inappropriate to build there an embassy of extreme design whether it was called Modern, Georgian, Renaissance, or whatever." The panel advised Johansen that his design was inadequate and asked him to yet again restudy the latest proposal and return with models and drawings that showed it "in relation to its neighborhood."

After examining Johansen's models in January of 1958, the AAP adjourned to executive session where Ambassador Joseph Satterthwaite, then AAP chairman, stated his dissatisfaction and Hughes "advised the panel that he could not in good conscience approve it for construction." The panel members then agreed to select a new architect for the job. They recalled Johansen into the meeting and informed him that the design was out of character for Dublin, the elevations were artificial insofar as they suggested a sun-protective treatment not required by the climate, and the building lacked a solidity that was considered more important in Dublin than a glass cage type of design. Instead of firing him, however, they gave *him* the choice of continuing with an entirely new design or leaving the project. He said he understood the reasons for the rejection, and he chose to continue "in a new direction."[15]

A month later Johansen returned with still another design and the panel was once again flatly unenthusiastic. Members objected to the fenestration, the scale of facing materials, and the total use of glass on the ground floor. The overall design was again unacceptable and the AAP agreed that Johansen needed design assistance from individual AAP architects. Although it remains unclear what role the AAP played in the following revision, the design presented in May finally pleased the panel. Inspired by Celtic towers and other landmark buildings in Dublin, Johansen returned with a cylindrical scheme.[16] The shape actually did make sense for the triangular site bordered on two sides by roads. Johansen was enthusiastic about the project, and at last the panel shared his optimism.

Other architects who presented similar schemes were less fortunate. Thornton P. Ladd, for one, had proposed a circular consular office building for Niagara Falls in January 1958, but the AAP said then that the circular design was better suited for a chapel, an airport, or a restaurant. The panel admonished Ladd not to think of his project as "a showplace," but rather as "a simple and dignified building" and pointed out that a "circular plan is inappropriate for offices in which the conventional rectangular desks would be used."[17] Members also expressed concern that round buildings would be difficult, if not impossible, to expand, and all of the new embassies were supposed to be expandable. But they overlooked these issues at Dublin. They also overlooked previously expressed objections to defensive-looking architecture. Amman was not the only project criticized for its resemblance to a stockade. The AAP had similarly rejected a proposed design for Kabul because of its "fortress-like" appearance.[18] Modeled at least partially after a medieval keep, Johansen's scheme still won the panel's guarded approval. Despite the reservations expressed at the various meetings, Hughes defended the scheme when it came under critical attack from Hays the following year.

In August of 1959, after the Dublin embassy project was already well into its third year and FBO had already paid Johansen more than $35,000 in fees, Wayne Hays saw a photograph of the model and told Hughes to drop the project.[19] He likened the design to "a modernistic mausoleum," and in a moment of special levity, he declared "that thing looks about as much like a Celtic Tower as I do a jet airplane." One colleague, Clement J. Zablocki, Democrat from Wisconsin, compared it to "a series of flapjacks with a pat of butter on top," and another, Alvin M. Bentley, Republican from Michigan, likened it to Stonehenge. Hays refused to believe Hughes's assertions that Irish officials had enthusiastically approved the project and claimed that it was certain to ruin relations between the two countries. Efforts to explain the Irish precedent for distinguished round buildings and curvilinear designs fell on deaf ears.

Hughes continued to support the scheme, although his boss, Deputy Under Secretary Henderson, expressed some willingness to abandon the project if the Hays Subcommittee specifically stated its opposition to the design in a written report and was thus willing to take the entire blame for cancellation. Hays was too savvy to fall into such a trap; he insisted that the project did not deserve to be funded, demanded a "review right" over future projects, and argued persuasively that "good taste" is not an exclusive possession of architects.[20]

When word of the standoff reached William Wurster in San Francisco, he wrote to Hughes expressing his dismay over the proposed Dublin design and what he called the "demagogic attack" on Hughes. Wurster, who had replaced Richard Bennett on the AAP late in 1958, did not urge Hughes to stand fast, however. Instead, he asked if it would be possible to change the design, even at the cost of paying two design fees. "It might be this very design which would blow up the whole wonderful program," Wurster wrote.[21] Others were similarly concerned about FBO's future. Hughes reported to the AAP about the budgetary problems and congressional opposition to the program a month later in October, and the AAP agreed to call Johansen to Washington to be briefed.

In January 1960, Henderson met with members of the panel and stressed to them the importance of "the maintenance of a proper relationship on such matters with the Congressional groups."[22] He expressed special concern about Dublin, directed the panel to think about ways of modifying the design to accommodate Hays's objections, and suggested a meeting between panel members and the Hays Subcommittee. Meanwhile, the architect's response to this delicate political situation was to return to his drawing board to devise another scheme consisting of *double*-twisted interlocking precast concrete units, a scheme that was even more complicated (and costly) than his previous design (fig. 109). Hays was not impressed. He had no intention of giving in until he stood to gain from the situation, so the building program remained unfunded. Until John F. Kennedy moved into the White House early in 1961, nothing happened to resolve the controversy over the design, dubbed by John Rooney as "The Drum."[23]

USING HIS VENDETTA against Hughes to enhance his own political position, Hays announced that he would never approve funds for FBO as long as Hughes headed the office. He then circulated unsubstantiated rumors that Hughes had profited from the sale of government property in Bermuda. He also let it be known to various reporters, off the record, that the State Department was in trouble as a result of its "ugly" and inappropriate architecture. Though he did not want to do it, Henderson had to fire Hughes, who was packed off to the U.S. Operations Mission at La Paz (he later became consul general at Ciudad Juarez). James Johnstone replaced Hughes in 1961. When Johnstone took over, he carried the added rank of deputy assistant secretary of state for foreign buildings, a sign of FBO's recognized importance. Henderson retired in 1961 when the Kennedy administration took charge and filled top slots at the State Department with its own people. (Before leaving the department, Henderson made one final overseas tour when President Eisenhower sent him to Africa to select sites for more than a dozen new embassies.) Amidst the administrative reshuffling, Rooney maneuvered his protégé Crockett into the position of assistant secretary for administration.

In retrospect, Hughes's stubborn and arrogant attitude toward political necessity remains puzzling. His refusal to order changes in the Dublin scheme, already seriously questioned by an AAP that was on the verge of recommending that the architect be fired, was perhaps the clearest example of his obstinacy. Writers unfamiliar with FBO's history later praised Hughes for "keeping politics out of architecture;" they overrated his role as an architectural patron and policy innovator, claiming erroneously that he established the AAP and selected the architects.[24] While Hughes did defend FBO architecture and the design review process, his refusal to modify Dublin grew out of his own personal unwillingness to cooperate with Hays and reflected his general attitude that cooperation represented a violation of administrative prerogatives. True, Hays was equally arrogant, but he held FBO's purse strings.

The arrival of Johnstone and Crockett signaled the start of a warmer relationship between the Executive branch and the Congress. When Hays described the architecture of the Madrid embassy as "ugly American," for example, Crockett agreed with him, admitting that Madrid represented "the worst of American modern." Both he and Johnstone vowed to work closely with Hays, and Hays praised both of them for wanting to cooperate with Congress. "Frankly, the average Congressman couldn't care less about your building program," he told the witnesses from the department; but he emphasized that whatever the program was, he had to be able to justify it before the entire House. He assured them that he was not hostile to the State Department, that he recognized that the department had no constituency, and that he wanted to be "fair-minded and friendly" to its interests. He also deplored those in Congress who found "it popular to use them [the department] as a whipping boy," but conversely deplored those in the department who saw no need to cooperate with Congress. "We are working for the same thing you are," he declared with obvious sincerity, "to put the best foot of the United States forward around the world."[25] Later, when Hays praised Crockett and Johnstone on the House floor, he expressed the hope that his praise would not "hurt them down in the State Department." He went on to say that he often had the impression that when State Department staff members developed rapport with members of Congress, the department moved immediately to get rid of them. He repeated his hope that his praise would not cost Johnstone or Crockett their jobs.[26]

The immediate result of this new-found harmony was a revised FBO design policy, announced by Crockett in May 1961 when the AAP met for the first time under the new administration. Once he appointed himself chairman of the advisory panel, Crockett made it clear that he would be a hands-on administrator. Johnstone's memorandum of the May meeting mentions that he and Crockett met with members of the panel—Lawrence Anderson, Roy Larson, and William Wurster—to discuss with them "the necessity for the Department to be more sensitive to architectural style, economy of construction and operation, functionalism and security." The new policy included these key points: planning should be practical, with special attention to functional needs and the suitability of design to the environment of each post; architecture should not be controversial—neither overly experimental or modernistic ("The ostentatious and monumental type of building will be avoided in the interest of achieving more reserved architectural character."); designs should be symmetrical and buildings should harmonize with their surroundings; buildings should be efficient to operate and easy to maintain; buildings should be planned for the possibility of expansion; and security (mentioned for the first time as a design concern) required "utmost consideration."[27]

Crockett had certainly cleared the new policy with Hays. "As a matter of fact," his notes say, "[Hays] commented that if the Department followed this policy, he didn't think it would ever have any problem with his Committee." Johnstone's notes mention how "gratifying" it was to see how quickly the architects understood the implications of the political situation and "accepted the new policy."[28] Of course, the architects understood that if they failed to agree to the new guidelines the advisory panel might be permanently dissolved, and they thought it foolish to endanger the program over one project or another. More than anything, they wanted to preserve a program that had benefited so many architects and held the potential to continue to do so.

Recognizing the risk that the AAP could be axed as part of a compromise between the department and Hays, the AIA stepped up its lobbying effort in 1961, when its president, Philip Will Jr., wrote to newly installed Secretary of State Dean Rusk on behalf of the AIA board of directors commending the building program and asking Rusk to retain the AAP. Will emphasized that the success of the program was due largely to the department's use of "highly qualified architects," and he told Rusk that the AIA was recommending the FBO model "to other government agencies concerned with public buildings at home." At the same time, Will also wrote to architects who had participated in the FBO program, asking for information on ways to strengthen it.[29]

By coincidence, Will was a long-time friend of newly appointed Deputy Under Secretary of State Roger Jones, who was subsequently called to testify before the Hays subcommittee. In his testimony, Jones referred to his friendship with Will and the fact that Will, as AIA president, had provided him with useful advice. When Rep. E. Ross Adair (R-Ind.) asked why it was necessary to maintain the AAP, Jones strongly defended the advisory panel and the architect selection process.[30] Johnstone also defended the new design policy and denied charges that AAP members were "running things" at FBO.

The AAP survived, but Congress made it clear that it wanted to see a move away from the open and often impractical architecture of the 1950s. The new design policy, the first official revision in the policy since Kenworthy outlined it in 1953, represented a pragmatic political compromise between State Department officials, who wanted to get on with their program, and members of Congress, who wanted to have greater say in its administration.

THE NEW PRESIDENT was dealing with matters of far greater import than the Dublin embassy, but he did have a strong general interest in improving "Irish-American relationships," and a particular interest in highlighting his own Irish heritage. Just after the disastrous Cuban invasion, and amidst the Berlin crisis, Ambassador Stockdale wrote to President Kennedy again to say he had heard rumors that Congress might allow plans to proceed for Dublin. "I can't think of anything which would give the staff and Irish-American relationships a bigger or better shot in the arm than its construction."[31] The political and diplomatic urgency of the situation demanded Kennedy's intervention, because the embassy project was so eagerly anticipated by Dubliners and had taken on symbolic significance at home and abroad. According to Johansen, he and Kennedy knew each other from Choate and also from Harvard. There is no evidence suggesting that the prior association affected the fate of the Dublin project, but it is possible that Hughes and others were deferential to the architect because of real or imagined presidential patronage.

As long as Hays maintained his standoff with the State Department, nothing could happen in Dublin. An indication that Hays might yield, however, came in September, when Rusk wrote to the president telling him that Hays "would withdraw his personal objection if you sent him a note indicating your approval of the design."[32] Soon after, a White House aide telephoned Johnstone to learn more about the project. By his own account, Johnstone "hurried to the White House with pictures, drawings and plans," that were then shown to the president. Kennedy saw two alternate façades—the single-twisted version and the more experimental (and far more expensive) double-twisted version. He selected the former.

Johnstone drafted a short letter from the president to Hays, and the letter was signed by Kennedy: "While I agree that the design will not please all tastes," it stated, "the delay and expense involved in redesigning the building indicates that we should go ahead with the present design." Three days later, Hays wrote back to the president thanking him for his letter, assuring him that he wanted to follow his wishes, and indicating that he would advise Johnstone to "proceed with the present design according-ly."[33] Though Hays's subcommittee colleagues, notably Edna Kelly, had also objected strongly to the design, Hays was able to convince them all to reverse themselves, which they promptly did.

Johnstone naturally saw the reversal as a victory for FBO and the State Department, but Hays saw the test of strength as a demonstration of con-gressional authority and a personal vindication. In his terms, he won the battle when the president of the United States was forced to acknowledge his singular importance by personally asking him to relent in his objec-tions and to allow the project to proceed.[34] This was a sweet success for the farmer's son from Flushing, Ohio.

THE MOST STRIKING characteristic of the new Dublin embassy, what makes it stand out from the cityscape and call attention to itself, is its roundness. In early photographs of the building, especially those taken at night when the cylindrical drum was illuminated from within, it seems to be more void than solid, and the wall surface appears to undulate or move as if the build-ing were rotating slowly on its axis (fig. 110–1). It is a small building, but a visually dynamic one, set off against an oddly-shaped plaza dotted with trees (and now also with security barriers). The embassy has two stories below ground, with garage, commissary, and mechanical equipment housed there, and three stories above, with a spacious circular lobby that extends to a clerestory above roof level. According to embassy staff members, the 50-foot-diameter rotunda, flooded with natural light in the daytime and spotlit at night, has worked unexpectedly well as a reception area and an entertainment space. Corridors ring the central space, with wedge-shaped offices lining the perimeter (figs. 112–3).

The exterior is surrounded by a dry moat crossed by two rusticated stone walkways over which visitors approached and entered the build-ing when it was new (fig. 114–5). (Now, all visitors enter through a single entrance to pass through security.) Over the main entrance is an ornate gold eagle, nothing so big or so fearsome as the London bird, but enough to underscore the building's special purpose (fig. 76). The building's base of rusticated granite blocks, combined with the drawbridge-like entry and the rock-lined moat, links the very contemporary building thematically to earlier Irish monuments.

The precast modules, fabricated out of reconstructed limestone and bush-hammered to the architect's specifications in Holland, were carefully transported on barges to Dublin. The vertical supports twist at angles of 90 degrees, enclosing large rectangular panes of flat fixed glass, alternated with narrow, rectangular operable windows. (For the *double*-twisted scheme, the supports would have twisted at 180 degrees, and the glass panels would have sloped and curved.) Though not a large or prepossessing building, the embassy has established a strong visual identity for the United States in Dublin. In that regard, it has been successful even if some reaction to it has been more puzzled than appreciative. Still, it is hard to understand how the architect arrived at such a scheme when he admits that he was instructed by FBO "to get lost in the old brickwork of the surrounding existing buildings." He answers this question himself by noting that prominent buildings in Dublin were built of limestone, not brick, and that he merely reconstructed the limestone in precast elements. The round form certainly had local precedent, and furthermore, although the Royal Georgian Society rejected his design, other Dubliners had urged innovation, remarking to him, "Why be so coy? We really want to see how the USA builds."[35] Johansen used the newest methods and materials to accomplish just that.

Even after Hays gave his okay, however, the political situation was not totally resolved. Because of the delay, the cost of the project had climbed from $880,000 to $1.1 million. When Johnstone appealed to Hays's nemesis Rooney for the necessary appropriation, Rooney refused, saying that he had already appropriated funds for Dublin and would not do so again. Despite his earlier negative remarks about the site, he did not stand to gain by obstructing the embassy's construction. But his animosity toward Hays was intense, and he flexed his own political muscle by refusing to supply the funds as asked.

Since FBO could sell surplus real estate and use the proceeds for its building program, Johnstone managed to arrange the sale of property in Paris and Antwerp to finance the new construction at Dublin. In a cable to the White House before the ground-breaking ceremony in 1962, Ambassador Stockdale stated, "This occasion probably most important single tangible act in history Irish-American relationship. Most of credit rebounds to President whose efforts culminated ten-year plan to get it going."[36] Construction was completed in May 1964.

All of the major journals reviewed and generally praised the completed building, and R. Furneaux Jordan declared in *Architectural Review* that the project was most definitely "not a stunt." In 1969, An Taisce, the National Trust of Ireland, awarded the embassy its highest honor "for effective development of a prominent corner site on a main city approach, for sympathy of scale with existing environment and interest of character, without imitation of surrounding buildings, and for integration with existing trees and street setting."[37]

The Dublin embassy was probably the last project on which an architect enjoyed the luxury of being able to explore the sculptural possibilities of concrete or the ambiguities of glass. Because Johansen pushed new technology to its limits in his final design, it is hard not to conclude that he was trying to design a building that would be hailed as innovative and ingenious by his fellow architects. The embassy commission was his first nonresidential project and he wanted it to be noticed. It certainly did not reflect the supposed design preferences of Hays, or the design policy adopted by FBO in 1961. In the end, congressional criticism of the proposed Dublin design had no discernible impact on the final scheme. As Hays suggested in his earlier remarks, most members of Congress cared little about the building program and had no real interest in architecture.

The resolution of the Dublin crisis did not instantly resolve FBO's financial woes. To the contrary; despite support from Hays, Congress failed to pass a 1962 authorization bill that called for $31,806,000 for a period of two years, a compromise from the originally requested amount of $40,180,000 over a period of four years. Naturally, each time the amount was reduced, additional projects were suspended or scrapped. The Hays subcommittee had unanimously approved the bill, using it as a means of imposing a number of new restrictions upon FBO operations. The new bill stipulated allocations by region, barring FBO from shifting designated funds from Europe, for example, to Africa. Wording in the bill objected to the creation of residential or residential/office compounds where Americans abroad lived together segregated from the life of foreign cities, and it insisted upon the government purchase and use of American products wherever possible. For the first time, the bill included a permanent authorization for the operating costs of the building program, and it also eliminated all references to the Foreign Service Buildings Commission, which had lingered on as a vestigial remnant from the days before its functions were replaced by FBO.

The 1962 bill passed the House, and was well on its way to passing the Senate in the mid-summer when two senators added an amendment to the bill barring the construction of foreign chanceries in residential areas of the District of Columbia.[38] This issue affected affluent Washington neighborhoods where residents objected to the increased traffic and obtrusive antennas associated with diplomatic office buildings. Local lobbyists managed to convince Fulbright to attach the measure to the funding bill although the House had already passed its bill. Any such amendment, seemingly unrelated to the original House version, was almost certain to send the bill to a conference committee for a resolution of differences. Both Hays and Fulbright miscalculated the impact of the amendment, thinking the bill could pass regardless. Instead, with little time remaining in the session, it was sent to conference where it died. With no funds, FBO lost yet another year of its program.

The lack of funding may have disappointed Anderson, Larson, and Wurster, whose AAP meetings ceased, and harmed architects such as Victor Lundy, who had been retained by FBO to design an embassy in Colombo, or the firm of Hellmuth, Obata & Kassabaum, similarly retained to design an embassy in San Salvador. But those most hurt were Foreign Service officers trying to establish or upgrade American representation in African and Asian capitals.

By adding an amendment that jeopardized the authorization bill, Congress sent a loud message to the State Department to clamp down on privileges enjoyed by foreign missions in the U.S. capital. Under pressure to assist the many nations seeking suitable sites in the downtown area, the department responded by establishing an enclave for foreign chanceries in northwest Washington on a 47-acre site, formerly occupied by the National Bureau of Standards. Owned and maintained by the State Department, the property became a planned development large enough to accommodate chanceries of twenty-two foreign nations, all encouraged to design embassies that reflected their own indigenous architectural themes—more or less the opposite of the department's policy with regard to U.S. embassies. (The result is an enclave already partially filled with the embassies of Austria, Bahrain, Egypt, Ghana, Israel, Jordan, Kuwait, and Singapore.)

Reintroduced in 1963, the authorization bill asked for a total of $49,824,000 over a period of two years—$26,324,000 for the purchase, construction, and long-term lease of facilities abroad and $23,500,000 for operations and property maintenance. The bill passed House and Senate committees, but ran into opposition on the House floor from members who described it as an example of unnecessary foreign aid that benefited foreigners, not Americans. Critics questioned why money was going to FBO when it would have been better spent by agencies like the FBI. They further argued that money should be spent for domestic building that might relieve domestic unemployment, and they condemned spending tax dollars in "unstable" places. "The net result," according to Rep. Albert W. Watson (D-S.C.), "could very well be that we would be constructing office buildings for some renegade governmental official such as Castro to confiscate....I believe it the better part of wisdom for us to continue to lease our facilities in these foreign countries until such time as these nations indicate a greater degree of responsibility and permanence."[39]

Watson's worries were not unfounded; several new American embassies, including the compounds in Baghdad and Mogadishu, were attacked and seized amidst political upheaval soon after they were built. (The $35 million compound in Mogadishu, built over the objections of Hays and other House members, was invaded and stripped by local gangs after the forced evacuation of Americans from Somalia in 1991.) There were reasons to question expensive new construction projects in "unstable" places, but those were often the places where such facilities were most needed—not just to proclaim the American presence, but to provide convenience and security for American personnel abroad.

After a two-year hiatus, the AAP reconvened in May 1963 to discuss the status of FBO operations. The May meeting was significant because of its discussion of major issues, namely the implementation of the new design policy, and because of the unusual guest list that included Wayne Hays. Not only did Hays join the meeting in the afternoon for discussion, but his entire House Foreign Affairs subcommittee joined the architects and FBO staff members earlier at a luncheon hosted by Secretary of State Dean Rusk (fig. 116). Rusk expressed "his hope that buildings would not be ostentatious or controversial," and told the guests that in his opinion, the best buildings were those that were simple and durable.[40] Crockett chaired the meeting and advised the panel architects—Anderson, Larson, and Wurster—that he intended to move ahead with new construction slowly, that he planned to contain costs, and that the future "avoidance of controversial architecture" did not mean that good design would not be supported. He cited Dublin as an example of the continued commitment to good design and mentioned that the Irish press had "enthusiastically praised the new Embassy building." He called for an end to "wasteful planning," noting that FBO had on hand approximately $1 million worth of unused plans. Above all, he stressed the need to avoid congressional criticism, and expressed his hope that the department would continue to enjoy the support of the AAP and the larger architectural community. "The cornerstone of our policy," he said, is "to have the best architects produce the best buildings."[41] The luncheon meeting was a milestone event because it marked the rare occasion on which high-ranking administration officials, congressmen (and one congresswoman), and architects met face to face.

After the luncheon, AAP members met to review back business, including projects in Montevideo, Colombo, and Madras, all of which had been suspended. They also looked ahead to forthcoming projects that included an "urgently needed" office building in Saigon and projects in Kabul and Tabriz. One project singled out for particular attention was John Carl Warnecke's proposal for Bangkok, a project that had received wide publicity and praise when it was first proposed in 1957 (fig. 55).[42] But six years later Wurster called it "theatrical," compared it to circus scenery, and declared it "inappropriate for American representation." He even decried its use of local themes, saying that diplomatic architecture should not "talk down to local architecture." Johnstone said that the *klong*, the lotus-shaped lake surrounding the building, was impractical and made the building difficult to secure. Publicity surrounding the design caused many to assume that the project was built; acquaintances even told Warnecke that they had seen it in Bangkok and liked it. But political developments coupled with the dramatic shift in FBO's architectural outlook contributed to the demise of this project and affected the designs of those that followed.

At the same May meeting Johnstone asked AAP members to review and comment on brochures from several architects, including Robert F. Beatty, whose "modest accomplishments," they said, qualified him only to design a "school or minor project." They talked about the possibility of naming Mies van der Rohe or Kallmann, McKinnell & Knowles to design a new embassy in Buenos Aires. But Johnstone and Crockett had other things in mind, as did Hays, who joined the afternoon AAP session for the first (and probably only) time. Hays introduced himself to the architects, saying that he was "neither an architect nor a critic, and wished only to assure that utility and reasonable cost" were features of new foreign buildings. He mentioned recent negative press reports concerning the New Delhi embassy residence (by Stone), and emphasized to panel members how hard it was for him "to get a bill through Congress with...press like this." The architects recognized his predicament. Speaking for the group, Wurster agreed that "a building should work," and "its cost should be reasonably in keeping with its purpose," but he also suggested that it "should be beautiful." Hays wanted to reassure everyone that the pending legislation would pass and that FBO would soon be back in business. He made an effort to impress the architects with his sincerity, following up his appearance with letters to each architect emphasizing his cooperative attitude. Judging from Wurster's response, the panelists accepted his reassurances and eagerly looked forward to the task of reviewing new work. If they saw that they were being politically pushed, they did not say so.[43]

Congress finally passed the 1963 bill in July, granting the foreign building program another lease on life. With the green light to move ahead, the AAP met in January 1964 and recommended architects for new projects in Buenos Aires (Mies van der Rohe or Eduardo Catalano), Islamabad (Geddes, Brecher, Qualls & Cunningham), Manila (Charles W. Callister), and Montreal (Catalano or Ulrich Franzen). Panelists at that meeting included Philadelphia architect Roy Larson, MIT dean Lawrence Anderson, and Washington University, St. Louis, dean Joseph Passonneau, who had joined the AAP in 1963, succeeding Wurster.

As the program was getting back into action, two events served as disturbing portents of things to come. The first occurred in August 1964 when Johnstone reported to the AAP on recent findings on the subject of embassy safety. He cited the need for perimeter fencing, reduction in glass areas, and protection of openings at new embassies, hoping, he said, that such changes could be accomplished "without obvious offense to the host country or misrepresentation of our own fears."[44] He specifically asked the AAP to consider security when reviewing new designs. Deputy Under Secretary Crockett reiterated the department's concern for security at a luncheon attended by Anderson, Passonneau, Wurster, and FBO officials. He suggested that panel members should visit posts abroad in order to better understand the facts. Then, in a move that might have pleased (or perturbed) the panelists, Crockett noted that it would be appropriate "to commission each of the Panel members for the design of a project after their service on the Panel."[45] His offer certainly sounded like a "reward" in exchange for cooperation. Although there is no evidence that the offer became official policy, there is evidence that it later became at least unofficial custom.

A 1981 audit of FBO's procurement program, for example, notes that despite a stated policy "to seek a different architect for each major project in order to spread the business in the private sector and to avoid charges of favoritism toward a particular firm or area of the United States," a review of recent contracts showed that "four former panelists who had completed their panel service since 1974 had received 11 contracts totaling $2.3 million out of $14 million (or 16 percent), awarded during fiscal years 1978, 1979, and 1980."[46] The report did not suggest improprieties, but stated that FBO needed to be more careful in documenting its selection process. In addition to those who served on the AAP and subsequently won major FBO commissions, including George Anselevicius (Bissau), Joseph Esherick (La Paz), and William Caudill (Riyadh), others, including Eero Saarinen (London and Oslo), William Wurster (Hong Kong), Lawrence Anderson (Taipei), John Lyon Reid (Algiers), Harry Weese (Accra), Hugh Stubbins (Tangier), and George Hartman (Kuala Lumpur), had already won FBO commissions prior to their appointment to the panel. Architects with prior experience were clearly most useful to FBO, but as the auditors noted, such awards and appointments did raise questions about "insider" advantage.

The second foreboding event occurred in March, 1965, when panel members Anderson and Passonneau were invited to lunch in the elegant State Department dining room by Under Secretary of State George Ball. There, Ball asked them to recommend a commission for Robert Beatty, whose qualifications they had previously rejected.[47] Beatty happened to hail from East Liverpool, Ohio, where he had practiced architecture for thirty years; more importantly, he was a Hays constituent. Hays wanted Beatty to have an FBO job and the department wanted to accommodate him. Johnstone decided to offer him the embassy in the small and remote African capital of Niamey (Niger) (fig. 117). Although they scoffed at the idea of hiring Beatty, they agreed to Ball's request. Similar requests followed. In fact, Beatty was later selected again in 1972 to design the embassy in Wellington (fig. 118). Hays's political intervention might have been more marked if President Nixon had not called for a construction freeze that stopped all new work at the height of the Vietnam War.

Hays ignominiously fell from power in 1976 amidst scandals involving a pretty private secretary and charges of payroll abuse and corruption. His congressional colleagues welcomed the revelations of personal misconduct; some compared Hays to a "skunk" and others described him as "meaner and nastier" than anyone on the Hill. Although Hays was best known in Congress for the power he had amassed as chairman of the House Administration Committee, news accounts of the scandal quickly led to investigations into his dealings with FBO as chairman of the Foreign Affairs subcommittee. Reports detailed how he and his crony, Orlan "Clem" Ralston, "used the FBO as a private travel agency and as an employment service for certain of their friends and associates." The *Washington Post* described FBO as "Hays' private duchy," and revealed how Mexican builder and entrepreneur Marcos Russek, a Hays friend, headed firms that had received more than $5 million worth of construction and real estate contracts from FBO over a period of five years. Firms controlled by Russek built embassies in Mexico City, San Salvador, and Guatemala City. For the Guatemala City project, he was allowed to resubmit his high bid to undercut the lowest bidder long after the bids were closed. Furthermore, based on no competitive bids at all, his firms won contracts to build U.S. consulates in Mexico at Tijuana, Guadalajara, Monterrey, and Nuevo Laredo, all of which were then leased back to the State Department for more than $2.5 million. The result was a "bonanza" for Russek, though it was not suggested that either Hays or Ralston profited financially from the deals.[48]

Ralston, named FBO director in 1974, arranged frequent "inspection" trips for himself and Hays. When the pair flew to the Dominican Republic in January 1976, for example, it was not to inspect a stone wall at the American embassy, as claimed, but to allow Hays to obtain a quick divorce. Hays wanted the divorce so he could marry a staff assistant whose sister also worked for him and whose father had been retained by Ralston as a consultant to FBO.

Though ridiculed for his brash behavior and viewed as a boor by

232   ARCHITECTURE OF DIPLOMACY

Foreign Service officers and State Department officials alike, Hays was not the simpleton that critics supposed him to be. To the contrary, he effectively represented his constituents and was a savvy judge of public opinion, even if his candor sometimes discomfited his foes, and even if his talk was often corny or "politically incorrect." Whatever his aims, Hays worked tirelessly to increase the influence of the House of Representatives in matters of foreign policy. The 1975 decision to change the name of the Foreign Affairs Committee to the Committee on International Relations was part of a broader effort to attain a status comparable to that of the highly respected Senate Foreign Relations Committee.[49] Hays used his oversight of FBO as a forum for comment on U.S. foreign policy, and to the extent that he could, as a means of influencing that policy. Thus the foreign building program, always a component of foreign policy, was even more directly affected by policy debate during the 1960s and early 1970s, with Hays at the pinnacle of his power.

SHIFTS IN POLITICAL GEOGRAPHY, not to mention wars and civil strife, had real impact on the planning, cost, and implementation of the FBO program, as did the delays caused by the policy disputes between Hays and the State Department. One such dispute focused on the purposes of U.S. involvement in Africa. After State Department officials admitted to him that U.S. policy in Africa was to encourage independence among former colonial possessions and to create new American allies, Hays declared that new African nations were not really U.S. allies but were merely masquerading as allies to collect aid money. In a review of voting records at the United Nations to determine whether or not Ghana, Guinea, and Mali deserved new American buildings, Hays showed that the three nations consistently sided with the Soviet Union against the United States. This indicated to him that American aid to these countries was failing to accomplish its goal and was therefore being wasted. Hays could not control the allocation of aid funds, but he was in a position to keep Agency for International Development (AID) workers and others attached to U.S. missions from getting office space and housing. When FBO asked for funds to build a house for the American military attaché in the Central African Republic, for example, Hays said that the United States had no business maintaining a full embassy with an ambassador and a staff of thirty-two in a nation with no discernible strategic value. He vetoed funds for the house and callously declared, "Let him live in a mud hut!"[50]

Some of Hays's questions needed to be asked, particularly when the United States found itself facing a rapidly changing world map, a proliferation of new nations, and deepening involvement in Southeast Asia, and also when eye-catching architecture seemed increasingly impractical and self-indulgent. He was only being sensible, for example, when he asked if it was prudent for the United States to build embassies in capital cities that were being moved about on the map like chessmen. When Brazil shifted its capital from Rio de Janeiro to Brasilia, the United States had to build a new embassy there. The African nation of Dahomey was another country that relocated its capital, from Porto Novo to Cotonou, a site that lacked all basic necessities, including water and power. Pakistan, too, moved its capital—to Islamabad—soon after the United States had opened its new embassy in Karachi. Hays also questioned expanding the foreign building program in "unstable" places. He warned that Somalia, for instance, would not last ten years as an independent nation. When FBO requested $1.3 million for an embassy compound in the Somali capital of Mogadishu in 1962, Hays ridiculed the request, claiming, with some reason, that "the biggest industry in Somalia would be the American Embassy."[51]

Hays's objections prevented FBO from building many new buildings and delayed other projects that the State Department considered urgent. He called South Vietnam "a bad gamble" when FBO director Johnstone came before his subcommittee asking for funds for a new embassy in Saigon in 1963, though Johnstone described U.S. office buildings there as "absolutely the worst" in the world. Johnstone advised the subcommittee that architects Curtis & Davis had been retained to design a new embassy for Saigon in 1956, that their completed plans had already been approved and paid for, but that the project had been suspended awaiting funds for more than four years. Hays responded by criticizing the administration for "pouring so much money in there." Two years later, when terrorists bombed the existing facility, President Lyndon B. Johnson took the unprecedented step of sending special legislation to Congress authorizing $1 million for construction of a new and properly fortified Saigon embassy to make certain that there were no further delays in the construction of the facility that had been a top priority on the FBO agenda for *nine* years.

Having its program constantly under review and its projects always involved in negotiations meant that FBO operated in a stop-and-go mode throughout the 1960s and well into the 1970s. In a major shift from its most active period in the mid-1950s, when it met nearly monthly, the AAP met only once or twice a year during the 1960s and considered only a handful of projects. It met more frequently in the 1970s, but many projects presented to the panel were never built, including embassies in Phnom Penh (designed by Eliot Noyes in 1960), Beirut (designed by McCue, Boone & Tomsick in 1971), Taipei (designed by Anderson, Beckwith & Haible and Campbell, Aldrich & Nulty in 1971), and Belgrade (designed by Raymond & Rado in 1971) (fig. 119). Others that were delayed for years included embassies in Colombo (initially designed in 1961) and Dakar (initially designed in 1965). Robert Madison's Dakar project was suspended for seven years. Then, in 1972, Madison's firm won a new contract and started again; the building was completed in 1977. Victor Lundy's Colombo project was not completed until 1985, twenty-four years after the architect submitted his first design (figs. 120–1).

The distinguished Raymond & Magonigle chancery compound at Tokyo was a casualty of the 1960s, demolished to make way for a much larger high-rise facility in 1971 (Cesar Pelli and Gruen Associates). Others that were built lacked the flair of earlier buildings and showed the impact of administrative indecision and political intervention, as well as rising concern about security. The 1960 Montevideo project (I. M. Pei), for example, suffered from repeated changes to its program affecting the size and shape of the embassy, and according to its architect, compromising its design. Its ponderous proportions and use of exposed concrete combined to produce an undistinguished building that brought no credit to the United States.

Members of the AAP were particularly dismayed when they were asked to approve the Omaha firm of Henningson, Durham & Richardson for the prestigious project at Brasilia in 1971.[52] As evidence of the importance of the commission, AAP member Lawrence Anderson had traveled to the new Brazilian capital to inspect the site with FBO chief architect Thomas Pope in 1967. Especially after rumors suggested that the French had retained Le Corbusier to design their embassy there, architects expected FBO to retain a prominent "name" for the U.S. project, for which AAP members proposed Mies van der Rohe, Gunnar Birkerts, Kallmann & McKinnell, and Louis Kahn; they were particularly keen on Kahn. But FBO director Earnest Warlow asked the panel to review a list of alternatives headed by the Henningson firm. Anderson reviewed the various brochures and advised Warlow that the Henningson firm's work failed to meet FBO standards. John Lyon Reid, the San Francisco architect who had replaced Roy Larson on the AAP in 1965, reiterated Anderson's concern stating that he, too, had reviewed the firm's qualifications and did "not find them worthy of consideration." Warlow overruled the panel, however, and awarded the job to the Omaha architects (fig. 122). Reacting to Warlow's decision, Joseph Passonneau resigned from the AAP in protest, declaring that the AAP was being subverted by political deals. In his letter of resignation, Passonneau wrote: "All of our difficulties have increased as the architects have had to work under increasingly restricting budget and security requirements." He continued: "I have made the point on a number of occasions that 'security' can make for powerful architecture. But it is difficult and probably impossible at the same time to make buildings cheap, secure and architecturally distinguished."[53] The impact of Passonneau's resignation, however, was negligible; no one took up his cause.

In terms of the overall history of the embassy building program, an era ended when John Rooney retired from Congress in 1975, having chaired the subcommittee on State Department appropriations for thirty years, and when Wayne Hays resigned his congressional seat in September 1976 after twenty-eight years in the House.[54] Hays's departure came exactly thirty years after Congress funded the postwar building program and exactly fifty years after Congress first recognized the need for government-owned embassies in 1926. Not surprisingly, Ralston departed soon after Hays. President Jimmy Carter appointed William L. Slayton, a city planner and former executive vice president of the American Institute of Architects, to head FBO. Slayton brought a new style and attitude to the office when he took charge in January 1978, and he aimed to reestablish the diplomatic importance of landmark buildings. Unfortunately, problems with the management of the overseas construction program did not disappear during Slayton's tenure. Instead, they multiplied. Larger and more expensive projects had the potential for larger and more costly mistakes and security loomed as an ever-growing concern.

CHAPTER ELEVEN

Targets for Terror

ARMED WITH AN ARRAY OF GRIEVANCES, protesters attacked American embassies as the United States deepened its involvement in Vietnam in the mid-1960s. Mobs stoned the embassy in Moscow, breaking two hundred windows. Crowds broke all of the lower windows at legations in Budapest and Sofia, and pulled the Great Seal of the United States down from above both entrances. Violence reached a new level when terrorists killed three embassy employees in an attack on the Saigon embassy in 1965. Such incidents provoked anger and dismay in Congress and led to calls for better overseas security. The Saigon attack was the first incident that claimed lives, and it forced the State Department to rethink the risks associated with the design of its diplomatic buildings.

Vandals who threw rocks at the glass-walled U.S. consulate in Frankfurt in the 1950s created only a nuisance.Even when ten thousand Bolivians stoned the embassy in La Paz in 1959, the attack seemed an isolated event. But security was becoming an increasing concern, a fact reflected in FBO's 1961 rejection of architect Victor Lundy's preliminary design for an embassy in Colombo because it featured open balconies and glass walls. Then, in 1965, an incendiary bomb wired to the exterior grille at the U.S. Army Mission in Guatemala City underscored the vulnerability of buildings that featured screens or grilles, as so many American embassies did. The deaths of embassy personnel at Saigon and the growing threat of anti-American violence elsewhere forced the department to increase perimeter security with high walls and fences, and prompted the testing of blast-proof construction materials, such as laminated glass. Meanwhile, FBO continued to plan and build projects in potential "hot spots" including San Salvador, Dhaka, Islamabad, and Mogadishu.

Throughout the 1970s, terrorists targeted American embassies—with murderous assaults in Khartoum (1973), Athens (1974), and Kuala Lumpur (1975). By 1976, after U.S. Ambassador Francis Meloy was assassinated in Beirut, the State Department upgraded its special office for combating terrorism and was dealing with the constant threat of more violence. The 1979 crisis in Tehran, during which the Iranian government made no effort to provide assistance to the American hostages, showed that American diplomats could no longer rely on local authorities for protection. The department moved to increase Marine guard detachments at embassies; FBO built guard stations for the Marines outside of existing facilities at sensitive posts and installed security checkpoints in embassy lobbies. High steel fences were erected at Munich, Madrid, and Brussels (fig. 123). Protesters scaled a poorly designed older fence to enter embassy grounds in Jakarta as recently as 1994 (fig. 124). FBO retrofitted other properties, notably London, Oslo, Dublin, and The Hague, with surveillance equipment and concrete vehicle barriers thinly disguised as planters (fig. 111). The windows in Dublin were coated with a gold laminate for sun control and blast protection. There and elsewhere USIS entrances were locked and barred from use, forcing all traffic through one secured door. To make its architecture less vulnerable, FBO prohibited the use of exterior sun screens and stilts, both popular hallmarks of modernist design in the 1950s.

Twenty years after Harry Weese designed the embassy in Accra he returned to Ghana to assess his landmark embassy building for FBO (fig. 125). He was asked to look for ways to enclose the ground floor, but he found that renovation was unfeasible. Because of the stilts, the open plan, and the central stairway, the building did not meet new security guidelines. Eventually, FBO was forced to move the embassy offices and abandon the Weese building.

The threat of terrorism forced a fundamental change in the thinking about U.S. embassies, which were viewed until the 1970s as prominent and accessible public buildings to be seen, used, visited, and admired by American citizens and their foreign hosts. Furthermore, until the hostage crisis in Tehran, they were viewed as inviolate. As these assumptions became less and less realistic, embassy architecture gradually became less distinctive in design, less open, more defensive in plan, and less accessible in location. The glass box, once symbolically important, was no longer useful as a design paradigm. Moreover, the entire design process required increased scrutiny as public safety and security became paramount. Architects, though, were reluctant to part with past practice. They had enjoyed tremendous leeway in designing embassies in the 1950s, when the grand gesture was applauded. Now, they were reluctant to share design decisions with engineers and others, including users, whose views they so often disdained. Schemes that might have been approved earlier, in deference to the architects' whims, were no longer so quickly accepted, but some architects continued to produce designs that ignored practicalities.

Dozens of projects were in the works in 1980 after William Slayton became head of FBO and took charge of the advisory panel, renamed the Architectural Advisory Board (AAB). Two of these projects illustrate the reluctance of some architects to deal with practical realities. At a board meeting in May of that year, Weese presented a design for a staff apartment complex in Tokyo featuring a wide-open pavilion with a large reflecting pool, dubbed a "kiddie drowning pool" by members of the FBO staff. Weese was reminded that families would be living in the apartments and that the open space would be used by children at play. He replied that he imagined the space otherwise, as a realm of tranquillity. "You can go commune there and become a better negotiator," he suggested, dismissing the children as an apparent nuisance.[1] Frank Schlesinger's proposed design for Marine guard residences in Port-au-Prince was equally impractical. He presented a scheme of apartments linked by open-air walkways. When asked why residents should have to be soaked by Haiti's driving rain on their way to do laundry or to eat, he said that a similar plan was typical at tropical resorts. He was reminded by Slayton that the Marine compound was not a resort.[2]

Slayton was not a Foreign Service professional, so he came to his position at FBO in 1978 as an outsider. Work in city planning and real estate development had led him into urban renewal. From 1961 to 1966 he served as commissioner of the Federal Urban Renewal Administration, precursor to the Department of Housing and Urban Development (HUD). He moved over to the AIA in 1969 to champion the cause of AIA constituents, namely American architects. Though he was neither an architect nor an engineer, Slayton was closely connected to the design profession when he came to FBO. He had a strong interest in hiring top firms and creating high visibility projects that boosted professional accomplishment, and he strongly supported a National Building Museum plan to showcase FBO architecture in a proposed exhibition (later canceled) initially scheduled to coincide with the museum's opening in 1980. The large commissions he controlled also increased his personal influence within the profession until he was replaced with a career Foreign Service officer in 1983. In 1980 alone, Slayton's "talent" included: Frederic Bassetti (Lisbon), William Caudill (Riyadh), Araldo Cossutta (Salisbury/Harare), Ezra Ehrenkrantz (Budapest), Joseph Esherick (La Paz), Frank Gehry (Damascus), George Hartman (Kuala Lumpur), Robert Marquis (San José), Richard Meier (Santiago), William Metcalf (Cairo), George Notter (Helsinki), James Stewart Polshek (Muscat), James Ream (Port Moresby), George Rockrise (Manama), Alan Y. Taniguchi (Georgetown), Benjamin Thompson (Ottawa), and Harry Wolf (Abu Dhabi and Doha). Some projects were just beginning and others were already under construction. Of these eighteen projects, ten were built, although two eventually acquired different architects.[3]

Frank Gehry's was one project that was never built. It represented a clash between art and practicality, or more specifically, between an artistic personality and a very dangerous place. Gehry presented a preliminary design for an embassy in Damascus in 1980. His scheme included a starkly modern building with a wide courtyard entrance. AAB discussion focused on how people crossing the open expanse would enter and leave the building without becoming possible terrorist targets, how the ambassador would safely get in and out, where and how to park the ambassador's car to protect it from tampering, whether or not an outside eating area would be secure, whether or not anyone would even want to eat outside, and how to coordinate the office installation with the adjoining American school and its playing field. The architect seemed bothered by the discussion that had little to do with what he considered to be the artistic merits of his design. The panelists seemed bothered by Gehry's new-found fame. When someone suggested a chain-link fence as a way of containing flying soccer balls and asked Gehry, possibly facetiously, if it might "ruin the design," the architect replied coolly, "You don't know my work."[4] (Chain-link fencing was a Gehry trademark, famously used at his widely publicized residence.) Maybe Gehry, like Louis Kahn earlier, could have created an embassy recognized as a true American original, but maybe neither was particularly well suited to the necessary compromise associated with this sort of project.

With public access control the number-one priority, spiked rails were added to window bays at the embassy Frederic Bassetti designed in Lisbon. Terrorists attacked it with mortar launchers soon after it opened in 1983, but the building repelled its attackers (fig. 126). Also in 1983, FBO completed a new embassy in Kuala Lumpur. Designed by Hartman-Cox, the building has no windows within fifteen feet of the ground, its site is wrapped in a nine-foot wall, and its balcony rails are bulletproof shields (fig. 127). According to George Hartman, the embassy was actually a reinforced concrete pillbox disguised as a house. "It looks friendly," he said, "but it's built like a fortress."[5]

The 1983 suicide bombs that killed scores at the Marine Guard quarters and at the American embassy compound in Beirut marked a shocking escalation of violence and precipitated a turning point in the U.S. response. In the decade between 1975 and 1985, there had been 243 attacks and attempted attacks against U.S. diplomatic installations. The attacks at Beirut, coupled with the overall vulnerability of U.S. property, personnel, and information, prompted a reorganization at FBO and an overhaul in diplomatic security. Congress authorized a study of FBO and the future of embassy design in 1984. That study, prepared by the National Research Council (NRC) and its Building Research Board, faulted the State Department, in part, for failing to integrate improvements in electronic information handling and office automation with upgrades in security and building design.[6] It warned that the combined threat of terror, espionage, and sabotage, together with the need to accommodate sophisticated telecommunications systems and increased numbers of non–State Department agencies within embassy buildings, would add to the complexity and size of future embassies. As the NRC was compiling its research recommendations into a report, another panel, the Advisory Panel on Overseas Security, issued its report in June 1985.

Secretary of State George Shultz had appointed Admiral Bobby R. Inman, USN (Ret.) to head the Advisory Panel on Overseas Security, the blue-ribbon panel that came to be known as the "Inman panel." Inman was former head of the National Security Agency and had also been second in command at the CIA. The panel's report called on Congress for a massive increase in funds for security upgrades and new construction. It specified new and more stringent security standards to be implemented at all U.S. embassies regardless of location and identified more than a hundred buildings needing major security overhaul or replacement. Additionally, it called for the creation of a new Bureau for Diplomatic Security within the State Department and a Diplomatic Security Service charged with an array of new security-related functions. [7]

Together, the two reports prompted immediate congressional action on a legislative matter that had been depoliticized by the viciousness of the Beirut bombing. Congress approved a five-year plan with a $2.1 billion authorization for security improvements, and Inman's name came to be associated with the new standards recommended by the NRC, though he did not author them himself. Even before the standards were fully formulated or enacted, embassy projects showed a heightened concern for security. Instead of trying to fit into the landscape and conceal security features as architects had done at Lisbon and Kuala Lumpur, architects moved toward massive and imposing structures that dwarfed surrounding buildings and spaces. Two such embassies were built at Dhaka (Kallmann, McKinnell & Wood, 1983–89) (fig. 128) and San José (Torres, Beauchamp & Marvel, 1985–89).

Public access controls were not enough; electronic locks, steel doors, and other delay devices may have thwarted angry mobs and intruders, but they offered only limited protection against bombs. The new Inman standards stipulated a minimum setback of 100 feet from surrounding streets and blast-proof construction. While embassies had been routinely sited in the heart of downtown areas, often near other key government buildings, the revised rules recommended remote sites, optimally fifteen acres in size. Other new requirements included perimeter walls, electronic vehicle arrest barriers, electronic locks, cameras, and monitors. Architects had to eliminate all hand-holds within fifteen feet of the ground (so no one could climb up or attach anything to the exterior walls), and they had to incorporate blast standards for walls and windows (the window area was limited to less than 15 percent of the total wall area). The standards also required safe havens for all embassy personnel including foreign nationals. While they provided no protection against missiles or air attack, they seemed to be a suitably strong response to past ground attacks. The emphasis was on construction of new embassies; with appropriations of $948 million, sixty-one new projects were underway by the end of 1986.

However, the Inman program was never fully implemented. Full implementation would have meant a wholesale replacement of U.S. embassies around the world. If the new standards seemed excessively rigid and if Congress endorsed a package of standards that were ultimately too costly to pay for or too impractical to enforce, some explanation lies in other events that unfolded just as the new standards were being proposed. Two scandals broke in 1985 and both seriously damaged the credibility of FBO, giving Congress more than enough reason to doubt the State Department's ability to properly and safely manage its overseas interests. One scandal involved shoddy construction at the American ambassador's residence in Giza; the other concerned "technical penetration" of the new American compound in Moscow.

FBO commissioned Washington architect William H. Metcalf to design an ambassador's residence just outside of Cairo at Giza in 1975 (fig. 129). Spurred by the wishes of the American ambassador and trying to take advantage of a picturesque Nile River site, Metcalf designed a handsome two-story villa modeled, he said, after a Mississippi River house. Having grown up on the banks of the Mississippi, he much admired the site, but he was sorely disappointed in the outcome of the project. Construction began in 1979, but the local builder had little experience and the FBO supervisor proved to be incompetent. FBO director Slayton allowed the project to absorb more than its share of funds and provided no adequate oversight despite stern warnings from the architect. Elegant furnishings, including custom-made parquet floors and specially woven carpets, were already approved when a 1982 on-site inspection revealed the house to have such terrible deficiencies that construction was halted. Plagued by inept workmanship and shoddy materials, the house was uninhabitable—and moreover, not worth fixing. One contractor was fired; the other fled town to avoid prosecution. FBO was left with an embarrassing blunder that had cost $3.6 million. GAO published a devastating critique of the Giza project, and Rep. Jack Brooks (D-Tex.) held public hearings on the Hill. Although the State Department later sold the property for a profit, its reputation suffered as a result of the scandal, and a fine property was lost.

The embarrassment caused by Giza was nothing, though, compared to the humiliation produced by Moscow. President Nixon initiated the Moscow project in 1969. As part of the policy of *détente,* the United States and the Soviet Union were to exchange embassy sites in Washington and Moscow. Before U.S. experts even realized the strategic value of the property, it seems, the White House offered the Soviets a large, hilltop site with a commanding view of the capital city below. In exchange, the United States accepted a far more constrained and less advantageous site in Moscow. Negotiations dragged on as the Soviets held firm to demands for control of their project in Washington and also considerable authority over the American project in Moscow. Pressure from the Nixon White House prompted the American ambassador to sign a 1972 agreement that ultimately allowed Soviet work-men to construct much of the U.S. project.

Charles Bassett of Skidmore, Owings & Merrill's San Francisco office headed a Moscow design team that included architects and engineers from SOM and Gruzen & Partners. The program called for a self-contained compound consisting of 134 staff apartments, a school, a shopping con-course, Marine quarters, and an office building (fig. 130). To convey some American flavor, the architects recommended exterior walls of red brick. The Soviet workmen were going to lay the bricks under U.S. supervision. If trouble loomed ahead, no one noticed. In an article he wrote in 1984, just after leaving FBO and before Soviet listening devices were discovered in the office structure, FBO director Slayton proudly claimed credit for negotiating the construction contract himself. He even boasted of the decision to "teach the Russians how to lay brick" by providing them with American know-how and American tools.[8] A year later American inspectors discovered that the walls of the nearly completed chancery were filled with Russian "bugs." Russian workers were barred from the site and construction halted. Though the housing was completed and occupied by 1987, the $23 million office building was not. Critics lambasted official incompetence and naiveté, plan-ners tried to figure out how to complete the costly and urgently needed project, and members of Congress launched an effort to move the Inman program, including new embassy design and construction, out of the State Department and over to the Army Corps of Engineers. That effort failed; the department retained control over the program, but it set up a separate construction agency to handle subsequent work at the Moscow chancery. That work consisted of the removal of three stories of the building and their replacement with four new ones redesigned by architects at HOK.[9] Given the security requirements that surrounded the building materials, all of which were specially packed and shipped from the United States, the added cost of imported labor and U.S. supervision and the impact of the delays, on a per-square-foot basis the building was one of the most costly ever constructed.

To enforce the Inman recommendations, the State Department would have had to abandon its downtown embassies, including London, Paris, and Rome, in favor of more secure locations distant from government and business centers and generally far from town. Even if there had been agreement that such a wholesale shift in U.S. representation made sense, the price tag would have been so high that it would have been impossible. But pressure to insure against another "Beirut" and the conviction that terrorism was a localized problem that could be thwarted by a deliberate show of force did lead to full implementation of the new standards at some twenty-two projects built in the late 1980s and early 1990s.

The embassy compound at Mogadishu was one of the first projects designed during what some FBO staff architects now refer to as the "dark ages of Inman." In 1984, FBO commissioned Oudens + Knoop, the firm that had collaborated earlier in the design of the ambassador's residence in Seoul and other FBO projects, to complete work that had been initiated in 1959 and never completed due to political instability in Somalia. The Somali compound spread over nearly fifty acres and adjoined another fifty-acre tract used as a golf club—though the terrain consisted of nothing but dirt. For the compound Stuart E. Knoop designed a chancery, a USIS library, a health unit, dining facilities, shops, and additional buildings for the Office of Military Cooperation and the Marines. The buildings were completed and occupied in 1989. While the architect used local themes and patterns in detailing gates, walls, and grilles, these were made of reinforced concrete and steel, unlike earlier ones made of concrete blocks or wrought iron. Knoop describes the perimeter wall as "gigantic." (figs. 131–4) The landscape plan called for preservation of the natural ecology with the addition of drought-resistant shrubs and shade-producing vines. Before any bougainvillea could take root, though, work was once again interrupted by anarchy and local civil strife. The compound, barely completed, was abandoned in 1991 when Marines and Navy SEALs completed a harrowing military operation, airlifting Americans by helicopter to the USS *Guam*. James K. Bishop, the U.S. ambassador who supervised the evacuation, sadly described how Somali marauders scaled the walls as the last helicopters departed, blasting open the embassy doors with rockets, looting the buildings, and killing the many Somali employees and their families deserted by the fleeing Americans.[10]

The embassy compound at Sanaa was another of the early Inman projects (fig. 135). Designed in 1986 by CRS-Sirrine, it was completed in 1990 at a cost of $28 million. With nearly windowless foot-thick exterior walls, it represents a fundamental change from the glass-walled projects of the fifties. It is typical of the massive new projects that combine offices, residences, and even schools and recreation facilities on a single walled site. The same firm designed comparable installations in Riyadh and San Salvador. At Amman, the partnership of Perry, Dean, Rogers designed a compound consisting of a gatehouse, an office building and annex, an ambassador's residence, an American club, Marine guard quarters, a service annex, and a motor pool. The buildings are notable for their color and surface animation, including fine stonework, but few Jordanians will ever get close enough to admire the craftsmanship (figs. 136–7). The compound is larger than six football fields and is surrounded by a nine-foot wall; it is hardly inconspicuous and is not intended to be. Similarly large compounds were built in Nicosia (Kohn, Pedersen & Fox, 1987–92) and Kuwait (RTKL, 1992–96) (fig. 138).

It is hard to imagine how projects of such scope and size could fit comfortably into any foreign landscape. Given the perceived risk, however, and the need for such an array of facilities, it was not hard for the State Department to justify the choice of large and relatively remote sites—dismissing doubts raised for so many years by critics such as Wayne Hays, who had referred to such installations as "ghettoes" that kept Americans insulated from the very people they were supposed to be seeing and getting to know. Congress had always urged FBO to make its buildings approachable so that foreigners would feel comfortable about the United States and about its substantial foreign presence. But it is not easy to disguise an elephant. New site requirements mandated large-scale installations, and design controls made the new compounds even more imposing, if not forbidding. Though not every project was a compound, even new office buildings were built as walled enclaves. Examples include: Manama (ROMA, 1981–90), Muscat (James Stewart Polshek, 1981–89), Bangkok (Kallmann, McKinnell & Wood, 1994–96), Georgetown (Alan Y. Taniguchi, 1983–91), Pretoria (Eduardo Catalano, 1982–92), La Paz (Joseph Esherick/Leo A. Daly, 1980–94), Santiago (The Leonard Parker Associates, 1987–94), Caracas (Gunnar Birkerts, 1991–95), Lima (Arquitectonica, 1992–96), Bogotá (Integrus, 1987–96), and Singapore (The Stubbins Associates, 1994–97) (figs. 139–

44). In addition, a chancery annex and a properly built ambassador's residence (The Architects Collaborative, 1987–95) joined the already completed office tower in Cairo (William Metcalf, 1982–89).

What sets Inman projects, both compounds and enclaves, apart from earlier buildings is their colossal size, their relative isolation, and their cost. According to State Department security experts, the core of each building is virtually the same; all that really varies, they say, is the exterior "decoration." Such projects offer architects little design leeway; even top designers cannot do much to make a citadel look inviting. In terms of its massing and surface treatment, the embassy in Lima is one of the most imposing. It is also one of the most daring. Rather than taking its scale from its users and visitors, it responds to the larger Peruvian landscape and the Andes Mountains, beyond. The Miami-based architects present their office building as a literal billboard, best seen from a distance and best understood as environmental art (fig. 141). Patterned with a grid of real and imaginary windows and topped by a band of brightly colored triangles that connect to the mountain backdrop, it is dramatic, if not inviting. Limited in what they could do, other architects turned to ever more rich-looking and costly materials to embellish public spaces and make designs distinctive. Leonard Parker's sleek and highly polished marble interior walls and floors at Santiago contrast sharply with the more severe exterior (fig. 142).

Regardless of where they worked, embassy architects faced the challenge of reconciling the Inman standards with a preexisting design policy that emphasized respect for locale and accommodation to local building conditions and materials. The Spokane-based firm Integrus designed the chancery in Bogotá as part of a facility that includes a motor pool, a Marine guard residence building, tennis courts, properly screened communications equipment, and a service area for consular visitors (fig. 143). FBO gave Integrus only two design directives: adhere to the Inman standards and devise an architecture that portrayed openness, freedom, and some sense of the American spirit. The first directive was spelled out in detail, the second was up to the architects to interpret. According to Gerald Winkler of Integrus, "The design was driven by the Inman standards, but we still tried to create a friendly piece of architecture."[11] The unusual aspect of the design is that visa applicants wait and also transact business in a shaded, trellised outdoor area. They do not even enter the building; they complete their transactions through teller windows like those at banks in an outdoor "room," which works well, according to the architect, except when it rains. How a walled enclave that bars most public access can be "open" or user-friendly is hard to know, but the architects worked within the given

constraints. Behind its stone inner wall, the building is predictably organized according to a prescribed plan. In Colombia, where metal detectors
are ubiquitous, security at the embassy is not unusual; but the well-designed
plaza is a real asset to the embassy.

Alan Y. Taniguchi had more design options in Georgetown (Guyana),
where his project was smaller and the perceived risk was lower (fig. 144).
Taniguchi's problem was to fit a three-story, 40,000-square-foot building
onto a relatively small site located in a national historic district largely made
up of buildings constructed during the years of British colonial rule. Former
dean of the School of Architecture at the University of Texas, he first visited
Guyana in 1981 to assess the site, the climate (hot and humid), the soil and
drainage (both poor), and the local scene. The project was far along before
enactment of the Inman standards, and the State Department decided to
exempt it from the 100-foot setback requirement, allowing it to proceed.
Still, the architect had to rework his design. To mirror local architecture,
he initially proposed a design featuring screened verandas accessible to the
offices through French doors. In the revised scheme he retained the wooden-
screened verandas and Victorian detail but wrapped the screens around a
heavily fortified concrete core with walls twelve to sixteen inches thick. He
eliminated the French doors and punched "portholes" in the blast-proof
walls for light. The screens, which echo the local Demerara style, hide the
heavy walls, enliven the façade, and as Taniguchi says, "humanize" it.[12]
The embassy was completed in 1991 at a cost of more than $12 million.
There are those who find fault with architecture that conceals its purpose
and those who object to the use of false windows and the like, but such
criticism misses its mark when a building, like an embassy, has more than
one purpose. A stripped-bare Inman building would have about as much
visual appeal as a power plant.

The Inman-mandated policy to situate embassies at remote sites had
mixed results. At Amman, for example, the embassy moved from a tight
downtown site to acres of scrub desert at the far city limits. Once it became
home to the U.S. embassy compound, though, the remote locale attracted
new development, including apartments, luxury villas, shops, and public
transportation, turning the former "tomato patch" into an exclusive district.
The same was true elsewhere, as in Bogotá, where a new embassy attracted
office and apartment development to a relatively undeveloped area that the
city wanted to improve. This does not mean that embassies in Amman or
Bogotá are conveniently located, but it does suggest that "remoteness" may
be only a temporary problem in some places.

At Lima, the threat of danger kept people from visiting the American Embassy when it abutted a busy downtown street and was surrounded by Peruvian tanks and armed soldiers to protect against bombs and attacks (fig. 145).[13] (Unfortunately, neither tanks nor soldiers were present at the Japanese ambassador's residence when guerrillas seized the building and took its occupants hostage in 1997.) Who wanted to work in such a building? Who even wanted to visit it? To escape from the danger and congestion of downtown and to procure a large enough site, the State Department purchased a polo field located in a Lima suburb. Worried residents opposed the move, fearing (rightly, as it later turned out) that the new U.S. embassy would attract congestion and danger to their residential neighborhood. They protested the project as an intrusion, but to no avail. The location policy has undeniably changed the perceived centrality of the U.S. diplomatic presence. Ironically, the new suburban embassy, highly fortified as it is, may be no more accessible or inviting than its downtown precursor. In some ways the suburban alternative is an improvement, in other ways, obviously not.

Recognition that no building can be perfectly protected, combined with a general lack of funds, forced a reevaluation of the Inman standards. Privately, State Department officials described new security requirements as "overkill," but they were initially bound to implement them. Realizing that it would never be possible or practical to implement all of the standards everywhere, the department gradually moved away from a policy of blanket enforcement to one of site-by-site evaluation. FBO greeted the decision to ease restrictions with a sigh of relief. A willingness to waive specific requirements meant that symbolically important but "vulnerable" embassies could remain in cities such as Rome, The Hague, and Oslo, where office buildings abut streets and do not even approximate a reduced setback requirement (fig. 146). It meant that the department could rent and renovate existing buildings where new construction was unfeasible or undesirable—as at new posts in the former Soviet Union. And it meant that plans could proceed for major new construction in downtown Ottawa and for a competition to select an embassy design for Berlin.

When the Soviet Union suddenly collapsed in the summer of 1991, no one knew if the new nations would survive for days, weeks, or decades. The United States already maintained an embassy in Moscow, but found itself confronted with the challenge of establishing full diplomatic representation in the three Baltic nations and eleven other new independent states (NIS). The State Department wanted to move quickly to show U.S. support for the new governments and to forestall a resurgence of communism. Secretary of

State James Baker tapped a former ambassador, Nicolas M. Salgo, to select and acquire suitable office space at each NIS post. At first, there was talk of new construction and/or prefabricated units that could be flown in and assembled on-site, but Salgo and others familiar with the situations recognized that existing buildings were adequate, even preferable to modern-looking modules or new buildings that might take years to design and build. There was no legal precedent for the purchase of land or buildings in the Soviet Union. According to Kenneth Yalowitz, former U.S. ambassador to Belarus, the political strategy behind the embassy acquisition plan was "to get on the ground quickly, to recognize that these were independent countries, and to let them know that we took them seriously."[14] For that reason, "leasing made sense." By renting existing buildings rather than building new ones, the State Department was also able to bypass the stringent Inman standards, which applied only to new construction and to renovation work deemed substantial. It was a risk management decision; the security risk was outweighed by the need to move out of hotel rooms and into offices. Ordered by Baker to "Go yesterday!" and given a budget consisting of next to nothing, Salgo flew to the Baltic states in the fall of 1991 and worked his way east looking for decent and "distinguished-looking" bargains, as close to occupancy-ready as possible (fig. 147).[15] His personal preference for traditional architecture played a key role. He chose at least four properties that were former Komsomol (Communist Youth) headquarters—in Tallinn (Estonia), Vilnius (Lithuania), Kiev (Ukraine), and Yerevan (Armenia). The Tallinn property had been the U.S. legation before 1940. According to one FBO architect who inspected the properties, the sight of the American flag back atop the former legation was enough to make "old-timers weep." The building in Kiev was far too large for projected U.S. needs when it was leased, but by 1996 it was already too small. Like Moscow, Kiev was planned as a larger post than the others; still, its projected staff of forty grew to over one hundred. All of the other new posts were supposed to be small, under thirty people. All subsequently mushroomed in size to become "full-service embassies" almost overnight.

In Riga (Latvia), Salgo approved the former Ministry of Architecture and Engineering building, one of the oldest buildings in the city and one said to be widely admired by Latvians (fig. 148). In Minsk (Belarus), he found a handsome classically detailed building with a pedimental porch and columns. It was almost a replica of the White House. Instead of painting it white, though, it was repainted sky blue (fig. 149). Salgo was able to offer some reciprocal assistance to the new nations trying to establish their own diplomatic representation in Washington, but he had little to offer in terms of cash. Timing was all important, he said. In his estimation, "it made a hell of a difference" to show up first because good properties were scarce and prices soared when other nations came in pursuit of similar facilities. In Minsk, the Russians and Germans followed the Americans and took buildings flanking the U.S. embassy on either side.

Salgo moved on to Chisinau (Moldova) (fig. 150), then Almaty (Kazakhstan), Baku (Azerbaijan), Tbilisi (Georgia), and Yerevan. The building in Baku was formerly a medical library, before that a casino, and before that a brothel. Five opposition parties were removed from the former Komsomol building in Yerevan to make way for the new U.S. embassy. The Georgian prime minister helped Salgo win approval to lease an architectural prize in Tbilisi, a nineteenth-century mansion with reception rooms decorated in gold leaf and marble. Facilities were less sophisticated as the State Department team moved farther east to Bishkek (Kyrgyzstan), Tashkent (Uzbekistan), Dushanbe (Tajikistan), and Ashgabat (Turkmenistan). FBO decided to construct a prefabricated building at Ashgabat and another in Bishkek.

Not everyone shared Salgo's preference for downtown "landmark" buildings. Former FBO director Joseph T. Sikes was one who found the old buildings less than satisfactory and described the acquisition process as "politically driven." [16] But even Sikes admitted that time did not permit a more extensive selection process. It may seem odd that the State Department did not use the occasion of the Soviet collapse to showcase democracy through architecture as it did in the 1950s, but with the Cold War no longer driving decisions, display was a less important factor and the urgency of moving out of hotel rooms and into actual office space took precedence. Furthermore, Congress would have had to approve the funds needed to finance new construction, and new embassies would have taken many years to build. Though there is little institutional memory concerning foreign buildings, Secretary Baker may have recalled what happened when many African states became independent in the 1960s and the State Department proposed construction of an array of new embassy buildings. Members of Congress doubted the region's stability and questioned the wisdom of capital investment in places such as Bangui (Central African Republic) and Mogadishu. In public hearings, they examined every department request in detail. Subsequent events, including the ransacking of the Mogadishu compound, reinforced those doubts, and the department did not want to raise similar concerns about the former Soviet satellites. The sudden decision by Kazakhstan's president Nursultan Nazarbayev to relocate his capital from Almaty to the remote northern city of Akmola was further proof that investment in such places can be risky.

Where the leased properties may have reflected the past, the embassy in Bishkek was future-oriented (fig. 151). Sheathed in stainless steel, it featured modular components manufactured by Kullman Industries, better known for its stainless steel diners. The project is a joint venture between Kullman and the builder, M. F. Malone Company, and has included input from two design firms and FBO staff architects. To link the imported architecture to its host community, the U.S. ambassador solicited designs from local artists for a frieze motif that decorates the embassy's façade. Because it is relatively small, and because it brought with it paved roads and water and sewer service that opened up the area for development, the new embassy, the first to be built in Bishkek, was seen as a diplomatic asset to the United States. The stainless steel skin is certain to attract attention, but the possible association with roadside dining is probably no cause for concern in such a locale.

Neither this new design nor renovation schemes for NIS or Baltic states were presented to FBO's Architectural Advisory Board for review. By and large, design/build projects bypass the review process, though even Sikes was not sure why. It may have to do with the fact that contracts were awarded to teams consisting of developers and builders whose package deals include design services, it may reflect the fact that bringing experts together to review just an occasional design no longer made sense, or it may have been nothing more than expedience. A decade later, many of the leased NIS properties were replaced by newly built U.S. embassy compounds. These include new compounds in Yerevan, Dushanbe, Tashkent, and Tbilisi.

The U.S. consulate in Osaka (1981–87), designed by Kyoto-based architect Tatsuya Okura, was one other design/build job from that period (fig. 152). There has always been a tendency to keep small projects or those that are most remote out of the design review process, but the project in Osaka was neither small nor remote. Since the project involved an exchange of property (the obsolete consulate building in Kobe designed in the 1950s by Minoru Yamasaki), FBO solicited proposals that included land in Osaka, plus design, a financial package, and construction. The winning team offered the best site, the best value, and an architect, Okura, who had trained at Harvard and had worked for The Architects Collaborative (TAC). It is significant that the Architectural Advisory Board's role was diminishing when, as Sikes noted, it had been at one time such an asset and a "political bulwark." It is also significant that FBO grew immensely during the 1990s. With a staff of close to eight hundred in 1998, it had become a bureaucracy in and of itself—expanded, in part, due to the added complexity of its work.

The only major project built between the Inman period and 1998 was the Embassy in Ottawa, Canada. FBO built the new chancery downtown and close to Canada's parliament to underscore the mutual trust between the two nations and the symbolic importance of having a prominent presence in the Canadian capital.[17] The project was part of a bilateral agreement under which Canada built its new chancery on Pennsylvania Avenue in Washington, D.C. at the foot of Capitol Hill and under which the U.S. government transferred ownership of its strategically located, but obsolete, former Ottawa chancery to the Canadian government (see fig. 2, figs. 153–4).

FBO awarded the design contract for Ottawa to Skidmore, Owings, & Merrill (NYC) in 1994 after purchasing the site in 1993. It was the same site that had first been selected in 1979 when FBO commissioned Benjamin Thompson to design a new U.S. embassy in Canada. That original plan was abandoned in 1983 after terrorists attacked U.S. facilities in Beirut and all new embassy work was suspended pending a security review. By the early 1990s, when FBO began to search again for a suitable site in Ottawa, there was pressure to locate on a larger parcel farther from the downtown area to accommodate the new Inman security standards, but also strong feeling that a downtown site would better serve U.S. diplomatic needs in the Canadian capital. Canada was regarded as a reliable ally and the Department decided to err on the side of optimism and openness in moving ahead with the sliver of a site—only 205 feet wide—wedged between two major thoroughfares. The site did not provide for the 100-foot setback requirement. However, the site was ultimately selected because of its proximity to key government buildings, because residents near other suburban sites had made it clear that they did not want a U.S. embassy as a neighbor, and because local city planners had selected the downtown parcel for development—a chance to link Parliament Hill, on one side, to the Byward Market district, on the other. Inman setback requirements were waived to permit the project to proceed at that location.

The architectural team, headed by David Childs, faced a difficult task because the steeply sloped site was so narrow and faced very different environs on both sides. In addition, Canadian planners wanted the building to provide a rooftop feature that would help define the skyline, already marked by tower features at the National Gallery and the Château Laurier Hotel, and to accent the ceremonial route known as Confederation Boulevard. The solution was a long, narrow building that somewhat resembles a submarine topped by a dome-like tower that somewhat resembles a power plant cooling tower. Inside, however, the tower is a dazzling dome atop a narrow, corridor-lined atrium flooded with natural light.

The architects cleverly varied the building's two façades to reflect the different sides. The more formal façade faces MacKenzie Avenue and Parliament Hill. The opposite side provides the main entrance and faces Sussex Drive and the market district. In effect, the building has two fronts and no back. The original idea was to make a gracious gesture in both directions. Childs originally planned the atrium as a glass-walled space looking out toward Parliament Hill to emphasize the building's transparency as a diplomatic metaphor. But after the Oklahoma City bombing, in which the Murrah Federal Building was destroyed, he moved the atrium to the center of the building for necessary added security. He retained the effect of the glass wall, but placed behind it a concrete blast wall with punched windows. The wall still provides a sense of transparency despite the evident reinforcement, but the original idea that passersby would be able to see through the building from Sussex to MacKenzie has been lost.

When the Ottawa embassy opened in 1999, it was hailed as a positive diplomatic signal by the Canadian government. But it was not a sign of things to come. Indeed, it was the last major capital project of the post-Inman era; construction was financed by the sale of the previous embassy on Wellington Street, not from funds appropriated by the U.S. Congress. Aside from Berlin, also planned at that time, no new U.S. embassies were built on such small parcels of land in such prominent locations. What is most disappointing about the Ottawa project is the amount of security added after its completion. Jersey barriers now block lanes on the adjacent roads and the building reads more as an intrusion than an asset to what was envisioned as a busy market and residential neighborhood. There has been recent talk of removing some of the perimeter security that surrounds the building. The Ottawa embassy stands as a monument to good intentions at a moment in time when it was possible to imagine a U.S. embassy as a semipublic building with a recognizable civic purpose. It establishes a high-profile presence for the United States in downtown Ottawa—a rarity among recent embassies worldwide.

The threat of terror was less of a problem in Ottawa than in Berlin, where the State Department also planned to build a major new embassy. Although Inman standards would have required a suburban facility, a downtown location with immense symbolic importance was chosen. Located adjacent to the Brandenburg Gate on the Pariser Platz, where the Berlin Wall once divided the city, it is not only in the city's historic core and near Germany's major government buildings, but it is also the spot where the

U.S. embassy stood before World War II. By reclaiming the former embassy site, the United States sought to make a statement about the continuity of German-American relations. A move to a walled suburban compound would have conveyed a very different message, though such a shift was planned as recently as 1989. "It is of enormous political importance that the U.S. build on the Pariser Platz," declared Joseph Sikes. "The U.S. embassy belongs there, and anywhere else would be a mistake."[18]

The State Department signaled its desire to proceed with the historic site by holding a major design competition in 1995, the first since Eero Saarinen's design was selected for London in 1956. FBO retained Portland architect Donald Stastny as competition advisor with a jury consisting of the four members of the Architectural Advisory Board (Thomas Beeby, George Hartman, William Turnbull, and Cynthia Weese), former U.S. ambassador Joan Clark, former West Berlin mayor Klaus Schuetz, and architectural critic Robert Campbell. The finalists were: Venturi, Scott Brown and Associates; Bohlin Cywinnski Jackson; Kevin Roche John Dinkeloo and Associates; Robert A.M. Stern Architects; Kallmann McKinnell & Wood; and Moore Ruble Yudell.

The competition was most remarkable for its emphasis on "American" themes, explored in detail in the original winning scheme presented by Moore Ruble Yudell with Gruen Associates. According to its competition design guidelines, FBO envisaged the new embassy "as a tribute to contemporary American architecture—offering a statement to passers-by and visitors on the spirit of the United States." The guidelines further stated that the embassy should "display a public face that portrays an open, accessible government while accommodating security measures in an unobtrusive manner that does not detract from the architecture."[19] The winning architects responded with a design infused with a sense of U.S. history that had been (curiously) lacking in past projects.

As part of its plan to rebuild the area, the German government drew up strict design controls to which the new embassy had to conform. FBO guidelines also made it clear that the embassy had to respect the historic square and that "the square should not be misused for experiments." In American architectural history, references to ancient Greek and Roman buildings suggest democracy or a republican ideal, but in Germany classicism also carries connotations of the Nazi past, since Hitler specifically rejected modern architecture and used the classical orders to express totalitarian dominance.[20] Competition architects had to grapple with the many meanings associated with classical elements and the tension between the past and the present. Some entrants presented designs that recalled past

pomposity. Some confused boldness with empty experiment and presented designs that featured stage-set walls suggesting bombed-out ruins. The
Bohlin team offered a mix of sharply angled elements, including a huge
metal "cloud," and dubbed the assemblage a "garden." The Venturi team
presented a giant outdoor TV screen on which, they said, American culture
might be exhibited—a novel idea, but likewise an experiment.

When Gordon Bunshaft designed the German consulates for FBO
in the early 1950s—minimalist constructions of glass and steel that were
aesthetically elegant, transparent, and open—German critics objected to
the placelessness of those modern buildings. Moore Ruble Yudell wisely
avoided the negative associations of modernist minimalism and classicism.
Unlike the earlier SOM consulates, the winning Berlin embassy design was
marked by complexity and solidity. It was a courtyard building surrounding
a landscaped garden. Its diplomatic entrance was on the north façade on the
Pariser Platz, and what was to be a consular entrance was located around
the corner facing the Ebertstrasse. The architects explained the architecture
as an expression of democratic principles (citing "openness," "equality,"
and "diversity") and included specific references to the American cultural
landscape. Most of those features were subsequently removed as part of the
cost-cutting that removed many design elements, including the dome, for
example, originally proposed "as a symbol of our government's presence on
foreign land," a courtyard lodge, reference to the quintessential "American
house," and various gardens, references to the American backyard.[21] Even
after the winning design was selected, construction in Berlin was delayed
almost a decade while embassy officials negotiated with German authorities
to widen the proposed embassy's security perimeter by moving a major adjacent street and while the State Department explored its financing options.
The final scheme was far more timid than the original design suggested—
the result of necessary compromises and a major budget cut imposed by
Congress (see further discussion of this project in Chapter Twelve).

The Inman program called for an array of new construction, but of the
many projects envisioned at the outset, more than a third were dropped or
shelved, including office construction in Abidjan, Algiers, Ankara, Baghdad,
Beijing, Beirut, Cotonou, Damascus, Djibouti, Doha, Geneva, Guangzhou,
Istanbul, Izmir, Khartoum, Kingston, Rangoon, Seoul, Shanghai, and Tunis.
FBO's leasehold program was far larger than its capital program in 1998
and it looked then as if the capital program might end with Berlin, which
awaited funding at that time.

Committed to modernism, but directed by FBO to respect local custom
and tradition, American embassy architects faced the dilemma of finding a

useful past and expressing it in a modern idiom. Though early modernists had shunned historical reference and decoration, by the 1950s, in search of ways to innovate, they were attracted to "foreign-ness" and enthusiastically borrowed from other cultures. It is difficult, though, to fit large-scale projects such as office buildings into contexts in which local history and indigenous tradition may or may not offer useful prototypes. Embassy architects grappled with this problem. An architect who lifts motifs from the vernacular to add authenticity to new work runs the risk of trivializing tradition and possibly offending local sensibilities. Often it is the "home" audience, not the host, that most applauds the effort to find and express "exotic" themes. Sometimes both take pleasure in a solution, as at New Delhi, but at other times there is no evidence that attempts to "go native" are appropriate, appreciated, or even sincere.

In 1992 RTKL architects were charged with designing the sprawling new American embassy compound in Kuwait. Instead of presenting a single massive structure, they devised a scheme consisting of a series of smaller blocks connected by a tented open walkway. In a genuine effort to link the design to local building tradition, they compared the arrangement to a village and the tent structure to a Kuwaiti marketplace, or souk. In Kuwait, a nation that prizes high-tech construction and lavish materials for their association with wealth and grandeur, is the American effort recognized as an asset? Taniguchi's experience in Georgetown runs counter to the theory that expressions of a colonial past are anathema to former colonies. Perhaps Guyana is unusual, and perhaps admiration for what one Guyanese newspaper calls its "colonial heritage" is not universal, but it is nonetheless interesting that the Georgetown embassy is much admired locally for capturing something of the past in its modern garb.

Stone recycled the New Delhi design for years, never again referring to the Taj Mahal, and Stubbins took the screen from his Tangier consulate and applied it at the Loeb Drama Center in Cambridge. Sert's designs repeatedly featured exposed concrete contrasted with brightly colored vertical panels such as those he had designed for Baghdad, but he did not continually explain his work in terms of Middle Eastern tradition. Breuer worked with trapezoidal precast modules before and after he designed the embassy in The Hague, and Kahn's proposal for Luanda was based on a theme that he had studied for years. Embassy commissions played a pivotal role in many design careers, and individual designers reworked signature schemes, often using these large but distant commissions as proving grounds. These and many other examples suggest that the rationale for embassy architecture may have had less to do with locale and the exigencies of the building type than many of the architects suggested.

More troubling than the question of architectural sincerity is the issue of competence. Every building has its flaws, and the architect is only one of many people responsible for them, but it is surprising at times to see how easily architects escape blame for problems that can plague buildings forever. This can be explained in part by the low-profile nature of the profession—nonarchitects hardly ever know the designers of buildings other than major landmarks—and in part by a preoccupation with artistic production and personal flair that overshadows other aspects of the building process. Also, both architect and client pass blame to the contractor whenever possible. Stone made a triumphant return to practice after a prolonged slump when the new American embassy opened in New Delhi. Clients lined up to retain him after he won worldwide acclaim for the design, despite the fact that both the chancery and the residence had to be extensively modified for use. The residence, for example, lacked solid interior walls and offered no privacy to the ambassador or his guests; its bedroom closets were too narrow to hold hanging coats or suits. Workers in the chancery were regularly drenched as the courtyard's aluminum mesh roof failed to divert rain away from office corridors. And the glass walls, heavily screened, produced claustrophobic-feeling offices—a problem at numerous other posts.

Sally Cutler's observations on inadequacies in the consular residence at Tabriz, for example, illustrate the problems created by ill-conceived design. Cutler's family of four moved into the new house in 1965 when her husband was posted to the city in northwestern Iran. The architect, Edward Larrabee Barnes, had designed a handsome vaulted ceiling to capture local tradition, but as Cutler notes, the result was "an acoustical nightmare" in which "diplomatic secrets exchanged in whispers were clearly audible to persons standing thirty feet away."[22] Other problems included lack of accommodation for the array of servants who are a necessary addition to households in many countries (no place for them to sit or eat, no bathroom); lack of separation between living and dining areas, leaving no way to shield guests from the sights and sounds of servants at work; absence of a powder room, forcing the American ambassador and his wife to share the guest bathroom with hundreds of invitees to a reception in their honor; no children's play area; no drawers in the kitchen; no linen cupboard; and no place to store toys or the luggage that accompanies foreign travel. Access to the family sleeping quarters was only through the living room. Servants tidying bedrooms in the morning trekked through the living room with scrub buckets and linens, an unwelcome distraction to guests who might be there for a morning coffee party. The choice of white carpeting was "a disaster" in a country where dust and mud prevail, even more so in a region renowned for its attractive and durable carpets.

The architect must not be blamed for everything, certainly not for the choice of carpeting, on which he had no input. FBO ought to take the lion's share of responsibility for preparing the program and approving the architect's plans, and the post is at least somewhat responsible for failing to convey to the architect an accurate picture of climate and custom. But however blame is distributed, Cutler—and others such as Louisa Willauer—aptly question whether design flaws were "a deliberate rejection of service needs or simply a glaring oversight." As Cutler rightly notes, "Spouses of FSOs (at that time, all of them wives) were not part of the planning process, and it is they who know better than anyone the challenges of occupying a residence that serves both public and private purposes." [23] The Tabriz property has since been abandoned to revolution in Iran.

The new embassy at Dhaka so perturbed its staff—and FBO was so unresponsive—that the staff was forced to draw attention to its concerns by refusing to have the post photographed when FBO wanted to submit it as part of an application for a presidential design award. Criticism of Dhaka, like earlier criticism of New Delhi, Accra, Tegucigalpa, and Tabriz, adds to the stereotype of the embassy as an architectural "ego trip." Such projects explain the feeling in the Foreign Service that actual users are involved in planning and design decisions too little and too late.

Striking a balance between risk and representation is a dilemma that has faced architects of embassies since they were first built—most significantly since the early 1960s. The Inman standards were an attempt to remove risk from the equation, but as former assistant secretary of state for diplomatic security Sheldon J. Krys notes, "Perfect security means nobody's there at all." [24] If the original intent behind the new standards was to produce no-risk environments, the State Department now recognizes that some risk is inevitable and standards can only aim to produce low-risk or minimum-risk facilities. The challenge to architects has gradually shifted from the conceptual problem of representing American democracy and ideals to the logistical problem of turning a concrete bunker into a presentable (maybe even good looking) multipurpose office building. Ironically, FBO fired the architect Louis Kahn in 1960 after he presented a design for Luanda that resembled a medieval fortress. FBO director William Hughes told Kahn that embassies are supposed to attract people, not repel them: "We do not like our public buildings to be planned as windowless buildings, nor do we like them to have a fortress quality." [25] Thirty years after rejecting Kahn's design, the State Department reluctantly accepted the embassy-as-fortress as an unwanted necessity.

How architecture promotes America's interests or enhances its presence is another issue. Throughout the history of the embassy building program, friendliness and freedom were equated with architecture that was open and inviting. Architects boasted that their glass walls symbolized openness, even if they were often impractical and even if no buildings since Rapson's and Bunshaft's were honestly open to view. The best way to express an "American flavor," Belluschi told them in 1954, was not to explore recognizably American themes, but to examine local conditions and prepare designs to suit their sites. FBO made a political decision to view residents of the host country as the designated clients rather than, say, members of the American Foreign Service, the principal users, or members of Congress, who paid the bills. What distinguished the architecture was its newness, its grandness (not grandeur), and the inventiveness of its designers. More than anything else, what gave the embassies their American flavor was the originality of each project and the fact that each was an intentional celebration of individuality. This was especially important as a counterpoint to the presumed sameness and anonymity of Soviet projects during the Cold War years, but nearing the close of the 1990s, it looked as if that no longer made a difference. And subsequent events certainly made that clear.

Assessing the Inman era with hindsight, it is evident that there are several reasons for its overall failure in addition to those already cited. Faded memory of the Beirut attacks contributed, as did FBO's inability to effectively manage the large-scale projects. But the most important reason was lack of land. A building program grinds to a halt without land, and FBO never had enough sites for new embassy construction. FBO hired a private-sector firm, Svedrup Corporation, to manage its Inman projects and keep them on a necessary fast track. Although up to $1 million per month was spent on this effort, the results were slim because FBO could not find appropriate sites necessary for new construction at the scale mandated by the Inman standards. Just to comply with the setback, perimeter security, and collocation requirements officials were required to look for sites of ten to fifteen acres in size, and such sites proved hard to find and often harder to purchase. In addition, ambassadors often vetoed sites that were not to their liking.

In Sofia, for example, after the fall of communism in 1991, there were no clear titles to property and it was next to impossible to acquire a site for a new embassy. It took more than a decade to find a suitable site there and purchase it with a clear title. It took another three years to plan and build the new facility that finally opened thirteen years later in 2005—by which time the world had changed dramatically and the building program had entered a new phase entirely.

FIG. 140 (TOP): U.S. Embassy, Bangkok, Thailand. Kallmann, McKinnell & Wood (1994–96).

FIG. 141 (BOTTOM): U.S. Embassy, Lima, Peru. Arquitectonica (1992–96). Recent photo showing perimeter security

FIGS. 142a, 142b: U.S. Embassy, Santiago, Chile. The Leonard Parker Associates (1987–94). Interior and aerial view. A good example of an "Inman Embassy" project.

FIG. 143 (TOP): Proposal for U.S. Embassy, Bogotá, Colombia. Integrus
Architecture (1987–96).

FIG. 144 (BOTTOM): U.S. Embassy, Georgetown, Guyana. Alan Y. Taniguchi,
Architect & Associates (1983–91).

FIG. 145 (TOP): Peruvian soldiers guard the U.S. Embassy, Lima, Peru (1995).

FIG. 146 (BOTTOM): U.S. Embassy, Oslo, Norway. Parking along southeast side (1973). Little protects the building, which abuts city sidewalks and streets on all sides.

FIG. 147 (TOP): Ambassador Nicolas M. Salgo (far right) in Kiev, Ukraine in 1991 with team members (left to right) FBO architect James Capen, Mary Mochary, and John Shearburn.

FIG. 148 (BOTTOM): U.S. Embassy, Riga, Latvia (acquired 1991). Formerly the Ministry of Architecture and Engineering, this building will be replaced by a new embassy compound scheduled for completion in 2011.

FIG. 149 (LEFT): U.S. Embassy, Minsk, Belarus (acquired 1991), not currently in use. There are plans to renovate and re-open the building as the embassy chancery.

FIG. 150 (RIGHT): U.S. Embassy, Chisinau, Moldova (acquired 1991).

FIG. 151: U.S. Embassy, Bishkek, Kyrgyzstan. FBO (Kevin Lee Sarring, project architect). A joint venture between Kullman Industries and M. F. Malone Co. with FBO, 1998.

FIG. 152: U.S. Consulate, Osaka, Japan. Tatsuya Okura (1981–87). This replaced
Minoru Yamasaki's Kobe consulate of 1954.

FIGS. 153 & 154: U.S. Embassy, Ottawa, Canada. David Childs for Skidmore, Owings & Merrill (1994–99). TOP: MacKenzie Avenue façade with blast wall behind glass wall; BOTTOM: Sussex Drive façade with main entrance facing Byward Market district.

CHAPTER TWELVE

Since 1998

THE STATE DEPARTMENT'S OVERSEAS BUILDING PROGRAM changed radically after the suicide bombings at U.S. embassies in Nairobi, Kenya, and Dar es Salaam, Tanzania, on 7 August, 1998. While many suppose that the more recent events of 11 September, 2001 reshaped the program, it was the earlier events that started the process that produced the change. The bombings in East Africa represented a major turning point in the State Department's embassy construction program because of the shock of the devastation that killed 220, injured thousands, and destroyed prominent symbols of America's foreign presence (fig. 155). Congress promptly authorized funding for a vastly expanded capital construction program and also enacted specific security standards into law. As a start, Congress passed a $1.4 billion supplemental appropriation for security in October 1998 to expand the Diplomatic Security staff and to upgrade security infrastructure at posts abroad, with special focus on reconstruction needs in Nairobi and Dar es Salaam. The Department's original plans were to construct some 150 new embassy compounds by 2018, with $17.5 billion earmarked to meet that goal. That is out of a total number of 260 posts worldwide. Never before had the nation made such an investment in its foreign presence.

To accommodate this much expanded building program, the State Department reorganized itself after 1998—largely as a result of recommendations in two key 1999 reports: (1) *The Report of the Accountability Review Boards on the Embassy Bombings in Nairobi and Dar es Salaam,* commonly known as the *Crowe Report* (Admiral William J. Crowe served as chairman of the two review boards); and (2) *America's Overseas Presence in the 21st Century,* a report to the Secretary of State by the Overseas Presence Advisory Panel (OPAP).[1] Both reports lambasted FBO for failing to provide safe and secure workplaces for embassy personnel. The Crowe Report reiterated the largely unheeded Inman recommendations and questioned reasons for Inman's failure. As former chairman of the Joint Chiefs of Staff and also former U.S. ambassador in London, Admiral Crowe brought significant expertise to the task of assessing the damage and making new recommendations. His report stressed that safety had to outweigh considerations of convenience, history, or symbolism, and he condemned the demise of the Inman program and the inadequate accomplishments during the fourteen-year interval between the attacks in Beirut and the later attacks in Nairobi and Dar es Salaam.[2]

The OPAP Report questioned whether FBO was even capable of handling the challenge of building and maintaining the array of new facilities that was so urgently needed. Established by Secretary of State Madeleine Albright in 1999, the OPAP panel issued a report that harshly criticized conditions at U.S. posts worldwide and questioned whether FBO was set up to handle the demands of a large-scale capital building program to replace all security-deficient facilities. The panel suggested a new government-chartered corporation to replace FBO as a way of providing better management and oversight.

While some critics blasted Congress for failing to appropriate funds that were authorized for construction projects, others, including former Senator Rod Grams (R-Minn), blamed FBO for the failure of the Inman program. Grams criticized FBO's "poor record in effectively using resources" as a key factor in the failure of Inman. As chairman of the Subcommittee on International Operations of the Senate Foreign Relations Committee, Grams argued that it was not congressional inaction that led to the slowdown at FBO but rather that FBO was incapable of making good use of funds that Congress appropriated for new construction and security upgrades.[3] Grams voiced the same concerns as outlined in the OPAP report.

Expressing frustration with FBO and its inability to run the building program efficiently and effectively and calling for a greater focus on security, Congress enacted the Secure Embassy Construction and Counterterrorism Act in 1999 (SECCA), allocating $5.9 billion for embassy security over five years.[4] SECCA put into law for the first time security standards recommended in the Inman report but never legislatively mandated. These included the one-hundred-foot setback and the collocation requirement.

"There was nothing magical about the one-hundred-foot number," as former director of the Diplomatic Security Service Gregory Starr has observed; but as he noted, there is a significant drop in overpressure during a bomb blast at a distance greater than ninety feet. The one-hundred-foot setback allows for the construction of "pretty blast-resistant buildings at a reasonable cost," Starr said, adding that otherwise it would be necessary to build with twelve-foot thick walls and with other similarly undesirable specifications.[5] The one-hundred-foot number has remained the standard for most new embassies. In those very few instances where it was impossible to provide the one-hundred-foot setback, as in Luanda (Angola), Congress refused to fund embassy construction out of appropriated funds. The State Department was forced to fund the project out of proceeds of sale of property. The resulting building was built to one-hundred-foot blast specifications at a sixty-foot setback. Notable exceptions to the one-hundred-foot rule were Ottawa and Berlin. Ottawa was granted an exception before the one-hundred-foot setback became law in 1999. The Berlin project was held up for years while the State Department negotiated with German authorities to secure additional setback for the new embassy.

The collocation requirement stipulated that all U.S. government agency personnel be located on one site rather than scattered at different locations in or near a given capital. This further contributed to the need for large sites generally found outside city centers, sometimes at remote locales, but its purpose was to locate all employees on one facility to provide equal protection for all government personnel serving abroad. There was the expectation, too, that such a requirement would help control the rising cost of protecting and maintaining separate facilities.

And another feature of the SECCA legislation was the creation by Diplomatic Security of a list of the top eighty projects ranked by vulnerability—a list that serves as a guide to project selection and priorities for the capital construction program. Except under special circumstances, funds appropriated to the Embassy Security, Construction and Maintenance Account are earmarked only for these most vulnerable projects.

To indicate to Congress and outside critics that it would and could cope with the challenges ahead and to avoid the threat of FBO privatization, the State Department reorganized and renamed FBO in 2001, replacing it with the Bureau of Overseas Buildings Operations (OBO). The new bureau had a higher status within the State Department hierarchy and its director reported directly to the under secretary for management. The new director and chief operating officer of OBO, Major General Charles E. Williams, USA, retired, embarked on a vastly expanded building program with a redefined mission and a business model as its benchmark. Williams was a former soldier with a background in the Army Corps of Engineers. Secretary of State Colin Powell named him to head the building program in 2001 after the election that brought George W. Bush to the White House.

With an imperious style, Williams made extensive changes to the organization of the building program. He was a no-nonsense manager who fragmented the planning process as part of his effort to maximize speed and efficiency. He abolished the project management structure in favor of what has been described as a "sandbox" approach that segregated planning functions and minimized coordination among the various design and construction components of OBO. In 2004, he also abolished the Architectural Advisory Panel that had reviewed embassy designs since 1954, a loss greatly lamented by the design community that saw this as yet another move to marginalize architecture and critical oversight. Williams shifted OBO's focus to construction and product delivery and created an Industry Advisory Panel (IAP) to provide a different sort of outside professional input. Mostly, it seemed, he used the IAP to bring industry officials on board to approve his plans for design standardization and a design/build method of product delivery. He won high marks from Congress for meeting projected goals, for completing some fifty-four new diplomatic facilities between 2001 and 2007 and moving more than 16,100 U.S. government employees into more secure workplaces.

Williams's legacy lies in: (1) the long-range overseas building plan that defined the OBO construction program for six years; (2) the Capital Security Cost Sharing Program (CSCSP) that requires all U.S. government agencies to share costs of construction of overseas facilities; and (3) the Standard Embassy Design (SED), a building model that was already under development when he arrived at FBO but which he greatly expanded. Furthermore, Williams is linked to the massive new embassy compound in Baghdad that represents the excesses of a program driven by strategic and political demands often uncomfortably coupled with diplomatic objectives. Delays and additional follow-on projects on the Baghdad project led to Williams's resignation in December 2007.

The Standard Embassy Design and the design/build process has transformed America's foreign presence in the past decade. Unlike the process that defined embassy design and construction in earlier years, the new process took much of the guesswork out of the architecture. Nearly every project now starts with similar specifications tailored only in general program terms to the site. By definition, the new model is more efficient as a delivery system and takes into consideration lessons learned from past work. With competitive bidding, contracts are awarded on a lowest fixed price to contractors. Work must meet a fixed timetable and a fixed budget. This provides the State Department with certainty when it comes to cost, but it can result in compromises to the workplace and other compromises that put savings in the short term ahead of long-term considerations. It can, for example, add greatly to long-term maintenance costs, according to architects familiar with the program.

Given the risks associated with embassy construction and the distant and often remote locations involved, the system favors large international construction firms with extensive experience building overseas. Thus the number of firms participating in the program is small. Those who have participated most in the program include B. L. Harbert International, Caddell Construction Company, Inc., American International Contractors,

Inc. (AICI), Zachry Construction, and Framaco. B. L. Harbert, alone, is responsible for the construction of new U.S. embassies and embassy compounds in Abuja, Accra, Addis Ababa, Antananarivo, Brazzaville, Dili, Dubai, Khartoum, Kigali, Kiev, Lomé, Lusaka, Monrovia, Ouagadougou, Rangoon, and Tunis; the USAID office annex and Marine Security Guard Headquarters (MSGH) in Kampala; and consular compounds in Johannesburg and Karachi. While only American construction firms may work directly for OBO, they hire subcontractors who can hire labor locally. It is no surprise that a number of the firms have expertise in building military facilities worldwide and large-scale public institutions here at home.

The SED did not suddenly spring into existence fully developed. It began with the 1999 design for the U.S. Embassy in Kampala by RTKL, Architects (fig. 156). According to Patrick Collins, OBO chief architect, the design for the building more or less emerged from the exigencies of the site, which was steeply graded. The result was a three-part structure—two blocks separated by a circulation gallery with classified operations isolated on the upper level on one side. The Kampala project was built in less than two years via design/build, and it utilized local finish materials. As Collins notes, OBO experimented with similar schemes as part of early efforts to standardize the embassy delivery system. Designs for Sofia (completed in 2004), Yerevan (completed in 2005), and Abidjan (completed in 2005), for example, were similarly configured with classified operations separated from public-access offices by an open multipurpose space (figs. 157–60).[6]

It was Kampala, however, that caught the eye of General Williams, who was traveling in Africa with Secretary Powell in 2002 when he saw the Kampala embassy already completed; he immediately decided to use its design as a prototype. OBO hired the URS Corporation to take the scheme and work it into a generic model that could be used anywhere.

Joseph Toussaint, OBO managing director for program development, coordination and support, points out that architects and engineers proposed to Williams "that programs differed and that the design should flow from the program needs" and that variations in locale needed to be considered. But what Williams wanted, according to Toussaint, was "faster and cheaper," and with a mantra based on what he called "discipline," that is what he got.[7] It was simpler and better, Williams argued, if all sites were ten acres in size, so that also became a new standard.

Before the SED was fully realized as a building model, some embassy projects were designed to early standard criteria or pre-SED specifications. These included design/bid/build projects in Tunis (completed in 2002), Abuja (completed in 2005) (fig. 161), and Tashkent (completed in 2005) (fig. 162), and design/build competition projects in Nairobi and Dar es Salaam (both completed in 2003) (fig. 163). It also included the consular compound in Istanbul that opened in 2003 just in time to thwart a suicide bombing aimed at the old U.S. consulate that was particularly vulnerable (fig. 164). Terrorists who could not mount an attack on the new and heavily fortified U.S. consulate struck at a bank and at the British consulate, killing thirty, including the British consul general, and wounding 400.

By 2002 the full SED prototype was introduced. Although there was talk of small, medium, and large versions, nearly all projects built to SED specifications have been variations on the "medium" scheme that was originally envisioned as a building of 7,400 gross square meters at an original cost of $75 million. All of the models consisted of two parallel building blocks separated by an atrium. The early atria soared to three and four stories in height and featured skylights, but the standard was modified in 2006 to a two-story model (with no skylights) partly to comply more easily with code requirements. The atrium serves as a general circulation space, a meeting space, and often as an eating space, as the embassy's public services (e.g., cafeteria, bank) can be designed to open onto the atrium. It is also the buffer space between the two portions of the structure. With a core pre-approved for security, new projects had at first a twenty-four-month timetable that was later extended to thirty months. Even with thirty months, there was intense pressure on builders to begin construction before designs were finalized in order to meet the completion deadlines.

The SED consists of site-planning criteria, building plans and specifications, design criteria, adaptation methods, and contract requirements. Specifically, it outlines plans for the site, the main office building (chancery), annex building (if any), perimeter security (including walls and Compound Access Control facilities), warehouse, shops, utilities, recreation facilities, and Marine Security Guard Quarters. Thus SED does not refer to a single building but rather to an enclosed compound, usually on ten acres. Its size ranges from buildings that accommodate less than forty-five to more than 400 desks, with an average somewhere around 225—at a cost ranging from $75 million to $200 million, a figure that includes site acquisition and project costs and one that increases with time. According to OBO estimates, at least thirty percent of project costs are related to security. If site acquisition is added to that total, the percentage is higher.

By 2005, SEDs were completed in Phnom Penh, Kabul, and Cape Town (fig. 165). By 2006, there were SEDs in Astana, Bamako, Conakry, Dushanbe, Tbilisi, and Yaoundé (figs. 166–70). In addition, OBO built USAID facilities in Kampala, Phnom Penh, and Nairobi, and an annex in

Tirana (fig. 171). By 2007, OBO had completed SEDs in Accra (fig. 172), Algiers, Belmopan (figs. 173–4), Freetown, Kathmandu, Kingston (fig. 175), Lomé, (fig. 176), Managua, Panama City (fig. 178), and Rangoon, with additional USAID facilities in Kathmandu and Managua (fig. 177), and embassy annex buildings in Athens and Bogotá. By the following year, OBO completed another group of new facilities including SEDs in Port-au-Prince (fig. 179), Kigali, and Quito (fig. 180), USAID facilities in Accra, Bamako, and Kingston, the new embassy in Berlin and the megaembassy in Baghdad. By 2009, OBO had completed another group of new facilities including the embassy compound in Beijing and SEDs in Brazzaville and Skopje, consular compounds in Ciudad Juarez and Johannesburg, and office buildings in Kolonia and Koror. In the first four months of 2010, OBO completed new embassy compounds in Ouagadougou, Khartoum, and Antananarivo. This is a tremendous output for a single building program, particularly one that had as recently as the late 1990s produced at most two capital projects per year.

Well-secured compounds have accomplished the task of taking U.S. government employees out of harm's way and done so in a relatively brief time. The number of people moved to safer workplaces rose from 461 in 2000 to 20,458 by March 2010. The new delivery system enabled OBO to produce a record number of new embassies in record time from an average of one or two to eight or ten per year, completing seventy-one major new diplomatic facilities in the years between 2001 and 2010, of which fifty-two are completely new embassies. In addition, thirty-four projects are in design or under construction as of 2010, at a price tag of over $8 billion. Most posts have commented favorably on the new facilities, according to the OIG report that cites overall user satisfaction and praise for the design, beauty, space, and security of new facilities.[8] According to anecdotal reports, Phnom Penh, for one, is so admired locally that newlyweds pose for pictures in front of the building (fig. 181).

A report compiled in 2008 by the State Department's Office of Inspector General (OIG) strongly supports the use of the design/build process and the SED model, and credits much of the success of the Capital Security Cost-Sharing Program to both.[9] At the same time, the OIG has been critical of the SED for its failure to adequately address maintenance needs. Replacement parts are hard or impossible to locate locally and finding staff capable of operating and servicing the sophisticated heating, ventilation, and air-conditioning equipment has proven difficult, as the systems are often too sophisticated for those who have been hired to run them. For example, the building automation system (BAS) provides data on the operation of the heating, ventilation, and air conditioning systems in an embassy compound, but the BAS is too advanced for technicians in some countries, and finding able maintenance personnel has been a challenge. OBO recently changed its standards for facility managers requiring them to have educational degrees in engineering or facilities management to meet current needs.

Critics also point to the speed of construction as a cause of maintenance problems. Belmopan, for example, spent five weeks without air-conditioning "as a result of an accelerated [construction] schedule."[10] Another cause lies in the cost allocation since long-term maintenance costs are not figured into initial cost estimates. The remote locations selected for many of the new facilities pose additional problems. According to the OIG Report, the new location of embassies in Tbilisi and Zagreb, for example, was too far from the center of each capital for staff and contacts to be able to work effectively. A 2007 report from the Center for Strategic and International Studies, authored by diplomats and former diplomats *(The Embassy of the Future)*, was another to criticize the selection of sites so far removed from city centers.[11]

Architects are the most likely to identify the negative consequences of standardization because the standard model most compromises their creative work. John Chapman, an architect whose firm KCCT has worked on numerous SEDs, including Port-au-Prince, Kingston, Astana, Valletta, and Bucharest, and on other OBO projects in São Paulo, Luanda, and Tirana, points out that architecture "is more than what a building looks like. If it is well planned," he says, "people are proud of it and everyone enjoys it."[12] But Chapman concedes that standardization has "taken some of the life out of the buildings." Design is no longer a creative process, he argues, when designers cannot innovate as a way of solving planning, design, and engineering problems. Like others, he points to the advantages of design-bid-build as one way of bringing innovation back into the design process that now lacks competition and suppresses innovation.

One advantage of standardization, however, is that it reduces many of the mistakes evident in the post World War II years, when every embassy was different from start to finish and none of the architects had prior experience with this building type. William Miner, director of the Office of Design and Engineering Division at OBO, has noted "we don't need iconic architecture in a lot of places." To Miner it was evident from "day one" when he joined FBO in 1985 that some standardization was needed. "They were starting every project differently," he says, "and the process was very slow and inefficient, and we never learned lessons from past work let alone incorporated those lessons into future work." Former principal deputy assistant

secretary for diplomatic security Patrick Donovan reiterates Miner's sentiment. "It was a costly process and a burden to the taxpayer," he says, to
do it the old way, with each project unique. "We get that it's okay in some
places, as in London," he adds, "but not in most places such as Dushanbe
or Phnom Penh." According to OBO, the SED represents "a tool to enable
OBO to plan, award, design, and construct new embassy projects more
efficiently than in the past; to simplify the building process; and to provide
economically feasible facilities overseas."[13] It makes little sense to treat
each project as unique when so much is common to all.

The biggest problem with the SED does not lie with the security measures nor necessarily with how they are incorporated, but rather with how
they may be interpreted or misinterpreted. Massive new embassies can be
read as statements of fear and aloofness as much as statements of power
and confidence. Heavily fortified and imposing in size and scale, these new
walled facilities have redefined America's foreign presence, giving rise to
skepticism at times about its underlying global intentions—as has happened
in 2009 in Pakistan, where plans for a much enlarged U.S. embassy compound in Islamabad met opposition from those who equated the size of the
embassy project with imperialistic intent.

This same charge was leveled at the U.S. Embassy in Baghdad, the
colossal new compound on 104 acres in Baghdad's Green Zone (fig. 182).
As planned, the Baghdad compound is entirely self-sufficient, with no need
to rely on the Iraqis for services of any kind. It depends on convoys to
deliver food supplies, but the embassy has its own electricity plant, fresh
water and sewage treatment facilities, storage warehouses, and maintenance
shops. It was originally designed to include more than twenty-five buildings, including six apartment complexes with 600 one-bedroom units. Two
office blocks accommodate more than 1,000 employees. To date, it is the
costliest embassy ever, at over $840 million, and the largest in the world.
But the project, which opened in April 2008, has been beset by criticism
as a result of shoddy workmanship, structural deficiencies, and flaws that
have prompted the State Department's inspector general to recommend the
department seek a rebate of more than $132 million from the principal
contractor, First Kuwaiti Trading Company. The OIG blames former OBO
director Williams for creating a separate planning arm for the Baghdad
project, for providing poor oversight, and for pushing for speed at any cost.
Given its location in a war zone, the needs of this project were strategically
unusual, but the long-term consequences, including the future cost of maintaining such a facility, have been poorly considered.

Of the recent projects, embassies in Berlin and Beijing stand out as exceptions to the Standard Embassy Design program. Both capitals were deemed to be relatively safe from terrorist attacks but both projects are still built to high security standards, particularly Beijing, for which the buildings are enclosed in a walled compound within a diplomatic enclave. Berlin, by contrast, faces directly onto Pariser Platz, a major public space in central Berlin and stands almost adjacent to the famed Brandenburg Gate, a major German landmark and popular tourist destination (figs. 183–6). To its east, it abuts the DZ Bank, designed by Frank Gehry. Across the Behrenstrasse to the south is the Memorial to the Murdered Jews of Europe (2005) by Peter Eisenman, another more solemn public destination in the German capital.

As noted in Chapter Eleven, the State Department selected the Berlin site because on it stood the Bluecher Palace, acquired for use as the U.S. embassy just prior to World War II. As such, the site was associated with the American presence and the department wanted to maintain the continuity of that association by relocating at the same symbolic location to underscore American commitment to the newly reunified Germany and to maintain proximity to the nearby embassies of France, Great Britain, and Russia. Given the high-profile locale and the solidity of the bilateral relationship between Germany and the United States, the State Department decided to hold a competition to select a design for the new chancery—only the second in its history (the first having been the competition for London in 1956).

In 1995, when the winning design was selected for Berlin, there was relative calm in the security sphere. It was three years before the bombings in Nairobi and Dar es Salaam. That helps to explain the department's willingness to entertain bold and engaging ideas for the Berlin chancery. Since the capital program had more or less ceased to exist by the late 1990s, the Department financed the Berlin project largely through the sale of surplus diplomatic property, although supplemental funds were needed to complete the project. Like Ottawa, it is a major civic statement, if a much more muted one than that originally envisioned by its architects, Moore Ruble Yudell (MRY) of Santa Monica, California. Some of the competition entries were flamboyant, almost frivolous—with Vegas-style video displays on the exterior, for example—while others simply overplayed their scale and monumentality. The Moore Ruble Yudell scheme "was above all respectful of the context," according to architect John Ruble, who describes it as "more of an ensemble building than a landmark in itself."

Critics harshly criticized the 161,000-square-foot building when it finally opened on 4 July, 2008, after more than a decade in which German tempers flared over comments from the U.S. ambassador that some inter-preted as arrogant and after a major thoroughfare was moved to widen the security perimeter.[14] Congress refused to provide needed supplemental funds forcing a cut of 30 percent from the project's budget to limit the build-ing's size and to constrain its program. The cuts were visible in the finished project. For example, one floor was removed as part of the redesign process. Critics compared the final project to "Fort Knox" and derided it as "banal" and even "monstrous" for its massing, detailing, and choice of building materials. This came as a blow to the State Department for the very reason that the building was so far and beyond more accessible and more attractive than the typical SED project. Ironically, the SEDs, built in less prominent places, largely escaped criticism. It is difficult to read all of the criticism of Berlin as related to the architecture and easier to see it as political in nature, possibly even linked to anti-American feelings connected to the George W. Bush administration's initiative in Iraq that Germans opposed. Whatever the cause, the outrage spoke to the larger issue of America's image and how architecture communicates a message. What was most disappointing about the interpretation of that message was that critics so overlooked the new embassy's positive stance and missed its significance as an outstanding exception to existing policy.

The striking new embassy in Beijing is comparable to Berlin only because it was also designed by an architect whose design was selected by a juried design competition and built as part of a design/bid/build process. Otherwise it is entirely different. The U.S. Embassy in Berlin is part of the urban cityscape, with its entrance opening onto a busy public plaza, but the new embassy compound (NEC) in Beijing is a ten-acre walled complex comprised of five buildings—an eight-story chancery tower block, a three-story glass-walled atrium office building, a low-rise consular building, a Marine Security Guard Quarters structure, and a parking/utility structure—grouped around open courtyards, formal gardens, terraces, and informal water gardens.

It is located not on a busy downtown street, but northeast of the Forbidden City in Beijing's Third Diplomatic Enclave in the Liang Ma He neighborhood (figs. 187–8). The architecture itself is a fusion of East and West presented in a high-tech idiom. It is not contextual like Berlin but a bold and singular statement. The architect was Craig Hartman of Skidmore, Owings & Merrill, and the landscape architect was Peter Walker, both of San Francisco. The SOM project was part of a bilateral agreement between the United States and China to build embassies in Washington and Beijing simultaneously. Both nations needed modern embassy facilities. The United States, in particular, suffered with facilities in Beijing that were substandard in terms of functionality, life-safety, and security. President George W. Bush dedicated the Beijing embassy on the morning of the opening ceremony of the 2008 Olympics.

According to the architect, Hartman, "It seemed especially important that our embassy's architecture in some way reflect our cultural, social, and political values while at the same time being respectful of China—a country with an ancient and extraordinarily rich culture." The challenge, as he noted, was how to weave Chinese tradition together with "American civic values of clarity, optimism, and openness." Instead of designing one or two towering or monumental structures, Hartman designed one eight-story building, the chancery, sheathed in glass and "a series of discrete smaller buildings which are woven into a series of gardens and courtyards, all of which are connected by a narrow hutong-like walkway lined with giant bamboo."[15] The chancery office block is luminous by day and also at night, when illuminated. And as Hartman says, the two-story consular pavilion with its porchlike entry plaza provides a welcoming venue for visitors. The architecture also incorporates sustainability by holding storm water and purifying it through the lotus ponds, by using thermal inertia and daylighting to increase comfort levels and decrease energy consumption, and by providing white roofs and up-to-date mechanical systems that also reduce carbon dioxide emissions and energy use.

Nothing marks the new embassies such as Beijing as "American" as much as the art that is featured in them. A major asset, the art plays a key role in linking each new embassy to its host community and the United States to each host country. For Beijing, OBO's ART in Embassies Program (AIEP) provided a complete collection of contemporary paintings, prints, and sculpture on the theme of landscape. The collection includes works by Maya Lin, Cai Guo-Qiang, Betty Woodman, Robert Rauschenburg, and Hai Bo. Jeff Koons's colorful steel sculpture, *Tulips,* installed in the lotus pond in front of the consular pavilion, is on loan from the artist for ten years (fig. 188). OBO calculates its art budget based on a project's overall square footage and Beijing is the second largest (after Baghdad) in size. Overall, the investment in art in Beijing represents a sum of over $800,000, the largest ever spent at a U.S. embassy.

The ART in Embassies Program originated in 1963 as part of President John F. Kennedy's cultural outreach agenda. At first, its mission was to supply loaned art to ambassadorial residences, and that remains a major part of its mission. As AIEP curator Sarah Tanguy recently noted, "At any given

time, some 3,500 works by 3,000 artists with a total value of more than
$350 million are in about 180 ambassadors' residences worldwide."[16] But
the AIEP mission has greatly expanded since 2005 when the program began
buying art for all of the new U.S. chanceries, annexes, and consulates—not
only residences. AIEP buys art and commissions new works by American
artists, and as part of the effort to expand its mission of cultural diplomacy, it now also showcases works by local artists. Chief curator and acting director Virginia Shore makes a point, as she says, of selecting art that
"connects" to place. Thirty works by American and Algerian artists explore
cross-cultural influences between contemporary abstract American art and
Islamic art at the new U.S. embassy compound in Algiers, for example. The
permanent collection at the new embassy in Bamako features quilts, other
textiles, paintings, sculpture, and photography by Malian and American artists—works that create visible cultural connections between the two countries. Forty-two photographs by Malian youth, for instance, document daily
village life in Mali. Ethiopian artists as well as Ethiopian-American artists
will be among those whose work will be featured at the new embassy in
Addis Ababa. As a result of extensive meetings between AIEP staff and local
artists, curators, studios, and collectors, comparable collections are being
assembled for Khartoum and Ouagadougou. As Virginia Shore explains, it
is a "win/win" situation for the artists from all countries whose works are
shown because of the prestige associated with being included in embassy
collections and because of the chance for all to participate in a valuable cultural exchange program. Since 2005, AIEP has installed thirty-four permanent collections in new diplomatic facilities. As part of its American Artists
Abroad initiative, it has also sent some fifty artists to visit and discuss their
art in more than forty countries in recent years. In the past five years alone
AIEP spent some $20 million on art. The diverse collections of art in new
embassies and the programs that accompany the art make a strong cultural statement for the United States, a statement particularly amplified in
the context of standardized architecture that varies so little from place to
place. Currently only invited visitors and staff can enjoy the art, but AIEP is
increasing access by partnering with the Public Diplomacy office to develop
ongoing cultural outreach programming.

   In addition to works purchased by the ART in Embassies Program, the
nonprofit group Foundation for Art and Preservation in Embassies (FAPE)
also commissioned original works for Beijing, including sculptural installations by Ellsworth Kelly and Louise Bourgeois. FAPE was created in 1986
to assist the State Department in exhibiting and preserving fine and decorative art at its embassies. From its outstanding collection of original prints,

FAPE provides works by American artists, including prints by Frank Stella, Roy Lichtenstein, Chuck Close, and Alex Katz. The Joel Shapiro sculpture that stands outside the U.S. embassy in Ottawa, for example, was a FAPE commission for that site as was the Sol LeWitt mural installed at the Berlin embassy (see fig 186). FAPE, in fact, provided all of the art for Berlin after the art budget there was cut.[17] It has also assisted with restoration and conservation work at sites including the embassy residence in Prague and the chancery in Rome.

After General Williams resigned, Richard Shinnick became director ad interim of OBO in January 2008, bringing to OBO a new sense of openness and possibility. According to an inspector general's report completed at that time, Shinnick "quickly corrected organizational deficiencies and improved coordination and communication between regional bureaus, overseas posts, and other agencies."[18] In addition, he focused real estate operations on site selection and purchase, authorizing contracts for the purchase of new embassy sites in London, The Hague, and other high profile capitals. Shinnick had served as a Foreign Service officer as second in command to Richard Dertadian, who headed FBO in the 1980s, and also in London, where he conceived of an innovative program for purchasing property. He came out of retirement to take the helm at OBO when his experience and talent were needed.

The State Department wanted a new site in London because the chancery in London's Grosvenor Square is obsolete in terms of security, physical plant, and also in terms of its size and functionality. It has been evident for years that the facility needed a full overhaul; but it has been impossible to reconcile the needs of much enhanced security and much larger space for a greatly expanded staff with the existing structure designed in the mid-1950s by Eero Saarinen (see figs. 99–103).

Sadly, the inelegant security installations that surround the London embassy have interfered with traffic flow on surrounding streets and have impeded access to and from neighboring dwellings. Neighbors have long wanted the embassy to move to a new location, citing it as a major intrusion to the Mayfair area that is otherwise highly desirable as a residential area. Responding to that criticism and recognizing that only a new embassy could meet current needs, OBO embarked on a five-year search for a suitable new site and recently announced purchase of approximately five acres in Nine Elms, Battersea, a developing industrial area south of the Thames River.

The London project is especially important because of the prestige associated with the post, its high visibility, and the close relationship between the United States and the United Kingdom. Acknowledging that importance and recalling the design competition through which Saarinen's winning design was originally selected, OBO held a competition to select a design for the new site. Jurors were both American and British and included architect Frances Halsband, architecture professor Michaele Pride, landscape architect Peter Rolland, former U.S. ambassador Clyde D. Taylor, sustainability expert Thomas Hicks, British architect Richard Rogers, and chairman of the Pritzker Prize jury Peter Palumbo. Donald J. Stastny chaired the jury as its competition manager.[19]

After a preliminary review of thirty-seven entries submitted in October 2008, the list of competing firms was narrowed to nine and then to four firms: KieranTimberlake, Morphosis Architects, Pei Cobb Freed & Partners, and Richard Meier & Partners.

IN FEBRUARY 2010, THE JURY SELECTED as the winner KieranTimberlake, the Philadelphia firm whose remarkable design celebrates both openness and sustainability giving the new embassy a positive and future-oriented stance (fig. 189). The centerpiece of the scheme is a transparent eleven-story office tower in the shape of a cube designed to conserve and capture energy. Instead of high fences and impenetrable walls, the design relies on the landscape to provide the necessary defenses for a secure perimeter. The extent to which landscape is used for this purpose is a first for OBO. The way the design integrates the building with its setting and creates pedestrian-friendly grounds is a development worth celebrating. Moreover, the sophisticated sustainability features further underscore this as a project that merits praise. The new embassy will set a high standard for the many new buildings that are likely to be developed in its immediate environs over the next few years. The whole project is expected to be self-financed at a cost of some $1 billion, with completion expected in 2017 when the Saarinen building will be converted by its new owners to a new use—probably as a hotel or upscale apartment block. The new owner will be the Qatari Diar Real Estate Investment Company headquartered in Doha, Qatar.

The competition was not without incident. In what can only be described as a startling move, the two British judges, Rogers and Palumbo, made known after backing the jury's choice that they favored the Morphosis design, which appears edgier and less considered than the winning scheme. Christopher Hawthorne describes the Morphosis scheme in the *Los Angeles Times* as a "sagging embassy that is practically collapsing in on itself."[20] Architecture that is unsettling or simply unsettled has its place but not necessarily in connection with this building type. It is no surprise, however, that politics intruded upon this competition. After all, embassy architecture is part of a political process. It is likely that there will be a lot more noise about this project given its location and prominence.

With mid-century modernism in vogue, Saarinen's work has been celebrated in major exhibitions in the past several years. The recent decision by English Heritage to grant the Saarinen building a Grade II listing may limit its development options to some extent—the façade and lobby must be retained under the preservation protocol (it is not clear what will happen to the giant eagle). Getting top dollar for the existing building was key because the State Department plans to finance the new embassy project through the sale of its combined Grosvenor Square properties.

The renewed appreciation of midcentury modernist architecture focuses attention on the future of embassy projects in places like London, Dublin, and Oslo, where embassies are obsolete or fail to meet current security requirements. In The Hague, the City of The Hague commissioned a study to examine the history and the architectural merits of the embassy designed in 1956 by Marcel Breuer (see figs. 71–2 and 104–7). Although the building was locally despised for failing to fit in to its historic neighborhood and for its brutalist stance, it has more recently found favor among those who appreciate it as history, if not as a beloved work of art. The 2008 study recognizes the building as an asset to the city and recommends that it be recycled somehow into another use rather than razed when the U.S. Embassy moves to its new locale sometime in the next decade.[21] There is one proposal to restore the building and convert it to a museum called the Marcel Breuer Design Museum that will show and collect outstanding furniture. It is not clear, however, what will become of it or other embassies and consulates that were designed by modernist masters at the height of the Cold War. Harry Weese's embassy in Accra was supposed to be recycled as a women's center but apparently fell into ruin after the embassy moved to its new and secure quarters (see figs. 58–60 and 172).

It is not just the modernist buildings that the State Department is replacing. In Ottawa, the embassy building designed by Cass Gilbert was sold as part of the deal that led to the acquisition of a site for a new embassy there (see fig. 2). Although the old building was originally slated to become headquarters for the Portrait Gallery of Canada, it remains vacant, awaiting a new use. The State Department often sells real estate to finance new construction. For better or worse, it is up to new buyers to decide the fates of these former American landmark buildings.

Conservation and preservation are issues that the State Department is not ignoring, even if it lacks resources to hold onto some properties that are no longer useful. What it is doing is attempting to catalog its historic assets and attend to their continued needs through two new programs— the Register of Culturally Significant Properties and the Cultural Heritage Program.

The Register of Culturally Significant Properties was created in 1999 by Secretary of State Madeleine Albright. undersecretary of state for management Bonnie R. Cohen was instrumental in bringing it into existence. It now comprises twenty sites selected for recognition because of their distinctive design or their association with historical events or people—local history as well as American history. It represents recognition that the United States has major architectural, archeological, and artistic assets overseas. The listing does not provide protection but it is a guarantee of increased care and concern and respect for the locale where such assets are located. The faux-Georgian manor house known as Winfield House, the residence of the U.S. ambassador in London, is one such site. The eigtheenth-century Schoenborn Palace, which houses the U.S. Embassy in Prague, is another. Both are prized as local assets. Other listed properties that were purchased by the State Department for diplomatic use include: the Palazzo Margherita and its twin villas in Rome (see fig. 14); the old American legation in Seoul; the Hôtel de Talleyrand in Paris (see figs. 15–16); the Palacio Bosch, the American ambassador's residence in Buenos Aires; the ambassador's residence in Hanoi; the Villa Otium in Oslo (see fig. 3); Truman Hall in Brussels; Byne House in Madrid; the American Center in Alexandria; Villa Petschek, the American ambassador's residence in Prague; Villa Taverna, the American ambassador's residence in Rome; and the Hôtel Rothschild, the American ambassador's residence in Paris. U.S.-built properties on the register include: the U.S. Embassy in Tirana (1929) and the ambassador's residence in Tokyo (1926–31) (see figs. 7–8 and 12); the old Manila chancery; and two modernist landmarks, the New Delhi chancery (1954–59) by Edward Durell Stone and the Athens chancery (1956–60) by Walter Gropius (see figs. 53 and 74). In addition to those listed on the register there are dozens more already identified as candidates for listing.

It is the purpose of the Cultural Heritage Program to provide proper conservation and maintenance of the listed properties and other OBO properties that are cultural assets. Historic properties, sometimes acquired complete with antiques, valuable furnishings, and other art objects, pose special challenges in terms of conservation and housekeeping. In addition, donors have given valuable items, such as paintings and furniture, to the embassies as gifts. Caring properly for these items preserves their value, strengthens ties between embassies and the communities that surround them, and earns goodwill for the United States.

As an expression of individuality and site-specific problem solving, design excellence has not figured prominently in OBO's program since 1998 because the program has focused so exclusively on architecture's role as shelter. But there are signs that that is changing. The new London project is the boldest example. Another is in Bujumbura, Burundi, where in 2010 OBO broke ground on a new embassy compound (NEC)—OBO's one hundreth diplomatic facility. The project will be the first using bridging documents that will mandate specific design features. It is part of a larger effort at OBO to find ways to use design excellence to produce better buildings. Architects have also been retained to design a new embassy in the Wassenaar neighborhood outside of The Hague. The project will not be a standard SED, but, like London, will be tailored to its locale in a community that values good design.

OBO's green agenda first emerged from grass-roots efforts by architects, engineers, and site managers to better their projects. General Williams lauded the effort that was formally recognized as a priority by OBO's ad interim director Richard Shinnick and then embraced by his successor, Adam Namm, as a major step in a positive direction. In 2008, Shinnick announced the requirement that all future U.S. embassies must earn formal Leadership in Energy and Environmental Design (LEED) certification from the U.S. Green Building Council. London, for example, will be LEED Platinum (above the required Gold), it will be carbon neutral, it will feature a self-sufficient water system, and its design will conserve energy in ways that make it possible for the embassy to operate "off-grid" for an extended period. Making embassies more sustainable not only cuts long-term costs but also gives them greater autonomy, which augments their security. Beyond that, it wins approval from host governments whose own efforts to conserve resources are thus boosted. The first embassy to achieve LEED certification was Sofia, Bulgaria in 2007 (figs. 157–60). Sofia has realized a thirty percent reduction in energy costs and a twenty-one percent reduction in water use compared to similar buildings as a result of its "green" design. Lights turn off when not needed and lightshelves on the exterior bounce light into the interior to augment the daylighting inside. The location is easily accessible via public transportation, which is also an asset. In addition, the necessary security setback allowed OBO to provide a four-acre wildlife habitat that includes some 400 newly planted trees. It is significant, too, that one third of all building materials came from relatively close by—within 500 miles of the site. CMSS Architects designed the new building in collaboration with J.A. Jones, International, the design/build contractor. The total cost was approximately $78 million for a project totaling 184,472 square feet and including an office building, a warehouse, and a Marine Security Guard Quarters building.

In 2008, the sprawling new 43.2 acre SED compound in Panama City became the second LEED-certified embassy (fig. 178). It modified the Standard Embassy Design prototype to meet newly defined planning goals. Using innovative plumbing fixtures, for example, the building reduced water consumption inside by thirty-two percent. It also reduced outside water use for irrigation by fifty percent. On the exterior, too, it reduced the urban heat island effect by limiting the use of hard or paved surfaces around the buildings. Most building materials were acquired from local sources, and interior environments are carefully controlled to promote comfort and conserve energy. Like Sofia, the compound consists of an office building, a warehouse, and a Marine Security Guard Quarters building. This project cost $67 million. The architect of record was Einhorn Yaffee Prescott (EYP), the landscape architect was Langan Engineering, and the contractor was Caddell Construction. These are the first U.S. embassies to be recognized as sustainable sites in terms of water efficiency, energy consumption, building materials, indoor environmental quality, innovation and design, and other measurable criteria. More are in the works.

A 2009 report, prepared by the American Institute of Architects, provided OBO with a manifesto for design excellence comparable in general terms to the program that has been so successfully implemented by the General Services Administration over the past fifteen years. Compiled by a task force of leading experts, the AIA report, *Design for Diplomacy: New Embassies for the 21st Century,* calls on the State Department to improve its overseas buildings through better and more thoughtful design. [22] Senator John Kerry, chairman of the Senate Foreign Relations Committee, praised the report as a step in a positive direction. "We're all well aware of the changed world we live in and the need to have security," he said, "But I believe we can build embassies that are not only safe and secure, but embassies that also reflect America's values of openness, creativity and innovation."

OBO Deputy Director Lydia Muniz heads a team examining the challenge of how to incorporate design excellence into the OBO building program. As Muniz noted at a recent IAP gathering, OBO sees design excellence as a means of producing embassies that are not only secure and functional, but also good-looking and environmentally and civically responsible. Muniz acknowledges that recent results with standardization and design/build have been less than "perfectly satisfying," but she is looking ahead with what she terms a "real desire to go back to building designs that we are very proud of and that will last a very long time."[23] Already, the new initiative has produced the winning scheme for London—an impressive move by OBO. It is too soon to tell where else this new initiative will lead; but given the history of the past decade, it is notable that the State Department is engaged in this discussion now. It is notable, too, that a number of recent projects have won industry awards for design/build excellence.

With globalization, when we face the world, we face ourselves. What we see matters. Good design conveys good intentions. Well-designed buildings are good investments. They represent the best of modern technology, show our respect for countries that host us around the world, and provide safe and functional workplaces for U.S. diplomats and their colleagues from the array of U.S. government offices that are represented at posts abroad. The Standard Embassy Design may not suit all design critics because of its similarity to a big box store with its kit-of-parts approach. Like a Marriott hotel, it is predictable and predictably bland. But it has created a recognizable identity for the United States from Bamako, Mali, to Port-au-Prince, Haiti, where the new, self-sufficient, and soundly built U.S. embassy was among the only buildings to survive the January 2010 earthquake unscathed and ready to serve as a platform for relief efforts (fig. 179)

In the past decade of geopolitical change much has been accomplished to meet the challenges facing the United States in an ever more threatening world. No longer designed to welcome the public as they were sixty years ago, new embassies are now built for defensive purposes. But government buildings and monuments here at home have also assumed a similarly defensive stance. It may not be what everyone wants but it is definitely where we are headed. Whether such facilities can still be called "public" buildings is a good question. Even the U.S. Capitol is not totally open to the public, augmented as it now is by a visitors' center that carefully distances, processes, and screens its visitors. Whether new embassies still have a role in promoting public diplomacy is another serious question; architecture, like literature, art, and theater, has a role to play in a war of ideas. Whether these structures can be accurately described as "diplomatic" facilities is something else to ponder—do they support or impede the work of diplomacy? Hopefully, new embassies can address life-safety issues and also showcase new technology and design expertise as a way of speaking to a better future and not just to a fearful present.

The need for effective overseas representation has never been more apparent. The communications revolution makes it possible to imagine an embassy that is little more than a computer terminal equipped with interactive software; the internet may someday replace the diplomatic pouch. But buildings will remain important insofar as they augment security and to the extent that economic opportunity and cultural goodwill remain high on the political agenda. As long as people look to the United States for world leadership and as long as embassies reflect America's self-image and its commitment to other nations, the architecture of diplomacy will continue to matter.

Fig. 155 (TOP): Damage to U.S. Embassy Nairobi, Kenya (right) and collateral damage from terrorist attack, 7 August, 1998.

Fig. 156 (ABOVE): U.S. Embassy, Kampala, Uganda (2001).

Fig. 157 (LEFT): U.S. Embassy, Sofia, Bulgaria (2004). Entrance.

Figs. 158–60: U.S. Embassy, Sofia, Bulgaria (2004). (TOP): Rear view, (BOTTOM LEFT): cafeteria, (BOTTOM RIGHT): lobby (atrium).

Fig. 161: U.S. Embassy, Abuja, Nigeria (2005).

Fig. 162: U.S. Embassy, Tashkent, Uzbekistan (2005).

Fig. 163: U.S. Embassy, Nairobi, Kenya (2003).

Fig. 164: U.S. Consulate General, Istanbul, Turkey (2003).

Fig. 165: U.S. Consulate General, Cape Town, South Africa (2005).

Fig. 166: U.S. Embassy, Astana, Kazakhstan (2006).

Fig. 167: U.S. Embassy, Bamako, Mali (2006).

Fig. 168: U.S. Embassy, Conakry, Guinea (2006).

Fig. 169: U.S. Embassy, USAID Annex, Tbilisi, Georgia (2006).

FIG. 170 (TOP): U.S. Embassy, Yaounde, Cameroon (2006).

FIG. 171 (BOTTOM): U.S. Embassy compound, including new annex, Tirana, Albania (2006).

Fig. 172 (TOP LEFT): U.S. Embassy, Accra, Ghana (2007).

Figs. 173–4 (TOP RIGHT AND BOTTOM): U.S. Embassy, Belmopan, Belize (2007). Main entrance and side view.

Fig. 175 (TOP): U.S. Embassy, Kingston, Jamaica (2007).

Fig. 176 (BOTTOM): U.S. Embassy, Lomé, Togo (2007).

FIG. 177 (TOP): U.S. Embassy, Managua, Nicaragua (2007).

FIG. 178 (BOTTOM): U.S. Embassy, Panama City, Panama (2007).

FIG. 179 (TOP): U.S. Embassy, Port-au-Prince, Haiti (2008).

FIG. 180 (BOTTOM): U.S. Embassy, Quito, Ecuador (2008).

Fig. 181 (TOP): U.S. Embassy, Phnom Penh, Cambodia (2005).

Fig. 182 (BOTTOM): U.S. Embassy (chancery), Baghdad, Iraq (2008). This office building
stands within a compound with an expanse of 104 acres in Baghdad's Green Zone.

FIG. 183–4: U.S. Embassy, Berlin, Germany. Moore Ruble Yudell (2008). TOP: Overall view including the Brandenburg Gate. BOTTOM: U.S. Embassy, Berlin, Germany (2008) distant view from the Memorial to the Murdered Jews of Europe showing the proximity of the Embassy to the Brandenburg Gate and the Reichstag (left).

FIGS. 185–6: U.S. Embassy, Berlin, Germany (2008). TOP LEFT: entrance adjacent to DZ Bank facing Pariser Platz; TOP RIGHT: side view showing Sol LeWitt mural visible from the sidewalk.

FIG. 187 (BOTTOM): U. S. Embassy, Beijing, People's Republic of China. Skidmore, Owings & Merrill (2008), model. FIG. 188 (NEXT PAGE): View of lotus pond featuring sculpture, *Tulips*, by Jeff Koons, installed in front of consular wing.

FIG. 189: Proposed U.S. Embassy, London, England (2010). Winning competition entry by KieranTimberlake.

APPENDIX A

Deputy Assistant Secretaries and Directors, Office of Foreign Buildings Operations 1946–2001 and Directors, Bureau of Overseas Buildings Operations 2001–2010

Administrator	Title	Tenure
Frederick Larkin	Chief, FBO	1946–52
Leland W. King	Director, FBO	1952–53
Nelson A. Kenworthy	Acting Director, FBO	1953–54
William P. Hughes	Director, FBO	1954–61
James R. Johnstone	Director, FBO	1961–65
Ralph Scarritt	Director, FBO	1965–66
Earnest J. Warlow	Director, FBO	1966–73
Orlan C. Ralston	Deputy Assistant Secretary, FBO	1974–77
William L. Slayton	Deputy Assistant Secretary, FBO	1978–83
Harvey A. Buffalo Jr.	Deputy Assistant Secretary, FBO	1983–85
Richard N. Dertadian	Deputy Assistant Secretary, FBO	1985–91
Jerome Tolson	Deputy Assistant Secretary, FBO	1991–95
Joseph T. Sikes	Deputy Assistant Secretary, FBO	1995–97
Patsy Thomasson	Deputy Assistant Secretary, FBO	1998–2001
Charles Williams	Director and COO, OBO	2001–2007
Richard Shinnick	Director, ad interim, OBO	2008–2009
Adam Namm	Acting Director, OBO	2009–current

APPENDIX B

Prospective Architects Listed in 1954 Memo by Pietro Belluschi with Commissions Later Awarded

(CGOB = consulate general office building; CGR = consulate general's residence; COB = consulate office building; ER = embassy residence; NA = no award; OBC = embassy office building chancery; SH = staff housing; SOB = supplementary office building)

Architect	Project(s) Awarded	Architect	Project(s) Awarded
Aeck, Richard L.	NA	Kahn, Louis	Luanda COB
Anderson & Beckwith	Taipei OBC	Kennedy, Robert Woods	NA
Armstrong, Harris	Basra COB	Ketchum, Morris	Rabat OBC, ER
Aydelott, Alfred Lewis	Manila SOB	Keyes, Smith & Satterlee	Asunción OBC, ER
Becket, Welton D.	Warsaw OBC, SH	Kilham, Walter, Jr.	Kabul OBC
Breuer, Marcel	The Hague OBC	Koch, Carl	Belgrade SH
Cochran, Alexander Smith	Nagoya COB, SH	Kump, Ernest	Seoul SH; ER
Dailey, Gardiner	Manila SH	Lescaze, William	NA
DeMars, Vernon	NA	Lyndon, Maynard	NA
Goodman, Charles M.	Reykjavik OB	Matsumoto, George	NA
Gropius, Walter	Athens OBC	McCarthy, Francis Joseph	NA
Hare, Michael	Tegucigalpa OBC, ER	Neutra, Richard	Karachi OBC
Hatch, Don	Port-au-Prince OB; Caracas OB	Reid, John Lyon	Algiers OBC
		Rex, John L.	NA
Hill, Henry	Vienna SH	Rockrise, George	Fukuoka COB
Holabird & Root	NA	Rudolph, Paul	Amman OBC
Hutchins, Robert	Dakar OBC, SH, CGR	Sert, José Luis	Baghdad OBC, ER, SH

Prospective Architects, cont.

Architect	Project(s) Awarded	Architect	Project(s) Awarded
Staub, John	NA	Weese, Harry	Accra OBC
Stone, E. D.	New Delhi OBC, ER, SH	Wiener, Samuel G.	NA
		Wurster, William	Hong Kong CGOB
Stubbins, Hugh	Tangier COB, CGR	Yamasaki, Minoru	Kobe COB
Wank, Roland	NA		
Weed, Robert Law	Leopoldville CGOB, SH; Lagos CGOB, SH		

APPENDIX C
Architectural Advisors to FBO and OBO

Advisor	Tenure	Advisor	Tenure
Pietro Belluschi	1/1954–6/57	William W. Caudill	3/76–4/78
Henry R. Shepley	1/54–1/57		
		Francis D. Lethbridge	3/77–12/80
Ralph Walker	1/54–2/56	O'Neil Ford	4/78–12/81
		Donn Emmons	2/79–12/82
Richard M. Bennett	3/56–6/58	Charles Bassett	1/81–12/83
		Hugh Stubbins	11/80–12/84
Edgar I. Williams	1/57–2/59	Ralph Rapson	1/83–12/85
		Norman Fletcher	1/84–12/86
Eero Saarinen	7/57–5/60	Anthony Lumsden	1/85–12/87
		Bill Lacy	1/86–6/89
William W. Wurster	7/58–8/63	Charles P. Graves	1/87–12/90
		Charles W. Moore	1/89–12/91
Roy F. Larson	3/59–9/64	Thomas H. Beeby	1/90–12/94
		George E. Hartman	1/91–8/04
Lawrence B. Anderson	6/60–9/70	William Turnbull Jr	1/92–(d. 6/97)
		Cynthia Weese	1/95–12/96
Joseph R. Passonneau	9/63–10/71	Frances Halsband	4/98–12/02
John Lyon Reid	9/64–4/67	Jack Hartray	6/98–6/01
		Donlyn Lyndon	5/00–11/04
Charles W. Moore	2/71–3/76	Peter Rolland	4/00–7/05
		Larry Speck	9/01–7/03
George Anselevicius	9/72–6/75	Andrea Leers*	1/03–1/07
		Barton Phelps*	9/04–9/10
Joseph Esherick	3/76–2/79	Peter Bohlin*	11/04–11/09
Harry Weese	7/73–3/77		

*The Architectural Advisory Panel was officially abolished in 2004 although advisors remained under contract after that date.

APPENDIX D
Designated Chairmen of the Architectural Advisory Committee/Panel

Chairman	Other Position/Title Held	Tenure
Col. Harry A. McBride	Former Foreign Service officer	1/1954–4/56
Hon. Raymond A. Hare	Director General of the Foreign Service	4/56–7/56
Hon. Joseph C. Satterthwaite	Director General of the Foreign Service	6/57–1/59
Hon. Waldemar J. Gallman	Director General of the Foreign Service	1/59–5/61
William J. Crockett	Asst. Sec. of State for Administration	5/61–6/63

APPENDIX E

Selected Embassies and Other Foreign Buildings Built by the U.S. Government

(CGOB = consulate general office building; CGR = consulate general's residence; COB = consulate office building; CR = consulate residence; DCMR = deputy chief of mission residence; ER = embassy residence; L = legation; OBC = embassy office building chancery; OBCX = embassy office building annex; cmpd = compound; SAT = Office of the Supervising Architect of the Treasury; SH = staff housing; an asterisk indicates that the SAT was the probable architect)

Post	Project	Architect	Design Date
Accra	OBC/SH	Harry Weese	1956
Amman	OBC (cmpd)	Perry, Dean, Rogers & Partners	1988
Amoy	COB	Elliott Hazzard	1931
Ankara	OBC	Eggers & Higgins	1948
Antwerp	COB	Leon Stynen	1950
Ashgabat	OBC	FBO with consulting architects	1995
Asunción	OBC	Keyes, Smith & Satterlee	1954
Athens	OBC	Walter Gropius/TAC	1956
Baghdad	OBC (cmpd)	Josep Lluis Sert	1955
Bangkok	OBC	Kallmann, McKinnell & Wood	1994
Basra	COB/CR/SH	Harris Armstrong	1956
Beijing [Peking]	L (cmpd)	SAT	1905
Belgrade	SH	Carl Koch	1956
Berlin	OBC	Moore Ruble Yudell[1]	1997
Bishkek	OBC	FBO with consulting architects	1996
Bogotá	OBC	Mitchell & Giurgola	1967
	OBC	Integrus Architecture	1987
Boulogne	SH	Rapson & van der Meulen	1952
Brasilia	OBC	Henningson, Durham & Richardson	1971
Bremen	COB/SH	Skidmore, Owings & Merrill (SOM)[2]	1952
Brussels	OBC	FBO (Alan Jacobs), Paris	1948
Budapest	SH	Fry & Welch Associates	1978
Buenos Aires	OBC	Eduardo Catalano	1970
Cairo	OBC (I)	Metcalf & Associates	1982
	OBC (II)	TAC	1987
Canberra	ER	FBO (Paul Franz Jaquet)	1941
	OBC	FBO (Jaquet)	1946
	OBCX	Milton Grigg	1957
Caracas	OBC	Don Hatch	1957
	OBC	Gunnar Birkerts	1991
Ciudad Trujillo	ER	SAT	1945
Colombo	OBC	Victor Lundy	1961
Copenhagen	OBC	Rapson & van der Meulen	1951
Dakar	CGR	Moore & Hutchins	1954
	OBC	Madison & Madison International	1972
Dhahran	CG cmpd	FBO	1948
Dhaka	OBC	Kallmann, McKinnell & Wood	1983
Dublin	OBC	John Johansen	1957

---

1. With Gruen Associates; 2. With Apel

Selected Foreign Buildings, cont.

Düsseldorf	COB	SOM with Apel	1952
Frankfurt	CGOB	SOM with Apel	1952
Fukuoka	COB	G. T. Rockrise	1958
Geneva	OBC	OMNIPLAN, Harrell & Hamilton	1973
Georgetown	OBC	Alan Y. Taniguchi	1983
Giza (Cairo)	ER	Metcalf & Associates	1982
Guatemala City	OBC	Reed, Torres, Beauchamp & Marvel	1970
Hamburg	COB (annex)	SOM with Apel	1956
Havana	ER	FBO (Jaquet)	1939
	OBC	Harrison & Abramovitz	1950
Helsinki	OBC	Harrie T. Lindeberg	1936
Hong Kong	CGOB	Wurster, Bernardi & Emmons	1954
Islamabad	OBC (cmpd)	Geddes, Brecher, Qualls, Cunningham	1966
Jakarta	OBC	Raymond & Rado	1953
	SH	Wilkes & Faulkner	1978
Jiddah	compound	FBO	1952
Kabul	OBC	O'Connor & Kilham[1]	1958
Karachi	OBC	Neutra & Alexander	1955
Kinshasa (Leopoldville)	CGOB/SH	Weed, Russell, Johnson	1954
Kobe/Osaka	CGOB/ SH	Hellmuth, Yamasaki & Leinweber	1954
Kuala Lumpur	OBC	Hartman-Cox	1980
Kuwait	OBC (cmpd)	RTKL Associates, Inc.	1992
Lagos	CGOB/SH	Weed, Russell, Johnson	1954
La Paz	OBC	Esherick, Homsey, Dodge & Davis[2]	1980
Le Havre	COB/SH	Rapson & van der Meulen	1952
Lima	ER	FBO (Jaquet)[3]	1945
	OBC	Keyes & Lethbridge	1956
	OBC	Arquitectonica	1992
Lisbon	OBC	Frederick Bassetti	1978
London	OBC	Eero Saarinen	1956
Madras	CGOB	Burk, Lebreton & Lamantia	1961
	CGR	Ginocchio Cromwell Carter Neyland	1965
Madrid	OBC/ER	Garrigues & Middlehurst[4]	1952
Managua	OBC	FBO	1952
Manama	OBC	ROMA	1981
Manila	SH	Alden B. Dow	1956
	OBC	A. L. Aydelott	1956
Mexico City	OBC	J. E. Campbell	1925
	OBC	Southwestern Architects	1957
Mogadishu	OBC (cmpd)	Holden, Egan, Wilson, Corser	1964
	OBC (cmpd)	Oudens + Knoop	1984
Monrovia	L	SAT	1938
Montevideo	ER	FBO (Jaquet)	1940
	OBC	I. M. Pei	1960
Moscow	OBC (cmpd)	SOM and Gruzen & Partners	1973
Munich	CGOB	SOM with Apel, later with Sep Ruf	1952
Muscat	OBC	Polshek & Partners	1981
Naples	COB/ER	George Howe with Mario di Renzi	1947
Nagoya	CGOB/SH	Cochran, Stephenson & Wing	1956
Nairobi	OBC	A. Epstein & Sons, Inc.	1971
Neuilly	SH	Rapson & van der Meulen	1952
New Delhi	OBC/SH	Edward Durell Stone	1954
	ER	Edward Durell Stone	1957
	SH	Ginocchio Cromwell Carter Neyland	1965
Niamey	OBC	Robert Beatty	1964
Nicosia	OBC (cmpd)	Kohn, Pedersen, Fox	1987
Osaka	COB	Tatsuya Okura	1981
Oslo	OBC	Eero Saarinen	1955
Ottawa	OBC	Cass Gilbert	1928

1. Completed by Ballinger & Co.; 2. Completed in association with Leo A. Daly; 3. With Leland King; 4. With FBO regional office, Paris

Selected Foreign Buildings, cont.

Ottawa	OBC	SOM	1994
Paris	OBC	Delano & Aldrich	1929
Port-au-Prince	ER	SAT or FBO (Jaquet)	1945
	OBC	Don Hatch	1955
Port of Spain	COB	Mence & Moore	1953
	CGR	Mence & Moore	1954
Pretoria	OBC	Eduardo Catalano	1987
Quito	OBC	Vincent Kling	1955
Rabat	OBC/ER	Ketchum, Gina & Sharp	1956
Rio de Janeiro	CGOB[1]	Frank L. Packard	1922
	OBC	Harrison & Abramovitz	1948
Riyadh	OBC	Caudill, Rowlett, Scott	1980
Saigon	OBC	Curtis & Davis	1965
Saana	OBC (cmpd)	CRS-Sirrine	1986
San José	OBC	Torres, Beauchamp & Marvel	1985
San Salvador	L	SAT*	1920
	OBC	Hellmuth, Obata & Kassabaum (HOK)	1961
	OBC (cmpd)	CRSS-J. A. Jones	1987
Santiago	ER	Paul Thiry	1957
	OBC	The Leonard Parker Associates	1987
Seoul	SH	Ernest Kump	1955
	ER	Zo Za Yong and Oudens + Knoop	1974
Seville[1]	COB	SAT*	1930
Singapore	OBC	Jones & Emmons	1957
	OBC	The Stubbins Associates	1994
Stockholm	OBC	Rapson & van der Meulen	1951
Stuttgart	COB	SOM with Apel	1952
Tabriz	CGOB/CGR	Edward Larrabee Barnes	1958
Tangier	CGOB/CGR	Hugh Stubbins	1956
Tegucigalpa	OBC/ER	Michael Hare	1954
Tehran	OBC	FBO (Ides Van der Gracht)	1948
	ER	Homsey & Homsey	1956
The Hague	OBC	Marcel Breuer	1956
Tirana	L (compound)	Wyeth & Sullivan	1929
Tokyo	OBC/ER/SH	Raymond & Magonigle	1926
	SH (Perry House)	Raymond & Rado	1949
	SH (Harris House)	Raymond & Rado	1952
	OBC	Cesar Pelli and Gruen Associates	1971
	SH	Harry Weese	1978
Vienna	SH	Henry Hill	1955
Warsaw	OBC/SH	Welton Becket Associates	1957
	ER	FBO (Sal DiGiacomo)	1967
Wellington	OBC	Robert Beatty	1972
Yokohama	COB/CR	Jay Morgan	1932

1. Designed as exhibition pavilion

APPENDIX F

Completed NEC/NCC Projects 2001–2010
Alphabetical by Post

NEC = new embassy compound (not all are built to SED specifications); NCC = new consular compound; NAB = newly acquired building; NOX = new office annex

As of 2010, there are some 34 NEC/NCC projects in design/construction, including those in Mumbai, India; Surabaya, Indonesia; Suva, Fiji; Karachi, Pakistan; Sarajevo, Bosnia and Herzegovina; Valetta, Malta; Lusaka, Zambia; Tijuana, Mexico; Riga, Latvia; Addis Ababa, Ethiopia; Antananarivo, Madagascar; Bandar, Brunei; Libreville, Gabon; Djibouti, Djibouti; Dubai, UAE; Bucharest, Romania; Kyiv, Ukraine; Taipei, Taiwan; Monrovia, Liberia; Guayaquil, Ecuador; Belgrade, Serbia; Bujumbura, Burundi; Guangzhou, China; Monterrey, Mexico; and Malabo, Eq. Guinea.

Post	Type	Complete	Principal Architect
Abidjan, Cote d'Ivoire	NEC	2005	CMSS
Abu Dhabi, UAE	NEC	2004	HOK
Abuja, Nigeria	NEC	2005	DMJM-Berger
Accra, Ghana	NEC	2007	SOM
Algiers, Algeria	NEC	2007	Integrus
Astana, Kazakhstan	NEC	2006	KCCT
Athens, Greece	NOX	2007	Kallman McKinnell & Wood
Baghdad, Iraq	NEC	2008	Several firms including Berger Devine Yaeger; Sorg & Associates
Bamako, Mali	NEC	2006	Integrus
Beijing, China	NEC	2008	Skidmore, Owings & Merrill (SF)
Belmopan, Belize	NEC	2006	HOK
Berlin, Germany	NEC	2008	Moore Ruble Yudell
Bern, Switzerland	NAB/NEC	2008	Jordi Architekten (concept by ZGF)
Bogota, Colombia	NOX	2007	CMSS
Brazzaville, Congo	NEC	2008	Page-Southerland-Page
Bridgetown, Barbados	NAB/NEC	2006	Sorg & Associates
Cape Town	NCC	2005	Zimmer Gunsul Frasca (ZGF)
Ciudad Juarez, Mexico	NCC	2008	EYP
Conakry, Guinea	NEC	2006	Integrus

Completed NE/NCC Projects 2001-2010, cont.

Post	Type	Complete	Principal Architect
Dar es Salaam, Tanzania	NEC	2003	HOK
Doha, Qatar	NAB/NEC	2002	ERA
Dushanbe, Tajikistan	NEC	2006	Kullman Industries
Freetown, Sierra Leone	NEC	2006	Integrus
Istanbul, Turkey	NCC	2003	Zimmer Gunsul Frasca
Johannesburg	NCC	2008	Page-Southerland-Page
Kabul, Afghanistan	NEC	2005	Sorg & Associates
Kampala, Uganda	NEC	2001	RTKL
Kathmandu, Nepal	NEC	2007	Sorg & Associates
Khartoum, Sudan	NEC	2010	Page-Southerland-Page
Kigali, Rwanda	NEC	2008	Page-Southerland-Page
Kingston, Jamaica	NEC	2006	KCCT
Lome, Togo	NEC	2006	SOM
Luanda, Angola	NEC	2005	KCCT .
Managua, Nicaragua	NEC	2007	Page-Southerland-Page
Nairobi, Kenya	NEC	2003	HOK
Ouagadougou, Burkina Faso	NEC	2009	Page-Southerland-Page
Panama City, Panama	NEC	2007	EYP
Phnom Penh, Cambodia	NEC	2005	Page-Southerland-Page
Port-au-Prince, Haiti	NEC	2008	KCCT
Quito, Ecuador	NEC	2008	Yost Grube Hall
Rangoon, Burma	NEC	2007	SOM
Skopje, Macedonia	NEC	2009	HNTB
Sofia, Bulgaria	NEC	2004	CMSS
Tashkent, Uzbekistan	NEC	2005	HOK
Tbilisi, Georgia	NEC	2005	HOK
Tirana, Albania	NOX	2006	HNTB
Tunis, Tunisia	NEC	2002	Tai Soo Kim
Yaoundé, Cameroon	NEC	2005	Wanchul Lee
Yerevan, Armenia	NEC	2005	CMSS
Zagreb, Croatia	NEC	2003	HOK

NOTES

Abbreviations

AAB   Architectural Advisory Board
AAC   Architectural Advisory Committee
AAP   Architectural Advisory Panel
FAOHP Foreign Affairs Oral History
       Program
FSBC   Foreign Service Buildings
       Commission
HCA   House Committee on
       Appropriations
HCFA   House Committee on Foreign
       Affairs
mf/FBO miscellaneous file/Office of
       Foreign Building Operations
NBM   National Building Museum
       Archive

Introduction

1. Aline B. Louchheim, "The Government and Our Art Abroad," *New York Times*, 23 May 1948.
2. Howard Devree, "Modernism Under Fire," *New York Times*, 11 September 1949; Jane De Hart Mathews, "Art and Politics in Cold War America," *American Historical Review* 81 (October 1976): 777.
3. Mathews, "Art and Politics," 778.
4. "U. S. Architecture Abroad," *Architectural Forum* 98 (March 1953): 101. At that time, *Forum* was edited by Pierrepont L. Prentice, Luce's former classmate. Prentice is cited in congressional testimony in which *Forum* is praised. See House Committee on Appropriations [HCA], Subcommittee on Departments of State, Justice, and Commerce, Appropriations for 1955: Hearings on H. R. 8067, 83th Cong., 2nd sess., 29 January 1954, 338. See also W. A. Swanberg, *Luce and His Empire* (New York: Dell Publishing Co., 1972), 711.
5. *Foreign Service Journal*, 32 (August 1955), excerpt in file, National Building Museum Archives [NBM], Washington, DC. The author began assembling a file on embassy architecture in 1980 as a curator at the National Building Museum. Later, in 1982 and 1983, curators

Judith Lanius and Anne Nissen conducted a series of taped interviews with architects and diplomats. Though plans for the exhibition were canceled, the papers and audio cassettes remain in the museum's archives.
6. "U. S. Architecture Abroad," 102. Saarinen's project was in its preliminary stages of design in 1953, but the project was suspended and the new embassy was never built. See also Alexei Tarkhanov and Sergei Kavtaradze, *Architecture of the Stalin Era* (New York: Rizzoli, 1992).
7. William Z. Slany to author, 12 July 1990. See also Charles Frankel, *The Neglected Aspect of Foreign Affairs: American Educational and Cultural Policy Abroad* (Washington, DC: The Brookings Institution, 1965).

Chapter One: The Early Years

1. No longer in use as a diplomatic property, the old legation in Tangier is now a museum, the only foreign property designated a Historic American Building.
2. William Barnes and John Heath Morgan, *The Foreign Service of the United States: Origins, Development, and Functions* (Historical Office, Bureau of Public Affairs, Department of State, 1961), *passim*; Elmer Plischke, *United States Diplomats and Their Missions* (Washington, DC: American Enterprise Institute for Public Policy Research, 1975), 12ff, 87ff; Warren F. Ilchman, *Professional Diplomacy in the United States, 1774–1939* (Chicago: University of Chicago Press, 1961), 18ff.
3. Dorothy Werner, "The American Embassy Residences," *Arirang* (August 1976): 41–8.
4. Andrew L. Steigman, *The Foreign Service of the United States: First Line of Defense* (Boulder, CO: Westview Press, 1985), 17. On Hawthorne, see Charles W. Thayer, *Diplomat* (New York: Harper & Brothers, 1959), 131.
5. Grover Cleveland, *A Compilation of the*

Messages and Papers of the Presidents, 1789–1897, ed. James D. Richardson (Washington, DC: Government Printing Office, 1896-99); Barnes and Morgan, *The Foreign Service*, 173–86.

6. Graham H. Stuart, *American Diplomatic and Consular Practice*, 2d ed., (New York: Appleton-Century-Crofts, Inc., 1952), 47.

7. *American Embassies Mean Better Foreign Business* (New York: American Embassy Association, 1910), 3.

8. Rep. Frank O. Lowden, *Congressional Record*, 61st Cong., 3rd sess., 1911, 46:2098.6; cited in Orville M. Lewis, "An Assessment of the Adequacy of U.S. Representation Abroad," Mid-Career Course Thesis, Foreign Service Institute, Washington, DC, 18 December 1959.

9. Stuart, *Diplomatic and Consular Practice*, 46.

10. Paul S. Reinsch, *An American Diplomat in China* (New York: Doubleday, Page & Co., 1922) 19–20.

11. "New Embassy Building at Mexico City," *Foreign Service Journal* 2 (October 1925): 336–7; "United States Embassy at Mexico City," *Bulletin of the Pan American Union* 59 (December 1925): 1247–9; "United States Government Building at Rio de Janeiro," *American Architect* 124 (August 1923): 325–8.

12. Robert Lansing to Rep. Whitmell Martin, 10 June 1916, NBM.

13. For comments on Mukden, see Foreign Service Buildings Commission [FSBC], *Chronicles of Transactions*, Mukden, 1923, original bound volumes, untitled with un-numbered pages (5 vols.), FBO. For Antung, see *China Weekly Review,* 8 September 1923.

14. House Committee on Foreign Affairs [HCFA], *Foreign Service Buildings: Hearings on H. R. 15774,* 71st Cong., 3rd sess., 20 January 1931, 13; and Steigman, *The Foreign Service,* 124.

15. HCFA, *Amend the Foreign Service Buildings Act, 1926,* 70th Cong., 1st sess., 1928, H.-Rept. 541 to accompany H. R. 10166, 3.

16. Antoinette J. Lee, "Architects to the Nation: History of the Office of the Supervising Architect of the U.S. Treasury Department" (manuscript draft, 29 May 1987).

17. H. Rept. 541, 1–2.

18. "Foreign Buildings: Historical Sketch," Office of the Historian, Bureau of Public Affairs, Department of State, n.d., 9.

19. H. Rept. 541, 4.

20. HCFA, *Foreign Service Buildings,* 1931, 7.

21. Ibid.

22. FSBC, *Chronicles of Transactions,* 1928.

23. FSBC, *Chronicles of Transactions,* 1929.

24. Wilbur J. Carr, State Department correspondence, 21 May 1935, NBM.

25. "Agenda for 19th Meeting of the Foreign Service Buildings Commission," 2 February 1938, 5, included with HCFA, *To Provide Additional Funds for Buildings for the Use of the Diplomatic and Consular Establishments of the U.S.: Hearings on H. R. 5633,* 75th Cong., 3rd sess., 1938.

26. The suggestion that embassies should resemble the White House is cited in L. R. Sack, "Many New Embassies," *Pittsburgh Press,* 1 January 1928. See also: George V. Allen, "New Legation and Consulate General at Baghdad," *American Foreign Service Journal* (1936); Parker Hart, interviews with author, 18 December 1992, 30 January 1993, and 1 June 1993, Washington, DC; Loy Henderson, taped interview, 19 October 1982, NBM. 21; and Ronald I. Spiers, "The Moscow Embassy Report," State Department memorandum (unclassified), 27 October 1986, 1.

27. "The New U. S. Government Building in Paris," *Architecture* 70 (September 1934): 127.

28. Magonigle also designed the official seal of the AIA. See: John Burchard and Albert Bush-Brown, *The Architecture of America* (Boston: Little, Brown and Company, 1961), 377; and Harry F. Cunningham, Magonigle obituary in *Architecture* 72 (October 1935): 219.

29. Antonin Raymond, *Antonin Raymond: An Autobiography* (Rutland, VT: Charles E. Tuttle Company, 1973), 119.

30. "Diplomatic and Consular Establishments of the United States in Tokyo," *Architecture* 66 (August 1932): 90.

31. Raymond, *An Autobiography,* 114.

32. HCFA, *Foreign Service Buildings,* 1931, 11.

33. Ibid., 6.

34. Colonel T. Bentley Mott, "Our Homeless Diplomats," *Saturday Evening Post,* 13 October 1928, 26.

35. "The New U. S. Government Building in Paris," *Architecture* 70 (September, 1934): 128; "Les enrichissements de Paris, la nouvelle ambassade américaine," *L'Illustration,* supplement 9, 1933.

36. HCFA, *Foreign Service Buildings,* 1931, 12.

37. Two amendments to PL 186 were passed. The first was PL 145 (74-1) for $300,000 passed on 15 June 1935; the second was PL 260 (74-1) for $1,325,000 passed on 12 August 1935. HCFA, *Amending the Foreign Service Buildings Act, 1926,* 82nd Cong., 2nd sess., 1952, H. Rept. 1396 to accompany H. R. 6661.

38. See: Raymond, *An Autobiography*; and Joseph R. Passonneau, "Memorandum to Foreign Buildings Office Re: Inspection Trips to Tokyo and Paris," 1970, FBO. This document is part

of a collection of documents filed at FBO under "AAP miscellaneous" and "miscellaneous" hereinafter cited as mf/FBO.

39. "Report on the Present Condition of the Active Projects in the Foreign Buildings Office as of this Date for the 19th Meeting of the Foreign Buildings Commission," included with HCFA, *Additional Funds for Buildings,* 1938, 2.

40. "Agenda for Foreign Service Buildings Commission Meeting," included with *Additional Funds for Buildings,* 1938, 2–3.

41. *Additional Funds for Buildings,* 1938, 17.

42. Frederick Larkin, "Statement of Foreign Service Buildings Projects Recommended for Construction Under the Authorization of $5,000,000 Covered in the Bill HR 5633 Now Pending Before Congress," 3 January 1938, included with *Additional Funds for Buildings,* 1938.

43. Ibid., 2. See also Jesse H. Stiller, *George S. Messersmith* (Chapel Hill, NC: University of North Carolina Press, 1987).

44. *Additional Funds for Buildings,* 1938, 18–9.

45. "Foreign Service Buildings Act of 1926, As Amended Through June 19, 1952," document prepared for internal distribution at FBO, Office of the Historian, Bureau of Public Affairs, Department of State, n.d.

46. Information pertaining to Leland W. King Jr., is drawn from telephone conversations, letters, and interviews with author, including interviews at Bodega Bay, CA, July 1991, and Washington, D.C., July 1992 and April 1995. See also: "Wyatt Clinic and Research Laboratories Building," *Architectural Forum* 62 (June 1935): 525.

47. King's position was listed both as "Chief Architect" and "Supervising Architect." He served as acting chief when Larkin was out of the country, which was much of the time.

48. Larkin, "Statement of Projects," in *Additional Funds for Buildings,* 1938, 1–6.

Chapter Two: Postwar Expansion

1. Rep. Frances P. Bolton, *Congressional Record,* 82nd Cong., 2nd sess., 31 March 1952, 3209.

2. Melvyn Leffler, "National Security and US Foreign Policy," in *Origins of the Cold War,* ed. Melvyn P. Leffler and David S. Painter (London: Routledge, 1994), 20. See map illustrating proposed base requirements, 21.

3. Hans N. Tuch, *Communicating with the World, U.S. Public Diplomacy Overseas* (New York: St. Martin's Press, 1990), 5.

4. HCFA, Subcommittee on State Department Organization and Foreign Operations, *Foreign Service Buildings Act*

Amendments, 1962, 87th Cong., 2nd sess., 6 February 1962, 82.

5. House Appropriations Subcommittee, *Departments of State, Justice, and Commerce Appropriations for 1955,* 29 January 1954, 326.

6. David D. Newsom, *Diplomacy and the American Democracy* (Bloomington, IN: Indiana University Press, 1988), 125.

7. Leonard Mosley, *Dulles: A Biography of Eleanor, Allen, and John Foster Dulles and Their Family Network* (New York: The Dial Press/James Wade, 1978), 364.

8. PL 584, 80th Cong., 2nd sess., (1948), cited in Tuch, *Communicating,* 17.

9. Newsom, *Diplomacy,* 180.

10. "United States Objectives and Programs for National Security," 14 April 1950, cited in John Prados, *Keepers of the Keys: A History of the National Security Council from Truman to Bush* (New York: William Morrow and Co., Inc., 1991), 39.

11. Enrico Bruschini, *Palazzo Margherita* (Rome: Embassy of the United States of America, 1996).

12. Carlisle H. Humelsine to Fritz Larkin, personal correspondence, reprinted in "Uncle Sam Builds His Dream House," *Foreign Service Journal* 29 (August 1952): 24.

13. Johnstone, interview with author, Fairfield, PA, 16 October 1992.

14. H. P. Martin and William E. DeCourcy, "Extracts from Survey of the Division of Foreign Buildings Operations," (5 November– 20 December 1946), submitted to the Director General of the Foreign Service, 13 January 1947, 3, Office of the Historian, Bureau of Public Affairs, Department of State.

15. H. Rept. 1396, 4 (see ch. 1, n. 37). See also: "Notes on Foreign Buildings Operations," 15 March 1949, Attachment 5, 1, included in *Report of Task Force on Foreign Buildings Operations,* prepared under FBO Task Force Chairman, Belton O. Bryan, by the Office of the Historian, Bureau of Public Affairs, Department of State; J. E. Miller and N. J. Noring, "The Office of Foreign Buildings: A History," (unclassified), 23 April 1987, 5; and Barnes and Morgan, "Foreign Service," 18 (see ch. 1, n. 2).

16. *Department of State Bulletin* XI (17 December 1944): 798–800; Departmental Order No. 1301, Department of State, issued and effective 20 December 1944, and previous orders, No. 1218 of 15 January 1944, and No. 1273 of 6 May 1944.

17. H. Rept. 1396, 5.

18. Humelsine, "Uncle Sam Builds," 22.

19. Senate Foreign Relations Committee,

Nomination of Paul V. McNutt to be Ambassador to Philippines, Discussion of International Aviation Convention, Diplomatic and Consular Service, Foreign Service Buildings Act: Hearings on H. R. 6627, 79th Cong., 2nd Sess., 19 June 1946, 9–11.

20. Ibid., 14.

21. Hart, interview with author. Hart was later ambassador to Saudi Arabia, Kuwait, Yemen, and Turkey (1961–1968). See also: Parker T. Hart, *Saudi Arabia and the United States: Birth of a Security Partnership* (Bloomington, IN: Indiana University Press, forthcoming fall 1998).

22. HCA, Subcommittee on Departments of State, Justice and Commerce Appropriations, *Departments of State, Justice, and Commerce Appropriations for 1954, Acquisition of Buildings Abroad: Hearings on H. R. 4974*, 83rd Cong., 1st sess., 25 March 1953, 178. Jiddah was upgraded from a legation to an embassy, but the embassy is now located in Riyadh. Jiddah remains a consular post.

23. Hart, interview with author.

24. *The American Ambassador's Residence in Paris* (Paris: "Friends of 41" Committee, 1985). "Friends of 41" was the private group that financed much of the residence's restoration.

25. Alan Jacobs, interviews with author, 6 April 1993 and 14 April 1993. See also: Jacobs, taped interview, 16 May 1983, NBM.

26. Rep. John Phillips, *Congressional Record*, 82nd Cong., 2nd sess., 31 March 1952, 3207.

27. HCA, Subcommittee on Departments of State and Justice, the Judiciary, and Related Agencies, *Departments of State and Justice, the Judiciary, and Related Agencies Appropriations for 1958, Acquisition of Buildings Abroad: Hearings on H. R. 6871*, 85th Cong., 1st sess., 25 February 1957, 906.

28. HCFA, Subcommittee on State Department Organization and Foreign Operations, *Foreign Service Buildings Act Amendments, 1959: Hearings on H. R. 9036*, 86th Cong., 1st sess., 27 February 1959, 42. For further discussion of this property, see chaps. 5 and 6.

29. John Ely Burchard, "The Dilemma of Architecture," *Architectural Record* 117 (May 1955): 193.

30. Frank T. Bow, Sam Coon, and Prince H. Preston Jr., *Report on Foreign Buildings Operations, Department of State* [known as the *Bow Report*], House Appropriations Subcommittee, *Appropriations for 1955*, (29 January 1954), 1–9. See testimony of Nelson Kenworthy before Rep. Frank Bow regarding Brussels, 305. Further comments on Brussels cited in the *Bow Report*, 293.

31. King to author, Bodega Bay, CA, 16 January 1993. Though Goodman's model photograph is dated 1949, King suggests the project was begun a year or so earlier.

32. "Summary: Utilization of Private Architects, 1949 FY-1953 FY," included in King letter to author, 7 January 1992.

33. King to author, 16 January 1993.

34. King to Edward Stone, 17 July 1953, Personal Papers of Leland King, Bodega Bay, CA.

Chapter Three:
Modernism at the State Department

1. Victoria Newhouse, *Wallace K. Harrison, Architect* (New York: Rizzoli, 1989), 15–6. See also: Kenneth Frampton, *Modern Architecture* (London: Thames and Hudson, 1985), 220.

2. Projects financed through foreign credits are listed in a table included in House Appropriations Subcommittee, *Appropriations for 1954* (25 March 1953), 1215. The 95 percent figure comes from testimony by Deputy FBO Director Edward Kerrigan. House Appropriations Subcommittee, *Appropriations for 1955* (29 January 1954), 341.

3. Nelson Kenworthy, taped interview, 1982, NBM.

4. Michael Rosenauer, *Modern Office Buildings* (London: B. T. Batsford, Ltd., 1955), 120.

5. Carleton Sprague Smith, "Architecture of Brazil," *Architectural Record* 119 (April 1956), 187–94.

6. H. Rept. 541, 2.

7. Larkin, "Statement of Projects," *Additional Funds for Buildings*, 1938, 3.

8. "Progress Review," *Progressive Architecture* 32 (October 1951): 15; Kenworthy, taped interview, NBM.

9. The Havana project is described in *Progressive Architecture* (October 1951): 16; "U. S. Architecture Abroad," *Architectural Forum* 98 (March 1953): 104; "U.S. Embassy Office Building, Havana, Cuba." *Progressive Architecture* 36 (February 1955): 110–1.

10. H. Rept. 1396, 3. The cost of transporting materials came out of the dollar expenditure for this project, a portion of the $15 million dollar appropriation of 1946, of which only $1 million had been spent as of 1952. Such costs figured in congressional debate when Congress was asked to approve a new FBO authorization in 1952. See also: Senate Foreign Relations Committee,

Nomination; H. R. 6661, Protocols: Hearings on H. R. 6661, 82nd Cong., 2nd sess., 15 May 1952, 32–3; and "House Appropriations Subcommittee, *Appropriations for 1955,* (1954), 341.

11. See Newhouse, *Wallace K. Harrison,* 152; King, interview with author; Jacobs, interview with author; *Progressive Architecture* (October 1951): 16, 106–7; *Architectural Forum* (March 1953): 104; and *Progressive Architecture* (February 1955): 107.

12. Kenworthy, taped interview, NBM; Jacobs, interview with author; House Appropriations Subcommittee, *Appropriations for 1954,* (1953), 1218.

13. Kenworthy, taped interview, NBM; House Appropriations Subcommittee, *Appropriations for 1955,* (1954), 305.

14. *Bow Report,* 293.

15. House Appropriations Subcommittee, *Appropriations for 1955,* (1954), 338.

16. *Bow Report,* 293.

17. King, House Appropriations Subcommittee, *Appropriations for 1954,* (1953), 172.

18. Humelsine, Senate Foreign Relations Committee, *H. R. 6661,* (1952), 37.

19. Angier Biddle Duke, taped interview, 22 September 1982, NBM.

20. Jacobs, taped interview, NBM.

21. John Jova, taped interview, 6 May 1982, NBM.

22. *Bow Report,* 297. See also: Blake Clark, "This Congressional Junket Paid Off," *National Review* 13 October 1956, 15–6; reprinted in *Reader's Digest,* December 1956, 137–40.

23. Ralph Rapson, taped interview, 10 October 1982, NBM; Rapson interview with author, Amery, Wisconsin, 12 June 1995. For further information on this project, see *Architectural Record* (February 1949). Burchard and Bush-Brown cite this as one of the best of the "high-cost apartments" of the early 1950s in Burchard and Bush-Brown, *Architecture of America,* 493. As Rapson later noted, they should have used the phrase "high-rent" apartments, because the per square foot *cost* of the apartments was actually low. See also: *Journal of the American Institute of Architects* (October 1951): 161 and (November 1951): 208.

24. Rapson, taped interview, NBM.

25. Ibid.

26. See: Press release, Ralph Rapson and Associates, Inc., Minneapolis, MN, nd. Although undated, this release was prepared after 1955, because it cites the 1955 AIA First Honor Award. See also: "U.S. Embassy

Buildings," *Architectural Review* 118 (October 1955): 244.

27. "U.S. Embassy Buildings," *Architectural Review* (October 1955): 242.

28. Ides Van der Gracht to King, 2 November 1954, 2–3, King Papers.

29. "U.S. Architecture Abroad," *Architectural Forum* (March 1953): 106.

30. "Modernistic U.S. Embassy in Denmark is a Sensation," *New York Times,* 1 June 1954.

31. Van der Gracht to King.

32. Press Release, Rapson and Associates.

33. Rapson, taped interview, NBM.

34. Ibid.

Chapter Four: America Exports Democracy

1. See ch. 1. See also Raymond, *An Autobiography,* 124; and "French Embassy, Tokyo," *Architectural Record* 75 (March 1934): 249–51.

2. For a fuller account of these events, see: William Manchester, *American Caesar* (Boston: Little, Brown & Company, 1978), 459–544.

3. *Architectural Record* 77 (May 1934): 438–43.

4. William T. Breer to author, Tokyo, 17 August 1993.

5. Raymond was elected a Fellow of the American Institute of Architects in 1952 and won the Architectural Institute of Japan Medal of Honor for the Standard Vacuum Oil Company Houses in Yokohama in 1953.

6. Ladislav Rado, interview with author, Biscayne Beach, FL, 23 March 1993. See also: Rado, "Recollections," unpublished, 10 October 1978, collection of author.

7. The best source of material on Raymond's work and his intentions is his own *Autobiography.* John Winter's essay in *Contemporary Architects* provides a useful overview of his career and a list of his works. John Winter, "Antonin Raymond," in *Contemporary Architects,* ed. Muriel Emanuel (New York: St. Martin's Press, 1980). See also William Marlin, "Thinking About the Past in the Cause of the Future: A Conversation with Ladislav Rado," in *Architectural Record* 163 (May 1978): 119–24, an article useful for its illustrations.

8. Rado, interview with author.

9. Ibid.

10. Ibid.

11. Ibid.

12. Tatsuya Okura interview with author, Kyoto, Japan, 10 July 1993.

13. See: "Housing for the United States Embassy Staff in Tokyo, Japan," *Architectural Record* 116 (September 1954): 167; "In the Far East," *U.S. News & World Report,* 19 March 1954, 47; Winter, "Antonin Raymond," 659. On

the *Reader's Digest* building, see "Shockproof Office Building," *Architectural Forum* 96 (March 1952): 99–107; "Projects: Isamu Noguchi," *Arts and Architecture* 69 (June 1952): 26–7.

14. George F. Kennan, *Sketches from a Life* (New York: Pantheon Books, 1989), 121.

15. Lawrence K. Larkin, interview with author, Washington, DC, 31 July 1997.

16. For the 1952 amendments, see: H. Rept. 1396, 2. FBO has always attributed all of the German projects to SOM, and U.S. sources attribute the German buildings to Bunshaft, listing him as the partner in charge of design for at least some of the projects and listing Otto Apel as the consulting architect. But the German publication *Bauen + Wohnen* listed Apel as the principal with "Skidmore, Owins [sic] & Merrill" cited as associated architects (April 1956). See also: "Amerikanische generalkonsulate in Bremen, Düsseldorf, Frankfurt und Stuttgart," *Bauen + Wohnen* 10 (April 1956): 113–8; House Committee on Government Operations, *German Consulate/America House Program: Hearings before a Special Subcommittee of the Government Operations Committee,* 83rd Cong., 1st sess., 17 February 1953, 4, 6, 9, 19, 31 [hereinafter cited as *German Program Hearings*]; Carol Herselle Krinsky, *Gordon Bunshaft of Skidmore, Owings & Merrill* (New York: The Architectural History Foundation, 1988), 18; and Richard Guy Wilson, *The AIA Gold Medal* (New York: McGraw-Hill Book Company, 1984), 115.

17. Krinsky, *Gordon Bunshaft*, 19.

18. "Administrative Management Assistance Team Report," *FBO Buildings and Maintenance Handbook* (Washington: March 1979), 8.

19. *German Program Hearings,* 17 February 1953, 16; and House Appropriations Subcommittee, *Appropriations for 1955,* (1954), 388.

20. The preliminary design for the Frankfurt Consulate was published in *Architectural Forum* (March 1953): 110. See also: Krinsky, *Gordon Bunshaft*; and King to author, Bodega Bay, CA, 7 May 1992.

21. Minutes of the FBO Architectural Advisory Committee [hereinafter cited as AAC, AAP, and AAB] indicate that AAC members, Belluschi, Walker, Shepley, and McBride, considered the design of the "Caldwell" [sic] stabile on 19 October 1955 and advised SOM architect David Hughes to return with a better solution. *Note:* Beginning in 1957, the AAC became known as the Architectural Advisory Panel [AAP]. In the late 1970s it was known briefly as the Foreign Buildings Architectural Consultants, and it is currently known as the Architectural Advisory Board [AAB]. It is identified in this text as it was known at the time in question.

22. Anita Moeller Laird to author, Cape May, NJ, 21 January 1992. See also "Special Embassy Issue" of *Interior Design*, 29 (August 1958).

23. Robert Harlan to Judith Lanius, 2 April 1982, NBM. See also: Harlan to author, Freeport, IL, 8 March 1992.

24. Henry Shepley, memorandum of meeting at the Munich consulate, 4 October 1954, mf/FBO.

25. Harlan to Lanius.

26. *Architectural Forum* (March 1953): 109.

27. *Congressional Record*, 82nd Cong., 2nd sess., 1 April 1952, 3331.

28. C. L. Sulzberger, *A Long Row of Candles, Memoirs and Diaries, 1934–1954* (New York: The Macmillan Company, 1969), 456.

29. *German Program Hearings,* 17 February 1953, 33.

30. James Riddleberger, Ibid., 16.

31. Ibid., 7.

32. Hugo Leipziger-Pearce, "Architecture as a Political Weapon," *Journal of the American Institute of Architects* 14 (November 1950): 204–6.

33. For discussion of how modernism shifted its emphasis after World War II see: Peter Blake, *No Place Like Utopia: Modern Architecture and the Company We Kept* (New York: Alfred A. Knopf, 1993).

Chapter Five:
Modern Architecture Under Fire

1. Humelsine to Larkin, nd, reprinted in "Uncle Sam Builds," 24.

2. H. Rept. 1396, Table III, *"Foreign Buildings Operations, Distribution by Project of Proposed Authorization for Utilization of Foreign Currency Credits,"* 16–9.

3. H. Rept. 1396, 6.

4. Ibid., 3.

5. Senate Committee on Foreign Relations, *Authorization for Foreign Buildings, H. R. 6661,* (1952), 31.

6. H. Rept. 1396, 3.

7. H. Rept. 1396, Table I, *"Status of Foreign Credits and 1953 Program Utilization,"* 10. See also: Senate Committee on Foreign Relations, *Amending the Foreign Service Buildings Act, 1926,* (1952), 33.

8. Rep. Thomas B. Curtis, *Congressional Record*, 82nd Cong., 2nd sess., 1 April 1952, 3331.

9. Rep. William C. Lantaff, *Congressional Record*,

82nd Cong., 2nd sess., 31 March 1952, 3208.

10. Curtis, *Congressional Record*, 1 April 1952, 3331.

11. H. Rept. 1396, 20 February 1952, 1.

12. Senate Committee on Foreign Relations, *Authorization for Foreign Buildings, H. R. 6661*, (1952), 48.

13. *Congressional Record*, House, (82-2), 31 March 1952, 3204—10.

14. Kennan, *Sketches*, 159.

15. Senate Committee on Foreign Relations, *Authorization for Foreign Buildings, H. R. 6661*, (1952), 42.

16. Paul Rudolph, quoted in "UN General Assembly," *Architectural Forum* 97 (October, 1952): 144–5. For a review of comments on the new United Nations buildings, see also: "The Secretariat, A Campanile, a Cliff of Glass, a Great Debate," *Architectural Forum* 93 (November 1950): 93–112; Lewis Mumford, "The Sky Line," *The New Yorker*, 22 September 1951; "UN Completes the Link," *Architectural Forum*, 96 (April 1952): 104–10; "UN Assembly, How Do Architects Like It?" *Architectural Forum* 97 (December 1952): 114–5.

17. Pietro Belluschi to author, Portland, OR, 13 December 1991.

18. House Appropriations Subcommittee, *Appropriations for 1954*, (1953), 8.

19. "Excerpts from FBO German Files Covering the Consular-America House Program Indicating Determination of FBO to Stress Economy" (Appendix I, *Design Meeting at Bonn, Germany*, 8 September 1952), House Government Operations Subcommittee, Addendum to *German Program Hearings*, 17 February 1953, 82.

20. King, "My Experience with the Department of State, 1937-1954," personal memoir, unpublished, nd, enclosed in letter to author, 1 June 1993.

21. Mosley, *Dulles*, 312 (see ch. 2, n. 7).

22. King, "My Experience," 3.

23. See Foreign Affairs Oral History Program interviews by Thomas Stern with William J. Crockett (20–22 June 1990) and Idar Rimestad (22 June 1990), Georgetown University Library. [This collection is hereinafter cited as FAOHP.]

24. House Appropriations Subcommittee, *Appropriations for 1954*, (1953), 164–5.

25. House Government Operations Subcommittee, *German Program Hearings*, 2 June 1953, 14.

26. "Crippling Our Diplomacy," *New York Times*, 10 June 1953; reprinted in *Foreign Service Journal* (July 1953): 38.

27. King to Anne Nissen, 27 May 1983, NBM.

28. King, "Notes for statement at conference 9 July 1953 with Assistant Secretary of State, Mr. Wailes, and Mr. Wilber (Budget)," 7 July 1953, King Papers.

29. Ibid.

30. King, memorandum on "Design Criteria, Foreign Buildings Office," 10 July 1953, King Papers.

31. Webster B. Todd to Donold B. Lourie, 14 July 1953, from "Panel Background and Papers, TAP," mf/FBO. "TAP" stands for Thomas A. Pope, who was chief architect at FBO, and these were his files. Charles Rex Hellmann succeeded Pope when he retired, and Patrick W. Collins, currently the chief architect, succeeded Hellmann.

32. Kenworthy, taped interview, NBM.

33. Johnstone, interview with author, 16 October 1992.

34. Paul Serey, telephone interview with author, 26 May 1992.

35. Rado to author, Biscayne Beach, FL, 18 January 1993.

36. King, "Notes on Foreign Buildings Operations Architecture," 28 April 1992, King Papers.

37. Frederick Gutheim, "Washington Perspective," *Progressive Architecture* (November 1953), 4. Gutheim's reference to Saarinen was wishful thinking—Saarinen's Helsinki embassy commission was canceled by Kenworthy.

38. Ibid.

39. King, "My Experience," 1.

40. *Bow Report*, 292, 293.

41. Ibid., 295.

42. Kenworthy, memorandum to Edward T. Wailes, 23 October 1953, 1, mf/FBO.

43. "Statement of Department of State's Architectural Policy and Specific Functions of the Architectural Advisory Group for Foreign Buildings," nd., mf/FBO. This statement was presented to the AAC at its first meeting, 21 January 1954.

44. Kenworthy, memorandum to Wailes, 2, mf/FBO.

45. House Appropriations Subcommittee, *Appropriations for 1955*, (1954), 314.

46. Kenworthy, taped interview, NBM.

47. House Committee on Appropriations, Subcommittee on Departments of State, Justice, and Commerce, *Departments of State, Justice, and Commerce Appropriations for 1954: Hearings on H. R. 4974*, 83rd Cong., 1st sess.,

25 March 1953, 168.

48. Statutory authority to employ architects and architectural advisers was contained in the Foreign Service Buildings Act of 1926. A press announcement released on 14 January 1954 announced the employment of the four architectural advisers who were to be paid $40 a day plus travel expenses.

49. Statement of official policy submitted to members of the AAC, 14 January 1954, mf/FBO.

50. AAC Minutes, 21 January 1954, FBO.

51. Belluschi, memorandum to Kenworthy, Cambridge, MA, 27 January 1954, mf/FBO.

52. Mary Cremmen, "U.S. Embassies Around the World," *Boston Sunday Globe Magazine*, 5 January 1958, 27.

53. "New Face for America Abroad," *Time*, 11 July 1960, 34; Thomas W. Ennis, "Experts Design Many Embassies To 'Speak' in Many Languages," *New York Times*, 26 January 1958; and Ada Louise Huxtable, "Sharp Debate: What Should an Embassy Be?" *New York Times Magazine*, 18 September 1960, 36.

Chapter Six: Power Shifts

1. Ronald Palmer, interview with author, Washington, DC, 1 April 1994.

2. Stuart, *Diplomatic and Consular Practice*, 48 (see ch. 1, n. 6).

3. *Bow Report*, 292.

4. Edward D. Folliard, "U.S. Embassies Shock Travelers Abroad," *Washington Post and Times Herald*, 6 September 1955.

5. See Martin Weil, *A Pretty Good Club: The Founding Fathers of the U.S. Foreign Service* (New York: W. W. Norton and Co., 1978).

6. Joseph Alsop, *I've Seen the Best of It: Memoirs*, with Adam Platt (New York: W. W. Norton & Co., 1992).

7. Henderson, taped interview, NBM.

8. Ibid.

9. Henderson temporarily replaced Carpenter as assistant secretary when he returned from his post in Iran in January 1955. During his interim appointment, Carpenter became controller of the State Department. When Henderson was named deputy under secretary in August 1955, Carpenter became assistant secretary once again. See: House Committee on Appropriations, Subcommittee on Departments of State and Justice and the Judiciary and Related Agencies Appropriations, *Acquisition of Buildings Abroad: Hearings before the Appropriations Subcommittee*, 84th Cong., 1st sess., 14 February 1955, 201.

10. Eleanora W. Schoenebaum, ed., *Political Profiles: The Eisenhower Years* (New York:

Facts on File, Inc., 1977), 522.

11. Crockett, interview, FAOHP.

12. Ibid.; and Henderson, taped interview, NBM.

13. House Appropriations Subcommittee, *Acquisition of Buildings Abroad*, (1955), 285.

14. Johnstone, telephone interview with author, 18 May 1994.

15. House Committee on Appropriations, Subcommittee on Departments of State and Justice and the Judiciary and Related Agencies Appropriations, *Department of State: Hearings before the Appropriations Subcommittee*, 85th Cong., 1st sess., 25 February 1957, 906; House Foreign Affairs Subcommittee, *Foreign Service Buildings Act Amendments, 1959*, (1959), 42. For additional comment on this property, see also chs. 2 and 5.

16. House Appropriations Subcommittee, *Department of State*, (1957), 900.

17. House Foreign Affairs Subcommittee, *Foreign Service Buildings Act Amendments, 1962*, (1962), 28.

18. Crockett, interview, FAOHP.

19. Ibid.

20. Ibid.

21. Johnstone, "Comments Concerning Report of Deputy Undersecretary William J. Crockett dated 22 June 1990, to Georgetown University, Assn. for Diplomatic Studies," unpublished, Johnstone to author, 4 December 1993, Association for Diplomatic Studies and Training, Arlington, VA, and collection of author.

22. Johnstone, interview with author, 18 May 1994.

23. Johnstone, interview with author, 16 October 1992.

24. Ibid.

25. Ibid.

26. Ibid.

27. Bob Woodward and Carl Bernstein, "State Dept. Unit Viewed as Hays' Private Duchy," *Washington Post*, 14 August 1976.

28. House Foreign Affairs Subcommittee, *Foreign Service Buildings Act Amendments, 1959*, (1959), 28.

29. Crockett, interview, FAOHP; and Johnstone, interview with author, 16 October 1992.

30. "The Changing Philosophy of Architecture," *Architectural Record* (August 1954): 180–3.

31. Bruno Zevi is one conspicuous exception. While in the United States during World War II, he worked against the Fascists. After the war, he returned to Italy and a career that successfully combined architecture, journalism, and political activism—a rare combination.

Chapter Seven:
The Architectural Advisory Committee

1. Kenworthy, memorandum to Wailes, on "Foreign Buildings Architectural Advisory Committee," 17 February 1954, mf/FBO.

2. AAC Minutes, 12 March 1954, 3; AAC Minutes, 17 September 1954, 4.

3. AAC Minutes, 26 May 1955, 2.

4. AAC Minutes, 16 August 1955, 2.

5. Ibid.

6. AAC Minutes, 14 January 1955, 2.

7. AAC Minutes, 12 March 1954, 3.

8. For more on the Giza project, see ch. 11.

9. House Appropriations Subcommittee hearings, *Acquisition of Buildings Abroad*, (1954), 332.

10. AAC Minutes, 4 February 1954, 2.

11. Belluschi to Hughes, Cambridge, MA, 30 November 1954, mf/FBO; and Shepley to Hughes, Boston, MA, 30 November 1954, Shepley Papers. Henry Shepley's papers, a collection of letters and documents pertaining to Shepley's association with the State Department, are quoted with permission of Shepley Bulfinch Richardson and Abbott and the Shepley Family.

12. AAC Minutes, 12 March 1954, 2–3. The minutes should have used the word "dependence." The issue was surely not whether or not native help was dependable, but rather whether or not embassy personnel depended upon such help.

13. William Wurster, cited in "The Changing Philosophy of Architecture," *Architectural Record* (August 1954): 183.

14. Secretary of State John Foster Dulles, cable to the American Embassy, Jakarta, "Request for expediting construction of chancery, DJAKARTA." The cable was drafted by Henry J. Lawrence, Deputy Director, FBO, and approved by William P. Hughes, director, FBO. It is dated 25 August 1955 and numbered CA-1635, attached to AAC Minutes, 16 August 1955.

15. AAC Minutes, 16 August 1955, 1.

16. Dulles, cable to Jakarta, 25 August 1955.

17. Rado, interview with author (see ch. 4, n. 6).

18. King, testimony to Committee on Government Operations, *German Program Hearings*, 17 February 1953, 19. See: William L. Slayton, "In Search of Good Design: Selecting an Architect," *Inland Architect* (March/April 1984): 33.

19. The agenda is outlined in a letter from Henry J. Lawrence to Shepley, Washington, DC, 29 January 1954, Shepley Papers. Lawrence was deputy director (technical), FBO.

20. Contract data is drawn from a table titled "Chronological Listing of Architectural & Engineering Contracts Awarded through April 30, 1965," made available to the author by the Office of the Historian, Department of State. See also: Eustis Dearborn to Henry R. Shepley, Stamford, CT, 3 June 1955, Shepley Papers.

21. Shepley to Hughes, Boston, MA, 10 November 1958, and 8 December 1958, Shepley Papers.

22. See "Architects for Embassies," and "Present list of architects as shown by P. Belluschi's records," undated, but dated by content and by placement in the file to early 1954, Shepley Papers.

23. AAC Minutes, 19 August 1954, 1.

24. Ralph Walker to Paul Rudolph, New York, NY, 26 August 1954, Shepley Papers.

25. Belluschi to Lawrence, letter attached to AAC Minutes, 18 November 1954.

26. AAC Minutes, 14 January 1955, 2.

27. Walker to Rudolph, 26 August 1954; and William Hughes to Rudolph, Washington, DC, 21 December 1954, Shepley Papers.

28. *Architectural Forum* 107 (December 1957): 122.

29. *Architectural Record* 117 (May 1955): 189.

30. Hughes to Michael Hare, 30 August 1956; Hare telegram to Hughes, 31 August 1956; and Hare to Hughes, 17 September 1956, Shepley Papers.

31. Hare to Shepley, 31 August 1956, and Shepley to Hare, 14 September 1956, Shepley Papers.

32. Hare to Shepley, 17 September 1956, Shepley Papers.

33. Note signed "HRS" attached to letter from Belluschi to Shepley, 25 September 1956, Shepley Papers.

34. [Louisa] Whiting Willauer to Henry Shepley, 5 February 1958, Shepley Papers.

35. Esther Seaver, quoting Walter Behrendt to J. Edgar Park, 16 June 1938, in Thomas J. McCormick, "Wheaton College Competition for an Art Center, February 1938–June 1938," in *Modernism in America, 1937–1941*, ed. James D. Kornwolf (Williamsburg, VA: College of William and Mary, 1985), 31.

36. Hughes to Belluschi, with copies to Shepley and Bennett, Washington, DC, 10 September 1956, mf/FBO. See also: Hughes to Henderson and Carpenter, 10 September 1956, mf/FBO. With his request, he enclosed the 2 July 1956 issue of *Time* magazine, which featured an article on Saarinen and his work.

37. Henderson memorandum to Carpenter, 5 October 1956, mf/FBO.

38. Carpenter memorandum to Joseph C.

Satterthwaite, 23 July 1957, mf/FBO.

39. "Edgar I. Williams, Architect, Dead," obituary, *New York Times*, 3 January 1974.

40. Williams to Hughes, 3 February 1958, mf/FBO. For reference to Canberra, see House Appropriations Subcommittee, *Appropriations for 1955*, (1954), 328.

41. Edgar I. Williams, "Traditional versus Modern Architecture: A Paper Given on the Traditional Side," Municipal Art Society, New York, reprinted in the *Empire State Architect* (November–December, 1950): 4.

42. Hughes memorandum to Henderson, 23 May 1957, mf/FBO. For material on Goodman, see Carpenter to Satterthwaite, 23 July 1957, with memo from Hughes to the "Architectural Advisory Group," 11 June 1957, mf/FBO. Hughes provided biographical data on both architects from the *American Architects Directory: 1956*. Murphy was the architect of the Apostolic Nunciature (known popularly as the Vatican Embassy) in Washington.

43. Press Release no. 15, Department of State, 14 January 1954, mf/FBO.

44. The chief architect or someone from the architectural staff maintained the minutes of committee meetings. Following each meeting, minutes were distributed to members for review and correction, then returned to FBO to become part of an official record.

45. Kenworthy memorandum to Wailes, 23 October 1953, (TAP) mf/FBO.

Chapter Eight: The Program at Its Peak

1. Marcel Breuer, *Marcel Breuer: Sun and Shadow*, ed. Peter Blake (London: Longmans, Green and Co., 1956), 117.

2. Walker expressed these views in his two-part article titled "The Education Necessary to the Professional Practice of Architecture," *Journal of the American Iinstitute of Architects* 15 (February 1951): 71–6 and (March 1951): 119–25; and in a letter to Walter Gropius, 27 March 1951, Shepley Papers.

3. Hugh Stubbins, interview with author, Ocean Ridge, FL, 21 March 1993. "Yamasaki's Ode to Aluminum," *Architectural Forum* 111 (November 1959): 140–3.

4. See "US Embassy for New Delhi," *Architectural Forum* 102 (June 1955): 116, 118; "A New Public Architecture," *Architectural Forum* 110 (January 1959): 86.

5. Hughes to Rudolph, 21 December 1954, mf/FBO.

6. Shirley Temple Black, taped interview, 16 March 1982, NBM.

7. C. L. Sulzberger, "Foreign Affairs: The Care and Housing of Ambassadors," *New York Times*, 25 July 1965; and Sulzberger, *A Long Row of Candles*.

8. AAP Minutes, 19 August, 1957, 4; 23 September 1957, 2; 21 January 1958, 4; 15 December 1958, 6.

9. AAC Minutes, 16 August 1955, 2.

10. Vincent Scully, *Modern Architecture* (New York: Braziller, 1961), 36. John Jacobus, *Twentieth Century Architecture, The Middle Years, 1940–65* (New York: Praeger, 1966), 152.

11. Walter Gropius, *The Scope of Total Architecture* (1943; reprint, New York: Collier Books, 1962), 14.

12. Rapson, interview with author, Amery, Wisconsin, 12 June 1995.

13. AAC Minutes, 29 June 1956, 2; and Henry J. Lawrence to Gropius (The Architects Collaborative), 5 July 1956, Shepley Papers.

14. John Carl Warnecke, telephone interview with author, 6 October 1992.

15. Ron Robin, *Enclaves of America: The Rhetoric of American Political Architecture Abroad 1900–1965* (Princeton, NJ: Princeton University Press, 1992), 160.

16. AAC Minutes, 29 June 1956, 3.

17. "Architecture to Represent America Abroad," *Architectural Record* 117 (May 1955), 187–92; "Second Group of American Embassy Buildings," *Architectural Record* 119 (June 1956): 161–5; and "American Architecture Designed for Export," *Architectural Record* 122 (October 1957): 237–42.

18. Walker, "Practice of Architecture." See also: Gropius to Walker, Cambridge, MA, 19 March 1951, Shepley Papers; and Walker's reply, Walker to Gropius, New York, NY, 27 March 1951, Shepley Papers.

19. Belluschi, "Architecture and Society," *Journal of the American Institute of Architects* 15 (February 1951): 85–91. See also: Walker to Belluschi, dated March 1953, Ralph Walker Papers, George Arents Research Library for Special Collections, Syracuse University.

20. Belluschi to Burt Kubli, 17 August 1981, NBM.

21. Jean Paul Carlhian, interview with author at Shepley Bulfinch Richardson and Abbott, Boston, MA, 11 September 1992. See also "Shepley, Bulfinch, Richardson & Abbott," *Architectural Record* 125 (February 1959): 154.

22. Walker to Shepley, Belluschi, and Bennett, New York, NY, 20 September 1956, 3, Shepley Papers.

23. Saarinen to Hughes, 24 February 1959, mf/FBO.

24. Shepley to Hughes, 8 June 1959, handwritten note, Shepley Papers; Shepley to Hughes, 17 June 1959, Shepley Papers.

Chapter Nine: Architects Assert Themselves

1. See NSC document #98/1 (22 January 1951), *Foreign Relations of the United States*, VI, 1650–2; and Howard B. Schaffer, *Chester Bowles: New Dealer in the Cold War* (Cambridge, MA: Harvard University Press, 1993).

2. Henderson, taped interview, NBM.

3. King, memorandum to Stone, Washington, DC, 17 July 1953, King Papers.

4. The facts concerning Stone are taken from several interviews, all of which support one another. See: Jacobs and Kenworthy taped interviews, NBM, and subsequent interviews of Jacobs and King by author.

5. Stone to Shepley, 12 April 1954, Shepley Papers. The letter's salutation reads "Dear Mr. Shepley" and it is signed "Eddie."

6. E. D. Stone, *The Evolution of an Architect* (New York: Horizon Press, 1962), 21.

7. I. W. Carpenter, "Memorandum of Meeting with Architectural Advisory Committee at 12:00 Noon," 29 March 1955, mf/FBO.

8. Shepley, "Notes Regarding Embassies & Embassy Sites," Shepley Papers.

9. "US Embassy for New Delhi," *Architectural Forum* 102 (June 1955): 114–9. The New Delhi project was also featured in: *Architectural Record* 117 (May 1955, July 1957, February 1959, March 1959), *Architectural Forum* (January 1959), *Foreign Service Newsletter* (August 1957), *L'Architecture d'Aujourd'hui* (April 1958). *Architectural Record* (March 1959) featured the overall work of Stone.

10. AAC Minutes, 30 July 1956.

11. Stone, *Evolution*, 139.

12. Ellsworth Bunker to William L. Slayton, 10 February 1982, mf/FBO.

13. Elie Abel, "New U. S. Embassy Praised by Nehru," *New York Times*, 4 January 1959. See also Norma Evenson, *The Indian Metropolis* (New Haven, CT: Yale University Press, 1989), 229.

14. "The Work of Edward D. Stone," *Architectural Record* 125 (March 1959): 157; "A New Public Architecture," *Architectural Forum* 110 (January 1959): 84.

15. Stone, *Evolution*, 139. See also: "It's News When Wright Lauds an Architect," *Palo Alto Times* (nd), Shepley Papers. Stone saw this clipping in the paper while he was in San Francisco designing the medical center for Stanford University and sent it to Shepley enclosed in a letter dated 11 August 1955.

16. John Kenneth Galbraith to Anne Nissen, 7 December 1981, NBM.

17. AAC Minutes, 10 November 1955, and 7 March 1956.

18. Walker's observations are drawn from his travel notes, "Foreign Buildings Operations—Department of State, Memorandum to Col. Harry A. McBride, Henry R. Shepley, Pietro Belluschi," 11 August 1955, mf/ FBO.

19. House Committee on Foreign Affairs, *Foreign Service Buildings* (1931), 16.

20. Fello Atkinson, "U.S. Embassy Building, Grosvenor Square, London," *Architectural Review* 129 (April 1961): 254. John Darnton, "A Reckoning May Be Due For British Landlords," *New York Times*, 21 March 1993.

21. Notes from Shepley's trip to Vienna and London, 13 October 1954, mf/FBO. For reference to the long-range plan, see: House Appropriations Subcommittee, Hearings on *Appropriations for 1954*, 25 March 1953.

22. "Government-Owned Properties, 1953," appendix A, FBO document from King Papers. See also House Appropriations Subcommittee, Hearings on *Appropriations for 1954*, 25 March 1953. The United States sold its former embassy property to the Canadians in 1960 for $4.7 million and it became the Canadian embassy.

23. McLaughlin's papers and other biographical data are available at the Seeley G. Mudd Manuscript Library, Princeton University Archives, Public Policy Papers, Princeton, NJ.

24. AAC Minutes, 5 August 1955, 1–2.

25. Ibid., 2.

26. "Competition for U. S. Chancery Building, London," *Architectural Record*, 119 (April 1956): 121.

27. The specifications are outlined in "Winning Design for American Embassy in London," *Architects' Journal* 123 (12 April 1956): 340.

28. Atkinson, "U.S. Embassy Building," 254.

29. "New US Embassy for London," *Architectural Forum* 104 (April 1956): 146.

30. Marjorie Belluschi to author, Portland, OR, 2 April 1992.

31. Stubbins, interview with author.

32. Robert T. McLaughlin, interview with author, 22 November 1992. Differing accounts of the "runner-up" appeared in the journals. *Progressive Architecture* and the *Architects' Journal* reported that Stone was the official runner-up, or second place winner. This is at odds with the account in *Architectural Forum*, which reported that the jury narrowed the selection to three before picking Saarinen, and that "No other awards or rankings were given." See: "Saarinen to Design Embassy," *Progressive*

Architecture 37 (March 1956): 89–91;
"Competition for U. S. Chancery Building,
London," *Architectural Record* 119 (April
1956): 221–4; "New US Embassy for London,"
Architectural Forum 104 (April 1956): 139–45;
and "Winning Design for American Embassy
in London," *Architects' Journal*, 123 (12 April
1956): 340–2.

33. *The Architects' Journal*, "Winning
Design for American Embassy in London," 341.

34. All entries are illustrated in articles
cited above: *Progressive Architecture* (March
1956), *Architectural Record* (April 1956), and
Architectural Forum (April 1956). Entries by
Saarinen and Stone are shown in the *Architects'
Journal* (12 April 1956). Excerpts from the
Times cited in *Architectural Record* (April
1956), 221. See also the *Architects' Journal* (12
April 1956): 340.

35. AAC Minutes, 7 March 1956, 1.

36. Marjorie Belluschi to author, 2 April 1992.

37. Walker to Shepley and Belluschi, New
York, NY, 20 February 1956, Shepley Papers;
and Walker to Shepley, Belluschi, and Bennett,
New York, NY, 20 September 1956, Shepley
Papers.

38. AAC Minutes, 15 May 1956, 4.

39. For background on the London eagle,
see *Embassy of the United States of America*
(London: U.S. Embassy, 1989). It should be
noted that the 35-foot wingspan does not
obscure the entire façade of the building, as later
critics suggested. The overall width of the façade
is about ten times the length of the eagle, which
is mounted five stories above the ground. It is
possible to walk right up to the building and not
even notice the eagle up above, but it is also possible to be focused on it. For Saarinen's presentation, see AAC Minutes, 24 February 1958, 5.

40. For Shriver's comments, see taped
interview with Judith Lanius, 10 May 1982,
NBM. "New U.S. Embassy in London
Praised and Criticized," *New York Times*, 20
November 1959. For congressional comment,
see HCFA, Subcommittee on State Department
Organization and Foreign Operations, *Foreign
Service Buildings Act Amendments, 1959:
Hearings on H. R. 9036, 86th Cong., 1st
sess.*, 8 July 1959, 141; Senate Committee on
Foreign Relations, *Foreign Service Buildings
Act Amendments of 1963: Hearings on H. R.
5207, 88th Cong., 1st sess.*, 7 May 1963, 12;
HCFA, Subcommittee on State Department
Organization and Foreign Operations,
*Foreign Service Buildings Act Amendments
of 1963: Hearings on H. R. 5207, 88th
Cong., 1st sess.*, 27 February 1963, 92; and
HCFA, Subcommittee on State Department

Organization and Foreign Operations, *Foreign
Service Buildings Act Amendments, 1960:
Hearings on (H. R. 9036 and) H. R. 9998, 86th
Cong., 2nd sess.*, 26 January 1960, 28.

41. "Controversial Building in London,"
Architectural Forum 114 (March 1961): 81–5.
The *London Times* report is also cited in this
article (84). Saarinen's statement appeared
in "U.S.A. Embassy," *Architect and Building
News*, 7 December 1960, 6, and it was also
published in *Architectural Forum* (March
1961): 85.

42. Atkinson, "U.S. Embassy Building,"
258.

43. Roel van Duijn, "Bommen op het
Bezuidenhout," (Bombs on the Bezuidenhout),
NRC Handelsblad (Rotterdam), 28 February
1995, 11.

44. Walter H. Waggoner, "U. S. Embassy
Design in The Hague Protested," *New York
Times*, 23 April 1957.

45 Shepley, "Notes from Shepley's trip to Vienna,
etc," 15 September 1954, mf/FBO.

46. Walker, "Report of Travel to London,
Dublin, and The Hague," 11 August 1955, mf/
FBO.

47. AAC Minutes, 12 December 1955, 4, and 16
January 1956, 2. See also William Gehron to
the AAC, 13 February 1956, mf/FBO.

48. AAC Minutes, 16 August 1955, 2.

49. See: "A New Kind of Bearing Wall,"
Architectural Record 120 (December 1956):
171–6; "Suburban Office Building Near
Amsterdam by Breuer," *Architectural Record*
126 (August 1959), 125–34; "Recent Work
of Marcel Breuer," *Architectural Record* 127
(January 1960): 123ff; "N. V. Magazijn 'De
Bijenkorf' te Rotterdam," *Katholiek Bouwblad*,
no. 21, XXVI (September 1959); and Breuer,
Sun and Shadow.

50. AAC Minutes, 15 May 1956, 2.

51. Waggoner, "U. S. Embassy Design."

52. Walker to Shepley, Belluschi, and
Bennett, 25 October 1956, Shepley Papers.

53. For criticism of the new project in The
Hague, see "Gast-Architect in Nederland,"
Katholiek Bouwblad XXVI, no. 21 (September
1959), 324; J. J. Vriend, "Stap achteruit," in
"Gebouw voor Amerikaanse ambassade, Den
Haag," *BOUW*, 25 July 1959, 871; R. C.
Hekker, "Vreemde tegenstelling," in "Gebouw
voor Amerikaanse ambassade, Den Haag,"
BOUW, 25 July 1959, 872.

54. A. Buffinga, "Verschil van opvatting," in
"Gebouw voor Amerikaanse ambassade, Den
Haag," *BOUW*, 25 July 1959, 872.

Chapter Ten: Deadlock Over Dublin

1. "Astute Plan for New Embassies," *Life,*
23 December 1957, 111; "USA Abroad,"
Architectural Forum 107 (December 1957):
114–23; "The Architecture of Diplomacy,"
undated pamphlet distributed at the New York
exhibition cosponsored by *Life*, the New York
chapter of the AIA, the Architectural League
of New York, and *Architectural Forum* (New
York: December 1957); "Foreign Buildings
Program Receives Award," *Foreign Service
Newsletter*, 15 August 1957; and "Architecture
in the News," press release, American Institute
of Architects, 5 February 1954.

2. Henry Shepley to Hon. Christian Herter,
4 June 1958, Shepley Papers. See also: "State
Dept.'s Modern Design Program Abroad
Suffers Severe Setback Under Attack of House
Subcommittee," *Archiectural Forum* 111
(October 1959): 5.

3. House Foreign Affairs Subcommittee,
*Foreign Service Buildings Act Amendments,
1959*, 17 March 1959, 54.

4. Congress had amended PL 480 in 1954 to permit the disposal abroad of surplus American
agricultural products to generate foreign currencies for use by the government, and in 1958
it again amended that law to make such funds
specifically available to the State Department
for its building program. FBO did not utilize
such funds until fiscal year 1961, when $4.5
million was appropriated. Such funds were
limited, however, to use in India, Pakistan,
UAR, Israel, Yugoslavia, Burma, and Poland.
In Poland, for example, these funds were used
to finance the construction of an ambassador's
residence in Warsaw (1967). See: House
Committee on Foreign Affairs, Subcommittee
on State Department Organization and Foreign
Operations, *Foreign Service Buildings Act
Amendments of 1962: Hearings on H. R.
11880*, 87th Cong., 2nd sess., 31 January
1962, 54.

5. House Appropriations Subcommittee,
Department of State Appropriations for 1958,
29 January 1957, 880. See also: Jean Rylands
(Public Affairs Officer, U.S. Embassy, Dublin)
interview with author, Dublin, 10 August 1992.

6. House Foreign Affairs Subcommittee,
*Foreign Service Buildings Act Amendments,
1959*,17 March 1959, 81. Notes to the hearings
indicate that FBO intended to build the new
chancery in Dublin in 1962 and had estimated
the cost at $500,000.

7. Walker, memorandum of trip to Europe,
11 August 1955, Shepley Papers.

8. Grant Stockdale to John F. Kennedy,
Dublin, 16 May 1961, the Presidential Papers

of John F. Kennedy, President's Office File, Box
119A, John Fitzgerald Kennedy Library, Boston,
MA.

9. Stockdale to Evelyn Lincoln, Dublin, 17
May 1961, President's Office File, Box 119A,
Kennedy Papers.

10. John Johansen, letter to author, 29 September
1992, 2.

11. AAP Minutes, 13 May 1957, 2.

12. AAP Minutes, 24 June 1957, 3. See also:
"Bus Terminal and Office Building, Modern
Irish Architecture," *Architectural Forum* 102
(June 1955): 120–1. Well-known Irish architect
Michael Scott designed the bus terminal and
also collaborated with Johansen on the embassy
commission.

13. AAP Minutes, 23 September 1957, 1, 3, 5.

14. AAP Minutes, 4 November 1957, 5.

15. AAP Minutes, 21 January 1958, 3–4.

16. AAP Minutes, 24 February 1958, 3; 12
May 1958, 3.

17. AAP Minutes, 21 January 1958, 6. John
Lyon Reid also presented a design based on a
hexagonal plan for an embassy office building
in Algiers in November. Reid's project was never
built.

18. AAP Minutes, 12 May 1958, 2.

19. House Foreign Affairs Subcommittee, *Foreign
Service Buildings Act Amendments, 1959*, 29
July 1959, 236–7. See also *Foreign Service
Buildings Act Amendments, 1960*, 26 January
1960, 13.

20. House Foreign Affairs Subcommittee, *Foreign
Service Buildings Act Amendments, 1959*, 6
August 1959, 287, 292.

21. Wurster to Hughes, San Francisco, CA, 25
September 1959, mf/FBO.

22. AAP Minutes, 29 January 1960, 3.

23. Johnstone, personal memoir, "Dublin,
Ireland, American Embassy Chancery," nd,
Johnstone Papers, Fairfield, PA.

24. Jean White, "Critic Hays Hints Action
on Embassies; Hughes Shift May Free Overseas
Fund," *Washington Post*, 8 January 1961.

25. House Foreign Affairs Subcommittee,
*Foreign Service Buildings Act Amendments of
1962*, 15 May 1962, 171; 1 January 1962, 46;
and 30 January 1962, 5.

26. *Congressional Record*, House, 1 May
1963, 7500.

27. Johnstone, "Architectural Advisory
Panel," memorandum, 24 July 1961. See
also: Crockett, Memorandum to Roger Jones,
"Foreign Buildings Guidelines," 6 July 1961,
mf/FBO.

28. Crockett, "Foreign Buildings Guidelines," 6
July 1961, mf/FBO; Johnstone, "Meeting of the
Architectural Advisory Panel, May 5, 1961,"

memorandum, 5 May 1961, mf/FBO.

29. Philip C. Will Jr. to Dean Rusk, 26 January 1961; see also Will to Holden, Egan, Wilson & Corser, 1 May 1961, mf/FBO. This was a form letter sent to all of the architects who had participated in the FBO program. Architect Milton L. Grigg provided a detailed account of his experience designing the embassy in Canberra and he gave a copy of his letter to Johnstone. (Grigg to Will, 23 May 1961, mf/FBO).

30. House Foreign Affairs Subcommittee, *Foreign Service Buildings Act Amendments of 1962*, 30 January 1962, 21–2.

31. Stockdale to John F. Kennedy, Dublin, 21 July 1961, President's Office File Box 119A, Kennedy Papers.

32. Dean Rusk to John F. Kennedy, "Memorandum for the President," 9 September 1961, White House Central Subject File, Box 227, Kennedy Papers. See also: Johnstone memoir; Johansen to author, 29 September 1992; and Johansen, interview with author, 18 August 1992.

33. John F. Kennedy to Wayne Hays, 11 September 1961, White House Central Subject File, Box 227, Kennedy Papers. Hays to Kennedy, 14 September 1961, White House Central Subject File, Box 227, Kennedy Papers.

34. See Johnstone's memoir and interviews, and Johansen letter to author, 29 September 1992.

35. Johansen to author, 29 September 1992.

36. Stockdale to McGeorge Bundy, Dublin, 26 June 1962, National Security File, Box 118, Kennedy Papers.

37. R. Furneaux Jordan, "United States Embassy, Dublin," *Architectural Review* 136 (December 1964): 420–5. See also: "Sinewy Drum for Dublin," *Architectural Forum* 121 (August–September 1964): 143–7; "Johansen's Honeycomb Embassy Opens," *Progressive Architecture* 45 (September 1964): 216–9; and "For Eire, a new 'Celtic Tower,'" *Architectural Forum* 109 (November 1958): 127–31; and "Embassy of the United States of America, Dublin, Ireland," U.S. Embassy fact sheet, 1982, Dublin.

38. Senate Foreign Relations Committee, *Amendments to the Foreign Service Buildings Act of 1926: Hearings on H. R. 11880*, 87th Cong., 2nd sess., 2 August 1962 and 21 August 1962.

39. Albert W. Watson, *Congressional Record-House*, 1 May 1963, 7500.

40. AAP Minutes, 9–10 May 1963.

41. Ibid.

42. See: *Architectural Forum* 107 (August 1957): 157; John Carl Warnecke, "United States Embassy in Bangkok: The Story of Its Design," *Journal of the American Institute of Architects* (November 1958), 36-41; and "U.S. Embassy, Bangkok, Thailand," *Architectural Record* 124 (October 1958).

43. AAP Minutes, 9–10 May 1963, 4; Hays to Wurster, 29 May 1963, and Wurster to Johnstone, 3 June 1963, mf/FBO.

44. AAP Minutes, 13–4 August 1964, 2.

45. Ibid., 10.

46. Walt Kenney, memorandum, "Audit of Procurement Program, Office of Foreign Buildings (A/FBO)," Department of State, 25 January 1981, 4–5, Office of the Historian, Bureau of Public Affairs, Department of State.

47. AAP Minutes, 24 March 1965. See also: Joseph R. Passonneau, interview with author, 21 July 1992, Washington, DC.

48. For characterization of Hays, see Albert B. Hunt, "Hays and Foes on Hill Agree He's Not Nice and Not in Last Place," *Wall Street Journal*, 24 July 1972, 1. For revelations about the use of FBO to benefit Hays's friends, see Woodward and Bernstein, "Hays' Private Duchy." See also Paul Serey, interview, 26 May 1992. The Hays Papers are now at Ohio University, Athens, OH.

49. When the Foreign Affairs Committee changed its name, it also changed the name of the Hays subcommittee, known until 1975 as the Subcommittee on State Department Organization and Foreign Operations. It was renamed the Subcommittee on International Operations. Subsequently, the committee changed its name two more times.

50. Material on Africa is drawn in part from House Foreign Affairs Subcommittee, *Foreign Service Buildings Act Amendments of 1962*, 31 January 1962, 49; and *Foreign Service Buildings Act Amendments, 1963*, 27 February, 18–20, 22, and 6 March 1963, 84.

51. House Foreign Affairs Subcommittee, *Foreign Service Buildings Act Amendments, 1963*, 4 March 1963, 57. For references to Somalia, see *Foreign Service Buildings Act Amendments of 1962*, 31 January 1962, 147; and 28 February 1962, 137.

52. Earnest J. Warlow to Lawrence Anderson, 5 May 1970; Warlow to John Lyon Reid, 28 January 1971; Joseph R. Passonneau to Warlow, 29 January 1971, mf/FBO; Lawrence B. Anderson, "Brasilia: Problems in Housing the U.S. Mission," unpublished report, February 1967, collection of author; and Anderson, interview with author, Lincoln Center, MA, in July 1992. For comments on Kahn, see Passonneau to Warlow, 17 September 1971, Personal files of Joseph R. Passonneau, Washington, DC.

See also Thomas A. Pope to Anderson, 20 July 1967, mf/FBO; Anderson to Warlow, 15 May 1970, mf/FBO; and Reid to Warlow, 19 May 1970, mf/FBO.

53. Passonneau to Warlow, 17 September 1971.

54. Mary Russell, "Hays to Retire, He Cites Health, 'Harassment'," *Washington Post,* 14 August 1976. Rooney died in 1975, and Hays in 1989.

Chapter Eleven: Targets for Terror

1. Author's notes on AAB meeting, 6 May 1980.
2. Author's notes on AAB meeting, 12 May 1980.
3. FBO built the embassies (designed by the architects listed) in Lisbon, Riyadh, La Paz, Kuala Lumpur, Cairo, Muscat, Manama, and Georgetown. Esherick's La Paz scheme was significantly modified by changed security requirements and the Leo Daly firm joined the design team. Minneapolis architect Leonard Parker was later selected to design the embassy in Santiago, and David Childs of Skidmore, Owings & Merrill won the Ottawa commission after Thompson's scheme was shelved.
4. Author's notes on AAB meeting, 6 May 1980.
5. George E. Hartman, quoted in Carleton Knight III, "Design for Defense," *Washington Post,* 9 November 1985.
6. National Research Council, *The Embassy of the Future* (Washington, DC: National Academy Press, 1986): 22.
7. *Report of the Secretary of State's Advisory Panel on Overseas Security,* Department of State, Washington, DC, June 1985. The Panel consisted of: Admiral Bobby R. Inman, USN (Ret.) (Chairman), Sen. Warren B. Rudman, Rep. Daniel A. Mica, Ambassador Lawrence S. Eagleburger, Ambassador Anne L. Armstrong, Lieutenant General D'Wayne Gray, USMC, and Robert J. McGuire. In addition to establishing construction standards, in 1986 the department also created a Bureau of Diplomatic Security and a Diplomatic Security Service in 1986 in response to the *Inman Report.* See also: Steven Emerson, Charles Fenyvesi, and Melissa Healy, "Can U.S. buy embassy safety?" *U.S. News & World Report,* 14 April 1986, 22; and Harry Anderson, "Terror Stalks America's Diplomats," *Newsweek,* 19 May 1986, 45.
8. William L. Slayton, "Federal Architecture, Part Two: In Search of Good Design: Selecting an Architect," *Inland Architect* (March/April 1984): 33.
9. An artist's rendering of the new project is shown in "Design Unveiled for U.S. Embassy in Moscow," *Architecture* (April 1996): 27.
10. James K. Bishop, "Escape from Mogadishu, 1991," in *Embassies Under Siege,*

ed. Joseph G. Sullivan (Washington, DC: Brassey's, 1995), 149–66.

11. Gerald Winkler, telephone interview with author, May 2, 1997.
12. Alan Y. Taniguchi, telephone interview with author, April 10, 1997. Indranie Deolall, "Georgetown's Gothic Charm Influenced Design of New US Embassy," *Guyana Chronicle,* 20 April 1991. See also "Select Project Description: United States Embassy Office Building, Georgetown, Guyana," from Alan Y. Taniguchi, Architect & Associates, Inc., Austin, TX.
13. Frederick Cooper, "Nueva sede de la embajada de los EE.UU," *El Comércio,* 11 November 1992; and Calvin Sims, "Shining Path Rebels Step Up Terror Campaign in Peru," *New York Times,* 20 March 1995.
14. Kenneth Yalowitz, telephone interview with author, 11 April 1997.
15. Nicolas M. Salgo, telephone interview with author, 23 April 1997.
16. Joseph T. Sikes, interview with author, Rosslyn, VA, 1 May 1997.
17. Ibid.
18. FBO, "A/E Design Guidelines for the New Berlin OBC," FBO, April 1995, 3, .
19. See also Michael Z Wise, *Capital Dilemma* (New York: Princeton Architectural Press, 1998).
20. Moore Ruble Yudell/Gruen Associates, Technical Narrative and Drawings, United States Embassy in Berlin, United States Department of State, Office of Foreign Building Operations, FBO, 15 August 1995, .
21. Canada is an exception, but Canada's new embassy on Pennsylvania Avenue was designed to specifications outlined by the corporation that controlled the redevelopment of Pennsylvania Avenue, the street known as America's "Main Street." The massing of the building, even the classical elements that echo details from federal buildings on the other side of the avenue, were to some extent predetermined by the development package.
22. Sally Cutler to Patricia Waddy, Exeter, NH, 25 September 1990; and Sally Cutler to author, Exeter, NH, 23 November 1990.
23. Sally Cutler to author, Chevy Chase, MD, 13 July 1997. The insertion is Cutler's.
24. Sheldon J. Krys, interview with author, Washington, DC, 8 May 1992.
25. Hughes to Louis Kahn, Attachment to AAB Minutes of 19 August 1960, letter dated 26 August 1960, Washington, DC.

Chapter Twelve: Since 1998

1. *America's Overseas Presence in the 21st Century,* The Report of the Overseas Presence Advisory Panel, November 1999, http://www.state.gov/www/publications/9911_opap/rpt-9911_opap.pdf

2. Admiral William J. Crowe, US Navy (Ret.), interview with author, 9 June, 1999. See also: *Report of the Accountability Review Boards on the Embassy Bombings in Nairobi and Dar es Salaam,* January 1999.

3. Senator Rod Grams, "Vulnerable Embassies? Don't Blame Congress," http://www.afsa.org/fsj/jun00/grams.cfm.

4. SECCA legislation included in H.R. 3427, the Foreign Relations Authorization Act for FY 2000 and 2001 and signed into law in the Consolidated Appropriations Act for FY 2000.

5   Gregory Starr interview with author at Department of State, 29 April 2009.

6. Patrick Collins interview with author at OBO, 23 March 2010.

7. Joseph Toussaint interview with author at OBO, 13 May 2009.

8. Report of Inspection, Office of Inspector General, U.S. Department of State, "Bureau of Overseas Buildings Operations," Report Number ISP-I-08-34, August 2008.

9. Ibid.

10. Ibid.

11. "The Embassy of the Future," Center for Strategic and International Studies, 2007.

12. John Chapman, interview with author.

13. William Miner interview with author, OBO, 26 May 2009.

14. Kornblum citation Kevin Cullen, "Quarrel over U.S. Embassy Reveals Rifts in Berlin" *Boston Globe,* January 31, 2000, A1.

15. "Questions on the NEC in Beijing," Notes from interview with Craig Hartman via OBO to Julia Klemeit, Fall, 2009, courtesy of Jonathan Blyth, OBO.

16. Sarah Tanguy, "Artful Diplomacy," in *State Magazine,* March 2010, 38.

17. For more information on the FAPE collection in Berlin see "Art Collection, United States Embassy, Berlin, Germany." FAPE, n.d.

18. Report of Inspection, Office of Inspector General, Department of State, "Bureau of Overseas Buildings Operations," Jan–May 2008.

19. Stastny also served as manager of competitions that selected designs for Berlin and Beijing.

20. Christopher Hawthorne, "U.S. Embassy: An Outpost as a Signpost," *LA Times,* 21 March, 2010.

21. Wijnand Galema, Fransje Hooimeijer, *Bouwen aan diplomatie; De Amerikaanse ambassade in Den Haag,* Marcel Breuer, 1956–1959, Municipality of The Hague, The Hague 2008 (cultural-historic survey).

22. *Design for Diplomacy: New Embassies for the 21st Century,* A Report of the AIA 21st Century Task Force, American Institute of Architects, 2009.

23. Transcript of Industry Advisory Panel meeting, U.S. Department of State, Bureau of Overseas Buildings Operations, December 1, 2009.

SELECTED BIBLIOGRAPHY

Acheson, Dean. *Present at the Creation: My Years at the State Department.* New York; W. W. Norton & Co., 1969.

Argyros, George L. et al. "The Embassy of the Future." Center for Strategic and International Studies (2007).

Al Sayyad, Nezar, ed. *Forms of Dominance.* Brookfield, VT: Avebury, 1992.

"Amerikanische generalkonsulate in Bremen, Düsseldorf, Frankfurt und Stuttgart." *Bauen + Wohnen* 10 (April 1956): 113–8.

"Architecture to Represent America Abroad." *Architectural Record* 117 (May 1955): 187–92.

Barnes, William, and John Heath Morgan. *The Foreign Service of the United States.* Washington, DC: Historical Office, Bureau of Public Affairs, Department of State, 1961.

Bastlund Knud. *José Luis Sert, Architecture, City Planning, Urban Design.* New York: Frederick A. Praeger, 1967.

Bloom, Sol. *The Autobiography of Sol Bloom.* New York: G. P. Putnam's, 1948.

Burchard, John, and Albert Bush-Brown. *The Architecture of America.* Boston: Little, Brown and Company, 1961.

Burdick, Eugene, and William J. Lederer. *The Ugly American.* New York: Norton, 1958.

Campbell, Robert. "An Act of Architectural Hubris Meets Its End." *Boston Globe,* 13 August 1993.

Committee on Research for the Security of Future U.S. Embassy Buildings, National Research Council. *The Embassy of the Future: Recommendations for the Design of Future U.S. Embassy Buildings.* Washington, DC: National Academy Press, 1986.

"Competition for U.S. Chancery Building, London." *Architectural Review* 119 (April 1956): 221–4.

"Controversial Building in London, U.S. Embassy." *Architectural Forum* 114 (March 1961): 80–5.

Craig, Lois, and the staff of the Federal Architecture Project. *The Federal Presence: Architecture, Politics, and Symbols in United States Government Building.* Cambridge, MA: MIT Press, 1984.

"Diplomatic and Consular Establishments of the United States in Tokyo." *Architecture* 66 (August 1932): 85–93.

"Eyeful in Africa." *Architectural Forum* 111 (September 1959): 134–5.

"Five Current Projects." *Architectural Review* 122 (July 1957): 153–76

"For Eire, a New 'Celtic Tower.' " *Architectural Forum* 109 (November 1958): 127–31.

Forbes, J. D. "Shepley Bulfinch Richardson and Abbott, Architects, An Introduction." *Journal of the Society of Architectural Historians* 17 (fall 1958): 19–30.

Forgey, Benjamin. "Designs for Diplomacy in an Age of Terrorism." *Washington Post,* 20 May 1989.

Galbraith, John Kenneth. "For Public *and* Potent Building." *New York Times Magazine,* 9 October 1960, 34.

"Gebouw voor Amerikaanse ambassade, Den Haag." *BOUW* (25 July 1959): 871–2.

Geertz, Clifford. *The Interpretation of Cultures.* New York: Basic Books, 1973.

Gordon, Barclay F. "America Turns a Fresh Face Overseas." *Architectural Record* (December 1980): 96–113.

Gournay, Isabelle and Jane C. Loeffler, "Washington and Ottawa: A Tale of Two Embassies." *Journal of the Society of Architectural Historians* (December 2002): 480-507.

Greene, Graham. *Journey without Maps.* 1936. (Reprint, London: Penguin, 1980).

———. *The Quiet American.* 1955. (Reprint, London: Penguin, 1962).

Grossman, Elizabeth. "Architecture for a Public Client; The Monuments and Chapels of the American Battle Monuments Commission."

Journal of the Society of Architectural Historians 43 (May 1984): 119–34.

Halberstam, David. *The Fifties.* New York: Random House, 1993.

Hines, Thomas S. *Richard Neutra. and the Search for Modern Architecture.* New York: Oxford University Press, 1982.

Ilchman, Warren F. *Professional Diplomacy in the United States: 1774–1939.* Chicago: University of Chicago Press, 1961.

Inman, Adm. Bobby R., and others. *Report of the Secretary of State's Advisory Panel on Overseas Security,* Department of State, June 1985.

Inspector General's Office. *New Construction of Foreign Buildings Operations,* report of the Inspector General, A-85-3, Department of State, August 1985.

Irving, Robert G. *Indian Summer.* New Haven: Yale University Press, 1981.

"Johansen's Honeycomb Embassy Opens." *Progressive Architecture* 45 (September 1964): 216–9.

Jordan, R. Furneaux. "United States Embassy, Dublin." *Architectural Review* 136 (December 1964): 420–5.

Kaden, Lewis B. "America's Overseas Presence in the 21st Century," *The Report of the Overseas Presence Advisory Panel* (November 1999).

Kennan, George F. *Sketches from a Life.* New York: Pantheon Books, 1989.

Kennedy, Charles Stuart. *The American Consul, A History of the United States Consular Service: 1776–1914.* New York: Greenwood Press, 1990.

Kornwolf, James. D., ed. *Modernism in America: 1937–1941.* Williamsburg, VA: College of William and Mary, 1985.

Lardner, George Jr. "Unbeatable Bugs: The Moscow Embassy Fiasco." *Washington Post,* 18 June 1990.

Leffler, Melvyn P., and David S. Painter, eds. *Origins of the Cold War.* London: Routledge, 1994.

Loeffler, Jane C. "The Architecture of Diplomacy: Heyday of the United States Embassy-Building Program." *Journal of the Society of Architectural Historians* 49 (September 1990): 251–78.

_____. "Embassy Design: Security vs. Openness." *Foreign Service Journal* (September 2005): 44-51.

_____. "Fortress America." *Foreign Policy* (September/October 2007): 54-7.

_____. "The Identity Crisis of the American Embassy." *Foreign Service Journal* (June 2000): 18-25.

_____. "The Rows on Embassy Rows." *Newsweek* (International Edition) (July 7-14, 2008): 39-41.

Loth, David Goldsmith. *A Long Way Forward: The Biography of Congresswoman Frances P. Bolton.* (New York: Longmans Green, 1957).

Luce, Henry R. *The American Century.* (New York: Farrar & Rinehart, Inc., 1941).

Manchester, William. *American Caesar.* Boston: Little, Brown and Company, 1978.

Muravchik, Joshua. *Exporting Democracy: Fulfilling America's Destiny.* Washington, DC: The American Enterprise Institute Press, 1991.

"New U.S. Government Building in Paris." *Architecture* 70 (September 1934): 127.

"New US Embassy for London." *Architectural Forum* 104 (April 1956): 139–45.

Newsom, David D. *Diplomacy and the American Democracy.* Bloomington: Indiana University Press, 1988.

"Norway's Precast Palazzo." *Architectural Forum* 111 (December 1959): 130–133.

Oberdorfer, Don. *Tet.* New York: Doubleday, 1971.

"Overseas Diplomatic and Consular Buildings for the Office of Foreign Buildings, Department of State." *Journal of the American Institute of Architects* (June 1962): 67–76.

Pach, Chester J. Jr., and Elmo Richardson. *The Presidency of Dwight D. Eisenhower.* Lawrence, KS: The University Press of Kansas, 1991.

Plischke, Elmer. *United States Diplomats and Their Missions.* Washington DC: American Enterprise Institute of Public Policy Research, 1975.

Pope, Thomas A. "The Embassy, Symbol of the United States' Dignity and Strength, Courtesy and Respect." Washington, DC: *Alumni Bulletin, The Catholic University of America* 28 (April 1961): 3–5.

Raymond, Antonin. *Antonin Raymond: An Autobiography*. Rutland, VT: Charles E. Tuttle Company, 1973.

Robin, Ron. *Enclaves of America: The Rhetoric of American Political Architecture Abroad, 1900–1965*. (Princeton: Princeton University Press, 1992).

Schaffer, Howard B. *Chester Bowles: New Dealer in the Cold War* (Cambridge, MA: Harvard University Press, 1993).

"Second Group of American Embassy Buildings." *Architectural Record* 119 (June 1956): 161–5.

"Sinewy Drum for Dublin." *Architectural Forum* 121 (August–September 1964): 143–7.

Steigman, Andrew L. *The Foreign Service of the United States: First Line of Defense*. Boulder, CO: Westview Press, 1985.

Stern, Lawrence, and Walter Pincus. "Wayne Hays' Power Base: Political IOUs" *Washington Post*, 8 June 1974.

Stone, E. D. *The Evolution of an Architect*. New York: Horizon Press, 1962.

Stuart, Graham H. *American Diplomatic and Consular Practice*. New York: Appleton-Century-Crofts, Inc., 1952.

Sullivan, Joseph G., ed. *Embassies Under Siege*. Washington, DC: Brassey's, 1995.

Swanberg, W. A. *Luce and His Empire*. New York: Dell Publishing Co., 1972.

Thayer, Charles W. *Diplomat*. New York: Harper & Brothers, 1959.

"Three Buildings of the FBO." *Progressive Architecture* 43 (June 1962): 108–17.

Tuch, Hans N. *Communicating with the World: U.S. Public Diplomacy Overseas*. New York: St. Martin's Press, 1990.

"U.S. Architecture Abroad." *Architectural Forum* 98 (March 1953): 101–15.

"U.S. Embassy Office Building, Havana, Cuba." *Progressive Architecture* 36 (February 1955): 106–11.

"US Embassy for New Delhi." *Architectural Forum* 102 (June 1955): 114–19.

"USA abroad." *Architectural Forum* 107 (December 1957): 114–23.

Vale, Lawrence J. *Architecture, Power, and National Identity*. New Haven: Yale University Press, 1992.

Walker, Ralph. "The Education Necessary to the Professional Practice of Architecture." *Journal of the American Institute of Architects* 15 (February 1951): 71–6; and 16 (March 1951): 119–25.

Warnecke, John Carl. "United States Embassy in Bangkok: The Story of Its Design." *Journal of the AIA* (November 1958), 36–41.

Weil, Martin. *A Pretty Good Club: The Founding Fathers of the U.S. Foreign Service*. New York: W. W. Norton and Co., Inc., 1978.

Wilson, Richard Guy. "High Noon on the Mall: Modernism versus Traditionalism: 1910-1970." In *The Mall in Washington: 1791–1991*, ed. Richard W. Longstreth, 143–63. Washington, DC: The National Gallery of Art, 1991.

Woodward, Bob and Carl Bernstein. "State Dept. Unit Viewed as Hays' Private Duchy." *Washington Post*, 14 August 1976.

Wright, Gwendolyn. *The Politics of Design in French Colonial Urbanism*. (Chicago: The University of Chicago Press, 1991).

Additional Sources

Minutes and proceedings: Architectural Advisory Committee/Panel and Miscellaneous Files, Office of Foreign Buildings Operations, Department of State; Senate Committee on Foreign Relations; and House Committees on Appropriations, Foreign Affairs, and Government Operations.

Collections: American Institute of Architects Archives, Washington, DC; Foreign Affairs Oral History Program, Lauinger Library, Special Collections, Georgetown University, Washington, DC (also available at the Association for Diplomatic Studies and Training, Arlington VA); Louis I. Kahn Collection, University of Pennsylvania and Pennsylvania Historical and Museum Commission, Philadelphia; John F. Kennedy Papers, John Fitzgerald Kennedy Library, Boston; Robert W. McLauglin Jr. Papers, Seeley G. Mudd Manuscript Library, Princeton University Archives, Princeton University; National Building Museum Archives, Washington, DC; Eero Saarinen Papers, Sterling Memorial Library, Manuscripts and Archives, Yale University; Josep Lluis Sert Papers, Special Collections, Frances Loeb Library, Harvard University Graduate School of Design; Henry Shepley Papers, Shepley Bulfinch Richardson and Abbott and the Shepley Family; Edward Durell Stone Papers, Special Collections Division, University of Arkansas Libraries, Fayetteville, AR; Ralph Walker Papers, George Arents Research Library for Special Collections, Syracuse University.

IMAGE CREDITS

1 Photograph by Bill Hoffman, Department of State; 2–3 Department of State; 4 Hede Foto, Department of State; 5–8 U.S. Embassy, Tokyo, and Michael Marcus; 10 Department of State; 11 Author; 12 Department of State; 13 Courtesy Leland W. King; 14 Foto Cer Co., Department of State; 15–6 Department of State; 17 D. L. Dwyer, Department of State; 18–20 Department of State; 21 Courtesy Leland W. King; 23 Collection of Author, Courtesy of Catherine Jacobs; 24–30 Courtesy of Ralph Rapson and Associates, Inc.; 31 Department of State; 32–5 Courtesy of Ralph Rapson and Associates, Inc.; 36 Courtesy of Leland W. King; 37 Courtesy of Ladislav Rado; 38–39 Department of State; 41 Department of State; 42–5 Author; 46 Department of State; 47 Photograph by Robert H. Loeffler; 48 Courtesy of Ladislav Rado; 49 Department of State; 50 Courtesy of Paul Rudolph, FAIA;51–3 Department of State; 54 Photograph by Balthazar Korab; 55 Courtesy of John Carl Warnecke; 56 © 1977 Louis I. Kahn Collection, University of Pennsylvania and Pennsylvania Historical and Museum Commission; 57 Courtesy of Ralph Rapson and Associates, Inc.; 58–60 Courtesy of Harry Weese Associates, Architects; 62–3 Department of State; 64–5 Special Collections Division, University of Arkansas Libraries; 66 Megaloconomou Bros., Department of State; 67–8 Department of State; 69 Author; 71 Department of State; 73 Department of State; 74 Megaloconomou Bros., Department of State; 75 Author; 76 Photograph by Robert H. Loeffler; 77 Photograph by Balthazar Korab; 78–79 Department of State; 80 I. D. Beri, USIS, Department of State; 81 Department of State; 82 Photograph by Louis Reens, courtesy of the Josep Lluis Sert Collection, Frances Loeb Library, Graduate School of Design, Harvard University; 83 Laboratoire Agfacolor Officiel Modern Photography; 84–8 Department of State; 89 Courtesy of the Josep Lluis Sert Collection, Frances Loeb Library, Graduate School of Design, Harvard University; 90–3 Department of State; 94 Courtesy of Hugh Stubbins, FAIA; 95 Courtesy of Edward Larrabee Barnes, Architect; 96 Photograph by Robert H. Loeffler; 97 Department of State; 98 Courtesy of the Josep Lluis Sert Collection, Frances Loeb Library, Graduate School of Design, Harvard University; 99–100 Photographs by Balthazar Korab; 101 Photograph by M. Falco, Department of State; 102 Photograph by Balthazar Korab; 103 Photograph by Robert H. Loeffler; 104 Photograph by Jan Versnel for Department of State; 105 Photograph by Robert H. Loeffler; 106 Collection of Author, Courtesy of Ton Heijneman, U.S. Embassy, The Hague; 107 Photograph by Robert H. Loeffler; 108 Courtesy of Lawrence K. Larkin; 109 Courtesy of John M. Johansen, FAIA; 111 Photograph by Robert H. Loeffler; 113 Department of State; 114 Pat Monaghan, Fotoprint, Department of State; 116 National Archives; 117–8 Department of State; 119 Courtesy of Ladislav Rado; 120–2 Department of State; 123 Author; 124 Reuters/Mark Baker/Archive Photos; 125–6 Department of State; 127 Courtesy of Hartman-Cox Architects; 128 Photograph by Henry Wood; 129 Courtesy of Metcalf Associates; 130 Department of State; 131–4 Courtesy of Oudens + Knoop Architects, PC; 135 Department of State; 136–7 Richard Mandelkorn, Photographer; 138 Elizabeth Gill Lui © 2005; 139 Department of State; 140 Photograph by Mario Carrieri for Kallmann, McKinnell & Wood Architects, Inc; 141 Department of State; 142 Photograph by Eduardo Modolo for The Leonard Parker Associates; 143 Courtesy of Integrus Architecture; 144 Department of State; 145 Vera Lentz/NYT Pictures, The New York Times Company; 146 Department of State; 147–50: Photographs by James Capen, Department of State; 151–55 Department of State; 156 Elizabeth Gill Lui © 2005; 157–84 Department of State; 185–7 Photographs by Robert H. Loeffler; 188–9 Department of State; 190 Photograph by Timothy Hursley, Department of State; 191 Department of State.

INDEX

---

* *Unless otherwise noted, all consulates, embassies, residences, and projects are U.S. properties (abroad).*

This book is set in Sabon, a typeface designed in the 1960s by Jan Tschichold (1902-1974) based on the classic sixteenth-century fonts of Claude Garamond. Tschichold considered Sabon to be his masterpiece, and it is the font he is most often remembered by today.